PLUTOCRACY, CRONYISM & POPULISM

Facets of Neoliberalism in India

Edited by

Kamal Nayan Kabra

Vrajaindra Upadhyay

Vitasta

Let Knowledge Spread

Published by
Renu Kaul Verma
Vitasta Publishing Pvt Ltd
2/15, Ansari Road, Daryaganj
New Delhi - 110 002
info@vitastapublishing.com

ISBN 978-93-82711-71-1

First Edition 2017
Second reprint 2024
MRP ₹995

Cover and layout by Vits Press
Printed by Vikas Computer and Printers

In honour and memory of Bramhadev Sharma (1931-2015)
He was a highly versatile scholar, social thinker-activist, author, communicator, educationist, administrator who chose to identify himself with the lives, causes and struggles of the common Indian in general and tribal people in particular. He championed the cause of gram pachayats as the basic fulcrum of a really vibrant democracy.

Bramhadev Sharma was an IAS officer, a scheduled castes commissioner, mathematician, Vice Chancellor of the North East University, author of dozens of books concerned with development and rural and agricultural segments. He also brought out a unique periodical, *Gram Ganrajya,* and played a leading role in numerous struggles and people-centric movements. His fast at Rajghat for the enforcement of the constitutional rights of the tribal people through enactment of necessary legislation is a memorable occasion in India's rights struggle.We fondly remember his remarkable contributions to some issues of the *Alternative Economic Survey* and conferences of the Indian Political Economy Association.

Our salaam and respects to his memory.

Contents

List of Contributors

Kamal Nayan Kabra, Malcolm Adishesiah Chair, Professor, Economic Development and Decentralised Planning, Institute of Social Sciences, New Delhi; former Professor of Economics, Indian Institute of Pubic Administration, New Delhi

Vrajaindra Upadhyay, Professor of Economics, Department of Humanities and Social Sciences, IIT Delhi

Surajit Mazumdar, Professor of Economics, CESP, JNU

KS Chalapati Rao, Professor, Institute for Studies in Industrial Development, New Delhi. Email: chalpatirao@yahoo.com

Malabika Pal, Associate Professor, Miranda House, University of Delhi

Seema Sharma, Associate Professor, Department of Management Studies, IIT Delhi

Jayan Jose Thomas, Associate Professor, Department of Humanities and Social Sciences, IIT Delhi

Praveen Jha, Professor of Economics, CESP, JNU

Avanindra Nath Thakur, Teacher in a DU College

Seema, Research Scholar, Department of Humanities and Social Sciences, IIT Delhi

Ranja Sengupta, Third World Network. Email: ranja.sengupta@gmail.com

Paramjit Singh, Assistant Professor, Department of Economics, Panjab University, Chandigarh. Email: paramjiteco@yahoo.com

Balwinder Singh Tiwana, Professor, Department of Economics, Punjabi University, Patiala. Email: balwindertiwana@yahoo.co.in

Satyaki Roy, Associate Professor at the Institute for Studies in Industrial Development, New Delhi

RV Ramana Murthy, Professor, School of Economics, University of Hyderabad

Ashok Rao, President, NCOA. Email: kashokrao@gmail.com

SP Singh, Professor of Economics, Department of Humanities & Social Sciences, IIT Roorkee

Manali Chakrabarti, Professor of Economics, Institute of Development Studies, Kolkata

Reetika Khera, Associate Professor, Department of Humanities and Social Sciences, Indian Institute of Technology, Delhi

Sarbeswar Sahoo, Assistant Professor of Sociology, Indian Institute of Technology, Delhi

Sharanjit S Dhillon, Professor of Economics, Guru Nanak Dev University, Amritsar. Email: dhillon_sharanjit@yahoo.co.in

AK Arun, Senior Homoepath and Public Health Activist

Ajay Sehgal, Assistant Professor, Khalsa College, Amritsar

Tulsi Lingareddy, Senior Director, Research and Consultancy, EPW Research Foundation, Mumbai

Jagdeep S Chhokar, Professor, Dean and Director in-charge at Indian Institute of Management, Ahmedabad and is a founder member of Association for Democratic Reforms (www.adrindia.org), and the founding chairperson of Aajeevika Bureau (www.aajeevika.org).

Lal Bahabur Varma, Former Professor of History, Allahabad University and Manipur University and Editor, *Itihas Bodh* journal

The Editors wish to express their thanks to Publisher Renu Kaul Verma for her professional approach and highly presentable publication of the volume. We also express our sincere thanks to and appreciation for the editor, Papri Sri Raman. But for her expertise, this volume would not have taken such a form. We are deeply aware of the problems involved and care/ patience required for bringing uniformity of style by so many contributors. We are sure her work has made the volume really reader-friendly.

This volume is the result of the collective efforts of all the contributors who have given so much of their time, energy and expertise to make this book a success. Any formal expression of thanks to the contributors may be too much of a formality.

Preface

THE PRESENT volume represents continuation by the Indian Political Economy Association of its over two decades long series of publications of periodic *Alternative Economic Surveys* devoted to a critical, people-centric assessment of socio-economic changes experienced by India and her common people.

Such an assessment acquires a special significance as the country has lived for the last twentyfive years with the neoliberal economic growth, regulations and policies in the context of globalisation. Various political regimes during the period implemented these policies as a kind of a 'reform' agenda (tautologically treated as desirable rather than by evaluating them as positive contributors to the declared and accepted national democratic objectives and values which respond to the needs and aspirations of the masses by instituting a just and fair policy package). This was done with fairly pronounced me-too zeal, mainly to accelerate the rate of growth of GDP by relying on the agency of big private Indian and foreign corporate entities, of course, with active support of the state in various forms. It was carried out in the framework of market mechanism with open borders, as a member of the WTO and with close rapport with the World Bank and the IMF.

Before proceeding further we wish to refer to the overall rationale for and purpose of these reviews by the IPEA. These exercises are the joint products of the contributions made by scores of scholars, activists and socially-concerned citizens of India who examine these processes of state-sponsored, market-led and big organised capital led-expansion of economic activities, initially in a state-led indicative development planning framework. Post-1990, all such initiatives were replaced by neoliberal packages. These contributions explicitly adopt the framework of what may broadly be called a *people-centric* perspective and without the baggage of the neoliberal GDP-centric economic growth paradigm which was and still is being oversold to the third world including India.

It may be recalled that with her own deep-seated idiosyncrasies, India is also an important part of the story of how the post-World War, post-decolonisation part of the global story of modern industrial growth is a modern catching-up economic growth in a mixed economy statist model. This initial globalisation was thought of as the panacea for the centuries old stagnation and exclusion from the benefits of modernity. Ours is the story of how this was enacted.

It is well known that powerful external forces of the early industrialised global hegemonic centres operated more or less jointly with the Indian national state. It operated under the leading role of the small, organised, private corporate sector as the single richest economic and financial engine of growth, with its own typical narrow agenda despite postures to the contrary. The national task of development was viewed as that of catching-up with the rich, early industrialised countries. However, it more or less excluded the general run of the poor, deprived and discriminated majority of vulnerable Indians from any worthwhile and adequate access to the slew of welfare measures and services and capability-building exercises to empower them as minor but state-enabled participants and stake-holders in India's socio-economic development.

To add fuel to the built-in exclusionary tendencies, the perversion of the stated social objectives was accentuated by the joint collaborative use of concentrated power, resources and public amenities—especially by violation of the formal state regulations and tax collection measures. This is reflected in the massive, systemic near ubiquity of the black economy and perverted democracy as the money-muscle and mafia power jointly came to rule the roost.

Little wonder, India's fiscal impotence and external vulnerabilities reached break-up peaks by 1990.

Ironically, the post-1990 neoliberal regime enthroned those very sections which subverted the socio-economic transformative agenda of independent India by legalising the economic and political processes of market-determined and Indian and foreign private-corporates-led people-disempowering agencies of exclusionary but accelerated economic growth.

The intra-dominant policies and projects were manipulated by resorting to cronyism, binding together the super capitalists with top-level political and policy processes. Shockingly, these cronyist and corrupt practices percolated down to the decentralised populist measures too and robbed the masses of even the token benefits meant for them.

Thus, among the marginalised sections, particularly the adversely included rural, agricultural and informal sector, there are at least a crore of young men, and especially women, whose endeavours to join the workforce was sadly frustrated every year.They were also the victims of forcible land acquisition and are among the prominent categories of the adversely included sections that became regular victims. Their rights and future were sacrificed on the altar of consumerist, foreign exchange-guzzling, hugely unjust, largely metropolitan growth. (A National Crime Records Bureau report of 2012 says, as many as 256,913 farmers in India committed suicide between 1995 and 2010. *The Hindu* newspaper calls it 'the worst-ever recorded wave of suicides of this kind in human history' ncrb.nic.in/StatPublications/ADSI/ADSI2014/adsi-2014%20full%20 report.pdf. During the period of neoliberal policies, many estimates and other data sources place the number of farmer suicides to up to 800,000 persons and the tragic process is continuing.)

It is this story that the numerous publications of the IPEA have over the past twentyfive years or so up-fronted and shared with the general public. The mainstream development discourse and its policy and evaluation counterparts in India, as also many externally located agencies, have today come to recognise the all-too-starkly visible reality in some select parts only. One may draw attention to various national and international studies on poverty estimates and status in terms of access to and availability of public goods, services and facilities and discrimination against those who are at the lower ends of the distribution pyramid which is becoming increasingly obese and enlarged at the top.

The distribution and popular participation in development are among the issues systematically evaded, often by reposing faith in the so-called trickle-down processes and ignoring the powerfully operating gushing-up growth. Little wonder, the present crises dominated the defensive phase of globalisation following the continued persistence of various crises syndromes in most parts of the world. This lead to widespread disenchantment, particularly after the mini-depression of 2008, despite state supported corpulent financialisation of the global economy including its premature and anti-people expansion in India, which has changed the context of the development discourse here.

Now it is getting recognised even by the high priests of neoliberal policies-led growth as something oversold, one may say basically as snake oil. Actually It is these kinds of people-centric issues which appear to be the dominant concerns of the contributors of the Alternative Economic Surveys, including of those to the present volume, who have put together these essays in order to share how has India and her people fared under the neoliberal dispensation.

It may be pointed out that despite the dominant discourse, in bits and pieces enough insights are available across diverse sources to see at least in retrospect how a systematic weakening of and weaning away from a statist national social model of development was made. The operating model in India frequently tended to become a prisoner of its own short-run easy choices. These were dictated jointly by the electoral compulsions of managing popular support and top-level manipulative politicking by keeping on their side the sections which were becoming increasingly better off, organised and vocal.

This was required by the political classes which did precious little for the general masses except by way of tokenism and failed to provide even the minimum for their wellbeing and for enabling their participation in development both as agencies and beneficiaries.The two-way necessity of practical politicking for winning the favours of the money bags for financing increasingly costly and false issues dominated, emotionally surcharged electoral battles and for personal high voltage ambitions of the political-bureaucratic strata ensure the continuous hollowing out of the people's concerns from the policy agenda, which in any case, may not be an inevitable part of the neoliberal agenda.

The assumption that there would be active operation of the trickle-down processes and the poor and marginalised would be taken on board the development chariot and even the sustenance of a reasonably rapid, all round and well-balanced growth floundered on the hard rocks of the emerging growth dynamics and intricate interplay of local and MNC corporate interests and their political-bureaucratic collaborators cum mentors.

The narrow, sectional interests guided behavior, in fact, belongs largely to the domain of the all-encompassing black economy. It is this large-scale expanding deviance which made the powerful sections from every field of business and administration, policy-making and international collaboration increasingly hostile to the social goals and content and made the reality a bonanza for big private local and foreign oligopolies.

Historically it might be well to recall how the growth processes in India became divorced from social goals and outcomes. The inner logic of walking on so many feet simultaneously created a lot of tensions and contradictions which, on the one hand worsened the lot of the common citizens and on the other, enveloped India in a severe fiscal crisis and dependence on fresh bouts of external borrowing to pay its way in international economic and financial markets. Thus the social legitimacy of India's growth path, fiscal capability and financial solvency precipitously moved downward and severe political uncertainties and instability became the fate of the largest electoral democracy.

Clearly it was a practically operative coalition of various centralised forces spawning faltering, inadequate, costly, inappropriate and exclusionary economic growth during the muddling-through era. As is often the case with regimes facing blind alleys, it was those who managed to benefit from the pre -1990 regime at the cost of the common man, and national viability and solvency, by incurring the costs of wading through highly discretionary and evadable jungle of controls and regulations who also became the grave-diggers of the old regime and masters of the new market freedoms. It is they who operated the open borders and friendly and nearly subservient state, wearing a verbal fig leaf of social commitments at a great national-social cost.

Little wonder all that it achieves are its very own narrow sectional goals and agenda (as seen in relatively higher growth rates of GDP, notwithstanding the controversies around the growth numbers) to the exclusion and by imposing huge exogenously imposed short-run and long-term social and environmental costs and displacement of tribal people and peasantry from their hereditary lands.

The most shocking but largely bypassed in the mainstream discourse is the huge worsening of distribution of income, wealth and social power. The small size of the organised sector itself stands out as one of the most telling indicator of massive growth of multifaceted inequalities and intense adverse inclusion. Latest income tax and national accounts data show that in 2012-13, just an insignificant number of 193 persons, each averaging annual income in excess of RS 500 crore managed to corner an astronomical amount of Rs 454,793 crore, amounting to 20 per cent of the country's gross national income. These data show that 3.12 crore persons (just about 30 million out of one billion people), ie. around 3 per cent of the total population, netted an annual income of Rs 21.37 lakh crore according to their income tax returns. Further evidence shows how among these fortunate apex-located persons also, there is a great deal of deep income inequality. One wonders why the shocking extent and coverage of income inequality, in addition to that of land holdings and access to public goods and services, brought out by the 2011-Socio-economic Caste Census is becoming a victim of a conspiracy of silence. The rural people who barely managed to scrap through during the 1950s were estimated at about 17 crore but now they number more than 65 crore!

Let us consider what all the neoliberal quarter century in India has accomplished. GDP growth has been unprecedented, so has been the entry of FDI, mostly in the form of portfolio investment as a part of global financialisation. It has boosted the market capitalisation of the increasingly cocooned in narrow self-interest private corporate honchos. And as their inevitable socio-political and cultural counterparts, in the form of intensification of mass penury, insecurity and intensification of adverse inclusion and emptying of the social, political and cultural content of 'development' visible in India. *The dominant discourse simply bypasses these outcomes and processes of growing adverse inclusion and corruption/ degeneration of democracy into plutocracy, cronyism and populism.*

Given the shock therapy character of the adoption of the neoliberal policy package, it began its march with the adoption of two associated objectives. These were: One, to tide over the extremely delicate external payments crisis owing to unsustainable external borrowing, even for debt-servicing/financing Rupee projects on an increasingly growing scale. Second, to wriggle out of the fiscal crunch owing to the inability to collect adequate amount of taxes from the big corporates and high-networth individuals who were the chosen agents of growth under state regulations and support.

By replacing external borrowing by spreading red carpet for foreign direct investment (FDI) and by severely restraining people-empowering public spending and selling public sector assets to the big chosen private corporate entities, the two immediate crises were papered over, essentially by patch-work, time-serving remedies which left the underlying basic issues intact and even accentuated them.

By all round liberalisation in favour of big private capital, opening up the economy and liberalised industrial policy, the rate of growth of GDP too has been comparatively accelerated. Now some cosmetic, pro-poor, populist measures with the intent to paint the 'reforms' with a human face are being over-sold by means of high-voltage publicity. Both, the programmes and the tall claims on their behalf, fall far short of any worthwhile impact and sustained capability building capacity for ensuring even a minimum of human existence for the country's crores of endemically adversely included masses.

A huge fiscal burden was accepted in order to benefit the corporate entities and the better-off sections (the major beneficiaries of the public spending for infrastructure). However, even basic minimum of good and assured health and education facilities, minimum of basic amenities for our huge rural and slums populations and a modicum of social security even on par with our equally or more constrained neighbouring nations became victims of the neoliberal imperative of fiscal discipline!

With continued sway of the menacingly growing and indistinguishably intermixed black economy, polity and administration (with not-so-open involvement of various mafias), the private corporate sector and the super rich is sought to be legitimised. Thus, except GDP growth and unprecedented entry of FDI inflows in various forms, almost every socio-economic and cultural indicator meaningful for the people at large seem to have deteriorated, particularly in a comparative context—a situation of 25 crore versus 100 crore!

The political class joins hands with its cronies in private business as a collective group, the selling point being pro-business is pro-people! Both thrive on the grand alliance of huge bottom lines and decisive election outcomes in their favour only. This is a part of the processes that demonstrates how the largest global electoral democracy degenerated at the operational level into a virtual plutocracy, following the principle that those who have shall get more and those who have little will be further deprived (the Mathew Principle). One wonders if during any period during the post-independence era, the country has suffered such a bout of growing inequalities and top-end concentration of all the goodies that our mimetic economic growth, its associated consumerism and practical daily imitation of degenerate life styles from the rich world, is witnessing today.

Just a cursory mention of what is the treatment meted out to people during all these seven decades of 'democratic' governance and proto- and full-scale neoliberal growth for the pursuit of the status of a global economic and financial power house. Irrespective of costs, both financial and opportunity social costs and the sources of technology, the country is being readied for high speed and bullet trains (with borrowed money and technology), farm land displacing airports around the country, relatively low-priced ATF operated air services sustained by massive budgetary support while the masses have to travel in overcrowded trains with poor sanitation, overcrowded buses on unsafe roads in the interior length and breadth of the nation. Big ticket production of practically all the major makes of passenger automobiles far outnumber the production of public transport vehicles. Creation of fancy six-lane highways linking the already well-linked metros and other big urban habitats, a network of smart cities while about 70 per cent of the people living in rural India lack swachh civic services and sanitary facilities, including adequate and assured potable water supply. Digital India without home lights and unpaved rural streets full of dust and filth, let alone minimum pubic infrastructure for capability building facilities and education, heath services and social security. A complete social insurance package for the elected representatives with high levels of salaries in the midst of as low as under 2 per cent of GDP for social security public spending for the vast unorganised sector. It is the messages of this kind based on hard but often ignored facts which is sought to be conveyed through the present volume.

The mountebank analysts and lobbyists seem to overshadow the entire mainstream discourse and have come out with tendencious analyses of the nation's achievements, without an iota of reference to the enormous, in fact, incalculable costs imposed on the poor citizens. These sections orchestrate the chorus of 'no alternative' and 'viable' options. It is a modest attempt by the IPEA and the contributors to this volume to highlight that another set of world views and many alternative meaningful functional worlds are not simply possibilities but also high value imperatives.

—Kamal Nayan Kabra with many inputs by V Upadhyay

Introduction

OVER THE last few decades, the operational-level real commitment to social inclusion (specified in terms of a variety of democratic socio-economic objectives and outcomes of the development-related socio-economic interventions by the state) has gradually been eroded in the course of implementation of India's plans and policies. This happened particularly pointedly after the 1990s under the pretext of pragmatic adjustments to the 'compulsions' encountered by the state in managing its multifarious challenges and the pressure of global and national big business in order to accelerate economic growth, propagated as common national imperative. It was then that neoliberal policies were adopted as a result of the pressures and manipulations by powerful sections dominating the Indian policy scenario. They offered choices as the defining and guiding discourse for India's development and macro-economic management, but with a great deal of pressure from western governments and the World Bank-IMF duo. Thus the openly accepted social content of development and democracy (which was initially articulated in the First and the Second Plan which culminated in the adoption of Socialist Pattern of Society and their replacement by a number of populist programmes as cover-ups in the later years) remained expectedly far from realisation and moved towards further strengthening of the status quo.[1]

[1] The stated sum and substance of variously worded objectives in our democratic polity seemed to imply (of course, in terms of a different kind of terminology) genuine, fair and just inclusion of the overwhelming majority of the poor and vulnerable Indians gradually by launching development plans consisting of a series of measures for increasing the participation and empowerment of the common citizens. See the first two Five Year Plan documents of the Government of India (1952 and 1956, New Delhi). More or

Prime Props of Neoliberalism in India

A variety of assessments have over time attempted to show how economic growth as development could not benefit the common citizens. Gadgil (1968) was among the early ones to give vent to public disappointment from the social point of view. Even if some claims are advanced regarding some limited measure of improvement, overall there does not seem to have taken place any definitive or really significant breakthrough in terms of making a meaningful impact on the masses, especially on their larger absolute number. However, these judgmental views are rarely backed by commensurate facts and analyses covering the whole country and her people, except by means of a lot of quantitative data based on surveys and some tendentious estimates of the incidence of poverty, particularly those advanced by the national or the multilateral establishments.[2] (Mishra, Coyle and Spears, *Indian Express*, 14 October 2015)

In any case, the daily lived life experience of the poor people, mostly belonging to the SCs/STs or the Dalits in general, can hardly be captured by any numerical data as the actual experience of extreme discriminatory conditions of existence magnify the denials, deprivations and discriminations woven into the way these people were subjected to oppression and exploitation even after independence. How far the *equal fundamental rights* granted by the Constitution to citizens, including in an equal measure to Dalits and women belonging to these social groups, have become a reality on the ground cannot be adequately captured

---

less similar objectives were repeated in the subsequent Plans and other policy statements. It means under such a perspective, the masses were to be both the main actors in and contributors to development on the one hand, and fair and equitable co-sharers of the fruits of development in order to overcome their centuries old persistent adverse inclusion in society, on the other. Though by virtue of the salience accorded to GDP growth, the main design of development remained, in essence, economistic of the catching - up with the West variety and constrained owing to the relatively limited effective power of the state vis-à-vis the big private business and such like forces. But for popular consumption, it speaks of a number of subsidiary elements and loudly proclaims policies and programmes supposed to extend their coverage to the whole range of socio-economic and cultural activities and outcomes intended to benefit the weaker sections..

2 This position is validated even by popular press, owing to the award of economics Nobel to Angus Deaton who has been making such criticism of Indian data sources. See *Indian Express* articles by Mishra Udit, Coyle and Spears, 14 October 2015.

without supplementing the numerical estimates of various dimensions by sensitive qualitative descriptions of their life stories and experiences. Thus, the policies based even on the most comprehensive and reliable quantitative data barely touch the surface of the actual degradation and adverse social inclusion which continues to remain the fate of these sections. This position seems to hold, notwithstanding some positive changes, particularly owing to some bit of supply of public goods and services and some elements of affirmative state action.[3&4]

Thus, many such studies seem to suffer from the lack of a realistic picture capable of showcasing the actual living conditions and experiences owing to the character of existing social relations and the inability of state action to deal with socially entrenched authoritarian extra-legal practices. It is such factors which make many even well-meaning policies and programmes, apart from their tokenism, counterproductive in the course of their implementation. This is an additional factor to the often-recognised weaknesses of the policies arising from weak data and lack of credible theoretical explanation of the prevalent situation to help design a consistent policy and practical ways to carry it out.[5]

---

[3] One gets a vivid picture of the situation which persists in some measure even now, mainly by means of sensitive Dalit literature. For instance, one may refer to the path-breaking book by Tulsiram (a faculty of Jawaharlal Nehru University) in his autobiographical Hindi book *Murdahiya*, Rajkamal Paperbacks, 2015 where the grim scenario and highly demeaning experiences of daily life persisting during the 1950s, based on personal and family and village experience in UP, is brought out as it was experienced.

[4] See Bose, Arun p 85, 1989, where he quotes the Presidential address to the First Indian Communist Conference in 1925. It reads, 'no sooner (is) their economic dependence (arising from their "agrarian problem" of inequality in the ownership of land which imposes "helotry of the vast masses of the suppressed peoples") solved, the social stigma of untouchability is bound to disappear'. At that time, Bose asserted that these views 'are widely held by Indian Communists even to this day'. Even in 2015, neither have the inequality in land ownership, nor the many-faceted social discrimination, oppression and exploitation disappeared. One has evidently to look for a different set of factors in their unity to be able to deal some decisive blows against these modes of social existence, amounting to simultaneous operation of multiple apartheids.

[5] Some of them even have a problem with the values-related aspects, in so far as they treat social-economic equality as dispensable in preference to poverty reduction in the sense of enabling those arbitrarily treated as poor to be able to consume a little more of the essential prerequisites of survival: Bhagawti J 2006; Dahrendorf Ralf 2006.

Moreover, such studies and estimates proceed without so much as mentioning what is happening at the decidedly narrow top end as a related and often causal factor. What it means is that the approaches and interventions remain divorced from the implications and outcomes in terms of relative shares in the distribution of national income, wealth and political influence among various socio-economic, occupational and regional groups and their impact on state policies (Lister, Ruth, 2001). That is to say, inequalities and growing concentration of wealth and access to participation in various socio-economic and political processes in increasingly fewer hands can hardly be consistent with what is imperative for a decisive positive influence on what is possible and, desirable at the lower levels of socio-economic and political hierarchy. Such assertions and limited analyses often adopt a theoretical framework that is deeply and unquestioningly rooted in the mainstream development theories and policies, based on the view that economic growth by itself is a major essential pre-condition for improving the lot of the deprived and discriminated parts of the population. These largely apologetic and self-serving exercises proceed as though any alternative perspectives and methods of assessing the ground reality are either not relevant or are not feasible. Thus, they shut themselves off from perspectives which are endowed with really far-going and socially desirable positive potential.

In the present exercise, we hold that the Socio-Economic and Caste Census (SECC, GoI 2011) data have the potential to provide a reliable and credible data base for evaluating what has happened to the rural people in the name of development, over the entire period of development planning in post-independence India as it reflects the situation as it was found in the whole of the country and is reflected by data collected on the basis of door-to-door visits canvassing simple direct questions. Thus, we believe these data concerning rural people tend to show how the largest single group of Indians remain victims of endemic development deficit. After presenting some select, largely all-India findings of the SECC (though States' and SCs/STs data too are available in it), we try to present a comparative picture by going back to the situation as it existed during the 1950s.

In order to briefly see the extent and nature of change as reflected in the SECC data, we refer in the present exercise, to some fairly comparable facts concerning the conditions of rural India, particularly the rural poor. In the second section, we attempt to relate these findings to the nature and course of evolution of India's development in the constitutional-democratic framework by means of advancingsome hypotheses. The third section presents some evidence regarding massive concentration of advantages at the top from various sources. Finally, we come to the concluding part in which we attempt to understand the rationale and implications of these findings.

From 17 cr to 65 cr Victims of Absolute Poverty

The published results of the Socio-Economic Caste Census 2011 (SECC 2011) concerning rural India are seen as a mine of hitherto not available data. Departing from the plethora of survey-based data with a lot of irreducible limitations, now the SECC census data on an all-India comprehensive basis is available to us. Moreover, the SECC data questioned the respondents directly about their incomes and specific aspects of their possessions and situation (far more easy to understand and recollect than consumption whether in physical quantities or in terms of money spent, whether a week or a month ago). Consumption data without relating to housing conditions, level of market penetration and accessibility, education and health status can really conceal a lot and are a poor substitute for data on income, assets and access to socio-economic services and facilities. The SECC data are better equipped to throw light on the larger questions regarding how do the masses live and work and their living condition in their villages. Hence we take the view that the SECC data are likely to bring out comparatively sharply and clearly for the entire post-independence period the ground-level reality. Since there was no reference made to this or that plan or policy or schemes, but direct information about the present conditions as such were obtained, the responses are likely to be close to reality without much misunderstanding and bias. In any case, one has little reason to ignore or downgrade the significance of these data as they stand. A recent news report says that a task force of the Niti Aayog examined the possibility of using the SECC data for determining poverty-line and has kept the issue open (*Business Standard*, 28 March 2016).

The information brought out by the SECC cover a lot of hitherto rarely treaded ground, and in some major ways make good at least one limitation in terms of limited availability of comprehensive socio-economic data regarding many key aspects bearing on the outcomes of our development and macro-economic management, and bearing on the lives and living standard of the rural people. In so far as rural India still accounts for an overwhelming part of our population (almost 70 per cent) the comprehensive, ground-level and entire country-wide socio-economic information revealed by the SECC 2011 may well be taken as capable of improving the prevalent understanding/assessments of the country's economic condition to a considerable extent.[6] On the basis of the above data, in the following chapters we try to see how have rural Indians fared in the socio-economic space over the past seven decades of what is portrayed as democratic, development planning-directed growth of GDP and its impact on overall development in terms of some declared socio-economic objectives.

The facts brought out by the SECC tend to indicate a great deal of socio-economic betterment owning to the model, manner and mechanism of the actually highly partisan ground-level applications of the economic growth mechanism and its outcomes. True, for a small section of those who were already better-off, these decades have meant a real bonanza (as we try to capture by means of limited data available fairly readily in the public domain) but at incalculable human and social cost and by worsening the life time prospects of our enormously large sections of rural people, thus putting a series of question marks on the sustainability of such an economy and polity.

Rural India is presently home to about 17.9 crore households - HH (about 88.3 crore people) out of the country's total of 24.39 crore HH (120.24 crore people). The SECC data show that, about 65.8 crore people

[6] Many other sources of information such as the A Sengupta Commission Report regarding the lower sections of society, mostly forming part of the unorganised sector (absorbing almost 90 per cent of our work force) and many studies on specific aspects too, are available but there is no other study that can claim to cover the entire country in the way the SECC has done. True there are numerous poverty estimates but they are hardly a substitute as they seem to be based on concepts hardly consistent with genuine inclusion and development as a universal democratic right. See Manali Chakravarty in the present volume.

(about 13.34 crore rural HH), ie. about three fourths (74.49 per cent) of India's total HH, have the highest earning member having an income which is less than a sum of Rs 5,000 per month. This means, bypassing the marginal contributions which may be made by other family members, per month per family member may have only Rs 1,014 to spend, and each member's per day income is about Rs 34 at 2011-12 prices. Obviously, the other members too are likely to add to the family kitty, especially with the widespread prevalence of child labour and informal work, but, given the absence of other social support and security sources it is difficult to hazard a guess whether any notable difference on this account is likely.

The *Economic Survey 2014-15* of the Government of India reported per capita net national income of Rs 64,316, (this is according to the new series, calculated by the CSO on the basis of market prices while, according to the preceding 2004-05 series calculated on the basis of gross value-added, it was reported to be Rs 61,855). That is, per capita daily income of an average urban Indian is a sum of little over Rs 176, that is a little over five times the average daily share of one member (out of the highest earner's income) of the Rs 34 at current prices, as seen from the SECC 2011-12.[7] Can the contrast between the census data on the highest earner's income per family and the CSO calculated NAS data indicate a certain degree of disparity because the latter covers all the sector averages, particularly covering urban incomes? Given the huge and unprecedented chasm between inter-sector disparities in income, vast and growing rural-urban disparities (as the rural income is about one-fourth of the urban income—see Singh SP in the present volume) show how the rural economy is becoming steadily worse off, particularly owing to the steep decline in the share of agriculture in GDP (under 15 per cent) and with no notable emergence of non-farm and formal sector activities in rural India. The figure of a little below Rs 34 per day per person income mentioned above is not that of the total actual income, but the share in a family of about five (rounded off from the average as 4.93 members per HH) persons, from the upper limit of the highest earner single member's income, without counting what the rest of the members and transfer payments may or may not be contributing. Thus, it is more an indicator

---

[7] The divergence between the ground level data and the NAS data on such issues are well-known.

of the approximate level than of the actually obtaining level which, to an extent and in all probability, would be somewhat higher.

In addition to the above, the SECC also shows that a little less than 3.1 crore households (that means a little less than 15 crore people) are lucky enough to have at least one member whose earning per month is between Rs 5000 to Rs 10,000; that compared to more than 65 crore people with half the maximum family monthly income, we have a little fewer than 15 crore people who live in rural families with double the income available to the former. The main point of significance is that, according to the SECC data, *only 8.29 per cent of the rural households of about 5 members each are able to live in families whose highest earning member's income is between Rs 5,000 to Rs 10,000, that is per member's monthly income is of Rs 2028.40 and daily income of Rs 67.61 (all at 2011-12 prices).*[8]

Certain other findings of the SECC 2011-12, including for the villages as a whole in terms of their access to and availability to them of a number of socio-economic common infrastructure facilities capable of enabling the rural people to participate in the growth-related processes give a little more concrete perspective and meaning to what is being seen as abject, persistent increase in the number of people with pitiably low income. Only less than one-tenth of the families, that is about 1.73 crore households, supporting some 8.5 crore rural people have the privilege of a salaried job, mostly (about 1.1 crore) working in public sector and the government. The private sector rural employees constitute barely 3.58 per cent of the rural households sheltering some 5 crore individuals out of a total of approximately 21.65 crore. This fact may be taken together with another finding, showing that only about 29 lakh households (ie. about 1.43 crore persons) with members numbering about 1.93 crore, are engaged in non-farm, self-employed activities. What has happened to the traders, traditional crafts and skills based non-agricultural own-account enterprises and occupations under the grossly unequal competition of the modern and foreign industries may be inferred from these facts. The pitch seems likely to become tougher for these categories with the

---

8 Can these income ranges allow the people covered by them to qualify for the status of the 'middle classes' is debatable.

entry of MNC retailers and e-commerce platforms, restaurants and increasing ease of doing business in India by rolling of the red carpet for foreign direct investment (FDI) under the blanket 'Make in India' stance.

For a logical appreciation of the outcomes seen above, one may refer to the number of causal manual workers in rural India. The SECC shows some 9.16 crore households or about 45.15 crore rural people belong to this category. Little wonder even now that the unorganised-informal sector (treated by the authors of the *Economic Survey 2012-13* as an 'arena of exclusion') continues to maintain a tiny lead over the organised and highly cared for formal-corporate sector, in terms of making a contribution to GDP and in a big big way in terms of providing comparatively high level of but not adequately secure livelihoods. Then the number of cultivator households is found to be 5.93 crore or 29.23 crore people (NAS: 2013-14). As many as 56 per cent rural citizens are without land and only 40 per cent of the land has access to irrigation, showing the preponderance of dry farming. In some States, famed for so-called land distribution under land reforms, widespread landlessness is still the reality for more than two thirds of the rural people. Consigning to oblivion the most relevant programme of rural and farm sector development, that is land reforms and large-scale public funded and grass-roots level programmes of land improvement, today the focus is on compulsory and very inadequately and unfairly compensated land acquisition after decades of depriving the farmer and the SCs/STs of their meagre landholdings. There are hardly any regular programmes of land improvement as a state-supported pro-small and marginal farmers programme.

The SECC shows that India's landless population (3.87 crore households, that is 19 crore people) is of a staggering proportion and their major source of income is labour. About 31.5 crore rural people are illiterate, which is more people than the total rural population reported in the 1950-51 census. A huge number live in rural India without a structure that can be called a house except by way of courtesy (2.37 crore households accommodating 11.7 crore people). Only 5.92 crore people live in their own houses. The SECC also gives the breakup of information in terms of SCs/STs and a lot of information about the female segment of the population. By bringing in the Dalit and female dimensions, the SECC data tend to make a sad story sadder still.

To see how the conditions have changed for rural India, especially in terms of average income over the last almost seven decades, comparison has to be made with the early days of planning during the 1950s. We recall that on the basis of official data, Minhas (1971) in a study estimated that at 1960-61 prices, some 17.3 crore rural people had annual consumption expenditure below Rs 200 (per person, that is under 55 paise per day) while, those subsisting below Rs 240 (per person less than 67 paise per day) numbered 21.5 crore in 1956-57. Minhas refers to 'a distinguished Study Group' which recommended a standard of private consumption of Rs 240 (at 1960-61 prices) per capita per year as a bare minimum requirement (pp 69). Compared to mid 1950s, during 2011-12, the value of the Rupee in the domestic economy is seen to be around 2.37 paise. The per capita per annum consumption of a very large part of the population during mid-1950s was estimated to be so inadequate that these persons were described as suffering from 'infernal destitution' by Minhas, ie. below Rs 200 per annum. This meant that for these people, per day consumption level was below 55 paise per person and for those termed 'not so poor' it was below Rs 240 per annum, ie. below 66 paise per person (both at historical 1960-61 prices). Some 17.3 crore people belonged to the poorest group while 21.4 crore belonged to the latter, marginally better-off than the group suffering 'infernal destitution'. Presently, during 2011-12 we have seen that the per capita per day income, as shown by the SECC, stands at almost Rs 34, which converted into 1960-61 prices amounts to *about 92 paise per capita per day.*

One may assume that during this period, some improvement has come about in the access of the poor to public goods and services over the level we inherited from the British and the native rulers. Is this small increase commensurate with the marked growth in total and per capita income in real terms, particularly in a comparative perspective vis-à-vis the other better-off and the commanding-dominant sections in our domestic economy? Against the backdrop of the unaddressed and 'unsatisfied' basic needs issue, one has to judge what to make of the 'progress' made by the economy during this period.[9]

---

[9] The SECC data on some indicators of this kind too find a place in its published results to an extent but we have not included them in the present exercise, as the entire set of SECC findings have become a sort of victims of silence.

Making an arbitrary allowance for the income of the other members, one can surmise that since mid-1950s, at least the status quo has been broken, though too marginal and meagre to yield practical and visible gains at the cutting edge for those on the lowest rungs. *But a far more disturbing truth is that, compared to around 20 crore Indians from rural India at such a high level of multi-faceted vulnerabilities during mid-1950, presently, the number suffering such a fate is a little less than four times larger, around 65 crore people!* It may be noted that we had about 30 crore rural population in 1951, of which about 21 crore were living at sub-human levels in rural India. Apparently, a little more than three times the 1951 number of people have to manage, may be at a trivially higher level, to subsist at such outrageously inadequate levels of incomes, as their daily share of the highest earner member's *real income has failed to reach even one Rupee!*

During this period, the real GDP has taken a big leap of about 28 times and the nominal national income has taken a many times bigger jump of around 969 times (calculated on the basis of comparing the index number of net national income, NNP, at current and at 2004-05 prices, see *Economic Survey*, 2013-14: 2-3). Clearly this high jump in economic activities by and large bypassed and left out a huge majority of the people who elected so many times the governments which actively participate in the economy, with the promise and stated purpose to lead the nation to a better human social existence for those who lacked it as a historical legacy. These governments left out the very voters who voted them to power election after election from benefit of the budgetary measures and policies.

Development Devoid of Social Content and Democracy

How do we make some sense of such disturbing facts? It is a difficult exercise and too detailed and many-faceted to be backed up by a great deal of actual analyses of the plans, polices and their implementation over the last nearly seven decades and, of course, a bit too ambitious to be tried in the course of a short exercise. But one can make a quick attempt to reach some conclusions by way of some initial, tentative hypotheses derived from the findings of the SECC (which showed that about 65 crore persons live in families whose highest earner brought home less than Rs 5,000 per month at 2011 prices, and that over 45 crore rural residents are casual manual workers, about 20 crore are leandless and another large number have miniscule landholdings).

What the government calls progress is what we term as 'perverse and opposite outcomes' (in the sense of combining positive economic outcomes with negative social ones concerning the adversely included sections, whose need for development is incontrovertibly the most acute and urgent) of what has been officially declared to be the *intentions* or *objectives* of India's policymakers. The government has attempted a limited extent of 'development' (which we illustrated above with the help of the data brought forth by the SECC-2011) which may well be attributed to three major, fairly consciously chosen or accepted elements of the policy measures and plans adopted during the period and most prominently deriving considerably from the political economy of this era.

One reason for considering the *declared intent* from being vastly different from the *realised outcomes* is the primary reliance on the unregulated or poorly, half-heartedly and ineffectually organised market forces in their elemental logic and development administration by a bureaucracy descended from the Raj, with hardly any effective steps to thoroughly overhaul it. The market forces and the signals emanating from them were operationalised on the basis of private profit-oriented market decisions, made by the narrow socio-economic groups or classes on the basis of their elemental response because there were hardly any effective attempts to make them respond to a bare minimum of social discipline and imperatives under the plan priorities, as was declared in the Second Five Year Plan document. What occurred on account of informal and formal influences of big business and rampant irregularities associated with their operations, under what has been called regulatory seizure, was, in effect, what the existing market structure dictated owing to both market perversity and policy dictates.[10]

This situation forms an element of what is generally perceived to be the great divide between the 'stated' or declared and the 'real' operative objectives of India's national development—largely under many subtle and not-so-subtle influence of big private business and inter-government

[10] The Report of the Industrial Licensing Policy Inquiry Report, 1969 and the Committee on Controls and Subsidies.

foreign influences—either by means of the diplomacy of foreign aid or by means of the towering influence of the economics of growth as development directed know-how and political economy, structures, processes and relationships. The market supremacy-based pursuit of GDP growth as the basic focus/objective and indicator of development has essentially led to market outcomes increasingly towards further cementing of the existing adverse equations. It hardly needs reiteration that these relations operate under the inherited and deeply embedded situation of adverse inclusion (that is, non-reciprocal and unilaterally beneficial relationships in major socio-economic aspects) of India's millions of people (indeed the majority) in terms of grossly inadequate and uncertain social security and denies them fair and assured participation and access to the means enabling participation in various branches of production (employment failure) and their consequent inability to become buyers of the goods and services (home market failure) required to obtain a better life. These people were reduced to the status of mere bystanders to watch the economy grow, diversify and enrich those well-endowed and helped and supported by the state and market processes, but bypassing the neglected and poorly endowed masses.

Actually, the initial starting position and its socio-economic character in many spheres were reflected in the mixed structure of the embryonic market in India more or less right up to the 1960s (as reflected in the vast size of the unorganised sectors taken together), and thus enhanced the market power and access to the plan-related growth initiatives of already fairly evolved business-corporate entities (to an extent also of the higher educated urban-metropolitan intermediate strata) in India's hierarchical hide-bound economy, society and polity to further fortify the initial lead of relatively better-endowed sections over the rest of society taken in its totality.

The policy and socio-economic framework/structure and composition of the state was incapable of allowing the state power to address itself to the overall democratic socio-economic tasks required for inclusive development. Hence, a large degree of reliance on populism remained the key substitute for genuine, adequate and transformative interventions to equip and enable widespread participation in the socio-economic processes by access to adequate and appropriate provision of public and quasi-public goods and services, meant specifically for the lower rungs of the social pyramid. This kind of a situation and impasse became further aggravated as our democratic processes and players—in the absence of proper and operationally effective democratic mobilisation focusing on the felt, meaningful and genuine rights, even though marginally to begin with (instead of some distant promised basic re-structuring in a question-begging, unrealistic manner owing to the existing stranglehold of the ruling power equations and the politics, not so much of development but as a proxy for it)—gave essentially just a certain amount of hypocritical lip-service to the cause and concerns of these politically highly 'manageable' masses.

In this context, one is drawing attention to not just the usual power games but India's deep-seated social authoritarianism, deliberate and strategically schemed misuse of the traditions and apparent divisions and market-led electoral-administrative processes. In the course of time, the working of such factors and processes, virtually led to the further strengthening of the incipient dominance of plutocracy. Lack of adequate and assured livelihoods, over time, to a large section of the existing and incremental workforce, and no more than just a token provision of the socio-economic and quasi-public goods and services too were factors that worked negatively for the common men and their fair and just participation in development.

Then there was the growing inappropriateness of the bulk of the GDP (a bundle of goods and services whose nature and composition, that is its ingredients) that remained impervious to the needs, affordability and preferences of the rural and poor sections of society. Thus, the real content of growth in terms of impacting the choice of industries and product mix (prior to the next question of the choice of techniques) and its supply-determined sector-wise unbalanced structure intensified the initial imbalances and dysfunctions despite much larger overall levels of production.[11] In this framework, the poor, deprived and discriminated masses, without even assured food and nutrition, let alone social voice, were denied access to education, health and a modicum of other no-less-critical civic services and production-helping decentralisation, particularly

[11] See Kabra (2012) for elaboration of the concept of appropriate product mix.

in the villages and small towns where infrastructure facilities were hardly in a position to contribute in the process of development in any gainful and dignified capacity, whether in the polity or the economy (*Journal of Social Studies. Kabra, Kamal Nayan, 2013).*

Worse still, even protection of their traditional rights and meagre possessions, as illustrated by massive magnitudes of compulsory and unfair acquisition of lands and other resources traditionally available to the tribal people, rural poor and other small landholders, including those enjoying certain valuable rights over forests and other common property resources, were compromised. Even protection against police and high caste atrocities remained at the most perfunctory level, as so many civil rights activists have brought out.

What a democratically-elected government is conventionally expected to do, as a part of running a democratic state administration and a progressive fiscal system, is to provide more than proportionate share of the public and quasi-public goods and services to those numerically the largest parts of the electorate. Those whose need for such support is the greatest in order to overcome their backlog of inherited deprivations, discrimination and inadequacies (that is, adverse inclusion) are the ones who have remained most deprived.

This can be seen in terms of the current status of education, health, socio-economic, production-related and civic amenities for the rural poor as brought out by the SECC data, but not taken up in the present exercise. Not only this, but most such outlying sectors were disproportionately neglected in preference to the interests of the corporate investors and the urban rich and middle income groups (for facilitating uninterrupted growth of GDP), as reflected in the share of central government investment allocated to the power and transport sectors, directly feeding primarily the organised, large-scale, corporate-controlled segments of the economy, often on artificially low rates. Serious deficiencies in providing access to and construction of productive and civic infrastructure for the rural poor, enhancement of their capacity to enable them to contribute to and benefit from growth (the backlog of illiteracy—over 30 crore illiterate in rural India, which is equal to the total rural population in 1951 and 66 years as life expectancy which is lower than that in Bangladesh and Sri Lanka) became another factor not addressed as a part of the initial conditions. In qualitative terms, it is a kind of state and big business-engineered situation which has to be identified as the root cause of the woeful situation shown by the SECC data. No random great deals and great achievements of big businesses can be a substitute for an overall evaluation, taking the minuses and the pluses together, to be able to generate a balanced assessment of India's achievements.

Thus, what has been achieved by the big private corporate sector entities in terms of growth, diversification, technological modernisation and India's place in the global supply chains was done with the directly incurred cess by the entire society, specifically with the help and support of public policies, resources, support and differentially positive, discriminating pro-corporate policies. As we see in the chapter on tax expenditure (a euphemism for the bounties granted to the corporate sector and large income tax payers), this remains the largest item of public revenue use of the central government for a number of years and in the current Union budget it has exceeded Rs 6 lakh crore out of about Rs 19 lakh crore. (See Malabika Pal's contribution in the present volume.) All that the state sought from the private sector in return is by way of following public policy discipline about the nature of investment decisions, contribution to public exchequer by way of tax payments and decent lawful behaviour towards workers. These were systematically sabotaged and by-passed. This happened, thanks again to a combination of factors plaguing our polity, administration, business behaviour, external economic and business relations (generally identified wide ranging corruption and cronyism as the operative pragmatic model), drawing upon in good measure on the tendency of follower actors to try and adopt without much discreet adaptation of what has been seen as success stories (Kabra 2012-13).

The second prop of the mechanism of growth and development, the leadership role of the private corporate sector in association with the MNCs too failed to work for the goals of widely shared, fair and just inclusion of the hitherto adversely included sections. The growth strategy's assumption regarding the private corporate entities as the main actors and managers of the processes of economic growth ended up being mimetic industrialisation and creating some isolated outposts of limited modernisation, which turned out to be unrealistic and far from realisation. It is the private corporate entities which are the largest tax evaders, stashing undeclared incomes by various devices in the global tax havens and are also the largest defaulters on repayment of bank loans (the latest data show that nearly Rs 4 lakh crore have been written off from the liabilities of the large companies to the public sector banks alone). Compared to these transfers, voluntary or forced, the employment contribution in terms of decent jobs by these entities is catastrophically low. These too are thus simultaneously major parts of the story of how India's democracy and development have been emptied out of their promised positive potential of a genuine, fair and just, inclusive development (that is opposite of what we have broadly indicated above to be adverse inclusion).

Do these facts call for a serious rethinking about the basic premises of 'development planning' in India?

As mentioned above, the growth story has been reasonably impressive. What about its underlying assumptions? While planning for the growth of GDP as the main task of development planning, it was believed and propagated that the low level of living standard of the masses, poverty and inequalities would be reduced by means of the trickle-down effects of GDP growth (Sachs,1997 and Singh and Agarwala,1960). Did the much-hyped 'trickle-down theory' and the outcomes of a variety of populist pull-up policies and efforts addressed at the fringes of the problems of poverty, change the inadequacy of peoples' livelihoods? As we see below, what has happened is largely the *opposite of* the sort of expected 'outcome of development planning'. The growth has, fairly regularly and predictably, benefitted the rather narrow top tier of our social pyramid.

The above analysis points to the inability of the third prop of the Indian development game-plan—the guiding, corrective, disciplining and directly participating democratic role of the state—to prevent growth becoming the handmaiden of the better-off sections and marginalisation of the really needy, that is, the deserving, entitled masses. One may be led to infer that as a closely inter-related outcome of such growth, multiple and sticky, disparities-ridden pattern of income, wealth, prestige and privileges was accepted as at least an initial situation associated with the work of Simon Kuznets.

As mentioned above, the glaring inadequacy of the access to viable means of livelihood is made worse owing to continued neglect of the rural masses in terms of basic human needs, the right to life and development and with hardly any meaningful civic infrastructure like paved streets with drainage, water supply, electricity, school, medical facilities and a warehouse at a reasonable distance where the peasants with extremely poor housing can store what little food grains they are able to obtain during the post-harvest seasons and honest and accountable security personnel protecting them from local strongmen.

Let us recall how, initially, the growth exercise was led by the state with active plan-determined cooperation of the handful of giants of the private corporate sector. It was helped and supported by setting up of a whole range of public sector enterprises which undertook what the private corporate were either incapable or unwilling or both, at least initially, to do. Even today, these corporates are still enjoying a key place and strong voice in the economy and India's public policies. It was a process of growth (to begin with) led, supported and guided by the democratically-elected central government with a junior role for the State governments, more or less continually until 1990. However, during this period, the influence of and dependence on foreign capital, in the form of largely external credits, basically as fiscal support, even for financing projects and programmes with little or no foreign exchange outgo, and later on for servicing the past foolish borrowings, continually increased.

It generated a whole range of contradictions and traps, making its continuation highly problematic as both the foreign and Indian corporate giants were out to extract their pound of flesh. Thus, after 1990, the model of growth was decisively influenced and participated in by the market and global hegemons led by the powerful corporate conglomerates. One may maintain with considerable justification that the powerful place of economic growth in the so-called 'development strategy' and this strategy as the real face of India's growth story (necessitating for populist purposes various human masks) continued, with renewed vigour as a logical sequel to the changed complexion of the economy and socio-economic and global power equations by 1990. This change can be seen as one marked by relative weakening of the Indian state.

Political, Economic Processes & Forces Perverse Change

The top end of the growth story may be described in some details in order to get a better appreciation of the huge contrast that the Indian reality displays.[12] In the evolving totality of this model, practically most of the gains of growth, development, modernisation, big strides in industrial growth, increased availability of infrastructure facilities and participation in the global economy, without restrictions after 1991-92 were pocketed by a small but influential small top section of the country. Even the supplementary and tactical moves to make huge outlays in socio-economic and civic facilities and infrastructure were directed mainly to the industrial and urban-metropolitan segments to provide backward and forward linkages—both in their location, nature and links. These facilities were marginally connected to agriculture, rural areas and were ill-suited to the needs of the common citizens. These services and facilities turned out to be inadequate, inappropriate and in some ways counter-productive for the neglected sectors and sections of population (see 'Reaping the Bitter Harvest' referred to in footnote 12.) The upwards push to the overall national rate of savings and investment by measures of direct and indirect transfers and preferential access and allocation to the big organised corporate capital with skewed regional profile left the weaker, traditional and highly dispersed economic segments at the margins of the expanding economy. It was the case more or less right from the beginning in the 1950s and as the organised modernise sectors faced constraints and shortages, and delivered outcomes far short of the needs and on-commensurate with the support provided to them (the classic phenomenon of non-reciprocal responsiveness of India's corporate giants) the state rewarded them by greater allocations and more plentiful concessions and the vicious cycle continues even to this day when export performance of the corporate sector is making the nation face huge absolute volumeof current accountdeficit. Absolue amounts are relevant because the ultimate national burden of ensuring solvency and liquidity on global accounts are in terms of absolute volume of foreign currency

[12] For a relatively detailed list of the ways in which the top cornered the gains of growth see, Kabra: 2005-06, Box 1 'Reaping the Bumper Harvest in Disempowering the Masses', and its Contrast for the People at Large in Box 2, 'Reaping the Bitter Harvest' *Alternate Economic Survey*: 16-18.

required and not as a part and proportion of globally non-convertible and non- tradable national output flows.[13]

Thus, it is true that the rate of savings and investment increased from the low of under 10 per cent gradually to generally around and even above 30 per cent over time, helped and supplemented by growing inflows of what is called 'foreign aid' and continued helpful role of the state in various complementary forms. The growth of the organised segments of the national economy saw the share of the public sector in GDP rising up to 25 per cent of the GDP just as the share of the organised private sector increased—both quantitatively and qualitatively. This could not, however, change the qualitative nature of the pro-capital and pro-corporate outcomes that were highly skewed. Also, the diversity of the economy has increased, though it can hardly be claimed to have reached a sustainable inter-sector and inter-regional balance consistent with India's openly declared socio-economic high-sounding objectives, the country's requirements and imperatives.

The results of the SECC 2011-12 underscore the relative worsening and structural retrogressing, largely of the services sector. As a result both relative and absolute suffering of the rural population has increased. These were more or less expected outcomes of what we did and did not do. Everything seems to have happened more or less as scripted and logically, except for its public face with the usual icing of empty bravado over growth rate (indeed as a ray of hope in the midst of global gloom of slowdown and deflation), added by highly over-advertised populist measures, their characteristic duality and public response of growing scepticism.

The discussion above has clearly stated how the primacy of growth rate and utter neglect andpopulist cover-up of socio-economic indices responding positively to broader social concerns can hardly hide from the public view various perverse outcomes in relation to employment,

---

[13] Actually it is only verbal sympathies which are made available to the farmers in their lakhs who face enormous difficulties, particularly in the dry farming regions, on account of frequent failures of their mono crops. These misfortunes lead to re-enactment of the stories seen during the pre-independence days when the farmers were over-burdened with non-institutional usurious loans and were led to end their lives, leaving a huge overhang of non-repayable loans. Its cruel outcome has been our national burden of suicides by harassed and pauperised farmers, as never before.

equalities, reducing the intensity of endemic mass poverty, looming threats to ecological balance and neglect of basic minimum public services which have often reserveda shamefully low place for various global indicators of development by many global watchdog organisations.

These features remain the hallmarks of our growth, industrialisation and policies throughout the UPA and NDA regimes. Contrary to the letter of the law, in actual practice, a fairly ruthless socio-economic and political authoritarianism covered up under the neoliberal policies narrowed down and stifled the hypothesised potential of social wellbeing and were unable to lift the rickety boats of the masses along with the rising tide of economic growth, increased participation of the national economy in the global economy and pseudo-anti poverty programmes.[14]

We briefly sketch the structural retrogression of the economy and then present some facts about the rising share of 'profits' vis-à-vis the 'other factor' shares as pointers to growing concentration of wealth in the organised sector of the economy. Let us remember that all these features emerged not as 'aimless opulence', as some scholars call it, but as a built-in, historically tried, tested and preferred pattern and as the consequence of the emergence of plutocracy (Freeland: 2012). This is followed by calling attention to some dramatic indictors of the growing concentration of wealth which frequently hit headlines in popular media.

The growth of the Indian economy has seen a sharp decline of the relative share of agriculture (from about 60 per cent of GDP to under 15 per cent now, together with the share of the workforce deriving livelihood from it from about 60 per cent to under 50 per cent now). The major gainer has not been the manufacturing sector, as has been oft seen historically, but the services sector without a basis in the secondary sector: over 63 per cent of GDP and nearly 30 per cent of the workforce. The manufacturing sector remains the least gainer from the dwindling fortunes of agriculture and allied activities. Thus, as confirmed by the SECC data, a vast majority of the rural people, particularly the landless, casual manual workers (the single largest category of our people) have to make do with, jointly with the big farmers and related entities, who

[14] A big way in which these processes have shaped and structured the economy is visible in what is known as growing structural retrogression of the economy. (*EPW*, Shetty, SL)

obviously take a bigger portion of the small cake, that is under 15 per cent of the GDP.

Let us see this along with what is happening in one of the major organised segments of the economy—our factory sector. According to the Annual Survey of Industry data, the share of profits in gross value-added was 20.4 per cent in 1981-82 and saw a little drop to about 18.5 per cent in 1990-91. After the beginning of the process of liberalisation and structural adjustment, the share of profits in GVA began to rise, reaching 53.8 per cent in 2007-08. Then the global slowdown pulled it back to 48.6 per cent in 2008-09 and since then, it has not recovered, coming down to 46.2 per cent in2011-12. (*The State of the Economy: Overview* before the 2016 union budget, said, 'One conspicuous change over the four-year period from 2011-12 to 2014-15 was the decline in the shares of the public and household sectors in total GVA, which was fully taken over by the private corporate sector'. http://indiabudget.nic.in/es2015-16/echapvol2-01.pdf.)

Surely, one can see how it has climbed up to more than twice the level of 1981-82 with labour practices of pre-capitalist era, such as casual and contract labour, during this period. The share of emoluments to GVA declined to nearly half the early 1980s level—from over 40 per cent to 20 per cent. Out of the emoluments, the share of wages of the workers also stands reduced—from about 65 per cent to 46.5 per cent (ASI Summary Results: 2011-12 and *EPW*:2014,24 May, p 93). As if all this is not enough, despite the worsening share of the workers in total value-added and the heftily increasing collections by the captains of industry (including by means reminiscent of the gilded age of Europe and North America when practices similar to those of primitive accumulation assumed newer forms as by means of selling snake oil by robber barons or more generally as discussed in fairly exhaustive details by Ackerlof and Shiller, 2015 in their recent book, *Phishing for Phool*), in India, there is a growing clamour by employers (weak in hiring) to be entitled to have an unhindered right to back up their meagre record of hiring by the unfettered freedom to fire!

Since the official statistical machinery of India is so sparingly made use of to estimate the relative shares of different sections of the economy and society (despite a number of ways inherent in the economy to estimate the relative shares in GDP and value-added), we have to bring in this aspect by certain other means. Lately economists such as Thomas Piketty have openly expressed a certain disappointment that even the income tax data bearing on income shares of different income groups, as used to be made available earlier, are no longer shared with the public. Inany case, one may draw attention to a macro-economic indicator of rising incidence of wealth. The CSO provides (as a part of the National Accounts Statistics 2014, along with the national savings and investment data) the details of volume of the wealth that finds shelter in the form of Valuables (consisting of gold and precious metals but excluding gold, as this too is a popular form of unproductive stocking of wealth which naturally finds outlets in the black/grey economy to further widen the socio-economic chasms and adverse inclusion of the broad masses, both legal and undeclared). Lately, the magnitude of Valuables used for holding wealth has been reported to be around 4 per cent of the GDP. Surely such a huge cache of Valuable, largely stocked by the wealthy, is an indicator of the rich becoming richer and bypassing normal investments and other earning assets, except for appreciation on account of rising prices.

A number of international agencies periodically announce their estimates of the concentration of wealth in different countries, including India and the ranking of the wealthy. These are widely reported in the media. These reports tell us about the rising trend of concentration of wealth in the hands of a small number of high and ultra-high networth individuals or billionaires. According to the estimates reported in the World Wealth Report 2015, released by Capgemini and RBC Wealth Management, India contained the 11th largest population of 1.98 lakh millionaires in 2014, which shows an increase from the 2013 number of 1.5 lakh millionaires. Another estimate is by the Boston Consulting Group. This estimate puts 20 per cent of the Indian financial wealth in the hands of 928 individuals. (*Mint*, 17 June 2015). The report further clarifies that Indian households with financial wealth of more than one million US dollars own 36 per cent of the private financial wealth in the country. Anyone familiar with the ground situation in India would say that these estimates are hardly able to take note of the hidden financial assets of the unorganised sectors and in the black-criminal and political circles, particularly the parts that are held benami (that is in fictitious names) and are parts of the stashed away funds in the global tax havens.

Another recent report by Knight Frank Wealth (*The Indian Express* on 4th March 2016), shows how the number of ultra-high networth individuals, that is persons with $30 million or more in net assets, is rising rapidly in India. This group of Indians billionaires, residing mostly in Mumbai and Delhi, accounted for one per cent of the global ultra-high net worth individuals in 2005. Now they number 6,020, and account for 5 per cent of the billionaire population across the world.

Little wonder the estimates of illegal wealth held abroad in various tax havens and within the country, despite their limitations, show another dimension of the huge concentration of wealth in the hands of few and its counter-part of abject and inhuman poverty and deprivation for millions. And not just that. This kind of wealth, given its enormous volume, regularity of occurrence and involvement of the real fat cats may not reasonably be considered an outcome of marginal deviant behaviour in the main functioning of the economy, society and polity (so much so that it is extremely difficult to separate out the legal from the illegal).

We do not quote many estimates showing the illegal volume of black wealth as a rising proportion of GDP, mainly because their dramatic effect apart, the methods and theoretical basis of such estimates is far from logical and valid. These fail to make a distinction between stocks and flows and one is not clear about the price indices used for expressing them in monetary terms. As such, it may well be reasonable to consider this class of phenomena as 'inevitable' and in some ways, not openly recognised but nonetheless expected to grow rapidly in so far as circulates fast and occupies a prominent place in the actual model of the grey political economy of India. And, of course, this is consistent with the global trends.

One may just recall how 'black' money began as 'primitive accumulation' in laying down the foundations of enormous capital accumulation. This was the initial steps towards capitalist industrialisation and wrote the history of the modern world. Naturally, it built upon its own initial successes and over time took the form and salience that it has come to enjoy in the post-WWII world, covering the golden age of modern capitalism and thereafter right into the 21st century in all the economies. (See the two works of Ackerlof and Shiller and that of Chrystia

Freeland and William W Baker 2005.) This seems to be so because these are generally widespread practices indulged in by the rich and powerful, which in one way or another impacts the entire system.

In fact, many sociologists have begun to consider these as white collar crimes. This concentration of resources and everything that goes with it have the most serious and far-reaching ill effect in the form of making a mockery of democratic elections to choose the rulers. It forges strong bonds which knit together the political and the economc-finacial and organised crime's money, muscle and manipulative power (with deep and multiple linkages with the agencies enrusted with the task of maintaining law and order and making and unmaking of laws) and create the illusion of decision-making by governments representing the popular will as expressed by means of free, fair and frequent elections. These are signs of and facilitators of cronyism which, as we see below, extends to the grassroots in sofar as venal political underclass at lower levels manage the voting behaviour in favour of the politician-big business nexus.

While the attempts to regularly estimate the extent of inequalities are so few and far between, there are many attempt to arrive at some broad estimates of the underground grey political economy of India, including some global estimates by international agencies. Given the generally growing size of the black and grey mixed political economy involving the top echelons of Indian society, which are built on the foundations of undetected white collar crimes (apparently encompassing both solved and unsolved white collar crimes), it is clear that the size of such a regularly functioning deviance is itself a strong indicator of concentration at the top and the adverse effects of such shenanigans on the general public. Looking at this phenomenon from the perspective of intensification of neoliberal pro-capital social adverse inclusion in India over nearly a quarter century, one may fairly confidently infer that these policies of pro-business stance of the public agencies must have taken gross inequalities to newer heights.

One may easily catalogue some factors working against equity and people-empowering steps, such as low and stable taxation, light and business-friendly controls, crony processes of privatisation of public enterprises and the general tone and tenor of growth and investment-friendly governance, competitive wooing of investors by the governments of Indian States, relaxing close surveillance and monitoring provisions, lest it be considered intrusive; in brief, measures to improve the rates of return and lighting costs which may reasonably be considered pro-centralisation factors. As mentioned by the *Economic Survey 2015-16*, the regime has 'abandoned socialism with restricted entry'. And with the liberal bankruptcy law and the right to fire, it seems poised to 'replace it with capitalism'. All these, along with the long-established privileges enjoyed by corporate entities (which can now be floated even by a single individual! and extension of such protective umbrella to partnerships as well) amount to socialisation of risks and losses and bad debts and privatisation of profits. The new code about private-public partnerships also seems to move in the same direction. Thus, it can be said that extension of what were the initial steps popularly known as LPG (that is liberalisation, privatisation and globalisation) are the main policies common between the UPA and NDA.The main sales plank of these measures remains, of course, accelerated growth of GDP and the natural, neutral or non-partisan goal post of *sab kaa saaath, sabkaa vikaas* and the regimes post-1990 have all followed this growth path as a routine matter by treating the present challenges as landing the country into an 'impasse', most often described as there is no alternative (TINA).

Even the SECC data remains to be examined from the angle of relative shares of different groups, for estimating the extent of income and wealth inequalities. Is it that the questions inconvenient from the point of myth-making and selling about the real unjust and discriminatory character of the intensified neolibealism are best dealt with by simply maintaining stony silence about the extant situation and emerging trends, but in a framework of formal democracy and treating each one equally when it comes to making and enforcing laws, policies and respecting the voices of dissent.

Given the will and resolve to know the truth, even available facts can be interpreted to throw a good deal of light on the distances and disparities which divide the people from different walks of life and from each other. Take the facts regarding the official money supply in the form of legal tender currency notes of various denominations issued by the Reserve Bank of India in the form of currency notes of different denominations. It has been reported that currency notes of higher face value than Rs 100 are mainly Rs 500 and Rs 1000 notes. These high face value notes account for over 84 per cent of India's total legal tender money circulating in the economy. With the facts about the most widely prevalent income levels, for example as reported by the SECC census 2011, over 75 per cent of India's rural population have such abnormally low monthly income that the question of the high face value currency notes being relevant to them as medium of exchange, or store of value or as unit of account hardly makes sense. Thus it follows that for an overwhelming majority of people about 80 per cent of the currency notes have little chance of being relevant. These facts may not say much about the extent of inter se inequalities among various sections of people but what can be read off from them is startling enough: over 80 per cent of the currency notes in circulation actually circulates at the most among the top 20 per cent of the population (*Mint*, 16 March 2016). What can possibly be read from this set of data is that the economic transactions involving changing of hands of high denomination currency notes are hardly relevant for the daily economic life of over four-fifths of our population while for the black economy and corruption, these notes are the facilitators. Obviously those who are the users of this currency are the top echelons and it is for them and by them that the Indian economy seems to be working.

Before proceeding further, we sum up the substance of growth-related changes in India, initiated during the 1950s but continuing now under neoliberal policies initiated and managed by the UPA and NDA governments in their various forms since 1990. During these eventful decades unemployment, poverty, inequalities and environmental degradation, as closely inter-related elements, have worsened. These anti-development features (the position advanced by Dudley Seers in terms of inability to tackle these formidable foursome maladies) continue to persist with magnified magnitude and deeper complexity. What it shows is that economic growth in nominal terms (the motivating factor for the agents of growth) cannot cure the four serious headaches of poor countries.

One might note that the anti-development character of the economy is manifested in several other ways too. We may make a note of some. One, the huge nominal expansion of GDP was connected with just about thirty times the real GDP growth. It means the dragon of inflation devoured a lot of good possibilities. Two, it saw a thoroughly changed commodity and sector-wise composition, weighted against mass consumption wage goods, regional-spatial concentration and without much shaking of the huge size of the informal sector of great diversity. Similarly, agriculture and rural economy lost a great deal owing to the urban-industrial bias and even the industrial scene yielded place prematurely to the services sector characterised by 'half-real, half-illusory output' as a scholar of repute has described it.

All these changes mean a great deal of non-absorption of India's s fast growing labour force in production and income-distributing activities which can be considered decent and secure. The growing informality was accompanied by its mixing up with a seriously large illegal and semi-legal set of activities and transactions, involving the statutorily audited and formal-legal government and public sector and state enterprises. These latter still elude a reasonably credible estimate of their size and coverage. However, no one is in doubt about its menacing proportions and ubiquitous penetration and big role in real political economic decision-making.

Then, despite close ties with the rest of the world, Indian economy remains miles away from the ability to autonomously and through normal commercial channels take its place in the global economy. A combination of several such fleeting and regularly operating grey and black factors have led to massive inequalities, worsening the lot of the worse-offs and rewarding the non-functional and the corrupt. They are the speculators, political-administrators, rentseekers and the business classes playing with the resources and opportunities of the entire society but pocketing the gains derived from others' labour for their narrow family-kinship-political allies networks and keeping the gains outside the pale of public scrutiny by massive creative accounting. These trends are surely not a recent phenomena. It has been shown time and again by many that these are enduring and inherited features which took deep roots and extensive shape and have been continually flourishing from the very beginning of our tryst with an independent republic, as a nation practicing highly partisan development planning and denying special and preferential provision for capabilities-building arrangements in order to enable the leftouts to play an active, fully participatory development role. Among the seriously neglected aspects of our development initiatives, we started by referring to the findings of the SECC and need not recount the sorry state of affairs we have landed ourselves in.

The dispossessed and uneducated rural and slums residents have to continue spending their lives for generations without a minimum of civic amenities and clean and healthy surroundings. Neither the Swachh Bharat campaign, nor the latrines within homes initiative cover the grievous shortfall in quality of life and if successful, they can only add a wee bit to ameliorate the complete absence of a rights-based decent civic life provide locally by panchayats and municipalities. Similarly, the skilling programmes too face the stone wall of non-creation of employment and adequate meaningful work and income opportunities in the midst of big oligopolies-led growth with pan border trade in a world obsessed with its own bagful of problems. What the state could and ought to do is to make good the heavy shortfall of decentralised small men and women related rural and small town infrastructure and improve the productive low cost and appropriate infrastructure with desi innovations answering our problems. Looking for external, western technological leads is surely barking up a wrong tree. India has to be strengthened by supporting our jugaad initiatives. The idea is just to locate our problems, needs and potential and without the 'fall into and catch-up and follower' syndrome and replace adoption by fine-tuned adaptation and new breakthroughs for a real decentralised burst of entrepreneurial capabilities.

With low quality of health owing to hunger and malnutrition and virtual lack of education for a huge number (persisting even now after seven decades), hardly any discernible arrangements for land and water conservation and optimum utilisation, especially by introduction of dry farming techniques and crops, measures to provide to all the farmers cheap and assured crop loans (with credit-deposit ratio tilted in favour of agriculture, rural areas and a credible cover against the risks arising from the combined furies of the weather gods and the market processes), is urgently needed. At the same time ending the step-motherly treatment of the artisans sector (compared to the pampering of the better-placed corporate giants) for upgradation of their techniques, product-mix and markets for the artisans as a second string to the bow for the rural and farm population are necessary, to name only a few sorely missing elements to revitalise the genuinely needy parts of the economy on an adequate and effective scale. Rather than simply token populist measures, steps need to be taken to enable rural India to become major local suppliers of elementary-wage goods to eachother as a part of a better level of living. These are some elementary measuress in pro-poor changes which can over time make poverty a historical memory, small steps in all that Inidia tried as a part of its strategy of economic growth.

In the midst of the dynamics of such a constellation of adverse factors, the statutory reservation policy can at best give a rather small number of the congenitally mistreated sections of our citizenry nothing more than a limited toehold in the regular livelihood-related activities. They have to put up with the hostility of many, including those others who too remain worse-off owing to the corporate and foreign capital-friendly employment and agressive capital accumulation processes by a few. The western capitalist development discourse has been able acquire such a iron grip on the minds of the middle and articulate groups and their value-system that they simply refuse to accept anything not endorsed by the so-called developed nations establishment as logical, appropriate and people-friendly.

Conclusion

The facts brought out above clearly show that all the economic growth achieved by India during the preceding almost seven decades in GDP and the related aspects could not make any notable difference towards amelioration of the living conditions of a much larger part of rural population, compared to the total number of rural people in the early 1950s. The structure of the economy too became highly imbalanced. In a nutshell , all the facts derived from the all-India census show far more convincingly than the national level sample data, an arbitrarily determined largely sub-human level of poverty level income/ consumption data (surely incapable of qualifying as humane and just on any criteria , including overall macro-economic national economic capabilities). It shows that the post-independence economic development, including that during the neoliberal era, failed to move towards attaining the stated and publicly embraced social objectives capable of moving India decidedly and clearly towards an inclusive society. A quick comparison of the levels of living as revealed by the SECC-2011 and the situation seen in terms of the data available for the 1950s stand testimony to the widening chasm between the objectives and the achievements of 'growth' as a development model, based on the active involvement of all the organised state and non-state modern institutions. The state of poverty of India's rural citizens is too glaring an yardstick to deliver a positive verdict on the wide-ranging changes recorded during this era . Many international regularly-updated comparative assessments too confirm the bad news. The combined role of the market forces and the private big corporate capital, both Indian and foreign, geared towards rapid growth of GDP and industrialisation (with some selected elements of modernisation commensurate with the progress of science and technology under the active but varying role of the democratically elected government) drained democracy of its avowed content. What makes the story most unedifying is that the Indian growth model underwent constant modifications, but in the direction of further adding to the counter-productive outcomes during what came to be known as the neoliberal era. Ironically, the crowning in 2014 of a regime with a different political complexion from the ones that ruled the roost most of the time (except for one full term NDA I regime as the predecessor of the present NDA II) does not seem poised to make any bold qualitative departures.

—Kamal Nayan Kabra

Plutocracy's Ascent to Unbridled Power: Distorted Democracy & Development

— Kamal Nayan Kabra

SINCE 1990 India is experiencing competitive intensification of neoliberal policies for attaining higher and durable rates of economic growth and closer integration with the global market economies, led by G 7 countries and their MNCs. This neoliberal model of economic development was, according to its protagonists, expected to bring down gradually but certainly the number of arbitrarily and callously quantified number of Indians living below the poverty-line. Our examination of the course and consequences of neoliberal policies tends to show how these policies have transformed the Indian economy and polity, led and dictated by multifaceted dominance of plutocracy (that is a tiny minority of state-supported private corporate houses, closely linked in a variety of crony relationships with the inter-mixed top-level political, administrative and business top brass). However, in order to maintain the facade of formal constitutional democracy with a human face, governed by periodically elected governments, the neoliberal policies were accompanied by a number of widely publicised measures to help move the masses of people above the poverty-line.

These populist measures, instead of overcoming the adverse inclusion of the masses (that is the unilateral and non-reciprocal incorporation of the majority of labour force and small businesses in the mainstream economic and political spaces primarily to sustain the system of prevalent control over power, privilege and prestige), produced counter-productive outcomes. In the following pages we examine the core issues arising from India's neoliberal policies, and how the disequalising features got a new lease of life under neoliberalism. How India saw what was called 'development' and as a consequence, far-reaching changes without any movement towards real development. That is growth and many qualitative changes moving in directions opposite of equality and wider, fair, secure, reasonably rewarding participation, even in labour processes. That is, they had to remain in their growing numbers outside the formal organised activities, even by means of involuntary uprooting. However, for the captains of new organised sector work, they remained easily available as and when required, mainly for short periods and away from their homes. Thus they remained victims of the freedom of the market processes which was claimed to be the hallmark of the markets and their unregulated working, often with the state standing tall, formally or invisibly on the side of the market forces.

Unfair Participation

Given the dependence of the working masses (with their own great deal of diversities and differentiations and consequent inabilities to acquire collective or joint countervailing capabilities, let alone power and influence without a different perspective) on the markets dominated by the rich and powerful, both in the organised and unorganised branches of the economy, the possibilities of participation in growth could neither be fair, adequate and surely not capable of building over a period of time. Nor could these masses have or acquire the capabilities for relative independence in any sphere, including the legally provided but unprotected political and civil freedoms. Moreover, corporate and business sector growth in India remained volatile, unbalanced and non-sustainable, that is even in the organised parts of the formal sectors which remained additionally congenitally weak vis-à-vis the more powerful external players related to the Indian economy (MNC capital with multilateral capital standing by them).

Then India has continued an unjust and weak fiscal system of neoliberal governments which could neither satisfy the business classes fully, nor could provide support to the weaker parts of the society to be able to become self-supporting over time. How the corporate concerns and submission to them has divorced the state from its role as the leader of development to a mere supporter of the big guns in business is a story we do not have space to relate here (see various chapters in the present volume dealing with certain aspects of this important question). *A perverse fiscal system, stuck with a rather low tax-GDP ratio and exogenous arbitrary pro-corporate ceiling on fiscal deficit, can surely not be a leader of development, let alone a gamechanger.*

The Union Budget 2016-17 not only continues this commitment to the corporate sector but also shows little capability to increase direct taxes. Instead, by a whopping unjust tax impost of Rs 97 thousand crore of indirect taxes vis-à-vis the reduction in the intended collections of direct tax by about rupees one thousand crore, more of the government's anti-development thrust has been reinforced. This, however, is not the only regressive feature. Strongly anti-progressive or pro-people character of the state gets clarified by comparing the allocations for the benefit of the common citizens as against those intended to benefit, (under the camouflage of being growth-friendly) a tiny top strata.

The central message of the above narrative offers two greatly contrasting pictures of post-independence India, particularly as it has evolved after 1990 under the impact of neoliberal policy and administrative dispensation. An overwhelming majority of citizens have emerged as victims of adverse inclusion, manifested in extreme poverty, grotesque inequalities and inhuman discrimination and marginalisation. On the other side, inherited state policies have supported non-functional concentration of power, prestige and privileges in the hands of a rather tiny group of ultra-high networth families. We have attempted here to present the economic growth of India as a plutocracy of cronyism and populism as the actually operating and living character of post-1990 India.

How plutocracy, cronyism and populism join hands to make the Indians worse off over time is what we can end the exercise with. In fact, now it is a part of received wisdom to recognise that our democratic and regularly organised elections from village panchayat up to the parliament are fought and won by the major political parties and the wealthy on the basis of corpulent financial sources and purchased with TPA-based self-financed media support for false and hollow slogans. The known superrich business houses and families dominate the corporatised political parties as the bridge joining the economic and the political spheres by the glue of illegal, locally-held or stashed away unfathomable wealth. It is in these senses that we specifically maintain that, despite all the rituals of a parliamentary democracy and rule-based administration and justice system, private property and freedom of exchange-based relationship, that—is it is plutocracy that is calling the shots under the label of democracy. That India's so-called inclusive growth of GDP, laced by a plethora of populist measures (more for garnering votes to a much greater extent than distributing purchasing power), is not for sustaining the growth of our hitherto insufficient distribution of purchasing power of people.

Power of Plutocracy

The power of plutocracy has become so all-encompassing that the cultural sphere too has become subservient to the top corporate houses and their political cronies. For instance, some of the so-called most 'prestigious' literary awards and social science research have been instituted and awarded by the corporate houses, and they patronise many academic, cultural outfits, events and the means of mass communications. As a result, so-called intellectuals often reduce themselves to supplicants in the political and corporate durbars of the white collar criminals representing the gray political economy of India in the form of the unholy confluence of business and politics and mafia groups or the black and not-so-black economies. With some change of gear and tactical and strategic adjustments, it is a pro-big business (sans borders) growth policy involving the top, organised corporate business, political and bureaucratic classes (the top of our socio-economic pyramid) who are the real centres of power, capable of managing the democratically crucial numbers. *Yes numbers, as people do not matter when the numbers have been managed.*

This new architecture of dominance consists of the subtle and not-so-subtle influences and open arms-twisting by the G-7 countries and their dominant MNCs (often through the intermediation of the multilateral organisations dominated by these global powers who have mastered the techniques and strategies to ensure the fulfilment of their agenda under the domestic or local sovereignty-based, independent nations). Of course, this is done with active and articulate advocacy by Indian big business.

Thus, it was the proto-neoliberal policies up to 1990 and the increasing intensification of neoliberal set of policies disproportionately favourable to the interests, whims and fancies of the dominant sections which resulted in a successful policy coup in the 'biggest democracy of the world', with the help of some stated and unstated alliances, with growing elements of corporatism, clienteles and cronyism (a deadly combination).

The above story would, however, be incomplete if one were to leave out the rural scene from the power games of an electoral democracy, as it is the largest centre of votes. In this sphere, the big farmers, themselves morphing into big traders in farm produce, did cut out a somewhat comfortable junior niche for themselves, particularly in some parts of India owing to the inter-sector, inter-region compulsions and the changes brought about by the green revolution. When the big business requirements of natural resources in general and land, including forests and water resources in particular, brought forth a conflict between the corporate, services and modern infrastructure-related activities with the rural and farm sectors and tribal communities, a switch over from land reforms-based small farmer economy to the so-called green revolution and a growing process of compulsory land acquisition with token compensation as insult added to grievous injuries that went on merrily in the service of the GDP god (a notorious definition of public interest). Thus, vast sections of poor land owners, tribal people and the dalits who constitute the bulk of the downtrodden sections were deceived victims of growth and constitute the whole of adversely included Indians.

The New Land Laws, Bills

In the presently emerging modern late-industrialising, catching-up India, these people are an integral and major part of the post-golden era capitalism of late 20th and early 21st centuries world economy. They are able to participate mainly through the intermediation of the political and corporate business classes and the academia handpicked by the upper classes. Even when the counter-mobilisation by the land-losing classes became irresistible under the past over-exposed slogans and assurances of GDP growth as beneficial to all and sundry, a new land acquisition law to somewhat soften past practices was enacted.

However, even before it could become operational, this new law was placed in a cold storage and instead, has now been left hanging as a transferred jurisdiction of the State governments. This was done probably as the central government was emboldened by the enactment of blatant pro-capital labour laws by Rajasthan and limitation of the basic democratic rights of the people at the Panchayat level in Rajasthan and Haryana, in which the gram sabhas under pnchayats have a big formal role. There have been reports that vast tracts of land handed over to the SEZs have either remained unused or have been allowed to be used for real estate development. Newer means, such as industrial corridors, and construction of six-lane super highways connecting the already well-connected big metros too are leading to compulsory acquisition of farm land, even of the most fertile lands with irrigation facilities. Actually, mining in heavily forested areas providing tribal people their economic and cultural space too are falling prey to exclusionary and export-oriented growth. These livelihood and cultural identity-destroying so-called development practices are reminiscent of how industrial revolutions in the first world extracted a heavy cost from the original inhabitants in the past. Clearly, in addition to adverse inclusion in the economic sphere, such moves extend it to the cultural and political spheres at the village level, and cuts from under the feet the prospects of benefiting the poor qualitatively from the pseudo anti-poverty programmes. Various newly-enacted laws to debar the poor from participation as elected panchs, because they are not sufficiently educated (on account mainly of the no-availabilty of adequate and meaningful education in rural areas) in the local bodies at the village level (who have the legal authority to deny compulsory land acquisition) seems have a larger, malicious design to facilitate compulsory land acquisition as the better-off farmers and tribals can be silenced by a combination of force, fraud and monetary allurements.

Before concluding, let us briefly sum up in what sense and how far the character of the policies of the National Democratic Alliance, as revealed in the last two years, along with the earlier stints of governing, can be regarded as continuation of the United Progressive Alliance model of neoliberalism and what the western lobbyists think about it. The official NDA position can be seen in the *Economic Survey* 2015-16 (Finance Ministry GOI). It advances a nuanced position. It cautions against expectations of any 'Big Bang reforms... because of the dispersed nature of power in India and the absence of that impelling driver—the crisis'. Hence it sees 'a persistent, creative and encompassing incrementalism' in the direction of the 1990s-initiated policies/reforms, which have to be seen 'both as the guide for prospective action and the benchmark for retrospective assessment'.[1] Clearly, the changes in the direction of neoliberal reforms are not as fast and comprehensive as the Indian corporate bosses and highly-regarded westerners monitoring the Indian scene would ideally be happy with. For instance, Martin Wolf in the *Financial Times*, 16 March 2016, says: The post-2014 government of India 'represents continuity rather the pro-market transformation many supporters naively expected'. He goes on to assert that even though the government 'is centralised in the office of the prime minister... its orientation is more towards *management than to markets, and more towards projects than to policies* (emphasis added). It has shown no inclination towards radical privatisation or restructuring of inefficient public monopolies. It continues to spend large sums on inefficient subsidies'. Obviously, the western MNCs' agenda of neoliberal restructuring of India runs far ahead of what Indian big capital and its political arm finds doable.

---

[1] In so far as it highlights the role of institutions, particularly of the extractive economic and political institutions and relates them to power, prosperity and poverty. It indicates the need to turn a new and different page for understanding development than is practiced by the neoliberal orthodoxy, even though such an indication is not explicit in the volume that analyses the experience of many countries by means of carefully chosen comparisons and contrasts. However, the attention it gives to India is grossly inadequate and even, to say the least, lop-sided and biased in favour of the role of British colonial rule over India compared to the place India is assigned in the development discourse.

UPA/NDA: Not Much Different

One is still not sure how the NDA will be able to take itself ahead of the UPA in its commitment to and capability to carry forward the wishlist of markets-led big organised capital. So far, the markets do not seem to be clear about these possibilities and some individual tycoons have hastily voiced being sort of letdown, though in a guarded manner. It would be naïve and unnecessary to argue chapter and verse to show how the same old wares are being dusted and polished in order to claim a marked shift in the economy. With the surfacing of some dramatic cases of political and corporate shenanigans, even hints of crony equations, a replay of the same script cannot be written off, particularly as costly electioneering and media management in the midst of occasional political setbacks seem to unsettle the complacent. One can observe a somewhat accelerated trend of adopting measures which, while intended to accelerate growth, also directly lead to greater inequalities.

A kind of new form of populism for the upper income, richer business and urban sections is their strong aspirations to share the bonanza flowing from neoliberalism. We do not have space here to go into details of these new measures but our initial understanding tends to indicate that these measures would make the rich richer and the poor poorer. Such a formidable list includes the smart city initiative to make chosen pockets of the already comparatively better-provided-for cities even more liveable for the urban rich. The private partners entrusted with these projects are to be entrusted with large funds by the union government, bypassing the local self-government agencies. Measures requiring heavy investments to make certain chosen railway stations world-class, introduction of super-luxurious coaches, speedier trains and bullet trains costing billions of rupees and foreign exchange between two western Indian metropolitan cities would not only divert resources from the poorly-served regions and people, but also add directly to the incomes of the super opulent and the opulent sections. The astronomical sums to be borrowed from Japan for the bullet train project including buying equipment from Japan would push India into the quagmire of unsustainable borrowing as no amount of foreign exchange earnings from it are likely for servicing this debt. Perhaps no other project for the select few, except the plans to build dozens of new airports, would match the bullet train extravaganza. It is going to be something similar to the huge burden of about Rs 30,000 crore sunk in sustaining Air India, an airline which just cannot be used by 90 per cent of Indians.

Steps are on to also build about 25 new airports! Actually these kind of projects are extending the legacy of the expensive and corruption-ridden Commonwealth Games when millions of small towns and villages were not even provided with reasonable quality sports grounds and facilities. It can be argued that super highways linking the already linked up cities by extremely costly six-lane international class roads with other facilities and diverting compulsorily acquired land from the farm sector is surely a blow in the direction of greater inequalities. This socially adverse effect would become particularly unfair when viewed against the background of persistent and massive shortage of intra-village and inter-village roads of even rudimentary quality.

How private-public participation (PPP) ends with transfer of public resources and markets for public and quasi-public goods and services to the chosen private parties is something rarely taken note of from the equity angle. The much-hyped Goods and Services Tax (GST) so forcefully advocated by the big business groups and their lobby organisations will surely enhance the absolute amount and relative shares of public revenue extracted by means of indirect taxes that inevitably over-burden the common citizens. The dangers of such departures from the established political idioms—to even raising the impact on fair and just distribution of national income and wealth, particularly when direct tax revenue is lowered and some taxes such as Wealth Tax are abolished—clearly shows how the neoliberal regimes are anti-poor and pro-wealthy. Such moves are in effect, opposite of the principles of just and fair governance (progressive fiscal and other public policies).

Expectation and Reality

Even on a formal plane, the neoliberal theory expects to accelerate the growth and hopes that its positive spread effects, by means of a combination of some old and some new populist initiatives, the lower rungs of society and make them believe that they are being cared for. Thus, by various steps such as imparting skills to a large number of young persons, Jan Dhan Yojana, better delivery of subsidies by direct cash transfer to bank accounts made safer by legalised Adhar cards, philanthropy by the socially-responsive richer corporate bosses for financing better infrastructure and other civic and productive facilities, the government seeks to create an impression of more responsiveness towards the weaker sections. In this way, it is hoped the size of the informal sector will shrink, leading to a more integrated economic and social structure, particularly by greater integration with the global economy. May be, at the back of these theories there is a lingering faith in the replay of the Kuznets postulated outcome of relatively more equal distribution of income and wealth as the economy scales higher levels of per capita income.

However, neither theories nor empirical experience of the rich countries spread over about three centuries, and of many third world countries of about seven decades, lend support to such expectations without a qualitative change towards a social state (Piketty, Thomas 2014). It has to be realised that development is a normative, social and holistic people-centric, equity-fostering process. Hence, it is simply inconsistent with the neoliberal doctrine which is a sure way to intensify inherited inequalities. This is a conclusion writ large over the entire third world. In fact, it *is a pernicious impact of the theories and policies of neoliberalism that, generally the development discourse refuses to consider the growing socio-economic and political inequalities as the most serious problem of our time. The outcome is a fate worse than pre-capitalist exploitation, in so far even the potential for a better and richer life for a vast majority of citizens, feasible then may be impossible now.*

Our analyses shows a. supposedly self-regulated markets b. markets under state support and even pampered with domestic and foreign corporate capital c. markets and a capital-friendly non-social or sectarian state may stand compromised by its own self-imposed policies to limit both the amount of revenue from the corporate sector and more plentiful social spending by incurring large budget deficits.

With self-imposed fixed limit on the extent of such deficit, adopted in order not to hurt corporate growth by imposing tight financial market conditions for the private corporates, the NDA seems to be in a double bind. On the one hand, a light tax burden with rechristened bounties as 'tax expenditure' survives in the 2016-17 budget. On the other hand, no additional resource mobilisation by direct taxes and a hefty draft on the income of the common man by a huge burden of Rs 97,000 crore (and no assurance of lighter retail inflation) in taxes, the prospects of higher and effective pro-poor outcomes by means of the populist measures appear dim.

Obviously, under such tight fiscal constraints, the state has to limit its public welfare and direct investments to support development. But in India, the ruling classes have to win elections. Can cronyism at the top and populism at the bottom levels, without a viable functional middle, ensure political survival of the neoliberal regimes? For such political compulsions, the political parties continue with more of what has been perfected by them—cultivate the constituencies by helping them tide over difficulties and get some positive succour and thus reduce the danger of a backlash of the voters' wrath. One is referring to the lower level crony behaviour, critical for managing elections by corrupt use of money and public programmes of welfare (too limited to satisfy everyone) and hence their discretionary allocation to the chosen few.

Are Provision of Public Goods Biased?

The existing methodology and logic of such practices has been neatly summed up by RBI Governor Raghuram Rajan in a public lecture (the Twentieth Lalit Doshi Memorial Lecture on 14 August 2014, reproduced on the site of the RBI). Its starting point is that, 'Our provision of public goods is unfortunately biased against access by the poor'. Then, without giving enough , how do the neoliberals survive politically and win frequent electoral battles? A typical neoliberal concern indeed!

It has two parts: one at the national and States level. Even for this, one can cite Raghuram Rajan's lecture in 2008, when he showed a mirror to the captains of industry and trade. In the 2014 lecture he describes how a politico-economic market emerges and fills the vacuum left by rather minimal allocations made for public services. To quote him, 'The poor and underprivileged need the politician to help him get jobs and public services. The crooked politician needs the businessman to provide the funds that allow him to supply patronage to the poor and fight elections. The corrupt businessman needs the crooked politician to get him public resources and contracts cheaply. And the politician needs the votes of the poor and the underprivileged. Every constituency is tied to the other in a cycle of dependence, which ensures that the status quo prevails'.

Obviously, one can say that the politician works through bureaucracy and shares the loot and favours and also returns the favours by good, 'wet' postings and direct sharing of the loot.

The Art of Winning Elections

How do the political classes—who provide inadequate supplies of some of the most critical needs, such as the basic wherewithal for a good civic life for the largest part of the population and undersupply what is required for oiling the wheels of the small-sized, scattered but in its absolute size a huge production apparatus, which is the largest part of the economy, that is the non-corporate, unorganised and mainly non-urban segments—still manage to win and retain political power?

Winning successive elections is something basic to neoliberal India's poltical economy. Perhaps the phenomenon is still not convincingly explored. But its outcomes are visible in the form of a practical, shared, hegemonic operation of the modern economic and political machineries and a near convergence in favour of neoliberal policies. The Indian development experience, irrespective of the declared intentions and formal model, is operated by generally no-holds-barred and contesting politico-business capital with what is visible and occasionally comes out in the open, including the tip of the iceberg which shows just due to serendipity of the authorities. Its theoretical, ideological and operational corelates are also too complex to be understood in simplistic formulations, as one sees in many well-received studies of India's emerging political economy. Obviously, it would be presumptuous to claim that anything approaching such an exploration can even be attempted in an initial overview of the present kind.

> A little noted outcome of these practices was a weak fiscal strength, both when viewed in relation to many onerous heavy responsibilities facing the government as also in international comparative terms vis-à-vis some select other countries. Hence the observed fact of rather limited extent to which the state moved to overcome the basic constraints crippling the poor masses. One sees that now the agenda with which the neoliberal major parties woo voters has been reduced to 'water, roads and electricity (*paani, bijli, sadak*, now ironically a common popular

> name for all the public goods and common productive and civic services and considered 'development'). Obviously it suited the fat cats controlling the growth process and cornering its fruits. But it served an additional political and functional necessity, especially owing to the token, tout-infested and top-down character of various populist measures which were neither effective nor comprehensive enough to make the select, lucky beneficiaries viable participants in normal on-going socio-economic processes. Actually, even for these normal entitlements, the adversely included sections have to seek patronage of the political, administrative and informal touts who double up as politically- connected middle men and women, working under or on behalf of political bosses and parties, local dons and muscle men. The use of such devices and processes gave birth to various mafia groups, who helped the local businessmen-landlords, service providers and contractors win government contracts, make shoddy and inadequate supplies and amass huge fortunes and even win superficial respectability (as described above as lower end cronyism).
>
> Thus, even rural and urban social services and infrastructure support systems became victims of low level of allocations, reinforced by crony local plutocracy and criminals nexus who gang up to coax, cajole and coerce voters into voting for pro-corporate political classes. It is on account of such methods of manging power that the ruling parties can blatantly attack the meagre livelihood support available to the victims of chronic poverty. The latest move regarding MNCs' entry into the e-commerce platforms is an example of how the interests of some 45 crore small retailers can be ignored in order to attract foreign capital, essentially to sustain the over and unsustainable, and of course, harmful degree of over-linking with the rich and market-centric corporate capital-led economies.

The loss of political supremacy by any one single political party (the onset of the era of coalitions), and the changed, corporatised and family empire-based character of almost all the non-left parties (of course to varying extents) and more importantly, the big role of the leaders with known and demonstrated abilities to mobilise and amass such huge money power are major facets of India's emerging post-liberalisation phase of politics. In these processes, various special skills and capabilities and resources came to play a big role. These led to emergence of some political wheeler-dealer groups and touts, including mafia gangs, even mouthing and proclaiming certain highly emotive values. On the other hand, in the name of the poor and the deprived, empty slogans of rights-based entitlements to education, casual wage-work for 100 days, that is without social security and inadequate funds, have made these programmes yet another instance of populism. As indicated by the title of the present exercise, our hypothesis is that it is the inter-connected emergence of plutocracy, cronyism and populism, taken together which may well provide some useful clues for making a sense of the present socio-economic reality of India. With some cosmetic changes and some which directly further enhance inequalities, the NDA is continuing the pro-poor measures, at the same time adding additional punch to its neoliberal economic agenda.

Conlusion

By way of summing up, we maintain that the two regimes (the previous UPA and the present NDA) have followed policies which are significantly similar, though their packaging and selling are of different kinds. However, both have stakes in claiming to be different. As indicated above, a different kind of management, with attempts to improve, cannot be a substitute for substantive improvement in content. Brisk, business-like handling of projects can hardly fill the void and lacunae in the policy design.

The social trappings and sloganeering for popular consumption and for 'management' of the cadre can easily go overboard while just holding firmly to and extending the policies whose outcomes are matters of political management, false slogans, and the play of top-level and lower level plutocratic corruption, cronyism and populism. Actually the time may be fast approaching for new political equations, organisational revamping and programmatic responsiveness to the experience gained so far.

Though the political opposition to NDA is fairly active at the level of demonstrative action and statements, what the country needs is a theoretically sound reappraisal and attempts with a long-term view, rather than clutching at all the economic straws in the wind. Unfortunately, such deeper and pro-people moves do not seem to be emerging in India's political-economic scene. Without robust internal democracy, economic adjustments may require direct, non-conventional, well-organised grassroots activism that is shorn of elitist, dynastic, money-backed and partisan, commercially-oriented and media-powered leadership that is spontaneously emerging. Just as the nice phrases in the Preamble to the Constitution have remained a shallow outer covering so far, it is not unlikely that new approaches without a thorough correction may invite a relapse into muddling through phases of intermittent economic growth, with different political formations moving to and out of governments as costly experiments.

End Notes, References and Bibliography

1. Acemoglu D and James Robinson (2013), *Why Nations Fail: The Origins of Power, Prosperity and Poverty*, Crown Business, New York.
2. Agarwala AN and SP Singh (1960), *The Economics of Underdevelopment*, Oxford University Press.
3. Alternative Economic Survey Group (2004), *Magnifying Mal-development*, Indian Political Economy Association, Zed Books, London.
4. (2005-06), *Neo-liberal disempowering of Masses*, Indian Political Economy Association, New Delhi.
5. (2010), *Dis-equalizing Growth: Two Decades of Neo-liberalism*, Indian Political Economy Association.
6. (2011), *Economic Growth and Development: Deepening Divergence*, Indian Political Economy Association.
7. (2012-13), *Economic Policies: 'Gods' that Failed*, Indian Political Economy Association.
8. Bose Arun (1989), *India's Social Crisis: An Essay on Capitalism, Socialism, Individualism and Indian Civililzation*, Oxford University Press.
9. Corbridge, S and B Harriss (2001), *The Dialectics of Reforms: The Reinvention of Indian Liberalization, Hindu Nationalism and Popular Democracy*, Oxford University Press.

10. Cornia Andrea(2003),'Globalization and Distribution of Income Between and Within Countries', *Rethinking Development Economics,* edited book by Chang Ha Joon, Anthem Press, London.

11. Dahrendorf Ralf (2006), 'Inequality: A Necessary Price for Freedom', *Financial Express,* 2 February.

12. Freeland Chrystia, (2012), *Plutocracy: The Rise of the New Global Super Rich and the Fall of Everyone Else,* Allen Lane.

13. Gadgil DR (1967), 'Planning Without a Policy Frame', *Economic and Political Weekly,* Annual Number, February.

14. Gadgil, DR (1968) *Planning and Social Policy,* published by Directorate of Advertising and Audio-visual Publicity, GOI, (Gadgil address at the University of Gujarat), 23 November.

15. Government of India (1952) *The First Five Year Plan,* Planning Commission.

16. (1956) *The Second Five Year Plan,* Planning Commission.

17. (1969), *Report of the Industrial Licensing Committee* (S Duttt, Chariman).

18. (1979) *Report of the Committee on Controls and Subsidies,* (V L Dagli, Chairperson).

19. (2012-13). *Economic Survey,* Ministry of Finance.

20. (2014-15). *Economic Survey,* Ministry of Finance.

21. Kabra, Kamal Nayan (2001),'The Transition in India: From Market-manipulated State to Market Fundamentalist State during 1990s', *Social Science Research Journal* (2).

22. (2006) 'Development Thinking of Indian Planners: A critical Review', *IASSI Quarterly (*Now named *Contributions to Indian Social Sciences),* 24(3).

23. (2006) 'Indian Planning and Liberalization', *Economic and Political Weekly,* 5 October.

24. (2008), *High Growth, Rising Inequalities, Worsening Poverty: India's Development Experience,* Books for Change and Action Aid, Bangalore.

25. (2010), 'The Private corporate Sector: Major Influence on the Pattern of Growth – Annexure', *Two Decades of Neo-liberalism (Alternative Economic Survey, India),*pp 65-66.

26. (2012), Appropriate Development: People First, Institute of Social Science, New Delhi.

27. (2012-13), 'Current Status of the Black Economy: Greying of India's Political Economy', Neo-liberal Economic Policies: 'Gods' that Failed *(Alternative Economic Survey, India).*

28. V Upadhyay (1999).'Crony Capitalism and Era of Scams', *Alternative Economic Survey 1991-98*, Rainbow Publishers.

29. Minhas BS (1971), *Planning and the Poor*, S Chand and Co, pp 65-70.

30. National Commission for Enterprises in the Unorganised Sector (2007), *Report on the Conditions of Work and Promotion of Livelihoods in the Unorganized Sector*, New Delhi.

31. Paranjape HR (1985), 'New Lamps for Old! A Critique of New Economic Policy', *Economic and Political Weekly*, 7 September.

32. Stiglitz J, 'A Social Democratic Agenda for a More Dynamic Indian Economy', Jawaharlal Nehru Memorial Lecture [but from a development perspective, perhaps the greatest failing of WC (Washington Consensus) was that it was not concerned with development].

33. Baker Raymond W, 2005. *Capitalism's Achilles Heel : Dirty Money and How to Renew Free-Market System*, Wiley.

34. Breman Jan, Globalizaton, Poverty and Exclusion Xviii GB Pant Social Science Institute, Allahabad.

35. Breman Jan, 2015, *Politics of Exclusion in Economic development of India,* edited by Pulin B Nayak, Routledge.

36. Piketty Thomas, 2014, *Capital in the Twenty First Century*, The Belknap Press of Harvard University.

37. Additionally there are references to news reports, source details have been provided in the text itself.

Macroeconomic Overview Myths and Reality

— Surajit Mazumdar

A REMARKABLE 'improvement' in the macroeconomic situation, compared to what prevailed not too long ago, is often claimed to be the significant achievement of the present government. Attention is drawn in this regard to the dramatic reduction of the current account deficit, the equally spectacular end of a decade long phase of persistently high levels of inflation, the continued reduction in the fiscal deficit and finally, of course, the signs that Indian growth has not only recovered but, in fact, India is a shining beacon in a gloomy global economy.The evidence put forward in substantiation of the proposition of a return to macroeconomic stability does put the present government in a kind of Catch-22 situation. On the one hand it wishes to claim most of the credit for the 'recovery'—in other words, it seeks to make out that the improvement is the result of the Modi effect. On the other hand, the only way it can substantiate the claim of macroeconomic improvement is by suggesting that its beginnings predate the ascendancy of Modi or have causes that cannot be attributed to actions of his government.

The real truth, however, is one of continuity between the two regimes which indicates a continuing process of seeking to keep a crisis-ridden economy afloat at the expense of the common people.

The 'Revival' of Growth: Fact and Fiction

The Indian corporate sector and the Finance Ministry are, of course, nostalgic about the 'good old days' between 2003-04 and 2007-08 when high growth rates ruled—leading to a galloping growth of profits, and consequently, also a surge in tax revenues that rendered the fiscal situation relatively comfortable. Exports of both goods and services also grew rapidly even though imports also climbed steeply at the same time. Additionally, the corporate sector also drove an investment boom which saw the investment-GDP ratio climb sharply by over 8 percentage points in just five years. The growth process nevertheless bypassed the majority—symptomatic of which was the stagnation in real wages even in the rapidly growing corporate sector. The only saving grace in that situation was that within limits, some expansion of public expenditure was consistent with the FRBM objective of reducing the fiscal deficit even while tax rates were held down. All of this, however, ended with the onset of the global crisis. The 'growth revival' being talked about today, if it is happening, surely does not have any of the features associated with the earlier high growth except one—it offers no positive prospects for the common Indian people.

The story of the GDP growth rate rebound, which supposedly means that India has upstaged China to become the fastest growing major economy, is firstly based on a 'revised' picture of India's economy, resulting from the CSO's move to a new series of GDP estimates. This revision of course reflects no real changes in the ground realities of India's economy and the growth would be invisible to most people if they were to go by their actual experiences rather than the statistics. Indeed, it would be hard to find any other instance where the CSO's growth estimates have been met by such widespread scepticism and the debate about its accuracy continues without any sign of being settled.

The new GDP estimates effectively *lower* the level of the GDP in 2011-12 compared to that in the older series. The evidence, in fact, suggests that 2014-15 would have been the first year in which the new estimation method resulted in a *higher* GDP figure than the estimates that would have resulted if the series with 2004-05 as base year had been continued. These adjustments, of course, mean that the growth *rate* is boosted-up—but what does it say about the state of the economy in 2011-12, the base year for the new series? This was the second of the two successive relatively good agricultural years but was also the year in whose second half, the growth slowdown (particularly in manufacturing) became palpable. Both the old and the new series show that growth in the next year was relatively poor. So were 2011-12 and 2012-13 worse years for the economy than was hitherto thought to be the case?

While the lowering of the base year figure may have helped push up the growth rates in subsequent years, this effect kicked in, in a significant way in 2013-14—before the Modi government came to power. This posed a problem for the spin doctors of the regime, leading to even official scepticism about the growth rates as outlined in the *Economic Survey* of 2014-15 (Volume 1, p. 6). The contradictions in the government's position, however, emerge in sharp relief if we assess the subsequent two years' performance by the same yardstick—which make their growth rates as suspect as those of 2013-14.

The divergence between the manufacturing growth rates emerging from the new series and the Index of Industrial Production (IIP) has not only persisted but even widened. While manufacturing GVA at basic prices, as per the new series, is estimated to have grown by 5.5 per cent in 2014-15 and a whopping 9.5 per cent in 2015-16, the growth in the manufacturing IIP for the April-February period in both years was just 2.3 per cent and this followed a contraction by 0.8 per cent in the previous year (meaning, the level of industrial production is even now not very much different from the 2012-13 level and in per capita terms, lower).Overall the picture emerging from IIP data is of almost complete stagnation in industrial output for over 50 months. What is significant to note here is that, the ASI data shows that 2012-13 was the first year in a decade when employment in organised manufacturing actually contracted by nearly 4 per cent, and the subsequent year only saw a return to 2011-12 levels. Since employment should have a closer link to the volume of industrial production than with the 'value-added', it is likely that the organised manufacturing employment scenario was poor in the subsequent two years too.

If we look at the sector on which the largest numbers of Indians depend for their livelihood—namely agriculture—the last two years have been a disaster. Real agricultural GVA was negative in 2014-15 and rose by a measly 1.1 per cent in 2015-16 as the vagaries of the weather, volatility of international prices and moderation of support prices have hit the sector hard. Foodgrain production in 2014-15 was lower than in the previous three years and is not expected to show any revival in 2015-16. Cash crops like sugarcane and cotton have seen increases in production levels but suffered from declining prices. Indicative of growing distress in the agrarian sector is the sharp rise in suicides by farmers.

On the trade front too, if 2014-15 was bad, 2015-16 was even worse. The real growth of exports of goods and services, which would be a source of rising demand, was just 1.7 per cent in 2014-15 compared to a 7.3 per cent growth in 2013-14. In 2015-16, it is estimated to contract significantly and show a 6.6 per cent growth. On the other hand, the contraction in imports too has continued, with a massive a drop of 8.4 per cent in 2013-14 being followed by a mere 0.8 per cent in 2014-15, followed by another drop of 6.3 per cent in 2015-16.

The investment picture of the economy also remains bleak even in the new GDP series. Gross Fixed Capital Formation (GFCF) at 2011-12 prices is estimated to have increased by only 4.9 per cent in 2014-15 and 5.3 per cent in 2015-16—a far cry from the earlier high-growth period when the average growth per annum of real GFCF was above 16 per cent. The investment GDP ratio has continued to decline—coming down in both years. In 2015-16 it is estimated to have been 31.6 per cent (at 2011-12 prices) and 29.4 per cent (at current prices), in 2013-14 the corresponding levels were 33.0 per cent and 31.6 per cent respectively. In contrast to this, the real expenditure on valuables, which had contracted sharply (42.2 per cent in 2013-14) rebounded to increase by 15.4 and 13.3 per cent in 2014-15 and 2015-16 respectively. In other words, the stagnation in productive investment and the relatively greater attraction of unproductive assets continues to afflict the Indian economy.

Where the story of growth recovery is most out of sync with other data is in relation to the fiscal situation. In each of the three years from 2012-13, the budget estimates for revenues from all central taxes (including the share going to the States) made at the beginning of each year were, as a percentage of the new GDP estimates, almost identical. Moreover these were one percentage point below the level actually realised in 2007-08. Yet, as Table 1 shows, actual revenue realis.

Table 1: Revenue from Central Taxes and Central Government Expenditure as Percentage of GDP at Market Prices (2011-12 Base Year Series), Budget Estimates versus Actuals

	2012-13	2013-14	2014-15
Gross Tax Revenue (Central Taxes)			
Budget Estimates	10.83	10.96	11.04
Actuals	10.41	10.10	9.97
Shortfall (BE-Actuals)	0.42	0.86	1.08
Total Central Government Expenditure			
Budget Estimates	14.98	14.77	14.37
Actuals	14.17	13.83	13.46
Shortfall (BE-Actuals)	0.81	0.94	0.91

Source: Union Budget and CSO, Press Note on Advance Estimates of National Income 2015-16.

Even in 2015-16, revenue realisations have actually been significantly below the levels estimated in the Budget. However, the government managed to avert a major revenue shortfall by making use of the fall in international oil prices—repeatedly increasing taxes on oil and not passing on the entire benefit of the decline in prices to consumers. Additional realisations of excise duties—to the tune of Rs 54,000 crore above budget estimates—have been used to compensate for shortfalls in direct taxes. This, of course, has reinforced the already existing trend of government's increasing reliance on indirect taxes, relative to direct taxes. This extraordinary revenue mobilisation was, in fact, extremely important for the government meeting fiscal deficit targets because of another curious aspect of GDP trends in 2015-16, namely the sharp fall in nominal growth rates. As can be seen in Table 2, in 2015-16, nominal growth rates of both GVA as well as investment expenditure (GFCF) were actually below their 'real' rates—implying a deflationary situation, an unlikely companion of robust economic growth even under conditions of falling oil prices. Manufacturing and construction are two sectors where this is particularly pronounced.

Table 2: Annual Rates of Growth of GVA and GFCF

	2012-13	2013-14	2014-15	2015-16 (AE)
	GVA at Basic Prices			
At Current Prices	13.6	12.7	10.5	6.8
At 2011-12 Prices	5.4	6.3	7.1	7.3
Difference	8.2	6.4	3.4	-0.5
	GFCF			
At Current Prices	10.8	7.3	7.9	3.6
At 2011-12 Prices	4.9	3.4	4.9	5.3
Difference	5.9	3.9	3	-1.7

Source: CSO, Press Note on Advance Estimates of National Income 2015-16.

If all of this is taken into account, the real truth of the Indian economy appears to be not of revival but of the existence of a strong demand constraint arising from both domestic as well as international factors, which is being further reinforced through extremely restrictive fiscal policy. This policy thrust had been initiated by the UPA government well before the last general elections. Adding to this has been the extremely conservative attitude of the RBI, which has maintained interest rates at high levels. It is this persistent squeeze on demand produced by all of these that has combined with the fall in international commodity prices to produce the lowering of inflation and the current-account deficit.

Current Account and the Balance of Payments Situation

India's Current Account Deficit, which hit a peak level of 4.8 per cent of GDP in 2012-13, certainly did not emerge overnight but was a culmination of a trend that operated consistently for over a decade. The real culprit was the trade deficit—reflecting a faster rise of imports compared to exports. The initial source of this exceptional rise in imports was manufactured imports (capital goods and intermediates) reflecting a trend of increasing import-intensity of Indian production and, in particular, of the manufacturing sector. Subsequently the collapse of investment and slowdown of industrial growth served to check this trend but increases in international oil prices and rising gold imports (whose prices were also rising sharply) maintained the pressure on the current account deficit. International oil prices, however, stabilised by 2011-12 and then from June 2014 onward experienced a sharp decline of over 50 per cent till January 2015, and after a minor recovery, there was another dramatic decline between July 2015 and January 2016. Therefore, as can be seen in Table 3, India's oil trade deficit was reduced in the last three years but naturally the sharpest declines were in 2014-15 and 2015-16. It has been a different story with the non-oil trade deficit, which *increased* in 2014-15 as well as 2015-16 after experiencing a sharp decline in 2012-13. This difference between the oil and non-oil balance exists despite the fact that the movements of international gold prices in this period have followed roughly the same pattern as oil prices—declining in the last two years after a steep increase till 2011-12. Clearly, the revival in gold imports neutralised some of the effects of decline in prices, but India's exports have taken a hit in the same period along with intensified competition from cheap imports. Things might have been worse but for the jewellers' strike which led to a sharp fall in gold imports towards the end of 2015-16. Indeed, if the effects of reduction in oil and gold prices were to be taken out, the trade balance in the last two years would have been not much different from what it was in 2012-13.

Thus, the so-called improvement in India's external payments situation is not based on either an expansion of exports or a replacement of imports by domestic production. It does not, therefore, constitute a structural solution to the problem which could reduce the dependence on volatile capital flows to cover the deficit and vulnerability of the rupee. Adding to this problem is the picture with regard to the invisibles surplus, which has for long cancelled out a major part of the trade deficit. In the last decade, remittances from Indians abroad and IT services exports have contributed to the maintenance of a significant net surplus in invisibles earnings, the other part of the current account. This surplus appears to be now under increasing stress as net exports of services are facing a squeeze.

The widening of the non-oil deficit and the shrinking levels of exports are sure signs that the relatively favourable balance of payments situation is a temporary reprieve that, in turn, is heavily dependent on contractionary conditions—low international commodity prices and restrained domestic output and investment. Even with a favourable situation with regard to international commodity prices, maintaining

Table 3: India's Foreign Trade (in Million US Dollars)

Year	Exports			Imports			Trade Balance		
	Oil	Non-Oil	Total	Oil	Non-Oil	Total	Oil	Non-Oil	Total
2012-13	60,865.1	239,535.5	**300,400.7**	164,040.6	326,696.1	**490,736.7**	103,176	87,160.6	**190,336**
2013-14	63,179.4	251,236.3	**314,415.7**	164,770.3	285,443.3	**450,213.7**	101,591	34,207.0	**135,798**
2014-15	56,794.1	253,544.3	**310,338.5**	138,325.5	309,707.9	**448,033.4**	81,531.4	56,163.6	**137,695**
2015-16	29,183.9	231,953.0	**261,136.8**	82,662.3	296,933.9	**379,596.2**	53,478.4	64,981.0	**118,459**

Source: RBI, Real Time Handbook of Statistics on the Indian Economy (http://dbie.rbi.org.in/DBIE/dbie.rbi?site=publications#!2).

a manageable external payments situation would still mean continued pressure to pursue restrictive fiscal and monetary policies.

Inflation in India

Partly the moderation of inflation in the last two years reflects international price trends, particularly of oil. However, more than fuel, Indian inflation over the last decade was driven by food prices even as slack demand for manufactured products kept prices of manufactures relatively stable. That food price inflation was never caused by excess demand for food, resulting from high growth, has been proved by the backdrop to the decline in inflation rates in the last two years. In both, overall GDP growth was supposedly high while agricultural growth was extremely poor—circumstances that traditional wisdom would suggest, should have increased inflationary pressures. This is, in fact, partly reminiscent of the decade of the severe agrarian crisis which preceded the emergence of persistence of food price inflation. That crisis had resulted in a simultaneous depression of both output as well as demand and the latter, combined with a running down of foodgrain stocks, had kept price increases in check. The subsequent inflationary phase marked the end of the road for such a process. In the absence of support from public investment in agriculture, inflation itself became the only means for moderating the effects of increasing unviability of agriculture and fall in rural incomes. It was during the inflationary phase, therefore, that there was some stepping up of private investment in agriculture, limited improvement in agricultural growth and some increases in rural wage rates after more than a decade of complete stagnation. Food consumption levels also experienced some recovery from the squeeze that had been at work before, but only to the levels that had prevailed in the early 1990s—even this recovery has been tapering off.

The 2014-15 *Economic Survey*'s discussion of the future of Indian inflation paid particular attention to what is happening to rural wages—and somewhat shamelessly pointed to the sharp and continuous moderation in rural wage growth since 2011 as a factor marking a structural shift in the inflationary process. According to the Survey, 'rural wage growth can continue to decelerate, further moderating inflationary pressures'. The *Survey*'s analysis actually says more about how inflation

Figure 1: Private Final Consumption Expenditure Per Capita on Selected Food Items at 2004-05 prices, 1990-91 to 2012-13

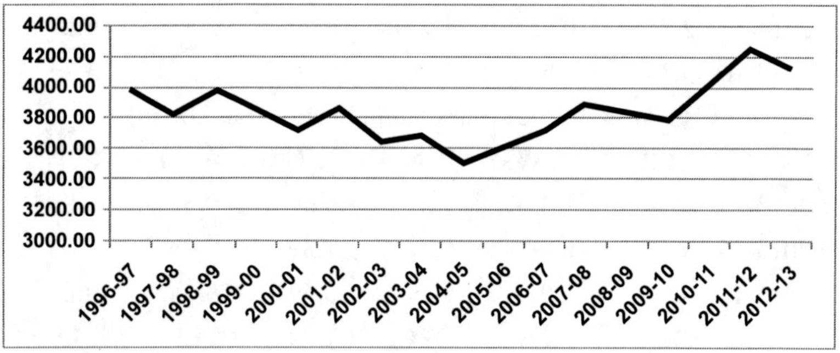

Source: CSO, National Accounts Statistics.

is being sought to be 'controlled'— at the expense of the agricultural sector and food consumption levels by holding down Minimum Support Prices and expenditures on MNREGA—than about its root causes. As such, like in the case of the current account deficit, the reduction in the inflation rate too does not represent a fundamental resolution of the problem and instead, is a reflection of the agricultural sector being pushed towards the brink.

Even after such a squeeze, food price inflation has not quite been tamed—only the rate of increase in prices has been reduced to an extent. As can be seen in Table 4, the moderation in the food price growth (and, therefore, subsequently of consumer price indices based inflation rates) emerged in the second quarter of 2014-15. However, after reaching their lowest levels in the same quarter in 2015-16, inflation rates again increased to a degree.

Table 4: Year-on-Year Increase in Monthly Price Indices, 2013-14 and 2014-15

Wholesale Price Index for Food Articles						
	APR	MAY	JUN	JUL	AUG	SEP
2013-14	6.08	8.25	10.27	12.29	19.17	18.68
2014-15	8.74	9.64	8.32	8.47	5.11	3.68
2015-16	5.90	2.74	3.12	-1.20	-1.02	0.84

	OCT	NOV	DEC	JAN	FEB	MAR
2013-14	18.34	19.69	13.73	8.85	7.94	9.57
2014-15	2.74	0.66	4.95	8.00	7.83	6.27
2015-16	3.33	5.55	7.89	6.46	3.35	3.73
	Consumer Price Index Combined (Rural+Urban)					
	APR	MAY	JUN	JUL	AUG	SEP
2013-14	9.39	9.31	9.87	9.64	9.52	9.84
2014-15	8.48	8.33	6.77	7.39	7.03	5.63
2015-16	4.87	5.01	5.40	3.69	3.74	4.41
	OCT	NOV	DEC	JAN	FEB	MAR
2013-14	10.17	11.16	9.87	8.79	8.03	8.31
2014-15	4.62	3.27	4.28	5.19	5.37	5.25
2015-16	5.00	5.41	5.61	5.69	5.18	4.83

Source: CSO and Office of Economic Adviser, GOI Ministry of Commerce and Industry.

Conclusion

For the common people of India, economic crisis has not been a temporary and recent development but something that they have lived through on a continuous basis in the period of neo-liberal reforms. The neglect of agriculture and the consequent agrarian crisis, along with limited growth of employment opportunities outside, maintained a situation in which there was a constant downward pressure on wages and other labour incomes, irrespective of the rate of growth of overall GDP. In the period of high corporate growth, wage stagnation contributed to the enrichment of the corporate sector and upper-income groups as the wage share in income generated fell continuously and a whole range of cheap labour and labour-intensive services were available.

Eventually, however, it is these imbalances which also produced the combination of food inflation, a severe demand constraint for the industrial sector, and a widening current account deficit. If there was inadequate investment (private and public) in agriculture and supporting activities, there was also excessive investment in manufacturing in relation to available consumption and asset demand which also tended to have an import-intensive character. These results of the fundamental imbalances in the growth trajectory made the Indian economy more vulnerable to the vagaries of international capital flows, particularly given the world economic situation emerging after the 2008 global crisis. The consequence has been that government, whether under the UPA or the BJP, have aggressively pursued policies which seek to solve the problem by *accentuating* rather than correcting the fundamental imbalances.

A direct all out assault on the interests of the common people in order to grant largesse to the rich and the domestic and foreign corporate elite—transferring private and public land, natural resources and other public assets to corporates at low prices, keeping wages low and tweaking labour regulations in favour of employers, curbing expenditures on subsidies, agriculture and the social sector while easing the tax burden on the rich and wealthy, transferring land, natural resources and public assets to the rich and the corporate elite cheaply and using all of these to 'sell' India to foreign investors and speculators so that they would bring their money to India —this is the formula for 'correcting' macroeconomic imbalances that is being pursued with savage intent.

Farmers' Distress, Suicides and Budget 2016-17

— RV Ramana Murthy

THE UNABATED suicides of farmers in India is an embarrassment in India's economic high growth story. The suicides, which began in the State of Telangana in 1997, quickly spread to Maharashtra, Karnataka, Madhya Pradesh, Punjab, Haryana, Rajasthan, and to Uttar Pradesh by 2013. A hailstorm in the northern State of Haryana that caused heavy crop damage has resulted in sizeable number of suicides, unusual to the State. Uniformly everywhere, the suicide victims are invariably small farmers. The farm distress is largely concentrated among cotton farmers in most parts of the country, though there are episodes where it has affected farmers growing a wide array of crops such as paddy, wheat, soy, ground nut, chilli, coffee and even shrimps. Most scholars have attributed the chronic indebtedness which led to the suicides to short term as well as long terms factors. Short-term factors are natural disasters, pest attacks and personal family situations; long-terms factors noted are increased dependence on private sources for credit in the light of falling share of institutional credit, price slumps caused by trade liberalisation, rising input costs—all of which are a result of neoliberal reforms undertaken since 1991. The decline of public sector research and technology development, entry of multinational companies in seed and pesticide markets, reduction of fertiliser subsidies, removal of public procurement have also led to increase in investment costs. The purported benefits of trade liberalisations did not accrue to the farmers.

The UPA I government, which came on a mandate to address some of these issues, introduced some policy correctives such as increased agricultural credit, revision of MSP (minimum support price) for wheat and paddy, loan waivers to farmers, ex-gratia to suicide victims' families in some States, increased PDS subsidy, MNREGA schemes, and several small benefits from different welfare programmes such as ICDS etc. A good run of normal monsoon years during 2004-10, along with other measures, enabled some agricultural recovery. While during this time the rhetoric about farmer suicides fell off the shelf, in reality the suicide of farmers continued in several States like Maharashtra, Andhra Pradesh, Karnataka and Madhya Pradesh. The recent hailstorm and the tragic suicide of Gajender Singh during a political meeting of the Aam Admi Party (AAP) meeting once again brought the issue back to centre stage. While it is a convenient weapon for the opposition parties to attack the ruling party, raising the issue in populist platforms cannot do any justice either to the suffering of farmers, nor ameliorate the causes. Even in the intellectual discourse, what is missing so far is a good understanding of the political economy of agrarian change that has occurred in India in the last one decade, such an understanding will give the fuller picture on why such deaths. Taking account of the diversity and complexity of the agricultural situation in the country, this paper attempts to build a meta-narrative of structural agrarian change and its political economy that helps to understand the agrarian distress and farmer suicides which have become chronic and endemic.

The Template of Suicides

The suicide narrative falls into three templates:

The first template: A typical small farmer owning less than 5 acres borrows money from private money lenders of up to Rs 1-1.5 lakh, to invest on irrigational assets like borewells fitted with submersible

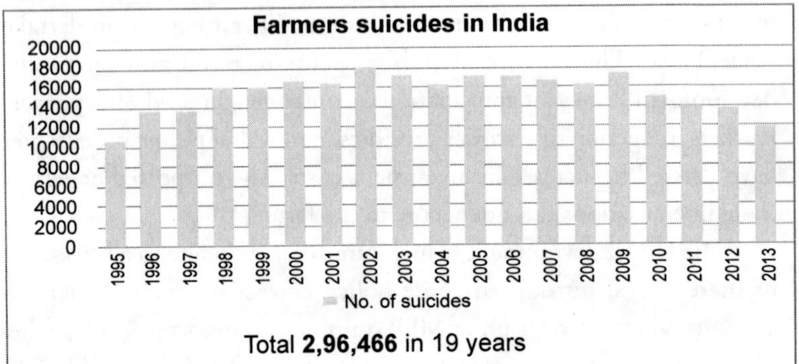

Source: NCRB 1995-2013 http://www.agrariancrisis.in

pumpset and from a bank for a crop loan. Tries inserting more than a couple of borewells, unsuccessfully, due to fall in the groundwater table in successive dry spells. With crop failure, and consumption needs of the family increases; further money is borrowed and the debt burden doubles in three years, crossing his asset value. Debtors prussurise to pay up and this ends in his suicide.

The Second Template: A marginal/small farmer, leases five to ten acres, sows crop like cotton, pays about Rs 60,000 rent per acre and incurs about Rs 150,000 on cost of cultivation; borrows further for borewell investment, borrows to a tune of Rs 2-3 lakh from private moneylender. Dry spells or excessive rains or pest attacks can lead to crop failure, turn this loan into a debt trap. He won't be able to pay the amount even after sale of his assets and reschedule the rest, to be paid though wage labour.

The Third Template: A marginal/small farmer borrows money to the tune of Rs 2-3 lakh to meet family consumption needs arising from health exigency/children's education/daughter's marriage. Crop failures due to environmental factors, fall in the market price owing to national and international market upheavals, leads to a debt trap.

Most farmer suicides fall into any one of the above three templates or sometimes in a combination of these. It is not difficult to list the causes as excessive risk in agriculture, rising cost of cultivation, falling terms of trade, rise in rents, absence of market support by the state, lack of agricultural extension services, inadequate coverage of bank credit, excessive dependence on private money lenders at exorbitant rates of interest, monopsonistic commodity markets and so on.

One also observes that the small farmer makes every possible effort to save his crop, trying alternative crops, reducing labour costs and so on. The debt portfolio is usually distributed among the money lender, commission agent, the fertiliser-pesticide dealer and the bank. The debt is incurred after pawning all assets like gold, bullocks etc. He is often left with the last asset—the small parcel of land, retained doggedly. Agricultural distress is not new to the Indian farmer. But it certainly is for a new class of farmers. It is not the medium or large farmer who is distressed, but actually it is the small farmer. Again, not every small farmer may commit suicide, but an exceptional subset of these burdened with other contingencies, who are at a higher risk, do. It is, therefore, the small farmer distress that should merit our attention. At the same time, excessive focus on 'suicide' may detract us from understanding the larger phenomenon of small farmers 'distress'. We need to separate those structural factors that make one group more vulnerable, in order to understand the phenomenon.

Changing Agrarian Structure

According to data on operational holdings from various rounds of the National Sample Survey, the share of marginal and small holdings, measuring less than 1 hectare and 2 hectares respectively, have increased to 63 per cent, commanding 40 per cent of land. If 19 per cent of semi-medium holdings, cultivating less than 4 hectares, are included, the share of small peasantry goes up to 83 per cent, operating 60 per cent of the land. The remaining 17 per cent of big holdings is owned by the upper peasantry who operate about 40 per cent of the land. Historical trends suggest that the bottom part of small peasantry in the agrarian structure is progressively growing; the upper segment is becoming lean and operating lesser land.

Except for a couple of States in India like Punjab, this phenomenon is common in India. The average holding in each size is also shrinking. The progressive marginalisation of operational holdings is happening from two processes. First, from the fact of property mutation—once large holdings are getting subdivided into medium and semi-medium farm holdings, medium holdings in turn are becoming small holdings. The second, landless labour have managed to buy small parcels of land, to become marginal and small farmers in several parts of the country.

The economic viability of small holdings is a widely debated issue. It is well known that most of the small land holders are peasants who use family labour and also wage labour. Thus, they are essentially petty commodity producers, while medium and large farmers are the typical capitalist farmers, using mostly hired labour with a different status. The difference is that the former are the ones aspiring to become capitalist farmers, while the latter are already capitalist. In the Indian context, given the sheer number of small size holdings, direct farm income is seldom adequate to support the consumption of the small farmer and his family.

Hence, he and his family members typically indulge in allied activists like dairying and wage labour. Wage labour becomes a default source of income when agriculture fails. Thereby wage employment is as important as farm income. However, there could be demographic factors such as having young children, or school-going children, having only one earning family-member, illness etc. that can cause reduced entitlement in an individual case. Some of the factors such as natural disasters can reduce more than one entitlement such as not only farm income but agricultural employment. Progressive mechanisation also reduces employment entitlement. Therefore, the prospects for small peasantry are certainly not very promising.

Structural Transformation

Liberal theory of economic development of the Lewisian type expects a structural transformation, with people leaving agriculture for better opportunities in the modern economic sector. The modern sector industry and services are expected to provide high wage opportunities to galvanise surplus labour away from the farm sector. The actual process of this prescriptive movement is much more tedious as choice of techniques in the modern sector progressively destroys job creation. The aspiration that the modern nation-state creates among people spurs a rural exodus in search of work. Marxist understanding on this provides more precise picture of the transformation. It imposes preconditions such as property rights, monetisation of transactions, general commodity production and emergence of wage labour and progressive destruction of petty commodity production. Migration of surplus labour, contingent on various factors, is a relatively quicker process for the agricultural labourer, while small farmers are straddled between farming and wage labour. Harshness of migration and love for stable rural life compels the small farmer to persist with farming. This usually gets encouraged by state intervention to promote agricultural production, access to modern institutions like banks, irrigation and technology. While compulsive land acquisition by the state for public projects displaces some, there is not much of such a threat at the macro-level. Thus, the small farmer succeeds in getting a foot-hold in commodity production and may earn a part of subsistence. The modern capitalist sector indulges in primary accumulation through squeezing the terms of trade for agriculture, which forces the agricultural sector to improve productivity, eventually through mechanisation. Small farmers eventually face investment crunch and, thus, are increasingly forced join wage labour. Isolated cases of success cannot be ruled out, there are always some exceptions. Farming can be taken up by large farmers or corporate houses, and this is a more complex process entailing both, distress as well as gainful experiences.

In contrast to this prescriptive movement, the share of the small peasantry leaving agriculture seems to be relatively low compared to a faster decline of large farmers and moderately medium farmers. According to the *Agricultural Census 2011*, about 2.6 crore farmers have left farming in the period between the years 2001-11, which is the highest recorded so far. There is also a migration of ten crore agricultural labourers from the farm sector; the overall agriculture-dependent workers' share has fallen from 56 per cent to 46 per cent in the last one decade, which has been the fastest decline in a decade so far. Available government data, thus, suggest some definitive process of structural transformation happening. When we collate this with the data on increasing share of small and marginal farmers, at least one thing becomes clear—that the lower segment of agrarian structure is not declining relatively. According to some field-level information, the movement is happening more from the medium and large agricultural households, often belonging to upper castes, who are getting better urban opportunities such as salaried employment and business opportunity. Landless labour and marginal farmers are migrating as construction and other unskilled labour. Small and medium farmers are unable to leave farming easily. However, it is the small farmers who are facing larger incidence of distress in agriculture while the medium farmer is able to diversify to less riskier options. Hence, one apparently paradoxical phenomenon is that despite the harshness of farming distress, small peasantry have lesser options to move out and hence, for some it becomes a do or die situation.

Green Revolution and Rise of Commercial Agriculture

There was a time when most farmers, small or big, were all subsistence farmers, who used to farm to meet their respective family's food needs. The village barter economy helped to access non-food goods and services. The developmental state in India, for the interests of urban industrial complexes, created markets and infrastructure beyond what the colonial state had created. Having tasted consumer goods and better standard of life, subsistence peasantry was progressively drawn into participation in commodity production to meet the rising cash needs in education, health and family consumption. Barter systems slowly disappeared, replaced by monetary exchanges. Labour migrations gave new options. Commercialisation of all transactions in a village life came to a completion. Introduction of Green Revolution and creation of institutional framework for faster adoption of new technology and rising market surplus for the modern nation was a decisive turn towards acceleration of capitalist relations. Medium farmers became successful capitalist farmers, by accessing bank credit, market inputs and hiring labour. The Green Revolution and subsidies helped this section in the early period to accumulate and diversify. All such facilities inspired small farmers to participate in commodity production, taking advantage of family labour to overcome lack of investment. They had to continue to also participate in wage labour to meet family subsistence. These are typical petty commodity producers, who inevitably face problems of lower productivity, lack of institutional access to credit, technology and market, and are often exploited by the trader. They survive through sheer over-exploitation of family labour and under-consumption. Arrival of bore-well technology and rural electrification undertaken by the state, in fact, democratised farming in such way that small farmers could bring their marginal lands under cultivation. It is the same borewells that sound their death knell, by eventually drying up and demanding more and more investment into deeper borewells until the ground water dries up completely, rendering their farms unproductive and investments fruitless.

Enter Neoliberalism and Decline of Agriculture

The deflationary policies of neoliberal regimes to integrate the Indian economy with global markets since 1991 have changed the fortunes of the agricultural sector. Decline of public investment, reduced allocation of farm credit, reduction of subsidies, abolition of agricultural boards which played key roles in market interventions, market access to global seed sellers and reduced budgetary allocations have meant greater market-led regimes for the farm sector. Though terms of trade in selective crops were maintained, for most crops prices became highly volatile and relative prices declined. Bank credit became highly iniquitous, which enabled the medium farmers to diversify towards poultry, large-scale diary, production of high-value added crops and diversification into agribusiness in several regions. There has been a new surge for diversification without any institutional support, though. Growth was sustained entirely by private investment in agriculture which seriously eroded the profitability. Small farmers lacking wherewithal to diversify continued to grow largely traditional crops, with increasingly low profitability and losses sustained during natural calamities.

An important aspect is that Indian farmers as whole failed to organise either as cooperatives or as a strong lobby on a sustainable basis. Medium and large farmers belonging to upper castes had occasional phases of showing muscle to push MSP for wheat and sugarcane. When the upper caste farmers left agriculture, the sector lost leaders who had effectively lobbied for the sector in the past. Farmers in general remained at the fag end of the value chain, left with residual risk arising from weather, quality and market vagaries, while other stakeholders could squeeze their share. Traders being always in small numbers, or farming as rings, operate as monopsonistic agents who dominate the exchange terms. In India, agricultural activity also bears the risk of inclement weather which industrial activities don't. New agricultural technologies of short duration crops have extensively promoted summer cultivation, which faces hailstorms and untimely rains affect the crops. The small farmer thus becomes the last and weakest link in the process, burdened with this residual risk. All the other stakeholders like banks, moneylenders, input suppliers and the wage labour take away their respective shares.

Farm Prices and Primary Accumulation

Recent studies using primary data has shown that except for high-value crops such as turmeric, sugarcane, tobacco, aromatic crops, rhizomes, fruits etc, for all traditional crops such as wheat, rice, jowar, millets, pulses, oilseeds prices barely cover the cost of production. The usual problem with agriculture in India is that if one crop has some profitability, acreage surges ahead and soon production overshoots the demand, bringing down the prices. Farmers have no mechanism to restrict supply by reducing acreage. Burdened with immediacy of debt servicing requirements, with no wherewithal to maintain inventories, farmers fail to take benefit of off-season prices, while traders do. Thus, seasonal price fluctuations always punish the farmers and reward the traders. Measures like the Kisan Credit Card scheme is hardly ever implemented. The institutional mechanisms to deal with issues like lack of infrastructure, investment capacity and inventory management, all key necessities in modern-day agriculture, are not there. Therefore, the prospect of capital accumulation has been doomed in Indian agriculture from the beginning. This lack of wherewithal is often described as 'urban-bias' against the rural farmer. In such circumstances, the small farmers' presence in overwhelming number adds to their collective misery due to uncoordinated production decisions and lack of institutional mechanism to deal with risk management. For crop after crop, we hear the stories of price crash. Prices are kept just over the cost of production without profits to the farmer. For the crops where state intervention exits, in terms of minimum support prices and procurement, the situation is a little better, say like for paddy, wheat and sugarcane. In most other crops, the state civil supplies corporations (and State Marketing Federations) have only marginal role. Thus, small farmers lack lobbying mechanisms in the overall structure which can address their distress.

One should also understand the kind of relationship which the agricultural sector tends to have with the modern non-farm sector. Agricultural products tend to have lower income elasticity of demand, which lead to lower relative prices in the long run. The agricultural sector, despite all efforts, tends to have lower productivity, which further denies avenues for farmers to make up incomes. Farmers, being in millions in number, are forever price-takers while industry tends to be price maker that enables them to tilt the relative prices in their favour. Agricultural prices fall behind non-agricultural prices, leading to lower accumulation of surplus. Industrial interests influence state policies more. The purported benefits of trade liberalisation will be taken by the traders more than its benefit being passed on to farmers. Thus, farming is bound to lose profitability and result in an exodus. Capital too flows out of agriculture to non-agricultural sectors (it may re-enter as usurious capital). We can see this happening as many large and medium farmers become commission agents, millers, money lenders, seed-and-fertiliser sellers and so on. There is an agribusiness built around agriculture, which pressurises the farmers as the latter are dependent on the former. In this process, the medium farmers tend to escape through diversification while small farmers get marginalised.

Ideally, capitalist development should provide opportunities for people to migrate out. The petty commodity producers, who cannot produce a profit, may eventually be forced to liquidate their landholdings and join the industrial working class. This is the resolution that happened in some of the developed capitalist countries in the 19th century. In Europe for instance, the agricultural imports from Americas ended the prospects of domestic farmers. Many emigrated to the New World, thus the agriculture-dependent population reduced. This option did not exist for post-colonial capitalist economies like India. The petty commodity production is fraught with crisis of viability. In several other developing countries, agricultural labour and the farming class have left farming to join the urban informal sector. The informal sector in urban areas, constituted of self-employed, however, is another area where the ambiguous existence of petty producers between the worker and the owner continues. Often, it is here that the migrant small farmer and agricultural labourer joins, without any profit.

Palliatives Don't Work

The response of the neoliberal state to the farm distress is to address it more in terms of welfare measures, rather than in terms of market interventions. As a response to civil society demand, the Andhra Pradesh government, for instance, came up with an ex-gratia programme to take care of victims' families in 2005, which made Rajashekhar Reddy, the then-chief minister (known as a saviour of farmers) recognise only one tenth of suicides as genuine. The UPA government too undertook measures such as revision of MSP as an election promise, along with the other schemes such as loan waiver and increased procurement by Cotton Corporation of India. But the crisis of cotton farming came back to square one after a brief respite, as wages and other input costs have risen again and the MSP was not revised on par. Export permits are given only after satisfying the needs of the domestic textile industry. The state, meanwhile, refused to acknowledge the actual number of suicides caused due to farm distress, it recognised just one-fourth. Many commented that ex-gratia would encourage more suicides. In fact, what it proved was that neither does the government encourage suicides nor is it capable of preventing suicides. Instead, activists from Non-government Organisations who were interested in solving farmer's distress leading to suicides (they have demanded ex-gratia) have been kept busy entrusted with overseeing implementation of the government ex-gratia. The root cause for the suicides lie somewhere else, populist understanding does not provide solution for problems which are actually deep-rooted.

Modi's Agri-budget 2016-17

The slowdown of the economic growth in the past two years and a continued poor monsoon for the second successive year has escalated the agrarian crisis in the country. It is feared that the farmer suicide rate may also go up. Probably, these fears compelled the Narendra Modi government to announce some measures to mitigate the crisis in the agricultural sector. Among the few measures are a revamped agricultural insurance scheme with a budget of Rs 5,500 crore, fast-tracking irrigation projects in States with a budget of Rs 20,000 crore, encouragement of organic manure and farming, soil testing facilities, model fertiliser outlets, computerised wholesale marketing, constructing rural connectivity with a budget of Rs 67,000 crore, farmers' welfare fund of Rs 35,984 crore. If we look at these measures from the question whether they can mitigate the situation, the answer will be both, yes and no. Irrigation projects in recent times are certainly enriching the contractors, but no significant area under net irrigation has been actually added in the recent past. Some improvements in the insurance scheme are being sought regarding reducing the delivery time, which is a welcome step. However, the insured amount per acre are too low to cover major share of the cost. Rural connectivity would reduce transportation cost for the farmer. Organic farming would certainly reduce cost of cultivation. But there is nothing in the policy of the government about the issue of non-viability of farming in the face of rising costs. The cost reducing measures would provide short term succour to the farmer, but are not adequate to solve the long term problem of stagnation of incomes.

The Way Forward

Farmers' suicides are a reflection of a much more deep-rooted structural problem in India. Farmers' distress is actually a distress of small farmers, rather than that of the entire farm sector. A worrying aspect is that the agrarian sector is becoming bottom heavy, with an overwhelming share of cultivation and the land resting with the small and marginal farmers. Commercialisation and capitalist transformation of India's agriculture is rapidly coming to completion in terms of commercialising all aspects of production and distribution. The larger dynamics of capitalist development subordinates agricultural sector, squeezing its terms of trade which lies behind the crisis this sector faces in India today. Petty commodity producers struggle to survive through self-exploitation of family labour and under-consumption. The small farmer is made the residual risk-bearer, burdened further during natural disasters. There is no real solution for the crisis of farmer in the capitalist development process.

One could contemplate two solutions. First is to command the prices through minimum support prices in such a manner that they give the farmer a decent income. Of course, a subsidy policy may become inevitable if prices are sought to be kept low. Hence, a substantial redistribution through taxation should fall in place. All these are politically infeasible for the current regimes in power, given the hegemonic direction of global capital. The second way is to organise the farmers into cooperatives, command bargaining power and generate internal economies of scale and scope. While this is a plausible solution, however, it is a socio-political challenge for farmers and activists in a caste-ridden country like India to make farmers of different castes to come on one platform in a village to form a cooperative. There should be encouragement to small-scale industrial units, which are traditionally labour intensive, located at the district level, which create non-farm employment that enable the surplus rural population to eventually leave agriculture.

Recommended Readings

1. Bernstein, Henry (2010), *Class Dynamics of Agrarian Change*, Fernwood Publishers, Kumarian Press, Sterling.
2. Chatterjee, Partha (2008), 'Democracy and Economic Transformation in India', *Economic and Political Weekly*, 19 April.
3. Lewi, Arthur (1954), 'Economic Development with Unlimited Supply of Labour', Manchester School, May.
4. Marx, Karl (1954), *Das Capital*, Vol I, part III, Progress Publishers, Moscow.
5. Mitra, Ashok (1977), *Terms of Trade and Class Relations: An essay in Political Economy*, Routledge, London.
6. Ramachandran,V K, Vikas Rawal, Madhura Swaminathan (2010), *Socio-Economic Surveys of Three Villages in Andhra Pradesh: a Study of Agrarian Relations*, Tulika, New Delhi.
7. Reddy, Narsimha and Srijit Mishra (2009) edited, *Agrarian Crisis in India*, Oxford University Press, New Delhi.
8. Sanyal, Kalyan (2007), *Rethinking Capitalist Development: Primitive Accumulation, Governmentality, and Post-Colonial Capitalism*, Routledge. London.
9. Sainath, P (2012), 'Farm suicides rise in Maharashtra, State still leads the list', *The Hindu*, July 3.
10. Shetty, S L (2008), 'Merging Policy Regime for Bank Credit Delivery and Tasks Ahead: A Critical Review' in *India Development Report* edited by R.Radhakishna, Oxford University Press, pp.112-133.
11. *Union Budget 2016-17* at indiabudget.nic.in/ub2016-17/bs/bs.pd

Growing Rural-Urban Divide in India

— SP Singh

RURAL-URBAN disparity in India still remains a key concern. In the post-1990-91 period, Indian economy achieved relatively faster economic growth, but its performance in improving the socio-economic status of rural households has been quite dismal. Currently, rural India comprises 69 per cent of the country's population, but its share in the GDP is only about 37 per cent, while urban India, with only 31 per cent share in the total population, commands about 63 per cent of the country's GDP. It is estimated that by 2020, the urban sector would contribute about 75 per cent of GDP, with only 35 per cent of total population (Ranjan, 2014). Rural India has low income level, poor quality of life and a weak human capital base. It has inadequate access to basic amenities like regular employment, clean and safe water, basic education, sanitation, shelter, road connectivity, electricity etc. What worries most is that the magnitude of rural-urban divide has accentuated during the neoliberal policy regime and the growth focus has shifted from rural to urban areas (Sharma and Singh, 2012). De-linking of growth with employment during this period significantly reduced the employment elasticity in various activities. Joblessness is particularly acute in rural India because agriculture has been growing at less than half the rate of the other sectors. Consequently, the gap between farm and non-farm income has widened. The lack of productive jobs in rural areas, especially in agriculture, pushes out a large number of poor rural workers to urban areas in search of better livelihood opportunities, and as a result, slums are growing rapidly in the cities.

It may be significant to note that the neoliberal policy regime has not only widened the rural-urban divide but also intensified intra-rural and intra-urban socio-economic divides. Those having better access to resources, education, health and social capital have better employment and income opportunities and thus grow economically faster than those who lack skills, education and income earning assets. Socio-economic disparities between and within the rural and urban sectors may have far-reaching economic, social and political ramifications.

Income and Employment Divide

The Central Statistical Office does not compile rural and urban break up of GDP on an annual basis. But it makes periodical estimation. As per the CSO estimates, the share of rural areas in the Net Domestic Product at factor cost has steeply declined from 62.35 per cent in 1970-71 to 48.09 per cent in 1999-00 (Sharma and Singh, 2012). The ratio of per capita income in urban areas to that of rural areas was 2.89 in 1999-00. Over the last one decade, this ratio has increased to more than 4.0. During the period from 1999-00 to 2011-12, there has been significant transformation in the Indian economy. The share of agriculture in gross value added (GVA) has declined from 23.8 per cent to 14.3 per cent, while its corresponding share in employment declined from 59.9 per cent to 48.9 per cent.

National Sample Survey reports show that during 2004-05 to 2011-12, 27.73 million jobs were lost in agriculture, while 24.38 million new jobs were created in the construction sector (GOI, 2013a). The share of construction in the GVA in 2011-12 was only 9.9 per cent, while its share in employment was 10.7 per cent, showing a shift from one kind of low productive activity (agriculture) to another kind of low productive activity (construction). On the other hand, some modern services, such as banking, insurance, and real estate contributed 17.7 per cent to the total GVA in 2011-12, while their share in employment was only 1.2 per cent. These facts indicate growing inequality among sectors and sub-sectors of the economy.

Table-1 summarises the trends in rural and urban employment growth rates from 1987-88 to 2011-12. It is significant to note that during the periods, employment grew much faster in urban than in rural areas. Apparently, the employment growth rate differential has been quite alarming between 2004-05 and 2011-12. No new jobs were generated in rural areas during this period, while jobs growth in urban area was as high as 5.67 per cent per annum. It may also be relevant to note that in spite of an average annual expenditure of Rs35-40 thousand crore on MGNREGS, the NSS results show that the employment situation in rural areas has not improved. The loss of jobs in agriculture seems to be primarily responsible for such a dismal scene.

Table 1: Trends in Employment Growth in India (per annum)

Period	Rural	Urban
1987-88 to 1993-94	2.03	3.39
1993-94 to 1999-00	0.67	1.34
1999-00 to 2004-05	2.29	4.44
2004-05 to 2009-10	-0.34	1.78
2009-10 to 2011-12	0.0	5.67

Source: Prepared from various NSS rounds on Employment and Unemployment in India.

Let's place these facts in the context of the overall manpower scenario that has emerged after 1999-00 (Table 2). The labour force increased from 385.53 million in 1999-00 to 428.7 million in 2004-05, with that of rural India going from 287.67 million to 313.5 million. During 1999-00 to 2004-05, urban labour force increased much faster (3.5% per annum) than the rural labour force (1.8% annually). In both rural and urban areas, female labour force increased faster than the male labour force during this period.

During 2004-05 to 2011-12, some 8.3 million people were added to the labour force. There was a net decline of 3.3 million people in the rural labour force and a net increase of 11.6 million people in the urban labour force. During this period, 20.30 million females left the rural labour force, while 17 million males joined the rural labour force. During this period, the size of the rural labour force decreased, while it increased in the urban areas. The structural change in the labour force that occurred during 2004-05 to 2011-12 implies that more rural females have left the labour force. Some of them might have joined colleges and universities to acquire education.

Up to 2004-05, rural India was the major contributor to employment generation. Between 1999-00 and 2004-05, 23.86 million new jobs were created in rural India; while in urban India, only 16.35 million jobs were created. Overall, 40.21 million additional jobs were created in the economy during this period, which comes out to be 8.4 million jobs per year. However, the scenario has changed after 2004-05. During 2004-05 to 2011-12, 2.8 million jobs were reduced in rural areas, mainly due to reduction in female jobs (for more details, see Table 2).

Thus, it seems that the decline in rural employment was mainly related to steep reduction in rural female employment. One reason for deceleration in female employment cited quite often is increasing enrollment of females in educational institutions. However, this is only partially true as work participation rate (WPR) of rural women has also declined in the age group above 25 years. Contrary to these facts, in urban areas, female WPR has significantly increased in all age groups, though it is still much lower than that of rural females (for more details, see GOI, 2013a).

Overall, it can be seen that during both the periods, growth in rural employment was much lower than that in urban employment. Decline in rural employment is a major cause for concern as it shows lowered labour absorption in agriculture. In Table 3, we find that the share of agriculture in total rural workforce has declined from 76.23 per cent in 1999-00 to 64.10 per cent in 2011-12, a decline of 12.13 per cent point, while corresponding percentage share of rural non-farm sector has increased. However, except construction, share of all other rural non-farm activities saw a fall. Share of construction sector in the total non-farm employment

Table 2: Rural-Urban Break up of Labour Force, Workforce and Number of Unemployed (in Million, UPS)

Categories/Survey Years	1999-00	2004-05	2011-12	Net Increase between 1999-00 and 2004-05)	Net Increase between 2004-05 and 2011-12
Labour Force					
Rural Male	203.07	219.0	236.0	15.93 (1.57)	17.0 (1.11)
Rural Female	84.6	94.5	74.2	9.9 (2.34)	-20.30 (-3.07)
Rural Total	287.67	313.5	310.20	25.83 (1.80)	-3.3 (-0.15)
Urban Male	80.85	93.2	101.8	12.35 (3.06)	8.6 (1.32)
Urban Female	17.01	22.0	25.0	4.99 (5.87)	3.0 (1.95)
Urban Total	97.86	115.2	126.8	17.34 (3.54)	11.6 (1.44)
Total Labour force	385.53	428.7	437.0	43.17 (2.24)	8.3 (0.28)
Workforce					
Rural Male	198.88	214.3	231.0	15.42 (1.55)	16.70 (1.11)
Rural Female	83.16	91.6	72.1	8.44 (2.03)	-19.50 (-3.04)
Rural Total	282.04	305.9	303.1	23.86 (1.69)	-2.80 (-0.13)

Table 2 (Contd...)

Urban Male	76.95	89.1	108.2	12.15 (3.16)	19.1 (3.06)
Urban Female	15.80	20.0	23.3	4.2 (5.32)	3.3 (2.36)
Urban Total	92.75	109.1	131.5	16.35 (3.52)	22.4 (2.93)
Total Workers	374.79	415.0	434.6	40.21 (2.15)	19.6 (0.67)
Unemployed					
Rural Male	4.19	4.7	5.0	0.51	0.3
Rural Female	1.44	3.0	2.2	1.56	-0.8
Rural Total	5.63	7.7	7.2	2.07	-0.5
Urban Male	3.9	4.1	3.6	0.2	-0.5
Urban Female	1.22	2.0	1.6	0.78	-0.4
Urban Total	5.12	6.1	5.2	0.98	-0.9
Total workers	10.75	13.8	12.4	3.05	-1.4

Source: Compiled from various NSS Rounds. Figures in parentheses are annual percentage increase/decrease in labour force and workforce between 1999-00 and 2004-05 and between 2004-05 and 2011-12.

Note: For 1999-00, figures are estimated from LFPR and WPR given in 61st Round, using 2001 population census data, while other figures are available in the 66th and 68th rounds.

has remarkably increased from 17.81 per cent in 2004-05 to 30.78 per cent in 2011-12 (Table 3).

Table 3: Composition of Rural Non-farm Employment (in %)

Sector	1999-00	2004-05	2011-12
Agriculture	76.23	72.58	64.1
Non-agriculture	23.77	27.42	35.9
Distribution within non-agriculture			
Mining & Quarrying	2.09	1.79	1.31
Manufacturing	31.15	29.47	24.07
Construction	13.96	17.81	30.78
Secondary	47.74	49.53	56.82
Trade, hotels	21.59	22.62	18.05
Trasport & Communications	8.66	9.11	7.97
Finance, insurance, real estates	1.52	1.76	0.50
Total Tertiary	52.26	50.47	43.18

Source: Compiled from NSS Rounds on Employment and Unemployment in India.

Over the period, rural-urban connectivity has improved, facilitating migration of poor workers from rural to urban areas. This process of migration actually shifts rural poverty to urban areas. It seems that distress migration of the workforce from rural to urban areas has increased. As per the population census 2011, the slum population in cities has increased from 5.24 crore in 2001 to 6.55 crore in 2011. More than 22 per cent of the urban population in 2011 was reported to live in slums (Government of India, 2013d). Many of them spend their nights on footpaths or under the flyovers and bridges. Their living conditions are more pathetic than that of their rural counterparts.[1] But distress employment situation in their villages compels them to move out to cities.

---

[1] In this context, Harsh Mander in an article on 'Nobody Chooses the Footpath' published in *The Economic Times* on 15 May 2015 rightly states: '...majority on streets are working men who left behind desperately improvised families in the villages to earn livelihood in the city. Most of them end up picking waste, driving rickshaws or casual workers on construction sites, earning irregular dirt wages. If they spend money on themselves to rent a roof, there would be no money left to send home.'

The second issue is related to the growth of urbanisation of rural areas. Urban economic activities are moving out of big cities to their surrounding rural areas, as land becomes more expensive in urban areas and environmental regulations become more stringent. High prices of agricultural land and better rural-urban connectivity due to improved transport and communication infrastructure have made the rural population living in the vicinity of cities economically better off than the average rural population. Therefore, if the households of rural migrant workers from the urban areas living in slums or on the streets and the population of urbanised villages are excluded from the estimation of per capita income, the rural-urban income divide would be much higher. Further, urban settlements and agglomerations, being densely populated, get the benefit of economies of scale. The high population density of cities helps to generate markets for various goods and services and thus attracts more investment and ensures better returns on investment. Better access to education and health facilities, economic and physical infrastructure, civic services and a wide range of employment opportunities in urban formal and informal sectors motivate the rural workforce to move to cities.

Rural-Urban Divide in Consumption

Rural-urban income data are not available on a regular basis. Hence, we use consumption data as proxy for income to study the levels of living standards in rural and urban areas. The National Sample Survey provides detailed data on per capita consumption expenditure on food and non-food items for both rural and urban households. Table 4 shows that the ratio of urban to rural real monthly per capita consumption expenditure (MPCE) has increased from 1.65 in 1993-94 to 1.71 in 1999-00 and further to 1.86 in 2011-12. It suggests that the disparities in rural-urban levels of living standards are widening.

Table 5 indicates that between 2004-05 and 2011-12, share of cereals in total consumer expenditure has significantly declined in both rural and urban areas. However, rural households spend relatively more on cereals than their urban counterparts. Except for beverages and fruits, percentage share of all other food items in total MPCE was higher for rural than urban households. In 2011-12, food shared 48.6 per cent

Table 4: Growth in MPCE (MRP) at current and constant prices since 1993-84, all India

Characteristic	1993-94	1999-00	2004-05	2011-12
MPCE: Rural (Rs) at current prices	286.10	486.16	579.17	1287.17
Price deflator for Rural sector	176	271	319	580
MPCE: Rural (Rs) at 1987-88 prices	162.56	179.39	181.56	221.93
MPCE: Urban (Rs.) current prices	464.30	854.92	1104.6	2477.02
Price deflator for Urban sector	173	279	338	599
MPCE: Urban (Rs) at 1987-88 prices	268.38	306.42	326.8	413.53
Ratio of urban MPCE to Rural MPCE at	1.65	1.71	1.80	1.86

Source: Government of India (2013b).

of total consumer expenditure in rural areas, while the corresponding percentage share in urban areas was only 38.5.

On non-food items, urban households' per capita spending in 2011-12 was more than double (Rs1,523.37) of what a rural household manages (Rs 661.61). The ratio of urban to rural MPCE on non-food is 2.30, while in case of food items, it is only 1.52. Since rural households spend relatively large share of their income on food, food inflation affects these households more than urban ones, who spend less proportion of their income on food. From 2004-05 to 2011-12, both in rural and urban areas, the percentage shares of clothing and footwear, conveyance, education, healthcare and other miscellaneous items have increased, while that of pan and tobacco, fuel and light have declined. It is interesting to note that rural households spend relatively more on healthcare, while their urban counterparts spend more on education. In urban India, the most prominent increases in share since 2004-05 appear to be in case of rent (1.4 percentage point) and conveyance (2 percentage point). The share

Table 5: Trends in Percentage Composition of Consumer Expenditure since 1993-94

Item Group	sector	Food		Item Group	Non-food	
		2004-05	2011-12		2004-05	2011-12
Cereals & Cereal substitutes	Rural	18.2	12.3	Pan, tobacco & intoxicants	2.7	2.4
	Urban	10.2	7.4		1.6	1.4
Pulses & products	Rural	3.1	3.1	Fuel & light	10.2	9.2
	Urban	2.1	2.1		9.9	7.6
Milk & products	Rural	8.5	9.1	Clothing & footwear	5.3	7.6
	Urban	7.9	7.8		4.7	6.5
Edible oils	Rural	4.6	3.8	Education	2.7	3.1
	Urban	3.5	2.7		5.0	5.7
Eggs, meat & fish	Rural	3.3	3.6	Medical Care	6.6	6.9
	Urban	2.7	2.8		5.2	5.5
Vegetables	Rural	6.1	4.8	Conveyance	3.8	4.5
	Urban	4.5	3.4		5.5	7.5

Table 5 (Contd...)

Fruits & Nuts	Rural	1.9	1.9	Consumer Services excluding Conveyance	3.8	4.5
	Urban	2.1	2.3		7.0	6.5
Sugar	Rural	2.4	1.8	Rent	0.5	0.5
	Urban	1.5	1.2		5.6	7.0
Salt & Spices	Rural	2.5	2.4	Entertainment	0.6	1.1
	Urban	1.7	1.7		1.9	1.8
Beverages etc.	Rural	4.5	5.8	Other items*	8.8	11.6
	Urban	6.2	7.1		11.1	12.0
Total Food	Rural	55.0	48.6	Total non-food	45.0	51.4
	Urban	42.5	38.5		57.5	61.5

* Include toilets articles, other household consumables, durable goods, taxes & cesses, other Misc. goods and services.

Source: Government of India (2013b).

of education also seems to be rising steadily in both the areas, though at a slower pace. In the rural sector the share of conveyance has risen by 1 percentage point, that of consumer services other than conveyance by a little less than 1 percentage point, and the share of entertainment, though much smaller, also appears to be rising.

Agricultural Distress and Rural-Urban Divide

Indian agriculture is in deep distress. During the last two decades, a steady decline in its share in the GDP indicates misery and deprivation in rural areas in general and for farmers in particular. Today, it is not only experiencing slow down in productivity and rise in input cost but also facing the volatility of the market and monsoon. Failure of technology, rainfall, crops and markets makes agriculture a less remunerative and more risky activity and consequently rising indebtedness among farmers adds to their distress.[2] Low profitability in agriculture appears to be one of the main reasons for widening the rural-urban divide, as livelihood of a little over 64 per cent of rural workforce still depends on agriculture. Rao and Suri (2006) observe that the model of development pursued in the wake of liberalisation policies all over India and shifting political focus towards the urban classes like the business people, traders, investors, professionals and salaried classes have also played a part in causing the present agrarian crisis.

The NSS conducted a Situation Assessment Survey of agricultural households in 2013 (70th round) after a gap of ten years. The 69th round of the survey was conducted in 2003. A comparison of these surveys indicates that during the last one decade, in spite of several policy interventions, the condition of agriculture has further deteriorated. As per the NSS report on Key Indicators of Land and Livestock Holdings in India (GOI, 2014a), the area under operational holdings has significantly declined from 107.65 million hectares in 2002-03 to 94.48 million hectare in 2012-13. Consequently, the size of the operational holdings has also

[2] The Expert Group on Agricultural Indebtedness (GOI 2007) also remarks: The support systems to farming have weakened, public investments in agriculture have declined and institutions have become unresponsive. In the absence of any breakthrough in cost reducing technologies, the rising input prices have made cultivation un-remunerative. The result is the manifestation of agrarian crisis, often, in the extreme form of distress that results in suicides by some farmers.

declined from 1.06 ha to 0.91 ha. Land area owned by farmers has also declined from 107.23 million hectares to 92.37 million hectares during the same period. This implies that 13-15 million hectares of agricultural land might have converted into non-agricultural uses during this period.

It may be significant to note that prices of agricultural inputs rose constantly over the years, while agricultural produce prices fluctuated across years due to global trade integration and supply and demand mismatch. Although the Government of India periodically announces MSP for various crops, but procurement by the government agencies remains abysmally low and varies across crops. For example, during January-June 2013, in case of paddy and wheat, two important cereal crops, percentage shares of cooperative and government agencies in the total quantity of paddy and wheat sold were 6 and 19 respectively (GOI, 2014b). The NSS 70th round shows that private traders and Mandies are the main platforms where agricultural crops are sold.

As per the NSS 70th round (GOI, 2014b) on situation assessment of farmers in India, during the agricultural year 2012-13, rural India had 90.2 million agricultural households, which constituted about 57.8 per cent of the total estimated rural households. Out of total agricultural households, 36 per cent held BPL cards and another 5 per cent possessed *Antyodaya* (extremely poor) cards. Thus, at the all-India level, 41 per cent farmer households were below poverty line.

Table 6 shows that at the all-India level, average income per agricultural household from all sources in 2013 was estimated as Rs 6,426 per month, which comes out to be Rs 214 per day per household. If we assume an average household of five members, then the amount would be only Rs 43 per person per day. Wages and salaries and non-farm businesses contributed 32 per cent and 8 per cent respectively to their average monthly income. Thus, on an average, 40 per cent income of farm households comes from non-farm activities.

Income distribution by the land-size indicates that about 69 per cent farmers (marginal farmers) get 56.74 per cent of their total income from non-farm sources. Small and marginal farmers (86.59% of total farmers) get nearly 50 per cent of their income from non-agricultural sources. This indicates that the contribution of agriculture and livestock to the total income of even farmer households is now quite low.

Table 6: Average monthly income from different sources, consumption expenditure and net investment in productive assets per agricultural household (July 2012-June 2013) in Rs

Size class of land possessed (ha)	Income from wages & salaries	Net receipt from cultivation	Net receipt from farming of animal	Net receipt from non-farm business	Total income	Total consumption expenditure	Net invest-ment in productive assets	Estd. No of agriculturaal HHs (()())
<0.01	2,902	30	1,181	447	4,561	5,108	55	23,857
0.01-0.40	2,386	687	621	459	4,152	5,401	251	28,7381
0.41-1.0	2,011	2,145	629	462	5,247	6,020	540	315,008
<1.0	**2,217**	**1,395**	**646**	**460**	**4,718**	**5,701**	**389**	**626,246**
1.01-2.0	1,728	4,209	818	593	7,348	6,457	422	154,810
<2.0	**2,120**	**1,953**	**680**	**486**	**5,240**	**5,851**	**395**	**781,056**
2.01-4.0	1657	7,359	1,161	554	10,730	7,786	746	83,964
4.01-10	2,031	15,243	1,501	861	19,637	10,104	1,975	33,519
10+	1,311	35,685	.2,622	1,170	41,388	14,447	6,987	3,199
All sizes	2,071	3,081	763	512	6426	6,223	513	902,039

Source: GOI (2014b).

Monthly consumption expenditure of nearly 70 per cent farmer households of India in 2012-13 was much higher (Rs.5701) than their monthly income (Rs.4718) (Table 6). The NSS surveys show that the percentage of indebted farmers has increased from 48.6 in 2003 to 51.9 in 2013. In 2003, prevalence of indebtedness among farmers was highest in Andhra Pradesh (82.0%), followed by Tamil Nadu (74.5%), Punjab (65.4%) and Kerala (64.4%). In 2013 also, the percentage of indebted farmers was highest in Andhra Pradesh (92.9%), followed by Telengana (89.1%), Tamil Nadu (82.5%), Kerala (77.7%) and Karnataka (77.3%).

NSS survey on Assets and Indebtedness in India (GOI, 2014c) shows that 46 per cent cultivators and 29 per cent *non-cultivator* households in rural areas were indebted during 2012-13; whereas in urban areas, 35.85 per cent self-employed and 20.96 per cent others were indebted. Table 7 shows that the incidence of indebtedness (IOI) was much higher in the rural (31.4%) than in urban (22.4%) areas. Further, it is higher among cultivators than non-cultivators.

The Expert Group (GOI, 2007) suggests that since the indebtedness among farmers may arise from time to time due to various factors like crop failure, natural calamity etc, there could be need for specific relief packages in such circumstances. In the event of natural calamities, rescheduling of loans of the affected households may be made. The Group also suggests that in the event of crop failure for two consecutive years in rain-fed areas, in addition to rescheduling of the crop loan, interest for the extended one year period should be waived.

The Union Budget 2016-17 proposes to set the transformative agenda for the Indian economy with nine distinct pillars, out of which two are related to agriculture and the rural sector. The government intends to double the farmers' income by 2022. This seems to be a distant dream, considering the current agrarian distress and budgetary allocation. Although allocation for agriculture is increased to Rs 35,984 crore (84% increase over the preceding year), it comes out to be only 1.82 per cent of the total budgetary expenditure (Rs1,978,060 crore). To double the income, it must grow at the compound annual growth rate (CAGR) of 14.87 per cent at constant prices for the next five year. Can farmers' real income grow at this rate? We have not yet been successful in achieving a targeted 4 per cent growth in agriculture on sustainable

Table 7: Incidence of Indebtedness (IOI) and Amount of Debt (AOD) for different Occupational Categories in Rural and Urban India

Rural				Urban			
Categories	IOI (%)	AOD per HH (Rs)	AOD per indebted HH (Rs)	Categories	IOI (%)	AOD per HH (Rs)	AOD per indebted HH (Rs)
Cultivators	45.94	70580	153630	Self-Employed	35.85	108714	303221
Non-cultivators	28.85	25741	89221	Others	20.96	82094	391724
All	31.44	32522	103457	All	22.37	84625	378238

Source: GOI (2014c).

basis. Since agriculture is a State subject, much of its its revival depends on the willingness and ability of the State governments to make real investment in agriculture, including irrigation; the central government has limited role in this regard.

As far as provision of agricultural credit is concerned, it has been increased from Rs 8.5 lakh crore in 2015-16 to Rs.9.0 lakh crore in 2016-17. It is of great interest to know how the credit earmarked from agriculture is being disbursed. How much of it is actually received by the farmers and how much of it goes to agribusiness companies? For example, if the entire targeted credit is received by farmers, then it will work out to be about Rs 95,000 per hectare of operated area. As per the 70th NSS round, average size of operational holding in India is 0.91 hectares and net income from cultivation and livestock per farmer household is only Rs 46,128 per annum. This indicates that only agricultural activities are not sufficient to generate enough income to repay the outstanding loan. There is need to prepare a comprehensive roadmap for raising the Indian farmer's income. If we want to think beyond food security and give our farmers a sense of income security, as stated by the Finance Minister in his budget speech, then there is need to bring a Farmers' Minimum Income Protection Act so that a minimum level of living for a farmer household may be ensured.

As 50 per cent of income of 86.5 per cent of total farm households (small and marginal) comes from non-farm sources, there is need to upgrade the education and skills of sons and daughters of farmers and create enough employment opportunities for them outside of agriculture to enhance their income. The measures suggested in the current budget for agriculture in particular and rural economy in general, such as, construction of farm ponds, soil health card, creation of additional irrigation facilities, crop insurance scheme, promotion of natural and organic farming and the 14th Finance Commission recommendation to allocate Rs 80 lakh per Gram Panchayat etc. can improve the economic conditions of rural India if these provisions are translated into actions.

Rural-Urban Divide in Quality of Life

Quality of life is the function of various socio-economic-cultural, environmental and physical indicators. Urban people have better access to education, health, sanitation, transport, electricity, banking, communication and many other services than their rural counterparts. According to NSS 69th round (GOI, 2013c), as against 95.3 per cent urban households having improved source of drinking water in 2012, corresponding per cent in case of rural household was only 88.5. The percentage of households who treated water before use was also lower in rural India (32.3%) than in urban India (54.4%). Regarding non-availability of washroom facility within the house, it is observed that about 62.3 per cent households in rural India and only 16.7 per cent of households in urban India did not have such facility. As far as sanitation facility is concerned, the survey indicates that 59.4 per cent rural households and 8.8 per cent urban households did not have access to toilet facilities. Further, only 38.8 per cent of rural households and 89.6 per cent of urban households had access to flush (sanitary) toilets. In case of access to other facilities also, rural households are far behind their urban counterparts. For instance, percentage of households having access to electricity was lower in rural (80%) than the urban (97.9%) areas. Similarly, about 53 per cent rural households did not have separate kitchen in their dwellings, while corresponding percentage in urban areas was only 34.

Access to drainage facility is another important indicator of quality of life. As per the NSS survey, 68.3% of rural households did not have 'improved drainage' facility while the corresponding percentage in urban areas was only 17.5. The survey further indicates that only 32 per cent rural households and 75.8 per cent urban households have a garbage disposal system. It may be pointed out that due to lack of safe drinking water, sanitation and drainage system, the intensity of water-borne diseases is higher in rural than in urban areas. Inadequate and inefficient delivery of these basic amenities in the rural areas puts enormous burden of disease on rural households, especially the poor households who are not able to afford costly water-purifying systems (Singh 2013). The water purifier market in India is growing at a CAGR of about 25% and is likely to touch Rs 70,000 million by 2015 from the Rs 32,000 million level two years ago (Das, 2013). Due to failure of public institutions to provide good quality of drinking water and other civic amenities to the masses, such private businesses are expanding rapidly in the country.

Improved water, sanitation and drainage facilities help to prevent water-borne/water related diseases and make it possible for people to lead a healthy and decent life. Contaminated water, open defecation, lack of personal and food hygiene and improper disposal of solid and liquid waste are key factors responsible for morbidity. Since, vector-borne diseases are mostly communicable in nature and have negative externalities, these can be effectively controlled only if all the rural people have access to basic amenities like clean water and sanitation. Therefore, rural-urban divide in the access to these basic amenities also explains, to a great extent, the differences in the health status of rural and urban households (Singh 2013). As per the SRS Bulletin (Census 2011), IMR in rural areas is 51 per 1000, while corresponding rate in the urban areas is only 31 per 1000. Similarly, CMR is 15.7 in rural areas and only 8.7 in urban areas. Birth and death rates are also found to be higher in rural (birth rate: 23.7 and death rate: 7.7) than urban (birth rate: 18.0 and death rate: 5.8) areas. Life expectation at birth in rural areas is 62.1 years, while it is 68.8 years in urban areas. As per the NSS 71st round (January-June, 2014), although on an average, expenditure per hospitalisation is higher in urban (Rs 24,434) than rural (Rs14,935) areas, rural people spend more amount of money on transport, escort, lodging etc related to patient treatment than their urban counterparts. The non-medical expenditure associated with per hospitalisation was Rs2,021 in rural areas and Rs2,019 in urban areas (GOI: 2015). Intensity of diarrhoea is higher in rural than the urban areas. It is estimated that around 37.7 million people of India are affected by water-borne diseases annually, 1.5 million children are estimated to die of diarrhoea alone and 73 million working days are lost each year due to waterborne diseases. The resulting economic burden is estimated at $600 million a year (www.wateraid.org).

Seeing the huge gap between rural and urban India in access to toilet facilities, *Swachh Bharat Abhiyan* (Clean India Mission) launched by the NDA government is a welcome step, though the previous UPA government had begun an upgraded total sanitation programme. The *Saansad Adarsh Gram Yojana* (MP Ideal Village Scheme) is also an important initiative in this context. How successful these and similar other schemes will be to reduce the gaps in socio-economic indicators of rural and urban India is yet to be seen.

Education and Skills Divide

Skills and knowledge are the driving factors in achieving faster, sustainable and inclusive growth and providing decent employment opportunities to the growing young population. Rural people possess relatively lower level of education and skills than their urban counterparts. A large number of them have either little or no job skills, which restrict their occupational mobility. NSS 71st round provides detailed information in this regard. Table 8 shows the percentage distribution of persons of age 15 years and above by general level of education for bottom 20 and top 20 per cent people by MPCE. It indicates huge disparity in the attainment of education across gender, economic status and rural-urban location. Among the bottom 20 per cent population, about 49 per cent in rural and 34 per cent in urban areas were reported to be not literate, while among top 20 per cent population, the percentages of such population were only 24 and 4.2 respectively. As far as attainment of higher education (graduate & above) is concerned, among bottom 20 per cent population, only 0.9 per cent rural and 3.6 per cent urban persons were reported to have attained higher education, while corresponding percentages of such persons among top 20 per cent population were 8.8 and 41.2 respectively. It can be concluded that education levels of poor persons in general and rural persons in particular are much lower than their counterparts.

Not only level of education among rural people is lower than that of urban people but also the quality of education is a concern. Although it is difficult to assess the quality, we can get an idea on the basis of per student expenditure on education, assuming higher the expenditure, better would be the quality of education. Table 9 shows average expenditure per student pursuing general education in 2014. The difference between rural and urban areas is quite significant up to higher secondary level education. An average urban student at the primary level education spent Rs10,083 per year, while his/her rural counterpart spent only Rs 2,811 per year. Gender difference is also significant in this context.

The rural-urban difference also exists in case of per student expenditure on professional and technical education. Table 10 indicates that on an average, an urban student spent relatively more on attaining technical/professional education for different courses as compared to a student from rural areas.

Table 8: Percentage Distribution of Persons of age 15 years & above by general level of education for bottom 20% and top 20% people by MPCE in 2014

Education Code	Bottom 20% by MPCE						Top 20% by MPCE					
	Rural			Urban			Rural			Urban		
	M	F	P	M	F	P	M	F	P	M	F	P
01	36.5	61.1	49.0	24.3	43.5	34.0	15.1	33.0	24.0	2.1	6.6	4.2
02	28.0	20.3	24.0	27.9	22.1	25.0	18.3	19.8	19.0	5.4	8.3	6.9
03	19.6	10.9	15.2	21.5	16.3	18.9	18.5	15.2	17.0	8.5	10.2	9.2
04	10.0	4.8	7.5	14.2	10.2	12.2	19.5	14.6	17.0	16.0	17.0	16.4
05	4.4	2.3	3.3	7.0	4.7	5.9	14.2	9.7	12.0	17.0	19.1	18.0
06	0.2	0.0	0.1	0.6	0.4	0.5	3.1	1.2	2.2	5.5	2.5	4.1
07	1.3	0.6	0.9	4.5	2.8	3.6	11.2	6.5	8.8	45.5	36.3	41.2
Total	100	100	100	100	100	100	100	100	100	100	100	100

Codes: 01= not literate; 02= literate & up to primary; 03= middle; 04=secondary; 05=higher secondary; 06=diploma/certificate; and 07 = graduate & above.

Table 9: Average Expenditure per Student Pursuing General Education in 2014 (Rs)

		Primary	Upper Primary	Secondary	Higher Secondary	Graduate	PG & above	Diploma
Rural	Male	3,061	3,603	5,568	9,820	11,306	13,017	15,209
	Female	2,512	2,813	4,534	8,012	11,813	16,715	10,706
	person	2,811	3,242	5,100	9,031	11,527	14,604	13,422
Urban	Male	10,604	11,864	13,781	21,681	17,480	19,090	23,040
	Female	9,489	10,940	13,284	18,442	16,161	16,565	21,947
	person	10,083	11,446	13,547	20,179	16,771	17,744	21,947

Source: NSSO 71st Round.

Table 10: Average Expenditure per Student Pursuing Technical/Professional Education for Different Courses and Type of Institutions in 2014 (Rs)

	Type of Institution	Medicine	Engineering	Management	IT/ Computer	ITI/ Vocational
Rural	Govt	57,292	40,828	39511	27094	13675
	Pvt Aided	76,383	61,516	60548	36401	30872
	Pvt unaided	91,391	69,439	69473	43453	30598
Urban	Govt	72,636	43,418	46050	29718	14508
	Pvt Aided	99,468	74,291	62778	54976	33567
	Pvt unaided	148,510	83,443	121150	59626	39166

Source: NSSO 71ST Round.

Table 11: Population in the age group 15-59 by status of vocational training received or being received in 2011-12 (in %)

Vocational Training	Rural			Urban			Total (Rural + Urban)		
	Male	Female	Person	Male	Female	Person	Male	Female	Person
Formal	1.6 (0.8)	0.9 (0.3)	1.3 (0.5)	5.0 (1.9)	3.3 (1.3)	4.2 (1.6)	2.6 (1.1)	1.6 (0.6)	2.2 (0.9)
Informal	11.1	5.5	8.3	13.7	4.3	9.1	12.0	5.2	8.6
No Training	86.4	93.1	89.7	79.4	91.1	85.0	84.2	92.5	88.3

Source: NSS 71st Round.

Note: Figures in parentheses are percentage of those receiving formal vocational training.

Government of India has launched an ambitious Skill India Mission to train 350-400 million people by 2022. A new National Policy on Skill Development and Entrepreneurship was also formulated in 2015 to give impetus to skill development and start-ups. National skills universities and institutes are proposed to be set up as centres of excellence for this purpose. The government also intends to integrate skills education with the formal school education system in at least 25 per cent schools within 5 years and to set up new ITIs in PPP mode and Kaushal Vardhan Kendras at the panchayat level. Union Budget 2016-17 makes a provision of Rs1,700 crore for skills development.

As per the NSS survey, only 2.2 per cent of total population in the age group 15-59 years was formally skilled, while 8.6 per cent got informal vocational training. The percentage of rural population with formal skill training is much lower than that of the urban population. Table 11 shows that about 90 per cent rural and 88 per cent of the urban population did not get any vocational training. Efforts are required for convergence between general education and skill development progrmmes, removal of multiplicity of institutional framework, training of informal sector workers, including agriculture and unpaid family workers, and setting up effective regulatory mechanism so that the Skills India initiative may not go the way the higher technical and management education in India has gone over the last two decades.

Financial Inclusion

Rural-urban divide also seems to exist in the access of banking services. A large number of rural households do not have access to these services. During the last decade, the government of India made efforts for financial inclusion of poor and marginalised sections. Introduction of Kisaan Credit Card (KCC) for meeting short-term credit requirement of farmers and making compulsory payment of wages to rural workers under MGNREGS through bank accounts are important steps towards financial inclusion. Several other government schemes, including old-aged pension, widow pension and self-employment schemes may also be considered crucial for financial inclusion of marginalised groups.

The government has constituted several committees to recommend appropriate policy interventions for extending banking services to hitherto unbanked households (for instance, the Nachiket Mor Committee, 2013 and the Rangarajan Committee 2008). In recent years, the number of bank branches in rural and semi-urban areas has significantly increased. As per the RBI database, the number of bank branches in rural areas has increased from 30,572 in March 2006 to 37,953 in March 2013, a net increase of 24.14%. In semi-urban areas, it went up from 15,274 in 2006 to 27,215 in 2013 (a net increase of 78.18%). During this period, the number of branches in urban areas and metros has increased respectively from 11,864 and 10,971 to 19,327 and 17,844 (62.90% and 62.70% increase respectively). This shows that growth in the number of branches was highest in semi-urban areas and lowest in the rural areas. In 2005, the RBI instructed banks to provide a 'no-frills' zero-balance account with minimum charges for other services. In 2009, RBI further directed the banks to prepare roadmaps to cover 74,200 villages with a population of more than 2,000 in each with one banking outlet by 2012 (Singh, 2014). The government also introduced the Business Correspondence (BC) model to extend the banking services to the unbanked households in the remote rural areas. NGOs, micro finance institutions, post offices etc are allowed to act as BCs.

In spite of all these efforts, a large number of rural households do not still have banking services. They mostly depend on non-institutional sources of credit. The 70th NSS round on situation assessment of farmers indicates that in 2013, only 60 per cent of outstanding loan of farmers was from institutional sources, which include banks (42.9%), cooperative societies (14.8%) and government (2.1%). In case of lowest size class of land possessed (less than 0.01 ha), the share of institutional sources was as low as 15 per cent.

Financial inclusion does not mean only opening of bank accounts and making credit accessible to the people; it is also seen as a major source of mobilisation of small savings and developing banking habits among the poor. Moreover, it is also critical for effective delivery of various government welfare schemes such as direct cash transfer to the intended beneficiaries. Although the financial inclusion drive was initiated by the UPA government, it was promoted to a mission mode by the NDA government with the launching of the *Jan Dhan Yojana* (JDY) on 8 August 2014, covering 75 million unbanked households by 26 January

Table 12: Progress of Jan Dhan Yojana as on 20 January, 2016

Banks	Number of accounts in Million			No of RuPay Debit cards (million)	Balance in accounts (Rs in crores)	With Zero Balance (million)
	Rural	Urban	total			
Public Sector Banks	89.1	71.0	160.1	138.2	24,180.79	31.78
Regional Rural Banks	31.2	5.1	36.3	26.2	5,286.66	26.26
Private Banks	4.5	3.0	7.4	7.0	1,170.33	39.80
Total	124.7	79.1	203.8	171.4	30,638.29	31.09

Source: Official website of Jan Dan Yojana.
Figures in parentheses are percentages to the total.

2015. The government considers the JAM Trinity (Jan Dhan, Aadhar and Mobile) as a 'game changing reform' that would help in delivering the development schemes with more efficiency and less leakages. The intended beneficiary of the welfare schemes needs a bank account linked with Aadhar and mobile number.

Table 12 shows that within a very short span, 203.8 million accounts were opened under JDY, with 61.2 per cent share in rural areas. Along with bank accounts, 171.4 million RuPay debit cards were also issued. These cards have in-built accident insurance cover of Rs1.0 lakh. National Payments Corporation of India (NPCI) provides a platform that connects all the banks and the telephone network operators to help a customer or any bank to access his/ her account with his/her mobile number. On an average, per account balance in these accounts is worked out to be only Rs 1,500.

JDY relies heavily on the Business Correspondence (BC) model for expanding banking network, especially in rural areas, where opening of new bank branches may not be economically viable. At this stage, it is premature to assess how successful this scheme would be in making the financial inclusion of poor households. However, it may be noted that just having a bank account does not ensure a household's financial inclusion. It is obvious from Table 12 that more than 31 per cent of the accounts opened under the scheme had zero balance. Most of the accounts might have been opened by the poor households due to the compulsion of getting bank credit, subsidies or wages under various government schemes and once the amount is withdrawn, such accounts remain idle. Poor households either do not have enough savings or they do not have a habit to deposit the savings in their bank accounts. Empirical evidence suggests that more than 80 per cent of zero-balance bank accounts are dormant (Singh, 2014). Another reason is that many poor workers are engaged in informal activities where they usually get their remuneration/ wages in cash. Due to lack of banking services at their doorstep, they have less motivation to put their savings in the accounts.

In order to know how much credits are received and deposits are made by banks, credit-deposit ratios (CDRs) are estimated since 2001(Table 13). On an average, CDR is highest in metros, closely followed by rural areas and lowest in semi-urban areas, though its

Table 13: Trends in Credit-Deposit Ratio in India since 2001

Year	Rural	Semi-urban	Urban	Metro	Total
2001	49.40	38.19	43.75	74.67	56.71
2002	55.02	41.93	48.44	71.81	58.39
2003	60.33	43.08	49.18	70.93	59.24
2004	56.34	42.83	51.46	67.66	58.25
2005	75.31	48.31	56.63	73.78	65.98
2006	88.22	57.84	64.15	76.25	72.39
2007	93.16	59.53	65.75	78.98	74.97
2008	106.50	59.50	65.47	75.72	74.37
2009	85.08	58.72	60.59	78.37	72.61
2010	91.63	59.91	62.82	77.41	73.34
2011	79.56	63.05	70.19	79.89	75.62
2012	77.15	62.70	67.18	87.85	79.02
2013	78.22	69.00	65.98	86.33	78.79
Average	76.61	54.20	59.35	76.90	69.21

Source: Prepared from RBI database.

magnitude varies across years. As far as a high CDR in metros is concerned, it is as expected because metros attract more investment and consequently money outflows from semi-urban and small towns to big cities.

In case of high CDR in rural areas, two points may be relevant to discuss. First, CDR may be high in rural areas, while volume of both deposit and credit may be low. For example, if in a metro city in 2015, total credit disbursed by the banks was Rs80 billion and deposit received by them was Rs100 billion, the CDR would be 80. Contrary to this, if in rural areas, credit disbursed by a bank was Rs8,000, while deposit received by it was Rs10,000, the CDR would also be 80. In this example, CDR is same but amount of credit and deposit is quite different. Second, CDR does not tell much about investment. There may be possibility that the credit received from the banks is used for consumption purposes. As stated above, a large number of farmers in India have their household consumption expenditure greater than their income, consequently, they borrow to meet their consumption needs. Although short-term credit flow to agriculture through KCC is meant for procuring farm inputs, it may also be used for other purposes, including marriages, purchasing motor bikes, cars etc.

Urbanisation of Rural India and Rural-Urban Continuum

Over the period, rural economy has become more integrated with the urban economy and the boundary between the two has largely blurred due to advent of modern transport and communication systems. As discussed earlier, rural economy is diversifying and slowly converging with the characteristics of urban economy. The rural non-farm sector is expanding and many practices of urban households are now being followed by the rural households. Globalisation has created new opportunities, challenges and threats to the rural socio-economic structure and livelihood options. Rural-urban distinction is now difficult to identify precisely due to greater rural-urban integration. Population census 2011 indicates that between 2001 and 2011, small cities and towns grew faster than the bigger ones. However, metro cities have created agglomerations, encompassing the large number of villages in their vicinity. Such villages are more urbanized and consumption habits of their residents have also changed and are converging towards that of their urban counterparts. Moreover, many people working in urban areas also live in rented houses in such villages, due to low rents and easy connectivity. Urban growth may have several implications for the rural populace. Expansion of cities and towns means shrinking of rural land, water and other natural resources and may create rural-urban conflicts. As stated above, between 2003 and 2013, more than 13 million hectares of operated land has declined, mainly due to its conversion into non-agricultural uses. With the urbanisation, water demand has also increased, putting more pressure on rural areas. The government envisages creating a hundred smart cities over a period of ten years in different parts of India, equipped with all the modern infrastructure, including smart buildings, roads, sanitation, sewerage, power backup, information technology and responsive public and private institutions. Make-in-India initiatives which focus, among other things, on expansion and upgradation of railways, defense, construction and manufacturing, may have both positive and negative implications for rural India, which require serious discourse and debate. No doubt, we need to make India a global manufacturing hub and generate 100 million additional jobs in manufacturing. But the point here is how to distribute the costs and benefits of this growth in society? Our past experiences show that rural people, because of lack of necessary skills and resources, have not so far got much direct benefits from development projects, while they are deprived of their land and bear the huge displacement cost. Moreover, sometimes, land acquired for a specific purpose may be diverted to other uses. For example, now the concept of Special Economic Zone is being viewed as a way to grab land. This is the reason why there is lots of opposition to the new Land Acquisition Act in India. Opposition is inevitable because farmers are not made partners in the development process.

Urbanisation can also provide new income opportunities to the rural people, as rural-urban linkages may generate more jobs for the rural workforce in urban formal and informal sectors. But this opportunity can be availed by rural India only when the capacity of rural youth in terms of education and skill is built. Due to lack of relevant education and skills, most members of rural households whose lands are acquired for development purposes, may end up with the job of security guard/ manual worker/Class IV employee in the enterprises built on their land.

It is significant to note that due to high cost of land in cities, companies are shifting their establishments and production units to small towns and rural areas. This is an important step towards urbanisation of rural India. The Credit Suisse Report (2012) estimates that almost 75% of the new factories during the last decade came up in rural India, contributing to 70% of all new manufacturing jobs created. No doubt, when a factory is set up in a rural area, it has a multiplier effect on the rural economy. Demands for local goods and resources increase and some additional employment opportunities are created for the rural people. However, it has been observed that most of the workers in such factories are hired from other places, especially from the urban areas because local people may not have the required skill.

Conclusions and Policy Imperatives

This paper shows that during the last two decades, socio-economic divide between rural and urban India has widened. Agriculture, an important source of rural livelihood, has been in deep crisis. Consequently its share in GVA and employment declined from 23.8 per cent and 59.9 per cent respectively in 1999-00 to 14.3 per cent and 48.9 per cent in 2011-12. During 2004-05 to 2011-12, the rural-urban difference in employment growth was quite alarming. During this period, there was no growth in employment in rural areas, while urban employment grew significantly. This implies that during this period, both GDP and employment growth trajectories have shifted from rural to urban areas, thus marginalising rural India. During this period, almost the entire loss of employment in the agriculture sector was compensated by jobs in the rural construction sector whose share went up from 17.81 per cent in 2004-05 to 30.78 per cent in 2011-12, indicating that growth in the rural non-farm employment is driven only by the construction sector. During the last 18 years (1993-94 to 2011-12), as against 54.1 per cent increase in real MPCE in urban India, the corresponding increase in rural India was only 36.52 per cent. Consequently, the ratio of urban to rural real MPCE increased from 1.65 in 1993-94 to 1.86 in 2011-12, indicating the widening of the divide.

Although agriculture is not equal to rural; it is still a key source of livelihood to 64 per cent of the rural workforce. Entire rural India is affected if agricultural output and income decelerate. The latest NSS survey on situation assessment of farmers reveals that average income per agricultural household from all sources in 2013 was estimated as Rs 6,426 per month. On an average, as much as 40 per cent income of farmer households comes from non-farm activities. It is significant to note that about 86.60 per cent of farmers in India get nearly 50 per cent of their income from non-agricultural sources. This clearly indicates that farmers are depending more on non-farm sources of income. It is also observed that about 70 per cent of farmer households have their consumption expenditure higher than their income. The NSS surveys show that the percentage of indebted farmers has increased from 48.6 in 2003 to 51.9 in 2013. In rural India, average indebted cultivator households in 2013 had an outstanding loan of Rs153,630 per household, while in case of non-cultivator households, the amount was only Rs 89, 221.

Rural-urban divide is also observed in case of access to basic amenities. Access to safe drinking water, sanitary facilities, improved sewerage system, uninterrupted power supply and clean energy is vital not only for improving the quality of life but also for achieving higher level of human development. Rural-urban divide in the access to these amenities also explains, to a great extent, differences in the health status of rural and urban households. As per the latest estimates, IMR, CMR, birth and death rates were much higher and life expectancy much lower in rural than urban India.

Expansion of cities and towns means shrinking of rural land, water and other natural resources, which may generate rural-urban conflicts. During the last one decade, more than 13 million hectares of operated farm land has declined, mainly due to its conversion into non-agricultural uses. The Make-in-India initiative of the government requires huge amount of land for developing smart cities, expansion of roads, railways, airports, industries and services. These developments can have both positive as well as negative consequences for the rural India. Therefore, efforts need to be made to minimize the negative consequences and promote the positive ones through well-design policies so that rural people may not only bear the cost of development but also share its benefits in an equitable manner. It is necessary to change the rural-urban divide into rural-urban continuum.

The solution of the problems of rural India lies both within agriculture and outside agriculture. Within the agricultural sector, the need is to make small and marginal holdings economically viable and environmentally sustainable through developing an institution of 'group farming', develop a supply chain system that benefits both farmers and consumers through effective linkage between 'farmers groups' and 'consumers groups', protect the farmers from technology, market and monsoon failures through setting up risk mitigation funds and crop insurance system. Outside agriculture, it is necessary to promote the rural non-farm sector by making substantial investment in five key areas—education, roads, healthcare, information technology and electricity. The investment in these areas will strengthen the rural-urban linkages and help in attracting private investment in rural manufacturing, agriculture and modern services.

References

1. Das, N (2013) A Study on Factors Affecting Consumer Purchase Decision of Water Purifier, *IJMBS* Vol. 3 (2). http://www.ijmbs.com/32/1/nilima.pdf
2. Government of India. 2005. Indebtedness of Farmer Households, Situation Assessment Survey of Farmers, *NSS 59th Round, Report No 498*, Ministry of Statistics and Programme Implementation.
3. Government of India. 2007b. *Report of the Expert Group on Agricultural Indebtedness* (Chairperson, R Radhakrishna), Banking Division, Department of Economic Affairs, Ministry of Finance.
4. Government of India (2013a). *NSS 68th Round*: Key Indicators of Employment and Unemployment in India, 2011-12.
5. Government of India (2013b). *NSS 68th Round*: Key Indicators of Household Consumer Expenditure in India, 2011-12.
6. Government of India (2013c). Key Indicators of Drinking Water, Sanitation, Hygiene and Housing condition in India, *NSS 69th Round*, July 2012-December 2012.
7. Government of India (2013d). Primary Census Abstract for Slum, Population Census 2011, Office of the Registrar General & Census Commissioner, India.
8. Government of India (2014a). Key Indicators of Land and Livestock Holdings in India, *NSS 70th Round*, January-December 2013.
9. Government of India (2014b). Key Indicators of Situation of Agricultural Households in India, *NSS 70th Round*, January-December 2013.
10. Government of India (2014c). Key Indicators of Debt and Investment in India, *NSS 70th Round*, January-December 2013.
11. Mishra N and Shankar R (2012). India Market Strategy: The Great Indian Equalization, Asia Pacific/Indian Equity Research Investment Strategy, Credit Suisse Report.
12. Ranjan NA (2014). Urban India to contribute 75% of GDP by 2020: Barclays. http://urbanupdate.in/in-depth/urban-india-contribute-75-gdp-2020-barclays
13. Rao P Narasimha and K C Suri 2006. 'Dimensions of Agrarian Distress in Andhra Pradesh', *Economic and Political Weekly,* April 22.
14. Sharma SSP and Singh SP (2012). *Growing Rural-Urban Disparity in Uttar Pradesh*, Serials Publications, New Delhi.
15. Singh K (2014). Jan Dhan Yojana: Ambitious but Ambiguous Plan, *Madhyam* *http://www.madhyam.org.in/jan-dhan-yojana-ambitious-ambiguous-plan/*
16. Singh, SP (2013). Water and Sanitation for Quality Life in Rural India, *Kurukshetra*, 61 (12).

Land Acquisition Bill 2015
Land as Corporate Entitlement

— Malabika Pal

LAND HAS been the focus of debate and discussion since the past decade when the violence in Nandigram and Singur in West Bengal had huge political ramifications. Although there had been persistent efforts by numerous people and organisations to get a new Land Law and an enforceable Rehabilitation Policy in place for many years preceding this, there had only been repeated drafting and re-drafting of policies by the government. After the left-front government's 2011 poll debacle in West Bengal, it became finally clear that the issue could no longer be glossed over. The nationwide protest brought to the fore many of the hitherto neglected instances from all parts of India and succeeded in putting enough pressure so that inputs were taken from many civil society organisations to frame the much-awaited Land Law, replacing the old colonial legislation. It took seven years and many rounds of consensus-building to finally arrive at what was called the Right to Fair Compensation and Transparency in Land Acquisition, Rehabilitation and Resettlement Act , 2013 (hereafter the

New Land Act) just before the parliamentary elections. Within six months of the enactment, the Bharatiya Janata Party came to power in May 2014 with a resounding majority on the promise of 'achhe din' or good days. There were some media reports about changes being considered to the New Land Act. However, the Land Ordinance that was promulgated on 31st of December 2014, came as a big bolt out of the blue, taking away in one step what decades of effort by many had yielded. There was a requirement in the New Land Act that within one year, thirteen other Acts will have to be brought within the purview of the New Land Act. The government took that opportunity to push through many other changes that purported to alter the essence of the New Land Act altogether.

The Land Ordinance of 2014 met with huge criticism. Although it was passed in the Lok Sabha in the earlier part of the budget session, it could not be passed in the Rajya Sabha where the government did not have majority. The Rajya Sabha was prorogued in March and the Land Ordinance was promulgated for a second time on the 3rd of April 2015. Some minor changes were introduced in the second Ordinance to make it appear that the government was responding positively to the sharp criticism against the first Ordinance. A new Bill titled Right to Fair Compensation and Transparency in Land Acquisition, Rehabilitation and Resettlement (Second) Amendment Bill, 2015 (hereafter the Land Acquisition Bill 2015) was introduced in the Lok Sabha on the 11th of May 2015. However, there was strong opposition and major parties staged a walk out. The Bill was sent on the 13th of May 2015 to a Joint Parliamentary Committee (JPC) consisting of 20 members from the Lok Sabha and 10 members from the Rajya Sabha with the mandate of giving its report on the first day of the monsoon session. The Ordinance was re-promulgated without any changes on the 30th of May 2015 to prevent it from lapsing. When it became difficult to get political muster to pass the Bill, the government decided to revise its stand by deleting most of the contentious provisions. With the opposition remaining determined, the government allowed the Land Ordinance to lapse on the 31st of August 2015 and deferred the Bill to the winter session of Parliament. The Bill is being considered by the JPC, which has been given many rounds of extensions.

The Land Acquisition Bill

The question arises, what would be the impact of the proposed changes that were sought to be introduced by the Land Acquisition Bill 2015? The New Land Act, which had replaced the 1894 legislation, was enacted after many previous attempts and amendments, two significant ones being the 1962 and the 1984 ones. In an earlier move, the Special Economic Zones Act 2005 was used to bring large tracts of land under industrial zones in the name of development. That met with huge resistance and the pressures of democratic politics came in the way of using it as a long-term measure. However, the recent move to use the ordinance route to do away with one of the crucial requirements of the New Land Act, namely, the social impact assessments (SIA) for a large number of projects, is clearly very short-sighted. It is important to note that it is only the urgency clause which permits acquisition without SIA. Although the urgency clause has been used covertly quite often, the Ordinances would have legitimised the acquisition of land for almost every conceivable 'public interest' overtly without any SIA, giving the impression that all the specified cases is 'urgent'. This was an extremely hasty move, particularly in view of the fact that there have been so many movements across India against forcible land acquisition and a lot of discourse in India and abroad scrutinising the Indian land acquisition law. In the past, we have witnessed that any move to compulsorily acquire land without considering the adverse effects on the community has led to a quick erosion of support for the ruling government.

In this context, it is worthwhile to compare the erstwhile Land Acquisition Act 1894 (hereafter the Old Land Act) and the Land Acquisition Bill, 2015. There are at least four reasons why one can say that the latter is draconian. The first and the most important is the removal of the requirement of SIA for a wide range of projects. It was important to scrutinise why the SIA process took so long and how it could be made time-bound and more comprehensive rather than doing away with it altogether. The basic economic premise underlying the undertaking of any investment project is that the benefits should outweigh the costs. The costs should include the compensation requirements, including rehabilitation and resettlement of not only the actual owners of a particular piece of land but also those dependent on that land for their livelihoods.

If the state is sincere in its promise of providing 'fair compensation' (as emphasised in the New Land Act), an approximate calculation of this must be done. If the state is to justify its acquisition in terms of national interest, an estimate of 'potential benefits' should be available for public scrutiny since eminent domain is being used to acquire the land in the first place. By doing away with the SIA requirement, was the state giving up this basic obligation which is required to make any acquisition a legitimate one? At least, the Old Land Act had a provision by which only projects that were economically efficient, in terms of enhancing total value, would be adopted. If the Bill with all the changes were to be passed in Parliament, any project would pass through the 'public interest' net by merely stating certain objectives. The removal of SIA would mean that the act of acquisition can no longer be questioned in a vast number of cases.

We note that it was the urgency clause [Clause 17(1) in the Old Land Act; Clause 40(1) in the New Land Act] that permitted acquisition without any SIA. While the Old Land Act did not specify the circumstances explicitly, leading to widespread misuse of the clause, the New Land Act purported to limit its scope by permitting only in case of 'national defence' and emergencies such as 'natural calamities'. The Land Acquisition Bill 2015 brought in many other categories. By the first Ordinance four more categories were added: namely rural infrastructure including electrification, affordable housing and housing for the poor people, industrial corridors and infrastructure and social infrastructure including projects under public-private partnership where the ownership of land continues to vest with the government. By the second Ordinance, there were three changes made to this part of the proposed amendment. Firstly, for industrial corridors it was specified that 'the land shall be acquired up to one kilometre on both sides of the designated railway line or roads for such industrial corridor'. Secondly, social infrastructure was deleted from the fifth category. Thirdly, for all the cases, it was specified that before the issue of notification, the appropriate government shall 'ensure the extent of land for the proposed acquisition keeping in view the bare minimum land required for such project.' The choice of four additional categories of purposes gave an impression that it is only in those small group of cases that these draconian changes would apply.

However, a close scrutiny shows that they were named so as to subsume almost all the major cases.

The second major change was the tremendous expansion in the scope of public purpose by bringing in the private sector in a big way. The words 'private company' was replaced by 'private entity' throughout the New Land Act. It elaborated by inserting in section 3: '(yy) "private entity" means any entity other than a Government entity or undertaking and includes a proprietorship, partnership, company, corporation, non-profit organisation or other entity under any law for the time being in force.' Also, by the first Ordinance, private hospitals and private educational institutions were no longer excluded from the definition of 'infrastructure projects'. However, this was reversed in the second Ordinance because of sharp protest. While the 1962 and 1984 Amendments made many changes, making it easy for the government to acquire land for private projects by using its power of eminent domain, these Ordinances made it the easiest route. This would be detrimental for the much-needed development of a land market in India.

The third major change has been the legitimisation of land acquisition for Public Private Partnerships (PPPs). The New Land Act brought in the acquisition of land by the government for PPPs with the requirement that prior consent of at least 70 per cent of the affected families was needed. The Land Ordinances removed the consent requirement and instead moved the acquisition for PPPs in case of infrastructure projects under the category where no SIA is needed. With one stroke, PPPs have been elevated to the preeminence enjoyed earlier only by national defence. In fact, it was this major change along with the change in definition of 'private company' to 'private entity' that would make land almost like an entitlement for the corporate sector. The enhancement of the scope of the power of eminent domain to circumvent the market mechanism and make land available to the corporate sector as an entitlement, without consideration of the costs and benefits would fundamentally alter the nature of the development process in India.

The fourth crucial change was the removal of requirements for consultation with the affected families. This was part of the SIA. Apart from judging whether the potential benifits of acquisition outweigh the social costs and adverse social impact, the SIA was entrusted to assess whether the proposed acquisition serves public purpose. The Expert Group had the power to recommend the abandonment of the project and to halt the process of land acquisition. The very rationale behind using eminent domain for acquisition of land is that some owners may be reluctant to part with land even if they are required for a larger public benefit. There could be strategic hold-outs which may delay the process. Since no SIA will be done in a large number of cases, the land losers would also not know for what purpose their land would be used. Since the local community would have various issues specific to their environment, consultation gives an opportunity to gather this valuable information. Society would definitely be worse off without such information since development understood in the truest sense, relates to the sustainability of life, livelihoods and the environment.

Reforms: Give Some and Take More Back

The argument that the complications in the New Land Act were making it difficult to acquire land was used to push through many other amendments which, in fact, made the acquisition process much more 'unfair' than what it was before the enactment of the New Land Act.

Most of the positive features of the New Land Act, like 'consent requirements' and 'return of land', if not used within five years, were done away with. Irrigated multi-cropped lands were excluded from the purview of acquisition for reasons of food security in the New Land Act. The first Ordinance removed that exclusion for the four additional categories of projects as well as national defence. Further, a provision under section 24 (2) which came to be called the 'retrospective clause' was added which stated: '...when an award under the said section 11 has been made five years or more prior to the commencement of this Act but the physical possession of the land has not been taken or compensation has not been paid the said proceeding shall be deemed to have lapsed and the appropriate Government, if it so chooses, shall initiate the proceedings of such land acquisition afresh in accordance with the provisions of this Act.' This was amended by the Ordinances to exclude the time spent in litigation where there has been a stay order or injunction. The second Ordinance introduced the provision for compulsory employment of at least one member of an 'affected family' of a farm labourer.

The 'employment' term is subject to interpretation regarding its nature and duration.

However, some of the major criticisms of the New Land Act have not been addressed. In particular, market price continues to be the benchmark which would determine the compensation amount. Even those who were happy with the progress made by the New Land Act in the area of consent, continued to argue that market price cannot be taken as a basis for the compensation amount. As any person who has ever delved into the property market would know, market price in India is quoted at much lower levels and a large portion is unreported to avoid stamp duty. If land owners are forced to part with land, without any SIA and without any consultation, at least they should be paid something close to the value they put on their land. The Ordinances took away the mandatory requirements of SIA and consultation and left the land loser with no option but to accept a payment which has been fixed arbitrarily, since India as yet does not have a well-functioning land market. Even if the aggrieved owner has the resources to engage in a long-lasting litigation, he would be handed down an award by the courts which also takes market value as a benchmark.

The more important question that arises is how has the nation come to this juncture where reforms in the name of development have become 'give some and take more back later'?

One important reason lies in the failure of the judiciary to act as a resort for justice as well as setting limits to the government so that it does not assume more powers than that vested on it by the people it governs. Unlike in the United States, in which each landmark judgment is scrutinised and sets a tone for what is conceived as 'fair' by society, in India court judgments tend to be left out of the mainstream discourse. An analysis of the maze of judgments reveals that courts have tended to let the important question of 'public purpose' be determined by the respective governments. In the case of *R L Arora v State of UP (AIR 1962 SC 764)*, the Supreme Court set aside the acquisition for a private company but through the 1962 Amendment Ordinance, the acquisition was legitimised. The petition filed challenging the validity of the Amendments was dismissed by the apex court. The case of *Somavanti and Others v State of Punjab (AIR 1963 SC 151)* has assumed landmark status and the majority opinion that even a hundred rupees of contribution by the government for a private project is adequate to justify use of eminent domain has been followed in innumerable judgments and has set the standard for what can be taken as public purpose. Even after four decades, the judgment of *Pratibha Nema and Others v State of MP (2003 10 SCC 626)* relied on this argument to justify public purpose. In recent times, people have taken to the streets and often preferred to resist acquisition on their own rather than opting for a legal remedy. In fact, when the first Ordinance was being planned, there ought to have been a change in the title of the New Land Act too. With the second Ordinance in force, the farmer is left with no 'right' worth its name, and there is no pretence of 'fairness' and 'transparency'. In fact, in this scenario, the courts have lost even the opportunity to act as the fair guardians of the rights of people.

Although the Land Ordinance was allowed to lapse and the Land Acquisition Bill, 2015 lies with the JPC (at the time of writing), the impact of the move is going to be far reaching. This is because the States have taken up the task of incorporating some of the provisions through amendments which would become operational after receiving the presidential assent. In fact, it was at a meeting of the Governing Council of the Niti Aayog held on the 15th of July, 2015, that the chief ministers of some non-Congress ruled States expressed a desire to pass legislation to circumvent the stalemate in amending the New Land Act. The vice-chairman of the Niti Aayog urged the States to emulate the example set by Tamil Nadu, which had an amended Act in place since 5 January 2015. By inserting a new section 105-A, some Acts related to Highways, Industrial projects and Harijan Welfare, would be excluded from the provisions of the New Land Act.

Other States have also started changing their land acquisition laws to incorporate the provisions of the Land Ordinance. The Gujarat Assembly passed a Bill on 31 March 2016, by which SIA and consent will not be required for acquisition for defence manufacturing units, canals, roads, schools and affordable housing. For industrial corridors, SIA will not be required but the consent clause still holds. Through insertion of section 23A, the district collector has been given the power to decide matters of land acquisition and compensation without enquiry. The retrospective clause of the New Land Act has also been amended to exclude the period of litigation or the period during which compensation lies unclaimed while computing the period of limitation. It is pertinent to note that this Bill was passed on the last day of the budget session, when the opposition members were not present in the assembly because the speaker had suspended them for two days. The Goa Assembly also amended the retrospective clause by stipulating that, where an award had been made and the compensation amount deposited in the government treasury or with any financial institution including the EDC limited on account of any acquisition, the same shall be considered valid. Further, there can be no litigation regarding the matter.

There are other ways in which States have diluted the New Land Act and gone beyond the provisions of the Ordinances. For instance, the Telengana government issued a series of orders over a period of six months by which, first it permitted acquisition by agreement (section 108 of the New Land Act permits this) and district negotiation committees were formed. By a second order, a district procurement committee was mentioned and monetary compensation included the value of land and property, costs of rehabilitation and resettlement, and perceived loss of livelihood. In return, the land owners would have to forgo their rights to the land through an affidavit and this included a clause that the landowner cannot approach a court challenging the acquisition. In the next two orders, the time limit for claims and objections was reduced from 15 days to 7 days and the payment of rehabilitation and resettlement costs was abandoned. Rajasthan has passed the Special Investment Region Bill, 2016 by which the State government 'may, by notification in the Official Gazette, declare any area of land, including an industrial area, to be a special investment region'. The Bill empowers the State to set up a board and a regional development authority which will develop and govern the areas, particularly the integrated townships along the Delhi-Mumbai Investment Corridor (DMIC). This can be construed as a way of getting around the New Land Act.

In conclusion, one can say that the provisions of the Land Ordinances created a situation in which there was no judicial review, no SIA, no referenda and no consent. Although the New Land Act remains unamended, provisions of the Land Acquisition Bill, 2015 are being rapidly incorporated in the legislative framework of the States. In fact, one can find indications that in their haste to move forward with the objective of development and attract investment, some States are willing to introduce measures which are more draconian than what was contained in the central Bill. Two-thirds of the Indian population live in rural areas, are severely debt strapped and have been committing suicide with astonishing frequency, irrespective of the government in power. In a democratic setup, can such a scenario be sustainable? Even from the point of view of investors, it would be a highly damaging legislation. The clearing of obstacles for acquisition is only the first step. The start of construction and operations will require the support of the local community and the public at large. The experience of the Tatas in Singur shows that at any point, there could be obstacles in the process of production. Only long-term solutions can lead to continued expansion in output which would lead to true 'development'. If this kind of short-termism is used to transfer a crucial resource from one section of the population to another as an entitlement, there can only be widespread social unrest, which would ultimately harm the investment climate of the country. When the 1962 Amendment Ordinance was promulgated to bring Nehru's temples of modern India into existence, we did not have a backlog of about sixty million people yet to be rehabilitated. Today, India cannot afford to push the development agenda in a way that we create a multiple of that number in a matter of a few years from now.

Counting the Poor

— Manali Chakrabarti

A NEW GDP measure puts India's GDP at 2.1 trillion dollars and it is slated to grow at close to 8% annually.[1] To put this in perspective—in 1991, the year the Indian economy was opened up and we embraced neo-liberal policies, the Indian GDP was about $275 billion which by the turn of the century had doubled to $481 billion. But the real growth of the Indian economy has been in the last 15 years which saw it increase by almost four-and-a-half times. One needs to remember that these include years which saw the greatest global recession since the 1930s. Thus, for the economy as a whole, the promised '*achche din*' seem to be happening and there are the numbers to prove it. The policymakers who have been rooting for further opening up and freeing of the economy have been justifiably sporting a smug expression with this quantitative endorsement of their position. The only vexing questionfor them is that all this growth does not seem to have translated to alleviation of poverty—the 'poor' people have been stubbornly impervious to this stunning growth of the

[1] http://www.livemint.com/Politics/xziKtmtOxBJntZb41p2hDL/India-GDP-seen-surging-74-in-data-that-has-puzzled-economi.html

economy. And this is disturbing, particularly given that the officials have not even been able to decide how many of them are there and, more importantly, how to identify them.

'Poverty Line' and a Brief History of Poverty Calculation

The last few years have witnessed a flurry of activity among academics and policymakers in trying to define poverty, determine what constitutes poverty, and where to draw the line below which people can be termed 'officially' poor. Popular media and academic journals have produced a plethora of articles on the various definitions of poverty and poverty lines. As is evident from Figure 1, the poverty line seems to be a rather *labile* concept with anywhere from 15% to around 80 % of the population under it. The NCAER study (2008) claims 15.6 % people to be poor, the Rangarajan Committee 2014 records every 3rd Indian to be poor, while the Economic Survey 2013-14 claims every 5thIndian to be poor. The Saxena Report (2009) instituted by the Ministry of Rural Development assesses every second Indian to be poor while the Arjun Sengupta Committee Report sensationally claimed that 4 out 5 Indians are poor! Let us delve briefly into the history of poverty measurement in India to make sense of this elusive poverty line.

Monthly Per Capita Consumer Expense (MPCE) Poverty Line

The Planning Commission had been seeking to measure the number of poor in the country since the 1960s and in the early 1970s a group of experts decided that the appropriate line should be set according to a minimum consumption basket including average monthly food consumption of 2,400 calories of food per capita per day in rural India and 2,100 calories per capita per day in urban India.[2]

But subsequently, the poverty line has simply been updated annually by adjusting for the inflation determined by the consumer price indices. And over the years, the numbers ceased to reflect the actual food (calories) consumption. This is because not only has the pattern of food consumption changed drastically over the decades,the cost of other components of the basket have risen disproportionately higher,[3] resulting in a situation where even the cost of minimum food required is

[2] http://sanhati.com/excerpted/805/

[3] http://planningcommission.gov.in/reports/genrep/himanshu.pdf

Figure 1: Poverty Estimates as Percentage of Population below Poverty Line in Recent Years

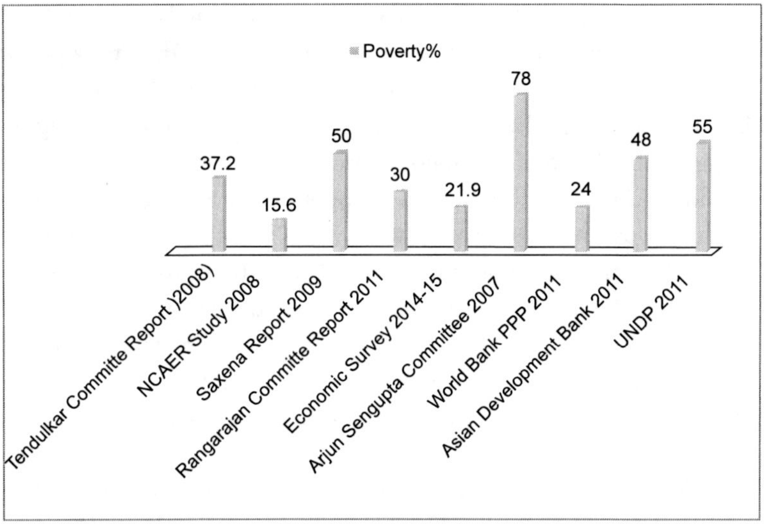

Source: Various reports on Poverty line estimation.

not covered by the 'official' poverty line. And yet the use of that line has been defended by the government and policymakers by simply assuming that the families have chosen to buy other items rather than the minimum required nutrition.These poverty lines also drew a lot of flak for focussing exclusively on food consumption norms, and ignoring expenditure on health, education and other basic needs.

Tendulkar Committee Report 2009

To correct some of the issues raised, the Planning Commission set up an expert committee under Professor Suresh D Tendulkar in 2005to review the methodology for official estimation of poverty and recommend changes in the existing procedures.[4] The committee submitted its report in 2009. The fundamental difference between the Tendulkar Committee's approach and the earlier approach was that it moved away from a purely calorie-based assessment of poverty to include other expenses like health, education, durable goods and entertainment. But the committee reduced the calorie intake requirement from 2,100 to 1,776 calories, in urban

[4] http://planningcommission.nic.in/reports/genrep/rep_hasim1701.pdf

areas and 2,400 to 1,999 calories in rural areas per person per day. This was apparently based on[5] the FAO (Food and Agricultural Organisation, a UN body) directive, which calculated that calorie intake norm of 1,770 Cal as a Minimum Dietary Energy Requirement (MDER) for a person engaging in 'light physical activity'. An example of this kind of activity is 'a male office worker in urban areas who only occasionally engages in physically demanding activities during or outside working hours'. It would be ridiculous to expect that a poor person in India would have the luxury to do sedentary office work. Most of them would be involved in very hard manual labour for inhumanly long hours to eke subsistence wages. The Tendulkar report also overlooked inclusion of the aged, destitute, primitive tribal groups, the disabled, single women, widows, and pregnant and lactating women in the category of poor—groups that the Supreme Court has already directed the Government of India to automatically include.

The total population of poverty worked out to 37.2 % for 2005 with these measures.Predictably, this new measure was decried by many as 'destitution line'. This led to setting up of another expert committee in 2012 chaired by C Rangarajan who headed the Prime Minister's Economic Advisory Council then.

Rangarajan Committee's Poverty Estimates 2014

The Rangarajan Committee which submitted its report in July 2014, determined poverty based on certain normative standards for adequate nourishment, clothing, house rent, conveyance and education and also some class based behaviourally-determined levels of other non-food expenses, food and non-food consumption. The energy requirement as calculated by Rangarajan is 2,155 cal per person per day in rural areas and 2,090 cal per person per day in urban areas. This is higher than the Tendulkar committee measures but significantly lower than the 2,400 cal in rural areas and slightly less than 2,100 cal in urban areas used by the earlier MPCE determined poverty levels. The new poverty line translates to a monthly per capita consumption expenditure of Rs 972 in rural areas and Rs 1,407 in urban areas in 2011-12-or, Rs 32 in rural areas

---

[5] Though the Tendulkar report do not make any reference to it but it has been cited by several experts criticising the report

and Rs 47 in urban areas on a per capita daily basis.[6] Like the Tendulkar Committee report, this report too invoked several responses,either vehemently disagreeing and equally forcefully justifying the poverty measurement. We daresay that another 'official' Expert Committee is on its way to resolve thisongoing conundrum!

Other Estimates of Poverty: Saxena Committee, NCEUS Report and World Bank Report

Three other Indian estimates are relevant here. In 2008, the Union (national) Rural Development Ministry set up a commissionwith NC Saxena as chair to examine alternative methods of estimating poverty. The commission reported its findings in late 2009. At the outset, the commission felt that monetary amounts specified by the Planning Commission for a minimal diet were too low. Instead of Rs 356 a month per person in rural areas, Rs 700 was considered necessary (Rs 1,000 in urban areas). The commission recommended that the proportion of the rural population living below poverty be raised to at least 50 percent. But even that figure was achieved by lowering the rural calories requirement to 2,100, the same as in urban areas, and if the 2,400 calories criterion had been kept, the percentage of India's rural population living in poverty would have risen to about 80 percent.[7]

The National Commission for Enterprises in the Unorganised Sector (NCEUS) was established in 2004 under Prof Arjun Sengupta, to examine ways to provide the welfare of the country's unorganised workforce. More than 90 per cent of workforce and about 50 per cent of the national product are accounted for by the informal economy. Most of them work as low paid agricultural workers, or in small manufacturing units and shops and as hawkers or delivery men and have no social security and little or no job security. In its study, NCEUS set an overall minimum of Rs 20 per day per person as its poverty cutoff and calculated that 77 per cent of Indians are 'poor and vulnerable'.

---

[6] http://www.business-standard.com/article/economy-policy/new-poverty-measures-rangarajan-used-nutrition-spending-and-consumption-behaviour-114070700956_1.html

[7] http://www.prb.org/Publications/Articles/2010/indiapoverty.aspx

The World Bank's poverty cutoff of $1.25 realigned by PPP estimate pegs Indian poverty at around 26% in 2011. And then that still leaves the UNDP report and several other national and international attempts to estimate poverty. See Box 1 and 2.

Box 1: Inconvenient-Just Move the Line

The whole exercise of estimating the poor and setting a poverty line reminds me of a very telling incident in the iconic novel *Catch 22,* probably the most influential piece of literature about the meaninglessness of war and its losses. Set in the Second World War, in this episode a disgruntled unit of air force bombardiers is dreading going over another meaningless mission to capture a godforsaken Italian town called Bologna. Untimely rains are delaying the mission and contributing to the already heightened emotions of the unit who seem to be spending most of the day anxiously looking at the bomb line on the map, indicating the location of Bologna.

When night fell, they (the bombardiers) congregated in the darkness with flashlights, continuing their macabre vigil at the bomb line in brooding entreaty *as though hoping to move the ribbon up by the collective weight of their sullen prayers.*[A]

One of the pilots exclaims in exasperation to his fellow unit member Yossarian(the hero of the novel):

'I really can't believe it', Clevinger exclaimed to Yossarian in a voice rising and falling in protest and wonder. 'It's a complete reversion to primitive superstition. They're confusing cause and effect. It makes as much sense as knocking on wood or crossing your fingers. They really believe that we wouldn't have to fly that mission tomorrow if someone would only tiptoe up to the map in the middle of the night and move the bomb line over Bologna. Can you imagine? You and I must be the only rational ones left.'

In the middle of the night Yossarian knocked on wood, crossed his fingers, and tiptoed out of his tent to move the bomb line up over Bologna.[B]

A. Heller, J Catch 22p136-137

B. Ibid

Box 2: This is not a 'Poor' Family

Just out of curiosity, I tried to assess the monthly expenditure of a contract worker in Kanpur city. The worker and one of his sons (not yet an adult) are the primary earning members of the family which constitutes of two adults and three children. Besides, the wife of the worker also contributes through regular piece rate work which she does from home, besides managing the housework. As is evident, the family does not buy any milk, nor any green vegetables and probably aptly have clubbed medicine, fruits and sweets together indicating that such expense is a luxury only availed by the sick. Buys two pairs of clothing per person, including uniform for the children. He does not have access to electricityand does not have a toilet either. For this bare minimum existence the percapita expense works out to Rs 68 per day per person –50% more than the 'urban' poverty line by Rangarajan committee. And this is afforded only by at least three individuals working, including the son who missed out on education to ensure subsistence for the family. The self-employed worker works for at least 12 hours every day. As is also evident, any unforeseen expense including a minor illness would cut into food and/or school fees. The family has no savings and hence should there be any major contingency (medical or otherwise) it would mean they would have to rely on moneylenders where the going rate of interest is 10% per month-for every 100 rupees borrowed Rs 10 is anyway deducted beforehand as the interest for the first month.[C]

Consumption for a family of 5	Monthly expense in Rupees
Grain	1,500
Pulses	550
Oil	450
Potato, Tomato, Onion &Garlic	600
Sugar	250
Tea	100
Spices	300
Detergent & soap	200

[C] This is a typical case and corroborated by several other workers whom we checked with

fuel	700
medicine, sweet, fruits	1,000
clothes	200
cycle repair	350
utensils	100
rent	3,000
mobile recharge	300
school fees	600
Total	10,200

Why so much of Noise regarding Poverty Line?

Poverty has been estimated for several decades now but till very recently, it remained an academic exercise not provoking much discussion beyond the experts. So why has it suddenly become so fashionable to speak, debate, contest and justify the poverty line? Probably the reason is that in 1991, the policy makers and the government ushered in liberalisation with a lot of fanfare claiming that this would be the dawn of a new era in the country's economy. For the last 25 years, the policymakers have been diligently implementing some of the standard (recommended by international financial institutions and applied uniformly, irrespective of national contexts) neo-liberal policies like 'privatisation, fiscalausterity, deregulation,free trade and reductions ingovernment spendingin order to enhance the role of theprivate sectorin theeconomy'.[8] It is significant that changes of political regimeeither in the centre or in the States, have had no effect on either the speed or the thrust of these policies and all the governments have claimed credit for completely obliterating the stigma of 'Hindu Rate of Growth'.

> Annual growth inGDP per capitahas accelerated from just 1¼ per cent in the three decades after Independence to 7½ per cent currently, a rate of growth that will double average income in a decade.[9]

---

[8] http://en.wikipedia.org/wiki/Neoliberalism accessed on 4.05.2015

[9] OECD report on India, quoted from http://en.wikipedia.org/wiki/Economic_liberalisation_in_India#cite_note-oecdindia2007-19 accessed on 4/05/2015

The Indian economic growth reached dizzying heights averaging 9% for the period between 2003 and 2007; it slowed down when the global economy came crashing in 2008.[10] There seemed to be nothing to mar the party except for a vexing question asked in some quarters whether the advantages of this 'miraculous' economic growth reaches all sections of society, especially the 'poor'? The official poverty estimates published by the Planning Commission conveniently showed a decline in absolute poverty levels from 36% in 1993-94 to 26% in 1999-2000 and the recent *Economic Survey* claims that only a fifth of the population are poor. And yet the visual evidence of widespread poverty, distress and squalor remain an irksome negation of the official claims of 'India Shining'. And not only visual evidence but statistical evidence indicates that the magnificent growth of the Indian economy has not only not trickled down to the poorest, if anything, it seems to have *gushed up* even more wealth to the elite.

Let us briefly see the effect of neoliberal policies on various sections of the population.

The Majority:

- According to the latest Human Development Report (2014) themed *Sustaining Human Progress: Reducing Vulnerabilities and Building Resilience*, India's HDI (Human Development Index)[11] is 0.586which places it 135th among 187 countries. Adjusting HDI for inequality (IHDI),[12] it falls by around 30% to 0.415. Further,

---

[10] http://en.wikipedia.org/wiki/Economy_of_India#Post-liberalisation_period_.28since_1991.29 accessed on 4/05/2015

[11] The HDR defines HDI as a summary measure for assessing long-term progress in three basic dimensions of human development: a long and healthy life, access to knowledge and a decent standard of living.

[12] *Definition of IHDI in HDR 2014*: The HDI is an average measure of basic human development achievements in a country. Like all averages, the HDI masks inequality in the distribution of human development across the population at the country level. The 2010 HDR introduced the Inequality-Adjusted HDI (IHDI), which takes into account inequality in all three dimensions of the HDI by 'discounting' each dimension's average value according to its level of inequality. The IHDI is basically the HDI discounted for inequalities. The 'loss' in human development due to inequality is given by the difference between the HDI and the IHDI, and can be expressed as a percentage. As the inequality in a country increases, the loss in human development also increases.

according to the Multidimensional Poverty Index (MPI),[13] 55.3% of Indians are multidimensionally poor and an additional 18.3 % are near multidimensional poverty—making the total poor count close to 3/4th of the population.[14]

- Nearly two million children under five die every year in India, one every 15 seconds—more than half die in the month after birth and 400,000 in their first 24 hours.[15]In 2010, the Infant Mortality Rate[16] of India was reported to be 47 at the national level, and varied from 51 in rural areas to 31 in urban areas.[17] Around 28 per cent of child deaths are linked just topoor sanitation and unsafe drinking water.[18] Nearly half of India's children — approximately 60 million—are underweight, 45 per cent have stunted growth (too short for their age), 20 per cent are wasted (too thin for their height, indicating acute malnutrition), 75 per cent are anemic, and 57 per cent are deficient in Vitamin A.[19]

The status of urban industrial worker is worse than ever before:

- The pattern of wage to profit ratio (a basic indicator of distribution of economic prosperity) in this period captures the rate of exploitation of industrial working class in the post-reform

---

13 Multidimensional Poverty Index (MPI), identifies multiple deprivations in the same households in education, health and living standards definition from HDR

14 HDR 2014

15 http://www.guardian .co.uk/world/ 2009/oct/ 04/india- slums-children- death-rate(back)

16 Infant mortality rate (IMR) is the number of deaths of children less than one year of age per 1000 live births. The rate for a given region is the number of children dying under one year of age, divided by the number of live births during the year, multiplied by 1,000.http://en.wikipedia.org/wiki/Infant_mortality(back)

17 *Children in India 2012-* Ministry of Statistics and Programme Implementation, GOI http://mospi.nic.in/mospi_new/upload/Children_in_India_2012.pdf

18 http://articles.timesofindia.indiatimes.com/2009-10-05/india/28104116_1_child-deaths-newborn-deaths-neonatal-diseases

19 http://articles.timesofindia.indiatimes.com/2013-08-08/india/41200919_1_acute-malnutrition-silent-emergency-world-bank-report

era. From around 2.73 in the late 1980s, the *wage to profitratio*has declined to 0.25 in 2012 – a spectacular 10 fold decline.[20]

- Out of the 472 million workers in 2011-12, 92 % are *informal workers,*ie. theyare employed either in the informal sector (83%) or are contingent workers (accounting for 58 % of the total organised sector employment) in the organised sector. This implies that these most workers do not even get the legal minimum wages (which itself is barely subsistence wages),let alone other facilities to ensure a dignified existence including health, education, housing, sanitation, safe work conditions.[21]

The agrarian sector has been in a state of crisis for decades now:

- The media is agog over the reasons behind the unfortunate suicide of a farmer during a recent Aam Admi Party rally. But Indian farmers have been committing suicide with alarming regularity for years now. *A total of 296,438* farmers have killed themselves in India since 1995. Most farm suicides have been linked to debt, a sharp rise in input costs, serious water crises, price volatility and crop failure due to pest attacks and disease.[22] In 2011, it was assessed that the suicide rate among Indian farmers is 47% higher than the rest of the population.
- Between 1991 and 2001, over seven million people for whom cultivation was the main livelihood, quit farming. The next decade,2001-2011, witnessed one of the largest migrations from rural to urban India, on a scale not seen in 90 years in the country. As economist K Nagaraj, professor at the Asian College of Journalism, Chennai puts it 'The migrations of these past 15-20 years are overwhelmingly distress driven, footloose and often disruptive of the lifestyle, roots and family bonds of the migrant'.[23]

---

[20] *Annual Survey of Industries* quoted from http://www.livemint.com/Opinion/53GWGOGWiVuqZibDu4hxnO/Is-Indias-labour-market-moving-towards-a-May-Day-situation.html

[21] *India Labour& Employment Report, 2014* quoted from http://www.rupe-india.org/58/deformed.html

[22] http://www.bbc.com/news/world-asia-india-28205741

[23] http://www.thehindu.com/opinion/columns/sainath/decadal-journeys-debt-and-despair-spur-urban-growth/article2487670.ece

The tribal and Dalit population have been the worst hit because of 'development':

- Between 60 and 65 million people are estimated to have been displaced in India since independence, the highest number of people uprooted for development projects in the world.'This amounts to around one million displaced every year since independence and of these displaced, over 40% are tribals and another 40% consist of dalits and other rural poor'.[24] Many of them have been displaced multiple times and only a 20-25% of them ever get resettled.[25]
- Millions of people are displaced regularly due to violence and armed conflicts which have been on the rise in the past decades. An estimated 526,000internally displaced persons(IDPs) were there in the country till 2013, states a UN-backed report. The report further said that this under-represents the real number of people displaced, since in Indi, IDPs tend to be no longer counted once official camps are closed, even if they remain in displacement. The report also states that IDPs lack access to clean water, adequate shelter, food security, clothing and health care.[26]

The dots above do not add up to a vibrant shining India aspiring to be a superpower. Instead, in many parameters, the country seems to be worse than the poorest regions of the world. So how does one reconcile a 2.1 trillion dollar economy with very high growth rates with this picture? We cannot, unless we consider the other section of this country—the elite. Let us see how the elite have fared in the last two decades.

The Elite

- India's richest 10 per cent have been getting steadily richer since 2000, and now hold nearly three-quarters of the total wealth of the country. India's 1 per centers—its super-rich—has been

---

[24] Working Group on Human Rights in India and the UN (WGHR) quoted fromhttp://timesofindia.indiatimes.com/india/India-uproots-most-people-for-progress/articleshow/13792551.cms

[25] Ibid

[26] http://articles.economictimes.indiatimes.com/2014-05-15/news/49873394_1_communal-violence-report-armed-conflict

getting richer even faster. In the early 2000s, India's top 1 per cent held a lower share of India's total wealth than the world's top 1 per cent held of its total wealth. That changed just before and after the global recession (though the world's super-rich are recovering) and India's top 1% holds close to half of the country's total wealth, equivalent of the country's 49 per cent GDP.[27] Figure 2 captures the wealth distribution.

- According to the Forbes billionaire list in the mid-1990s, there were only two Indian billionaires with a combined net worth of $3.2 billion. This number rose by 2012 to 46, with a combined net worth of $176.3 billion; by 2014, it reached 55, with a combined net worth of $191.5 billion. But even better days were to come as Forbes jubilantly announced: *For the first time the top 100 are all billionaires, with combined wealth of$346 billion, up more than a third from 11 months ago.*[28]
- According to a wealth report by the Kotak group and Ernst & Young,[29] the number of ultra-high networth individuals (UHNIs) having an investible surplus of over Rs 25 crore (Rs 250 million) rose 16 per cent to 1.17 lakh in 2013-14, and this is estimated to triple to 3.43 lakh in the next three years. The wealth of the UHNIs, which also includes professionals having an annual income of over Rs 3 crore, grew 21 per cent to Rs 104 trillion (Rs 104 lakh crore), and is estimated to grow four times to Rs 408 trillion in the next three years.

An important aspect to the wealth estimation quoted above is that it only covers the disclosed wealth and does not account for the illegally held wealth. As per the latest estimates released by the Global Financial Integrity (GFI)a, the cumulative illicit money moving out of India over a ten-year period from 2003 to 2012 has risen to USD 439.59 billion

---

27 ibid

28 http://www.forbes.com/sites/naazneenkarmali/2014/09/24/indias-100-richest-of-2014-are-all-billionaires-for-the-first-time/

29 http://www.rediff.com/business/slide-show/slide-show-1-117-lakh-ultra-high-networth-individuals-in-india/20140724.htm

Figure 2: Wealth Distribution in India total wealth 3.6 trillion $

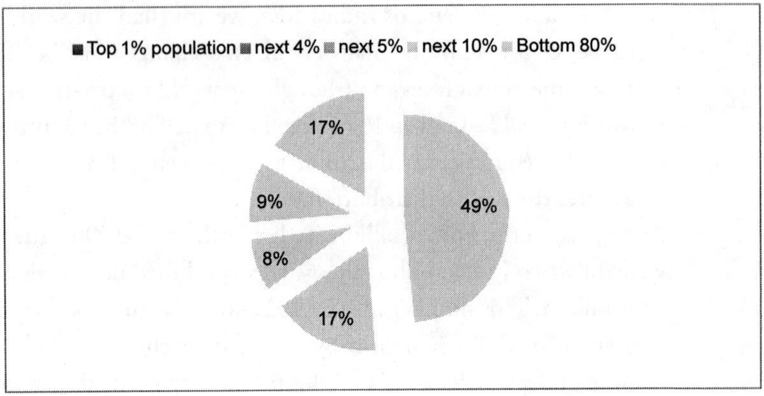

Source: Source: Credit Suisse's Global Wealth Databook 2014.[30]

(Rs 28 lakh crore). Obviously this is also held mostly by the super rich population, further widening the wealth gap.[31]

Why are the Poor, Poor ?

> When I give food to the poor, they call me a saint. When I ask why the poor have no food, they call me a communist.
>
> — Hélder Câmara, *Dom Helder Camara: Essential Writings*

As is evident from the above section, India probably is not truly one nation. In fact there are two extremely diverse nations in one geographical confinement—one of the super-rich (about 5% which in our country translates to over 6 crore people) and the other (95 %) of abjectly poor. This explains the apparent contradictions of various parameters of the economy. And we would like to argue further that the disparate economic access of these 'two' Indias are not unrelated, in fact, they are mutually responsible for the status of each other. The whole exercise of counting the poor is in fact eyewash to hide the real issue of extreme inequality, which

[30] http://www.thehindu.com/data/indias-staggering-wealth-gap-in-five-charts/article6672115.ece

[31] http://www.thehindu.com/news/india-third-on-black-money-list-report/article6696491.ece

has been increasing exponentially since the economic reforms. Poverty is not a condition afflicting the poor; it is not a quantitative measure of how to provide subsistence existence to the poor,which if perfected, would lead to gradual alleviation of poverty. It is not even merelya question of economic deprivation; it is actually a political issue. The poor have no say in the political dispensation of the economy which is evident by the various policies affecting them.

Jobless Growth

First of all, most of the growth so far has not even translated into jobs as is evident from Fig 3 below. In fact, in the highest growth years 2004-5 to 2009-10, the share of agricultural jobs shrank by over 6 %, manufacturing sector shed 5 million jobs and services created only 3.5 million jobs. Between 2005 and 2010, only one million jobs were created for almost 60 million new entrants to the labour market. And even these employment figures are inflated because they do not show disguised unemployment of various kinds.[32] Unemployment or underemployment itself renders majority of the population politically ineffective.

Figure 3: Comparison of GDP and Employment Growth 1973-2010

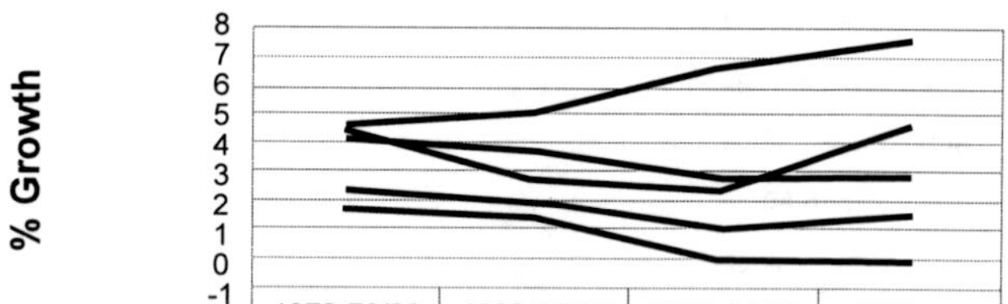

	1972-73/83 00 00/2009-10	1983-93/94	1993-94/99-	1999-
Primary Sector	1.7	1.35	0.05	-0.13
Secondary Sector	4.43	2.82	2.44	4.64
Tertiary Sector	4.21	3.77	2.85	2.83
Total Employment Growth	2.44	2.02	1.04	1.5
Growth of GDP	4.66	4.98	6.51	7.52

Source: Papola and Sahu *Growth and Structure of Employment in India: Long-Term and Post-Reform Performance and the Emerging Challenge*, ICSSR, 2012, pp4-8http://isidev.nic.in/pdf/ICSSR_TSP_PPS.pdf

[32] *Economic Survey 2013* quoted from http://www.newindianexpress.com/columns/2014/11/25/Decoding-Jobless-Growth/article2538969.ece

Let us briefly look at some of the recent policies, laws and budget allocations to further substantiate our point.

- *Government Spending on Social Protection and Health*
  In a country where almost 80 % people are poor and do not even have access to basic amenities one would expect that this would be the top priority for the government. And yet as Figure 4 below shows India has one of the lowest allocation for Social protection and health in the world, including sub-Saharan Africa.

Figure 4: Government Spending on Social Protection & Health Expenditure as % of GDP

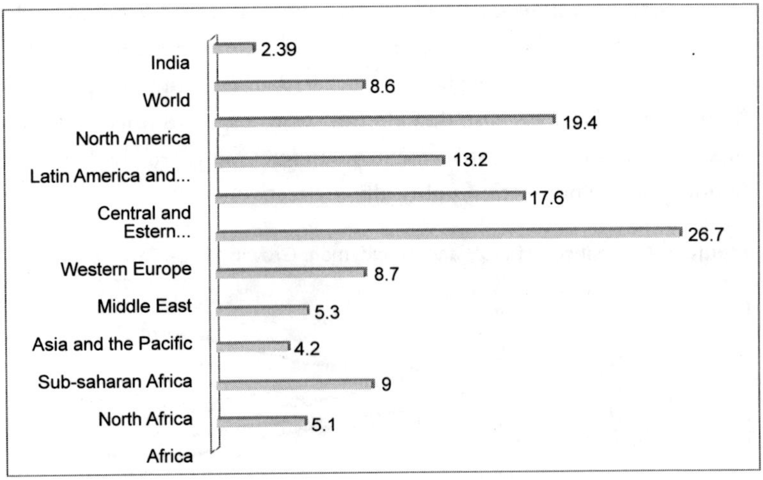

Source: *World Social Protection Report 2014-15.*

- *Decline in Budget Allocation for all Sectors and Schemes Affecting the Poor*
  The budget allocation for MNREGA is almost the same as last year which means in real terms it has actually gone down. There has been a 29% reduction in budget for children from 2014-15. There is a cut in the allocations in school-related schemes like the Sarva Shiksha Abhiyan (by 21%) and Mid-Day Meal scheme (by 30%). In the case of health, the overall budget allocation has been reduced from Rs3,9237crores to Rs33,152

crores.[33] About 2.3 crore children in India are malnourished and still the scheme that deals with malnourishment—ICDS (Integrated Child Development Scheme)—has seen a 54.19 per cent decrease in allocation. Overall there was a 55 per cent reduction in the budget for the Ministry of Women and Child Development.[34]

- *Budget Allocation to Agriculture Consistently Declining*
  A sector which supports over half of the country's population and feeds the whole population, and which has been in extreme distress for several years now, has been consistently allocated less and less resources by the government.The growth rate of agriculture has been constantly declining and so has been the budget allocation. In the Budget 2013-14, agriculture allocation was Rs 17,788 crore, which reduced to Rs11,531 crore in 2014-15 and in the 2015-16 budget estimates it stands at Rs11,657 crore. Further, the allocation for irrigation has been reduced by 58% over last year's Rs 1,797 core to merely Rs772 crore, out of which 40% would go for flood management.[35]

See Box 3: Feeding a Billion for an Argument for Universal Public Distribution System.

The Finance Minister,in his Budget statement, claimed that the objective of the present government is *'Wiping every tear from every eye'* and yet has reduced all relevant allocation for the same. There is a lot of pontification on leakages[36] of subsidies with 'accurate quantification' of various heads which do not reach the poor.[37] And yet, the policymakers find adequate resources to subsidise the wealthiest of this country—individuals and corporations.

---

[33] http://www.indiatomorrow.net/eng/food-security-elimination-of-hunger-low-priority-of-modi-govt

[34] http://www.counterview.net/2015/03/union-budget-allocation-for-children.html

[35] http://www.firstpost.com/business/budget-2015-left-rss-affiliated-farmer-unions-say-nothing-farmers-2129477.html

[36] Obviously a leakage also implies that the benefit of the subsidy is cornered by the 'non poor'

[37] http://indiabudget.nic.in/es2014-15/echapvol1-03.pdf

Box 3: How to Feed a Billion[D]

A *Tehelkaarticle* argues for universal subsidy and claims that the *Food Security Bill is not a spend; it is an investment, crucial for India's future and growth.* Relating from field experiences in UP and Chhattisgarh, the article notes that unlike a complete mess in UP, in Chhattisgarh almost every citizen was getting their food entitlement simply by the State removing targeted subsidies.

In the currentPDSsystem, there are 13 parameters to determine who is poor: how many sets of clothes a person has, whether they live in a*kachcha*or*pucca*house, whether they own a patch of land; possess a cow, and so on. This is then marked on a scale of 0-5 and a percentage of the poor who make it to that scale are computed as worthy to receive subsidies. No wonder the present sorry state of affairs in most States.

InChhattisgarh, because of universalization of beneficiaries, anybody who needs it can ask for it. The State has also taken away fair-price shops from private operators and given them to cooperatives, panchayats or women's self-help groups; raised the commission earned by these mediators; set up computerised ledgers in godowns. Further, it has sent out a diktat that all food-related grievances must be settled by district magistrates within 15 days and apparently, this has led to decline of leakages from 40 per cent to four.

The benefits also are visible, as a woman in Sarguja told *Tehelka*:

For the first time in our life, we are sure we have enough to eat. So instead of spending 15 hours a day trying to find money to buy roti and salt, we have started a cooperative and are running a dairy.

- *Subsidies to the Super Rich*

  The revenue foregone by the central government for the financial year 2014-2015 is a whopping Rs 589,285.2 crore, a figure higher than the fiscal deficit of Rs 512,628 projected for this financial year.[38] As Sainath sums it up '*But budgets only started carrying that annexure (revenues foregone) a few years ago, and we only have the*

[D] The entire box is from the article in Tehelkahttp://www.tehelka.com/how-to-feed-a-billion-and-why-it-pays/

[38] http://www.firstpost.com/business/budget-2015-why-cut-corporate-tax-but-not-personal-tax-mr-jaitley-2128125.html

data from 2005-06 to 2013-14. In those nine years, the corporate karza maafia amounted to Rs 36.5 lakh-crore...For those stricken by number-crunchitis: that works out, on average, to Rs 1,110 crore every day—for nine years. That's one hell of a free lunch.[39] If we add up the figures for 2014-15, it amounts to Rs 42.5 lakh crore or Rs 1,770 crore per day for 10 years. To add to this, the Union budget 2015-2016 has proposed cutting basic rate of corporate tax to 25% from current 30% over the next four years,[40] making corporate tax lower than personal tax.

- *Jan DhanYojna and the Non Performing Assets*
  The ambitious financial inclusion scheme announced by the Prime Minister on 15 August 2014 has led to opening of 147.1 million accounts, mostly in public sector banks. And yet, 9 months into the campaign, over 58% of the accounts (85 million) had zero balance.[41] On the other end of the spectrum, the outstanding loans for PSU banks stand at 22.13 lakh crore and most of them would be to the 'non poor'. Top 10 defaulters account for Rs 28,000 crore and over 433 borrowers have more than Rs 1,000 crore of outstanding loans,each amounting to Rs 16.31 lakh crore.[42]

Other major policies which would further disenfranchise the poor and pushed by the present regime include:

- *Dilution of Labour Laws*
  In October 2014, the Prime Minister unveiled aprogramme titled'ShramevaJayate', to support his 'Make in India'campaign. The major announcements include doing away with the system of labour inspection, instead the employers would be required to submit a self-certification of compliance online! A computerised lottery system will decide which factory is to be inspected and

---

[39] http://www.outlookindia.com/article/how-much-can-we-forgo-to-india-inc/291424

[40] http://www.livemint.com/Politics/ikph424Cm0V8pNao13uXbI/Budget-2015-Corporate-tax-reduced-from-30-to-25-for-4-yea.html

[41] http://www.livemint.com/Industry/xtd7YXbYZP20AQLRXn6nEP/More-than-50-Jan-Dhan-Yojana-bank-accounts-remain-empty.html

[42] http://articles.economictimes.indiatimes.com/2015-03-10/news/59970147_1_lakh-crore-loan-sanctioning-npas

which inspector will do the inspection. Inspectors will be required to file their reports within 72 hours of the inspection and any action will be initiated only after a proper scrutiny is made by a central agency, and on the basis of the compliance reports of the employer.The new regulations have rendered superfluous the role of the existing enforcement authorities like, the Employees' Provident Fund Organisation (EPFO), the Employees' State Insurance Corporation (ESIC), the Labour Welfare Department and even the Chief Labour Commissioner. Further,a draft proposal for small-scale industries has been put up on the Labour Ministry's website, exempting units employing up to 40 workers from at least 14 basic laws, which include exemption from the Factories Act, the Industrial Disputes Act, the ESI Act and the Maternity Benefits Act.[43] As we write this piece, the first of the new laws, combining four existing laws—the labour Code on Wage Bill 2015 is being finalised and experts claim that workers' safeguards are going to be eroded further by this restructuring.[44]

- *Land Acquisition Ordinance 2015*

  Seven decades after independence and as a result of several movements, agitations, resistance and sacrifices by the poor of this country, the UPA government was forced to replace the colonial era Land Acquisition Act of 1894. The new Act named *Right to Fair Compensation and Transparency in Land Acquisition, Rehabilitation and Resettlement Act, 2013*, was framed after consulting all stakeholders over seven years and two Parliamentary Committees. But even before the Act was implemented by either the Sate or the Union governments, representatives of the NDA government 'convinced' the President to sign on an Ordinance[45] to amend the LARR Act.[46] With a stroke of pen, rather than a parliamentary process, the present government has compromised

[43] http://www.frontline.in/cover-story/labour-under-attack/article6540729.ece

[44] http://scroll.in/article/725006/as-one-labour-law-replaces-four-existing-laws-is-something-lost-in-the-fine-print

[45] Actually on 31st December, 2014 so that it got enforced before the dawn of the new year!

[46] Right to Fair Compensation and Transparency in Land Acquisition, Rehabilitation and Resettlement, 2013

the safeguard provided for millions of affected people. Briefly the ordinance:

- Exempts special categories of projects from social impact assessment and obtaining consent from affected families
- Dilutes the requirement of utilisation of land within five years of acquisition, else to be returned to the owner.[47]
- Distinction between fertile/unfertile and irrigated/non-irrigated land has been done away with for acquisitions which would have serious impact on agricultural labourers and share croppers.[48]

- *Dilution of Forest Rights Act*

  Predictably the government has also brought key changes, diminishing the applicability of Forest Rights Act (FRA) for seeking statutory forest clearance for projects. The Environment Ministry has exempted plantations, notified as forests,after December 1930,[49] and not having tribal population as per 2001 and 2011 census for green approval of the projects.It would mean that the FRA provision will not apply to a large chunk of forest areas such as the one which the Odisha government acquired despite resistance from locals for India's biggest foreign direct investment project—the Posco Steel Plant in Jagatsinghpur.[50]

As is evident from the data above the 'economically' poor in our country not only have to deal with abject poverty and undignified existence, they also are completely disenfranchised in the present dispensation. Their lack of political voice in the formal system denies them any possibility of meaningful alleviation of their situation. In fact, the system is geared to further accentuate the inequality. The almost unbridled power of the rich make their sense of entitlement almost

---

47 A CAG report on SEZ tabled in November 2014 found that of the 45,635 hectares of notified land 38 % remain unutilized.

48 Data quoted from http://www.theweekendleader.com/Opinion/3556/why-land-ordinance-of-modi-government-is-anti-people.html

49 That is areas not recorded by the British as a Forest

50 https://www.opendemocracy.net/openindia/basudev-mahapatra/modi-government%E2%80%99s-war-on-environment

'inhuman', reflected most aptly by the twitter reaction to Salman Khan's conviction for killing one person in a hit and run case:

> *Kutta rd pe soyega kutte ki maut marega, roads garib ke baap ki nahi hai I ws homles an year nvr slept on rd@BeingSalmanKhan@ sonakshisinha*[51]
>
> — abhijeet (@abhijeetsinger) 6 May, 2015

Having no avenues in the formal system have pushed many of the most vulnerable to forces outside the system. Probably not surprisingly, the years of the most spectacular growth in the Indian economy coincides almost entirelywith ever louder and ever shriller dissenting voices from all over the country, the most significant being those of the Maoists in Central India.

In a meeting of Chief Ministers in 2010, then prime minister Dr Manmohan Singh reasserted that '*Naxalism remains the biggest internal security challenge facing our country*' and that '*it is imperative to control Left-wing extremism for the country's growth*'.[52] This, of course, is an assurance to the big business whose sentiments maybe summed up by the following quote of Anil Agarwal, the executive Chairman of Vedanta Resources, a global diversified metals and mining company headquartered in London:

> *If left-wing extremism continues to flourish in parts which have natural resources of minerals, the climate for investment would certainly be affected.*[53]

---

[51] http://timesofindia.indiatimes.com/entertainment/hindi/music/news/Salman-Khan-hit-and-run-case-Singer-Abhijeet-Bhattacharyas-tweets-condemned-as-insensitive/articleshow/47175616.cms

[52] http://www.thehindu.com/news/national/naxalism-biggest-threat-to-internal-security-manmohan/article436781.ece

[53] For a detailed treatment of big business assessment of Maoism please refer to Varman &Chakrabarti "Big Business and Indian Maoists' Alternate Economic Survey, 2011, pp 127-144

And the Home Minister of the time, P Chidambaram, assured that: '*The government was confident that the problem of left wing extremism would be overcome in the next three years.*'[54]

What is uncanny is that in spite of a change of government there has been no change in policy. Apparently the present Union Home Minister, Rajnath Singh, has also claimed that he can finish the Maoists in '3 years' by flooding Chhattisgarh with troops.[55] And history continues to repeat itself—just ahead of Prime Minister's visit to Chhattisgarh in May 2015, to sign two significant MOUs worth Rs 25,000 crore, there were reports of re-launching of the notorious State-sponsored militia Salwa Judum.[56&57]On 9th May 2015, business papers assured us that 'in a big push for infrastructure development in Chhattisgarh, MoUs worth Rs 24,000 crore were signed at Dantewada in the presence of Prime Minister Narendra Modi'.[58]

Governments may come and go but the actual *show definitely must go on*. And the 'poor' seem to have no say in it—they only foot the bill. And should they defy the rules, there is always the *iron fist*—the military apparatus of the state, to clobber them into submission.

---

54 http://timesofindia.indiatimes.com/india/Will-overcome-Maoist-problem-in-three-years-Chidambaram/articleshow/6233378.cms

55 http://www.hindustantimes.com/analysis/nda-is-pursuing-anti-adivasi-agenda-in-the-name-of-countering-the-maoists/article1-1260599.aspx

56 SalwaJudum claimed as a 'peace' movement, in Chhattisgarh between 2005 and 2009forcibly evicted 3.5 lakh Adivasis from 640 villages in anti-Maoist operations. Many Adivasis were incarcerated in 'camps' run by Judum members and state forces and subjected to brutal forms of torture and sexual violence. Further when it was succeeded by the state-led Operation Greenhunt from September 2009 onward, the Judum members found new identities as SPOs (Special Police Officers) who accompanied the security forces in 'area domination exercises', a euphemism for state terror. The Supreme Court in 2011 held that SPOs were unconstitutional and demanded their immediate disbanding but a significant section had already morphed itself into KoyaCommandos and the rest were regularised as police personnel by the state government.

57 Chhavinder Karma, son of the slain Mahendra Karma made this announcement on 5th May, 2015 http://www.countercurrents.org/cdro100515.htm

58 http://economictimes.indiatimes.com/news/economy/infrastructure/big-development-push-for-chhattisgarh-mous-worth-rs-24000-cr-signed-during-pm-narendra-modis-visit/articleshow/47212562.cms

Conclusion

For over two decades now the government, the policy makers and the media in tandem have been raving about 'Roaring India'[59], 'Shining India'[60], 'Growth Miracle of India'[61]; India apparently is poised to leap into a superpower status.[62] And yet, all these accounts have to grudgingly admit that in spite of the stupendous economic growth for over a quarter of a century now, majority of the Indians are miserably poor. In fact, the country seems to have been bifurcated into two different and mutually exclusive nations—one of the super rich comparable to the global elite and the other comparable to the poorest regions of the world. One third of the world's 1.2 billion poorest people live in India, according to the latest Millennium Development Goalsreportby the UN.[63] The rulers have been trying to address this impasse, by attempting to identify the 'poor' and implement targeted policy measures. But they have had practically no success in this endeavour. In the present piece we have tried to argue that this is because economic poverty and extreme inequality is merely the symptom of a deeper malaise afflicting Indian society. The poor are poor and continue to be so because they have no political voice in the present system. Therefore, trying to implement targeted poverty alleviation measures (even honest efforts) is akin to attempting to cure chicken pox by addressing every individual blister;an effort however glorious but doomed to fail.In fact, the whole exercise of defining poverty and identifying the poor to avoid 'leakages' obfuscates the real issue. As long as the structural political disparity exists (the disease) in society, poverty (symptoms) would also be there. Therefore,till the power equation changes the poor of the world would remain the 'Nobodies', as described poignantly by the recently deceased Uruguayan author Eduardo Galeano:

---

[59] http://daily.bhaskar.com/article/NAT-TOP-video-of-launch-of-make-in-india-in-germany-is-proud-moment-narendra-modi-4968862-NOR.html

[60] http://en.wikipedia.org/wiki/India_Shining

[61] http://www.economist.com/node/17147648

[62] http://fortune.com/2015/01/25/india-the-next-superpower/

[63] http://time.com/2999550/india-home-to-most-poor-people/

The Nobodies

Fleas dream of buying themselves a dog, and nobodies dream of escaping poverty:
That one magical day good luck will suddenly rain down onthem—will rain down in buckets.
But good luck doesn't rain down yesterday, today, tomorrow, or ever.
Good luck doesn't even fall in afine drizzle, no matter how hard the nobodies summon it,
Even if their left hand is tickling, or if they begin the new day with their right foot, or start the New Year with a change of brooms.

The nobodies: nobody's children, owners of nothing. The nobodies: the no ones, the nobodied, running like rabbits, dying through life, screwed every which way.

Who are not, but could be.
Who don't speak languages, but dialects.
Who don't have religions, but superstitions.
Who don't create art, but handicrafts.
Who don't have culture, but folklore.
Who are not human beings, but human resources.
Who do not have faces, but arms.
Who do not have names, but numbers.
Who do not appear in the history of the world, but in the police blotter of the local paper.
The nobodies, who are not worth the bullet that kills them.[64]

And history has taught us that rulers have never shared political power willingly with the masses.

[64] Eduardo Galeano, *Open Veins of Latin America: Five Centuries of the Pillage of a Continent*

Demographic Dividend Opportunities and Challenges

— Paramjit Singh and Balwinder Singh Tiwana

IT IS frequently assumed that the growth in population is an important stimulus to economic growth. The present phase of demographic changes in India has been characterised as 'advantage' for the economic growth, with an argument that due to the increasing proportion of young population in the total population, the dependency ratio is declining in India. But the demographic dividend, which India claims, is an opportunity as well as challenge. In order to cash in on the demographic dividend, the task for India is to utilise the potential workforce in productive activities by generating secure and long-term employment opportunities. But the recent employment situation shows that the growth of organised sector (both public and private) is negligible in India and most of the organised public sector has recorded negative employment growth. The withdrawal of the state from direct production activities is a serious concern for the common people in India. The actual picture of distribution of workforce shows that most of India's working population is employed in low productive agricultural activities.

The introduction of capital-intensive technology in the private and foreign capital-driven manufacturing and other activities has reduced the possibility of absorption of increased working population. The question of employability for both, the rising workforce and workforce already involved in low productive jobs, becomes very crucial for India. This paper is an attempt to examine India's claim of demographic dividend.

The first section of the paper deals with India's demographic features in order to look at the changing nature of the composition of population over a period of time. In the second part, we examine the question of demographic dividends and the growth dynamics, as well as the paradox of technological revolution and employability in India.

Demographic Profile of India

The world experienced a dramatic population growth during the twentieth century. The number of inhabitants doubled from 3 to 6 billion during the period of 40 years (from 1960 to 2000). In India, the population growth was more rapid during the same period. The population of India increased from 448 million to 1.04 billion during the above period and the recent census data shows that the population of India was 1.21 billion in 2011. In order to allay fears posed by high population growth, the demographers and economists have come up with the new idea that it is not the population size that matters but the age structure (Government of India 2012-13). In order to link the population growth with the economic growth, demographers use the 'demographic transition' and age structure of population as their tools for analysis.

In case of India, the data on selected demographic indicators (not relative to other nations but in absolute terms) shows improvement over a period of time. As far as health-related indicators are concerned, there has been a significant improvement in some of the key indicators. The annual growth rate of population shows a steady decline and it is likely to decline further in the future (see Figure 1). The decline of crude birth and death rate are positive signs for health and growth in the country. The decline in death rate has resulted in the increase in life expectancy in India, which in absolute terms has improved a lot since independence (see Figure 2).

The decline in infant mortality rate (another important indicator of health) is contributing qualitatively to the indicators of demography (see Figure 3).

Figure 1: Average annual rate of Population Change

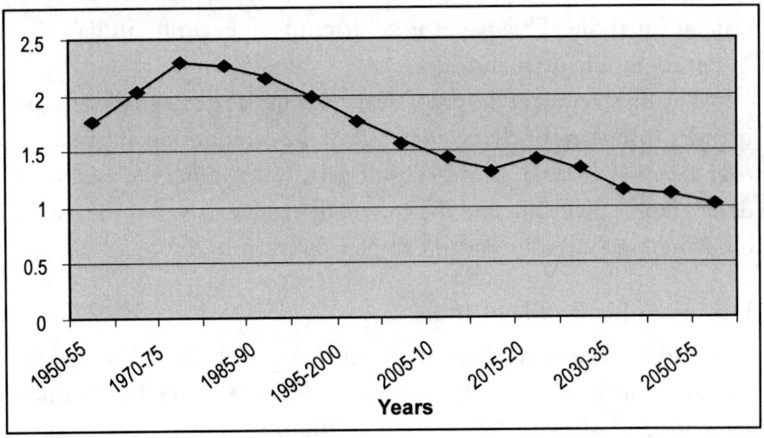

Figure 2: Crude Birth and Death Rate

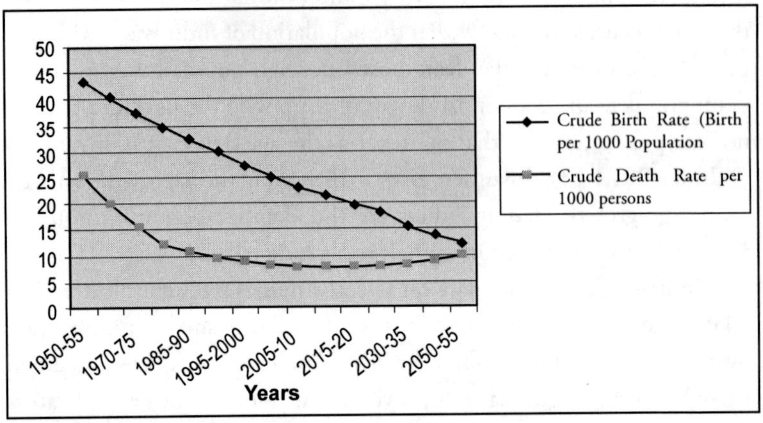

Source: World Population Perspectives, United Nation, 2010.

The other crucial qualitative indicator, which requires a close examination, is the literacy rate. To exploit the demographic dividend, India needs a workforce which is skilled and which can understand the complexities of production processes. As shown in Fig 4, the literacy rate in India has increased from 18.33 per cent in 1951 to 74.04 per cent in 2011. Along with literacy, the level of knowledge and skill also matters, as in many industrial and service sector jobs, skill requirements now are quite high. According to the experts, the demographic profile of India, in this respect also, is quite favourable.

Figure 3: Infant Mortality Rate

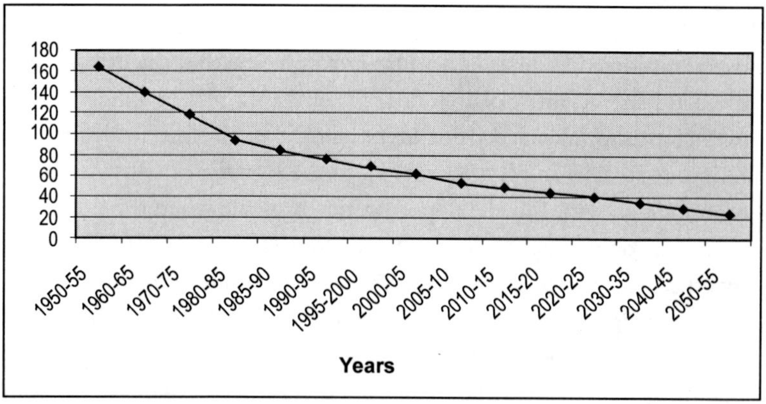

Figure 4: Crude Literacy Rate

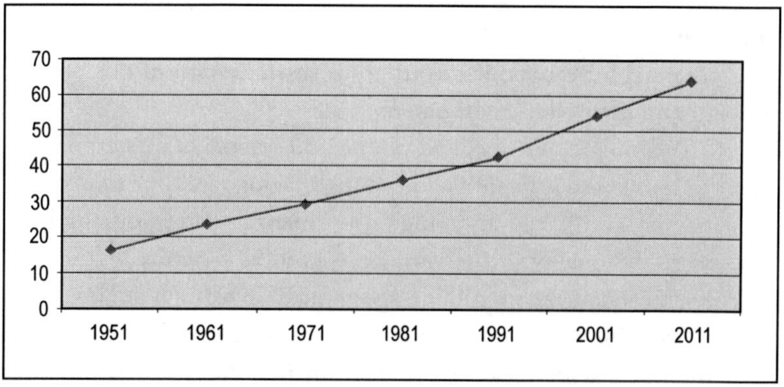

Source: Census of India, Provisional Population Tables, 2011.

Demographic Dividend and Growth Dynamics

It is an empirically well proved fact that the growth in per capita income is driven by the growth of labour productivity (what an average worker produces), and growth in employment. The rising proportion of population in the working age group is an advantage categorised as 'demographic dividend' for higher economic growth. The decomposition of population into the different age groups, ie. between labour force (15-64 age group) and those outside of it (usually old age dependent and dependent children), gives the estimate of the working-age population. The higher proportion of labour force age group has been considered as an advantage for long-term and sustainable growth.

The high working-age population in economic terminology has been considered as an asset because it is expected that the demographic dividend in the form of low dependency ratio allows higher surplus over consumption needed for investment. The decline in dependency ratio due to shift in age structure can have significant consequence for economic growth. But the opportunities available when the population enters the demographic dividend age requires initiative, in the form of investment and productive employment opportunities to absorb or cash on the budge, to accelerate the economic growth. The utilisation of demographic dividend is not an automatic process. There is no guarantee that the benefit of the demographic dividend will be exploited. As Bloom and Canning (2004) pointed out, there is nothing automatic about the link between the demographic change and economic growth. No doubt, the changes in age composition in favour of young population create the potential for economic growth, but the utilisation of this potential depends on the policy environment.

The demographic dividend can be understood as a determinant of growth in two ways. First, it allows a high saving rate (due to decline in dependency ratio), leading to high investment in education and health to ensure the quality of the workforce, seen as a necessary facilitator. Second, the increment in working-age population requires real investment in order to absorb this population in productive jobs by increasing the absorption capacity of existing units or by building the new units. *The historical experience of the East Asian progress has shown that the productive investment in education and health were the main determinant of higher economic growth.* Growth was further enhanced by adoption of export-oriented industrialisation strategy. *In all this process, the role of state was not only as a facilitator to private sector but also as an active and interventionist investor.*

Table 1: Trends in the Dependency Ratio in India (Medium Variant)

Years	Dependency Ratio	Child Dependency Ratio	Old-Age Dependency Ratio
1950	73	67	6
1960	76	70	6
1970	79	72	7
1975	77	71	7
1980	74	67	7
1985	72	65	7
1990	69	62	7
1995	68	60	8
2000	64	56	8
2005	60	51	8
2025	48	36	12
2050	50	27	22

Source: World Population Perspectives, United Nations, 2004.

At present, India is in the middle of a process to cash in on the opportunity created by the demographic dividend. The dependency ratio in India had begun to decline in the mid-1970s and it seems to be continuing for a long period. The data in Table 1 show that the old age dependency ratio was relatively stable up to 2005 and it started increasing afterwards. The child dependency ratio is the major contributing factor in overall dependency ratio. The data on child dependency ratio show the trend of secular decline after 1970s. According to these estimates, India has been in a phase of demographic dividend after the 1970s. But this opportunity, as mentioned above, requires active participation of the state in providing educational and health facilities to enhance the capabilities of the potential workforce. So far, however, the Indian state appears to lack in this commitment.

In India, the labour force participation rate of a young population (age group of 15-29) has recorded decline in rural areas for both males and females during 1999-2012. Still, it is more than 80 per cent in case of rural males in the age group of 20-24 and more than 95 per cent in the age group of 25-29 (see Table 2). But the workforce participation rate of both the age groups are not very high. The workforce participation rates for both the age groups (20-24 and 25-29) were 11 per cent and 12.5 per cent, respectively, during 2011-12 (Table 3). It indicates that though India is claiming the demographic dividend, it does not seem true in case of rural areas because the workforce participation of youth is very low. The situation is also the same or worse in case of rural women.

Table 2: Workforce Participation Rate of Youth according to Usual Status (PS+SS) (Per Cent)

	Age Group		
	15-19	**20-24**	**25-29**
Rural Male			
1999-2000	53.2	88.9	97.5
2004-05	52.9	89.1	98.2
2011-12	33.3	81.3	97.5
Rural Female			
1999-2000	31.4	42.5	49.8
2004-05	33.1	43.5	53.0
2011-12	16.4	29.7	36.9
Urban Male			
1999-2000	36.6	75.5	95.1
2004-05	38.1	76.9	95.7
2011-12	25.6	66.4	95.1
Urban Female			
1999-2000	12.1	19.1	21.4
2004-05	14.4	25.0	26.1
2011-12	8.9	19.7	25.3

Source: NSSO, Employment and Unemployment Situation in India, 68th Round, 2011-12.

As far as urban areas are concerned, the picture is not much different. In case of workforce participation rate of urban males, it has decline from 75.5 per cent to 66.4 per cent in the age group of 20-24 during

1999-2000 to 2011-12. Whereas in case of 25-29 age group, the percentage of workforce participation remained the same (95.1 per cent) during the given period. In case of young urban females, the participation rate was less than the participation rate of young females in rural areas for both 20-24 and 25-29 age groups. It was 11.1 per cent for the 20-24 age group and 13.7 per cent for the 25-29 age group during 1999-2000 and it has recorded 10.6 per cent in the 20-24 age group and 14.89 per cent in the 25-29 age group during 2011-12. Whereas in case of urban female youth, there was a sharp decline in work force participation rate for the age group of 24-29 from 39.9 per cent in 1999-2000 to 14.8 per cent in 2011-12.

Table 3: Workforce Participation Rate of Youth according to Usual Status (PS+SS) (Per Cent)

	Age Group		
	15-19	**20-24**	**25-29**
Rural Male			
1999-2000	9.4	12.2	13.4
2004-05	9.2	12.5	12.7
2011-12	6.0	11.0	12.5
Rural Female			
1999-2000	9.0	11.8	13.7
2004-05	8.8	11.1	12.4
2011-12	5.9	9.5	11.7
Urban Male			
1999-2000	9.0	11.8	13.7
2004-05	8.8	11.1	12.4
2011-12	4.2	10.6	14.9
Urban Female			
1999-2000	10.5	12.6	30.9
2004-05	12.0	11.9	31.5
2011-12	4.8	10.8	14.8

Source: NSSO, Employment and Unemployment Situation in India, 68th Round, 2011-12.

The implication of the above data is that the government's claim of demographic advantage does not seem quite true if we examine it on the basis of workforce participation rate of youth in both rural and urban areas, according to government surveys. Urban areas, which in most of the economic theories of development, have been considered as dynamic spaces to attract the young, are not able to attract the youth in the work force in case of India. The main reason behind the low-youth workforce participation rate in urban areas is that this so-called dynamic space is not able to provide enough decent employment opportunities to attract India's young population.

Policymakers and some economists claim that due to the opening up of the economy for foreign capital, the domestic human resources and working age population have got utilised efficiently, leading to improved growth rate of the Indian economy in recent years. However, it is very clear from the above data that the workforce participation rate of young population is not high enough to support the above argument.

Technological Revolution and Question of Employability

Employability becomes an important issue in the current phase of technology-driven economies. There are some crucial changes, which the world economies are experiencing in general, and the developing world in particular. These changes are associated with the rapid technological process, globalisation and liberalisation. The question of 'employability' becomes important due to the decline of industrial domination and rise of service and knowledge economies, necessitating a new form of preparation for the workers. There is a demand for a new type of educational structure to prepare the workers according to the demand of skill required for the new types of jobs emerging every day. The relevant issue for economies, particularly those that are labour-abundant like India, is that, can their service sector and high technology sectors have enough potential to absorb the vast amount of available youth workforce in the organised segments?

Conclusion

Since the 1970s onwards, the demographic transition of India has been considered as favorable for higher economic growth because the proportion of young population is increasing and dependency ratio is decreasing. But the utilisation of demographic advantage is not only a economic phenomenon, it is political also. It heavily depends upon the will of the state to use the potential workforce in an effective manner through provision of education and health facilities and generation of productive employment opportunities. According to the government's claim, the rising proportion of population in the working age group will be considered as the 'new growth driver' in the future. But the data of workforce participation rate of youth does not so far support this claim. Even if we agree with the government claim of possibilities of demographic dividend, then productive employment opportunities for the available workforce is a crucial factor in the nation's ability to utilise this dividend.

The utilisation of the working population is only possible if the state takes the real initiative in the form of investment in education and health and direct production activities. If India really wants to enter into the age of demographic dividend, then the most effective way is to provide productive employment opportunities to the rising proportion of young population. The government should directly intervene in the economy in order to build the industrial and infrastructural base to shift the population from low productive jobs to high productive jobs.

References

1. Bloom D E and D Canning (2004), Global Demographic Change: Dimensions and Economic Significance, *Nation Bureau of Economic Research Working Paper No.10817.*

2. Government of India (2013), *Economic Survey 2012-13*, Oxford University Press.

3. United Nations (2004), *World Population Perspectives*, United Nation Population Fund.

Appendix

Demographic Profile of India

Years	Crude Birth Rate (Birth per 1000 Population	Crude Death Rate per 1000 persons	Life Expectancy at birth (years)	Infant Mortality Rate
1950-55	43.3	25.5	37.9	165
1960-65	40.4	19.8	44.1	140
1970-75	37.5	15.0	50.8	118
1980-85	34.5	11.8	56.2	95
1985-90	32.5	10.9	57.7	85
1990-95	30.0	10.2	59.0	76
1995-2000	27.2	9.4	60.7	69
2000-05	24.8	8.7	62.5	61
2005-10	23.1	8.3	64.2	53
2010-15	21.3	7.9	66.0	48
2015-20	19.6	7.7	67.4	44
2020-25	18.0	7.7	68.7	40
2030-35	15.5	8.1	71.0	34
2040-45	13.6	8.9	72.9	29
2050-55	12.1	9.9	74.4	25

Source: World Population Prospectus, United Nations, 2010.

Employment Prospects in Neoliberal India

— Praveen Jha and Avanindra Nath Thakur

THIS PAPER seeks to examine the broad trends relating to employment conditions in the neoliberal reform era (since early 1990s). This has been attempted in the context of exploring the prospects of better livelihood conditions for the masses in general and labour in particular (with respect to changing policy of the Indian government during the last couple of years). In doing so, it primarily relies on secondary data sources such as National Sample Survey Reports for relevant years and the recent budget documents of the central government.

Since independence, India has made inadequate progress in terms of addressing the problems of poverty, unemployment and occupational structural transformation. In spite of the fact that during the first four decades after independence, there has been substantial focus on direct measures to overcome the obstacles in this regard, the achievements on these counts were, nevertheless, unimpressive. While the strategy of relatively autonomous development and public sector-led industrialisation during the same period resulted in respectable growth outcomes with reference to any appropriate benchmark, it remained far from satisfactory in regards to raising the livelihood conditions of significantly large section of people at the margin. Moreover, since early 1990s, that is during the era of neoliberal reforms, the aforementioned correlates of the well-being of the masses in general have come under further relative pressure. As is well-known, even today a significantly large proportion of the population of the country relies for their livelihood primarily on agriculture, under extremely fragile conditions.

Evidently, the prospect of any substantial shift in occupational structure away from agriculture seems remote in India, as in most developing countries, in the near future. In retrospect, the 'dual economy' models and other 'modernisation' paradigms that economists had hypothesised would result in a relatively smooth transition in occupational structure, seemed to have gone wrong. In fact, as discussed elsewhere in some detail (Jha, 2003), in most of the developing world, even when the increases in output of the non-agricultural sectors have been rapid, growth of employment in such sectors have been far from impressive. For India, the share of agriculture in total employment has reduced from 73 per cent in 1950 to about 55 percent now but this decline, over the same period, has been much slower than that in the share of GDP (59 per cent to 17 per cent). Also, some of the transfer of workers to non-agricultural sectors may not be due to any positive development but on account of distress diversification (particularly in a variety of self-employed services), and may also hide the fact that sections of them happen to be part-time agricultural workers as well. Hence, it would be reasonable to argue that in terms of labour absorption in the modern manufacturing or services sector, the country is not favourably placed and a major decline in dependence on agriculture, and the transfer of labour into decent livelihood options elsewhere, does not seem to be on cards at least in the foreseeable future.

In the given backdrop, it is of utmost importance to assess the implications of the globally ascendant neoliberal policy regimes for employment scenario and overall well-being of labour. Persistence of high levels of unemployment in different regions of the global economy during the recent decades of neoliberal reforms lend strong support to the view that the macroeconomic policies based on such doctrines are hardly consistent with a progressive employment agenda, even in the structurally more favourably placed economies, let alone in the more adverse circumstances prevailing in most developing countries. As is well-known, among the major premises of neo-liberalism was the argument that in the case of developing countries, the inward looking capital-intensive import substitution policy had resulted in a bias against agriculture and other employment-intensive activities, with respect to both the domestic and external markets, and thus labour utilisation had been well below potential. Advocates of neo-liberalism hoped that the pro-market reforms would rectify the above noted bias and facilitate a surge of investment, both from domestic and foreign sources, in labour-intensive projects with significant export-orientation. All the available evidence since the ascendancy of the neoliberal economic policy package confirm that the expectations regarding greater labour utilisation in the global economy, through changes in structure as well as intensity of employment have not been realised. On the employment front, it is important to look at some of the trends mirrored into the changes in the policy environment as mentioned above in the nations's official data system, ie. the NSS.

Worker Population Ratio (WPR) and Employment Generation

Worker-population ratio (WPR) is a broad indicator of the availability of job opportunities[1], and on the whole, there has not been much change in this rate for the last three decades (table 1 & 2). However, the WPR in different rounds of NSS show some fluctuations, mainly on account of macroeconomic policy shifts. For instance, the increased government expenditure and consequently expansion of employment opportunities in rural areas during the decade of 1980s is clearly visible on overall WPR in rural areas between 1983 and 1993-94; over this period the WPR in rural areas increased by one percentage point on the 'usual basis', two percentage points on the 'weekly basis' and more than two percentage points on the 'daily basis'. This rise in the WPR, particularly on 'CDS basis' indicates the expansion of work opportunities created by various self- employment as well as casual wage employment programmes.

---

[1] As is well-acknowledged, the impact of residual absorption of labour is also included in this ratio.

However, the neoliberal regime has been marked by a tendency to compress the overall public expenditure in rural areas. Therefore, the decade of 1990s experienced a decline in the absorption capacity in the rural economy as a whole and consequently a fall in the WPR was observed for both male and female labour during the same period. After a noticeable dip in this rate during 1999-2000, there was a marginal recovery in 2004-05[2] for both male and female (particularly for female workers in both urban and rural areas). But, for the next three rounds in 2007-08, 2009-10 and 2011-12, while the WPR for rural male increased marginally, it declined for rural female and this indicated an overall worsening of the employment generation scenario in the rural areas. Looking at the entire neoliberal era, ie. from 1993-94 to 2011-12, WPR remained stagnant. Now, if we exclude the employment opportunities created by MNREGA during the later period, one can infer that the ability of the rural economy to generate adequate work has remained very limited.

For the entire period from 1983 to 2011-12, the above rate marginally improved for both urban males and females. In spite of high and sustained GDP growth for the last three decades, the overall worker population ratio for a person as a whole does not show rise in any significant manner during the recent period (ie. between 2004 and 2012), which clearly indicates a situation far from satisfactory on the employment generation front. For the urban female, WPR has shown a marginal rise, taking the entire period from 1983 to 2011-12.

As regards the rate of growth of rural employment since early 1980s: it increased at an annual rate of 1.72% between 1983 and 1993-94 before it nose-dived to 0.66 per cent between 1993-94 and 1999-2000; subsequently, it picked up to 1.97 per cent between 1999-2000 and 2004-05 (a year of indifferent agricultural performance)[3] and then fell again significantly. In urban areas, the growth rate of employment between 1983 and 1993-94 was 3.10% per annum. And it was

---

2 After 2004-05, It is followed by a dip again even below the level of 1983 (37.4 per cent) in 2007-08.

3 However, taking the period from 1999-2000 to 2007-08 (a good agricultural year) this rate declined significantly to 1.27 per cent.

approximately the same for the next decade also (ie. between 1993-94 and 2004-05, although there was decline during the first half but recovery during the second).

The point worth emphasising here is that between 2004-05 and 2009-10, though the economy witnessed a high growth rate, total number of usual with subsidiary-status workers increased only by 2.3 million. This was in sharp contrast to the relatively significant expansion of around 60 million during the previous period between 1999-00 and 2004-05.During the period from 1999-2000 to 2004-05 male employment increased by 20.2 million in rural areas, while in the next period from 2004-05 to 2009-10 it rose by only 13.4 million. The corresponding figures for the urban areas were 15 million and 9.8 million respectively. Rural female employment, which rose by 18.3 million during 1999-2000 and 2004-05, registered a decline of 19.2 million between 2004-05 and 2009-10. In the urban areas, the female employment rose by 6.4 million in the first and declined by 1.7 million during the next period (Chandrasekhar and Ghosh, 2010). During the most recent period, ie. between 2009-10 and 2011-12 there was further deceleration in the rate of employment generation on yearly basis in rural areas (for rural male, annual increase was 2.11 million and for rural female it was an annual decline of 4.4 million as compared to corresponding figures of 2.63 and 2.12 during 2004-05 to 2009-10)). However, a marginal recovery in these rates was witnessed in urban areas for both male and female during the same period.

Thus, a clear mismatch between the high rate of growth of GDP and pace of employment generation indicates a significant fall in the elasticity of employment with respect to output. In other words, the key message that gets reinforced by the latest round of the NSS is that the transition to a high growth trajectory has not delivered much on the employment front. The data since early 1990s indicate that the increase in employment seems to occur when workers, especially female workers, are pushed into the workforce by increased adversity in their economic circumstances (eg. a bad agriculture year), and there have been few positive impulse for employment. Moreover, organised manufacturing and services appear to contribute very little additional employment creation, and the expectation that these would add significantly to the generation of employment opportunities once neoliberal policies succeeded in delivering growth has hardly materialised. On the contrary, there has been a significant dip in the absolute count of the workers in organised segments of the economy. These facts cumulatively suggest that, in the years of high growth, much of the increase in employment was in the categories of casual and self-employment which had extremely adverse distributional and social welfare implications (Chandrasekhar and Ghosh 2007; Jha 2009; Jha& Thakur 2013, Chandrasekhar 2010; Himanshu 2011).

Unemployment Scenario

The relevant data, since early 1980s show a clear worsening in this respect during the reform period. In rural areas, between 1983 and 1993-94, there was a significant decline in the unemployment rate on CDS basis, both for male and female. During the next decade, between 1993-94 and 2004-05, the corresponding rates rose sharply.[4] In urban areas, there was a small decline in unemployment over the longer period, ie. 1983 to 2004-05, for both male and female workers, but it was hardly adequate to compensate the considerable worsening in rural areas. As emphasised repeatedly, such trends are indicative of setbacks in generation of productive employment opportunities and deterioration in the quality of employment in the recent growth process.

However, some positive trends in the reduction in unemployment rate are discernible during the period between 2004-05 and 2011-12. In rural areas the unemployment rate for male workers declined from 8 per cent in 2004-05 to 6.4 per cent in 2009-10 and 5.5 in 2011-12. For rural females, the corresponding figures were 8.7, 8.1 and 6.2 respectively on current daily basis. Similarly, in the urban areas the unemployment rate for male workers declined from 7.5 per cent in 2004-05 to 5.1 per cent in 2009-10 and further to 4.9 per cent in 2011-12. For urban females, these figures were 11.6, 9.1 and 8 respectively. Given the trend of stagnant regular wage, increasing casualisation and persisting informality in the labour market etc., these quantitative improvements in the unemployment rates in the recent period do not, however, indicate better

---

4 In 2007-08, for male workers, it reached the level even higher than that of in 1983.

quality jobs. Moreover, decline in unemployment rate can be attributed more to the decline in labour force participation rate than to the creation of sufficiently more jobs. Besides, in rural areas, MNREGA played a significant role and looking at the overall capacity of the rural economy to generate additional employment, it can be inferred that whatever improvement on the employment front is visible in rural areas can be attributed to MNREGA rather than to the rise in the systemic capacity to absorb additional labour force during the entire period under consideration.

Status of Employment:

Chart 1: Status of employment in different rounds of NSS survey for rural male

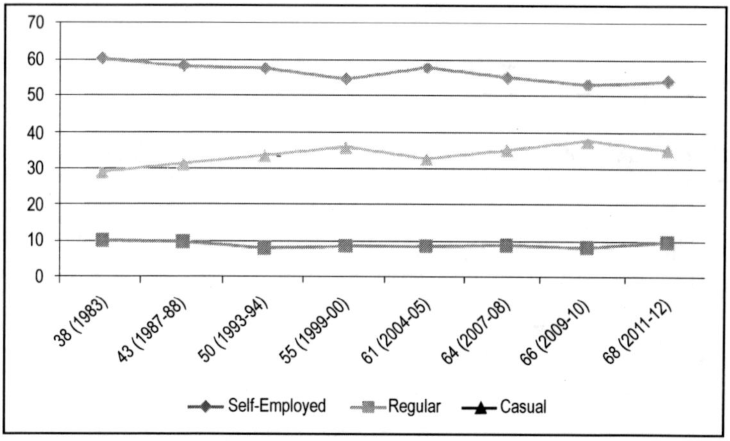

Chart 2: Status of employment in different rounds of NSS survey for rural female

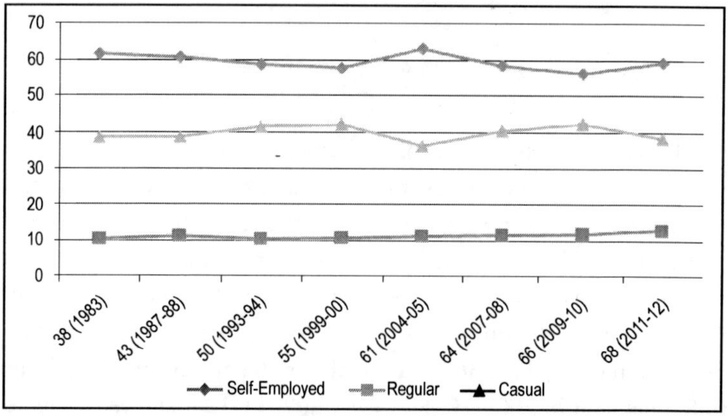

Chart 3: Status of employment in different rounds of NSS survey for urban male

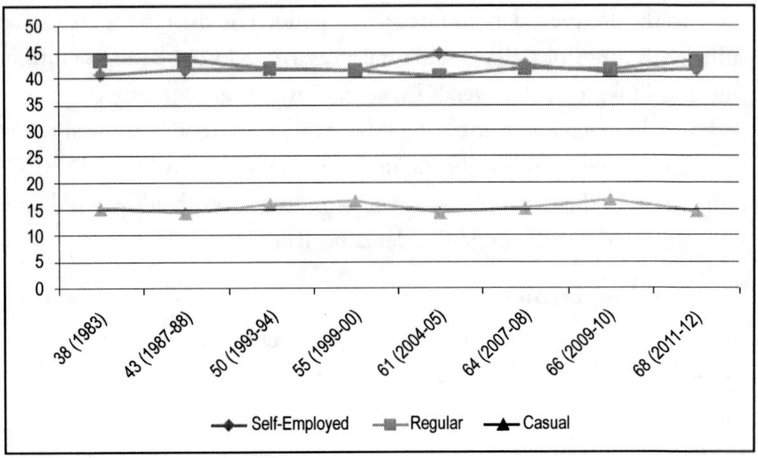

Chart 4: Status of employment in different rounds of NSS survey for urbanfemale

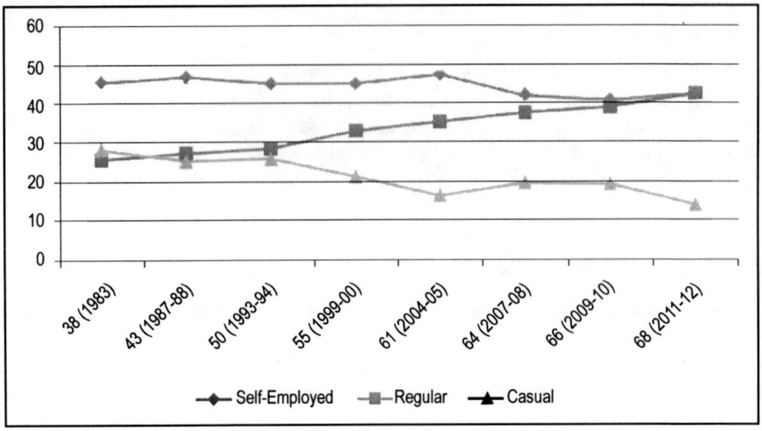

In regards to the quality of employment, there is hardly any doubt that over the period of almost three decades, a relative deterioration has remained one of the most visible characteristic of employment trends as captured in the NSS data. Regular employment as a whole has been under tremendous pressure during the last three decades, and it is instructive to look at the relevant numbers (table 5 and 6). For rural male, the proportion of regular employed was about 10 per cent in 1987, declined to 8.5 per cent in 2009-10. However, in 2011-12 it showed an increase and again reached at 10 per cent. Also, in urban areas, the share of regular employed in the male category remained more or less stagnant between 1999-00 and 2009-10 and clearly shows a significant decline between 1983 and 2009-10.

The marginal increase in regular employment during the period from 1983 to 2011-12, for both rural and urban females, was too small to raise the share of regular employed in total employment. We may also note that the annual increment in regular employment was about two million during 1993 to 2005, and it declined to approximately one million during 2005 to 2010.

Nevertheless, some sign of improvement in this regard is clearly visible during the most recent period from 2009-10 to 2011-12. However, the change in this regard has been too small to make any dent on the long-term gloomy scenario of relative worsening of quality of jobs both in rural and urban areas. Although the data for the 61st and 66th NSS rounds show that the rate of regular employment generation in the private organised sector has picked up recently, it is also clear that this was more than offset by decline in the share of regular employment in the rest of the economy. In fact, it is quite striking that over 80% of all new jobs created in the recent years have been of casual nature, with construction alone accounting for a substantial share.

In other words, in spite of the high growth rate in the Indian economy, the process of informalisation and casualisation in the world of work has been on the rise during the last two decades. A substantial segment of workers who are unable to find even casual employment often remain 'self-employed', which, to a large extent, is the same as being underemployed or disguisedly unemployed.[5] Further, it is quite clear that the process of casualisation and contractual employment has gained momentum in the organised sectors.

Modi Government and Prospects for Better Employment

Higher growth rates do not always necessarily imply the fulfillment of expectations about decent livelihood. In India, while for most of the years

[5] Eevidently, exception to such a trend would be a very small proportion of self-employed skilled workers who have done extremely well as self-employed, due to the opening of the new avenues like the expansion of ICT.

under the reform, the economy witnessed significantly higher growth rates, generation of a decent livelihood condition for overwhelming section of the population living at the margin is hardly discernible. Lower employment elasticity of the modern sector is not accidental but constitutes an inherent characteristic of the mainstream economic development (Patnaik 2007). Moreover, the conditions relating to employment has been even worse in rural areas as compared to urban areas for the entire period under the neoliberal reform. Though, some relief in rural India has been evident after the enactment of MNREGA (2006 onwards), it remains primarily restricted in helping them to sustain themselves economically rather than enhancing their livelihood conditions permanently. The *Economic Survey* (2014-15) also questions the performance of the economy in creating adequate employment opportunities. *'A cause for concern is the deceleration in the compound annual growth rate (CAGR) of employment during 2004-05 to 2011-12 to 0.5 per cent from 2.8 per cent during 1999-2000 to 2004-05 as against CAGRs of 2.9 per cent and 0.4 per cent respectively in the labour force for the same periods'* (Economic Survey 2014-15, pg 135). The Survey further states that, *'Self-employment continues to dominate, with a 52.2 per cent share in total employment. What is critical is the significant share of workers engaged in low-income generating activities. There are other issues of concern like poor employment growth in rural areas, particularly among females. Though employment of rural males is slightly better than that of females, long-term trends indicate a low and stagnant growth'* (Economic Survey 2014-15).

Arguably, any further promotion of the neoliberal agenda would affect, in all probability, the prospects of decent employment generation adversely. In other words, incentivising finance capital, prioritising the scope for the expansion of large businesses at the cost of small and marginal ones, shifting away the focus from the institutional reforms, dilution of labour laws, acquisition of lands in favour of large business projects etc. and above all a continuous decline in the relative share of public expenditures in rural areas and social sectors would, to a large extent, constitute obstacles rather than a solution of the problem in this regard.

Much in conformity with the broad foundations of neoliberal reforms the present NDA government seems committed to go a step further. Evidently, in the last year's Central Budget (2015-16), rural development and particularly agriculture did not figure with adequate attention. The allocation for the Ministry of Agriculture and the Department of Agriculture and Cooperation shows a decline. This decline is to the extent of Rs 1,713 crore from 2014-15 to 2015-16. Rashtriya Krishi Vikas Yojana, which has been the most important flagship scheme for the development of infrastructure in the agricultural sector, has witnessed substantial decline in budgetary allocation (from Rs8,444 crore in 2014-15 to Rs 4,500 crore in 2015-16) during the same period (CBGA report on Budget). Similar cuts were made in several other schemes such as the National Food Security Mission, National Horticulture Mission, National Mission for Sustainable Agriculture etc. However, in the latest Central Budget (2016-17) some reversal in these trends seemed evident. For instance, allocation for the Ministry of Agriculture including interest subvention, Rashtriya Krishi Vikas Yojana, and National Food Security Mission witnessed a rise in this Budget. Nevertheless, the extent of rise can hardly be considered appropriate as the total allocation under these heads still remained below the level that was realised in 2014-15. Moreover, taking into the account of negative employment elasticity of this sector for couple of years, increasing incidents of farmers committing suicides, and limitation in regards to growth in productivity of various farm products, the Budgetary allocation for this sector needs a sharp rise which in a given scenario seems a distant dream. Thus, persistent negligence of rural area in general and agricultural sector in particular will increasingly stress the employment opportunities and livelihood conditions of a large number of people living in rural areas.

One of the recent initiatives of the government is to focus on skill development, which would arguably provide better job opportunities. However, limited availability of quality jobs, rather than quality labour, seems to be the constraint which renders such initiatives to be less of a success. This is reflected in increasing unemployment rate among the educated and young age groups over the last decade, as indicated in various NSS rounds data. In India, because of its high population, even small enrollment rate in higher education is sufficient to bring significantly large number of educated persons into the labour force. The challenge is, however, to sufficiently increase the availability of regular skilled jobs in the secondary and tertiary sector. This requires a paradigm shift in the policy framework towards a more direct role of the government and providing strong institutional support for the people living at the margin.

However, the last Central budget shows a step backward in this regard. It seems that the idea of market fundamentalism is getting its root deeper in the overall economic structure of the country. A big corporate tax relaxation of five per cent also supports such hypothesis. It is generally argued that expansion of corporations would shift the workers from unorganised to the organised sector and thus will be instrumental in improving the quality of jobs in general. However, the experience of the Indian economy in this regard hardly facilitates any optimistic thinking. In spite of the fact that there has been a rise in the share of the formal sector in terms of total output, total share of employment in the informal sector nearly remained stagnant (92.7 % in 2004-05 to 91.9 % in 2011-12) between 2004 and 2012 *(Economic Survey 2014-15).*

Even at the risk of having a myopic view, one can hardly resist the temptation of judging the impact of the neoliberal policies at the completion of nearly two and half decades since its inception. This especially becomes an economic imperative at the current political juncture when the social urge for change has democratically elected a party with a large majority in expectation of 'Achhe Din'. An evaluation of the last two decades of neoliberal regimes reflects a visible decline in. government activities. Except a few significant policy initiatives such as the enactment of MNREGA, the negligence is prominent in rural areas as compared to its urban counterpart.The adverse implications of such policy changes are clearly reflected in the deteriorating working conditions of the workforce in general and rural labour in particular.

Disillusion about the prospects of those policies might be safely concluded to be one of reasons for 'change' of government. However, with the coming of new government, it seems that the tenets of neoliberal reforms have further deepened. More precisely, the broad direction of the first two full Budgets of the central government, prominent announcements regarding the future economic policies and several legislative initiatives, such as reforms in labour laws, amendment in land acquisition bill and hasty implementation of GST etc. reflect a sharp move towards a market fundamentalist regime. Therefore, given the downbeat experiences of market-led development in the last two decades, any improvement in the employment conditions in near future seems a distant reality. Moreover, lack of prioritisation of rural as well as the agriculture sector in government policies, along with the decline in the public expenditure in social sector, do not indicate a silver lining for betterment of livelihood conditions of this country's sizable section of toiling poor in the near future.

References

1. Chandrasekhar CP (2010): India's New, High-Growth Trajectory: Implications for Demand, Technology and Employment, presented at 52nd Annual Conference of ISLE, Dharwad, Dec 17-19.
2. Chandrasekhar CP & Ghosh Jayati (2007): Recent Employment Trends in India and China: An Unfortunate Convergence, www.macroscan.com, Apr 5.
3. *Economic Survey* (2014-15): Government of India, Oxford University Press.
4. Jha Praveen (2009): The Well-being of Labour in Contemporary Indian Economy: What's active labour market policy got to do with it? Employment Analysis and Research Unit, ILO.
5. Jha, Praveen (2003): Issues relating to Employment in India in the Era of Globalization, *Social Scientist*, Vol. 31, No. 11/12, Nov-Dec.
6. Jha & Thakur (2013): Employment and Unemployment: Contexts and prospects, in Zoya Hasan & Mashirul Hasan (Ed.) *Social Development Report 2012*, Oxford University Press, New Delhi.
7. Himanshu (2011): Employment Trends in India: A Re-examination, *Economic and Political Weekly*, Vol XL VI No. 37, September 10.
8. NSSO Reports, Various Issues
9. Patnaik (2007): A Model of Growth of the Contemporary Indian Economy, *Economic and Political Weekly*, Vol 42, No. 22, June 02-June 08.

Table 1: Worker-population ratio in rural areas

NSS ROUND	Rural Male				Rural Female			
	PS	*PS+SS*	*CWS*	*CDS*	*PS*	*PS+SS*	*CWS*	*CDS*
38 (1983)	*52.8*	*54.7*	*51.1*	*48.2*	*24.8*	*34*	*22.7*	*19.8*
43 (1987-88)	*51.7*	*53.9*	*50.4*	*50.1*	*24.5*	*32.3*	*22*	*20.7*
50 (1993-94)	*53.8*	*55.3*	*53.1*	*50.4*	*23.4*	*32.8*	*26.7*	*22*
55 (1999-00)	*52.2*	*53.1*	*51*	*47.8*	*23.1*	*29.9*	*25.3*	*20.4*
61 (2004-05)	*53.5*	*54.6*	*52.4*	*48.8*	*24.2*	*32.7*	*27.5*	*21.6*
64 (2007-08)	*53.8*	*54.8*	*52.5*	*49*	*21.6*	*28.9*	*23.7*	*18.7*
66 (2009-10)	*53.7*	*54.7*	*53.1*	*50.1*	*20.2*	*26.1*	*22.3*	*18.2*
68 (2011-12)	*53.5*	*54.3*	*52.6*	*50.4*	*17.6*	*24.8*	*20.7*	*16.9*

Source: Various rounds of NSS Reports.

Table 2: Worker-population ratio in urban areas

NSS rounds	Urban male				Urban female			
	PS	*PS+SS*	*CWS*	*CDS*	*PS*	*PS+SS*	*CWS*	*CDS*
38 (1983)	*50*	*51.2*	*49.2*	*47.3*	*12*	*15.1*	*11.8*	*10.6*
43 (1987-88)	*49.6*	*50.6*	*49.2*	*47.7*	*11.8*	*15.2*	*11.9*	*11*
50 (1993-94)	*51.3*	*52.1*	*51.1*	*49.8*	*12.1*	*15.5*	*13.9*	*12*
55 (1999-00)	*51.3*	*51.8*	*50.9*	*49*	*11.7*	*13.9*	*12.8*	*11.1*
61 (2004-05)	*54.1*	*54.9*	*53.7*	*51.9*	*13.5*	*16.6*	*15.2*	*13.3*
64 (2007-08)	*55*	*55.4*	*54.5*	*52.9*	*11.8*	*13.8*	*12.9*	*11.3*
66 (2009-10)	*53.9*	*54.3*	*53.6*	*52.2*	*11.9*	*13.8*	*13*	*11.7*
68 (2011-12)	*54.2*	*54.6*	*53.9*	*52.8*	*12.5*	*14.7*	*13.8*	*12.5*

Source: same as table 1.

Table 3: Unemployment rate in rural areas

NSS ROUND	Rural Male				Rural Female			
	PS	PS+SS	CWS	CDS	PS	PS+SS	CWS	CDS
38 (1983)	*2.1*	*1.4*	*3.7*	*7.5*	*1.4*	*0.7*	*4.3*	*9*
43 (1987-88)	*2.8*	*1.8*	*4.2*	*4.6*	*3.5*	*2.4*	*4.4*	*6.7*
50 (1993-94)	*2*	*1.4*	*3.1*	*5.6*	*1.3*	*0.9*	*2.9*	*5.6*
55 (1999-00)	*2.1*	*1.7*	*3.9*	*7.2*	*1.5*	*1*	*3.7*	*7*
61 (2004-05)	*2.1*	*1.6*	*3.8*	*8*	*3.1*	*1.8*	*4.2*	*8.7*
64 (2007-08)	*2.3*	*1.9*	*4.1*	*8.5*	*1.9*	*1.1*	*3.5*	*8.1*
66 (2009-10)	*1.9*	*1.6*	*3.2*	*6.4*	*2.4*	*1.6*	*3.7*	*8*
68 (2011-12)	*2.1*	*1.7*	*3.3*	*5.5*	*2.9*	*1.7*	*3.5*	*6.2*

Source: same as table 1.

Table 4: Unemployment rate in urban areas

NSS ROUND	Urban Male				Urban Female			
	PS	PS+SS	CWS	CDS	PS	PS+SS	CWS	CDS
38 (1983)	*5.9*	*5.1*	*6.7*	*9.2*	*6.9*	*4.9*	*7.5*	*11*
43 (1987-88)	*6.1*	*5.2*	*6.6*	*8.8*	*8.5*	*6.2*	*9.2*	*12*
50 (1993-94)	*5.4*	*4.1*	*5.2*	*6.7*	*8.3*	*6.1*	*7.9*	*10.4*
55 (1999-00)	*4.8*	*4.5*	*5.6*	*7.3*	*7.1*	*5.7*	*7.3*	*9.4*
61 (2004-05)	*4.4*	*3.8*	*5.2*	*7.5*	*9.1*	*6.9*	*9*	*11.6*
64 (2007-08)	*4*	*3.8*	*4.7*	*6.9*	*6.6*	*5.2*	*6.5*	*9.5*
66 (2009-10)	*3*	*2.8*	*3.6*	*5.1*	*7*	*5.7*	*7.2*	*9.1*
68 (2011-12)	*3.2*	*3*	*3.8*	*4.9*	*6.6*	*5.2*	*6.7*	*8*

Source: same as table 1.

Table 5: Status of Employment in rural areas

NSS Rounds (year)	Rural Male			Rural Female		
	Self-Employed	Regular	Casual	Self-employed	Regular	Casual
38 (1983)	*60.5*	*10.3*	*29.2*	*61.9*	*2.8*	*35.3*
43 (1987-88)	*58.6*	*10*	*31.4*	*60.8*	*3.7*	*35.5*
50 (1993-94)	*57.9*	*8.3*	*33.8*	*58.5*	*2.8*	*38.7*
55 (1999-00)	*55*	*8.8*	*36.2*	*57.3*	*3.1*	*39.6*
61 (2004-05)	*58.1*	*9*	*32.9*	*63.7*	*3.7*	*32.6*
64 (2007-08)	*55.4*	*9.1*	*35.5*	*58.3*	*4.1*	*37.6*
66 (2009-10)	*53.5*	*8.5*	*38*	*55.7*	*4.4*	*39.9*
68 (2011-12)	*54.5*	*10*	*35.5*	*59.3*	*5.6*	*35.1*

Source: same as table 1.

Table 5: Status of Employment in urban areas

NSS Rounds (year)	Urban Male			Urban Female		
	Self-Employed	Regular	Casual	Self-Employed	Regular	Casual
38 (1983)	*40.9*	*43.7*	*15.4*	*45.8*	*25.8*	*28.4*
43 (1987-88)	*41.7*	*43.7*	*14.6*	*47.1*	*27.5*	*25.4*
50 (1993-94)	*41.7*	*42.1*	*16.2*	*45.4*	*28.6*	*26*
55 (1999-00)	*41.5*	*41.7*	*16.8*	*45.3*	*33.3*	*21.4*
61 (2004-05)	*44.8*	*40.6*	*14.6*	*47.7*	*35.6*	*16.7*
64 (2007-08)	*42.7*	*42.0*	*15.4*	*42.3*	*37.9*	*19.9*
66 (2009-10)	*41.1*	*41.9*	*17.0*	*41.1*	*39.3*	*19.6*
68 (2011-12)	*41.7*	*43.4*	*14.9*	*42.8*	*42.8*	*14.3*

Source: same as table 1.

Challenges for Female Labour Participation in India

— Seema

THE STRUCTURAL changes occurring in India's labour market open up several new challenges. The first challenge is with respect to the labour force and workforce participation rates (LFPR &WFPR) in the country, which are relatively low and are also declining. [Labour force participation rate is the proportion of the population ages 15 and older that is economically active: percentage of total population modeled on ILO estimate. For India it shows as 54% in June 2016. http://data.worldbank.org/indicator/SL.TLF.CACT.ZS. In India, both labor force and workforce terms are used.]

Labour Force Participation Rate (LFPR)

Labour Force refers to the population which supplies or offers to supply labour for pursuing economic activities for the production of goods and services and, therefore, includes both 'employed' and 'unemployed' persons/person-days.

The estimates of LFPR in different approaches provide information on the following aspects: i) number of persons in labour force according to the usual status (ps) ie. by considering usual principal activity only,

ii) number of persons in labourforce according to the usual status (ps+ss) ie. by considering usual principal and subsidiary economic activity together iii) number of persons in labourforce according to CWS ie. number of persons either employed or unemployed on an average in a week of 7 days preceding the date of survey iv) number of person-days in labourforce according to CDS, ie. number of days on an average during the reference period of 7 days preceding the date of survey where a person was found either employed or unemployed.

Worker Population Ratio (WPR/WFPR)

The estimates of employed (or worker) according to the number of persons who worked for a relatively long part of 365 days preceding the date of survey. The work force, according to the usual status (ps+ss) includes a person who worked for a relatively long part of the 365 days preceding the date of survey and (b) those persons from among the remaining population who had worked at least for 30 days during the reference period of 365 days preceding the date of survey. The workforce measured in terms of current weekly status (CWS) gives number of persons employed on an average in a week of 7 days during the survey period.

The participation of the rural male in India in the labour market was 55.5% in 1983 and it has remained more or less same in the year 2011-12. As compared to the rural male, the participation rate of rural female is much lower. The LFPR for rural female had been 34.2% and has declined to 25.3% in 2011-12. In urban India, male's participation in the labour market was 54% in 1983 and it increased to 56.3% in 2011-12. On the other side, LFPR of the urban females is not only lower than that of their male counterparts but also lower than that of rural females. The LFPR for urban female was 15.9% in 1983 and it has remained more or less same at the level of 15.5% in 2011-12. These rates are also much lower in India in comparison to other developing countries.

The results of the 61st round (2004-05) of NSSO pointed to a reversal of the earlier trend of stagnation in employment growth. There was a net addition of 59.4 million[1] new jobs in the country between 1999-00

1 All the figures are based on the NSSO reports on the Employment and Unemployment in India and the figures have been arrived at using the proportions for Usual Principal and Subsidiary status only.

and 2004-05. Out of this 59.4 million, an increase of 25 million was on account of female workers. Questions had been raised on the quality of employment generated during this period. The reason was that out of this net increase of 60 million in workforce, around 50 million workers were self-employed workers.

Females accounted for a significant part of the increase in self-employment. Out of net addition of 25 million female in the workforce, 22 million were reported as self-employed (rural female-18 million and urban female-4 million). Papola (2008) named this workforce as the 'working poor' and Abraham (2009) called this growth in rural employment as 'distress-driven employment'. According to Abraham, 'Under conditions of distress, when income levels fall below sustenance, then that part of the normally non-working population is forced to enter the labour market to supplement household (HH) income.' Abraham (2009).

If we look at the sectoral data location and segment wise, we find that 83% of the working rural females in India were still working in the agriculture sector in 2004-05. Nisha and Ravi Srivastava (2010) called it as 'creeping feminisation of agriculture'. According to them 'male workers are moving out of rural areas but for women, this movement has been very difficult. One of the major factors which compel women to engage in agriculture is low level of education. About 86% of female agricultural labourers and 74% of female farmers are either illiterate or have education below the primary level.'

The results of the 66th round of NSSO (2009-10) showed that there had been a huge fall in the growth rates of labour force and workforce between 2004-05 and 2009-10. There was an addition of only around one million jobs per annum during this period compared to an addition of around 12 million jobs per annum in the previous period (1999-00 to 2004-05). During this period, India's GDP grew at an average growth rate of 9%, but the employment statistics showed opposite results. For the first time since 1973, in the history of these surveys, the female workforce showed a negative growth during this period. NSSO data shows, approximately 21 million women withdrew from the labour market during this period against net addition of 25 million women in the previous period. Out of the withdrawal of 21 million females from the labour force, 20 million were rural females, largely those who were self-employed. This was seen as reversal of the exceptional increase in the female labour force during 1999-00 and 2004-05 by many (Abraham 2009, Klasen and Pieters 2012, Thomas 2014).

The women who were opting out of the labour force reported their status mainly as attending education institutions and attending to domestic duties. Females attending educational institutions as percentage of the total female population increased from 22.2% in 2004-05 to 24% in 2009-10. The share of women involved in domestic duties (both 92&93 codes) has increased from 32% in 2004-05 to 38% in 2009-10.

Many studies (Chandrasekhar and Ghosh 2011; Rangarajan et al 2011 etc) have found 'Missing female labour' as the single most important component for the slowdown in the growth rate of labour force in India during the period 2004-05 to 2009-10. Different reasons were quoted by these researchers for such a huge fall in FLPR during this period. These were: (a) increase in the level of rural income indicated by high growth rate of real per capita household expenditure in rural India, observed during the latest two rounds of NSSO Household expenditure surveys. As a result, rural women engaged in casual work/unpaid work in agriculture might have withdrawn from the labour force and may have got engaged in domestic activities (b) A tremendous rise in the student population ratio is one of the reason for women not entering the labour market (Rangarajan et al 2011, Thomas 2012, Chandrashekhar and Ghosh 2013) (c) The reportedly low female labour force participation in India is partly on account of the methods employed to measure women's work.

One of the main reasons is a substantially high proportion of females reporting their activity status as 'attending to domestic duties'. In 2011-12, 35.3% of all rural females and 46.1% of all urban females in India were attending to domestic duties. National Income Accounting or other statistical systems do not recognise domestic activities by women in their own households as economic activities. This probably undervalues women's contributions in the official statistics (Mazumdar and Neetha 2011). (d) This may be due to various forms of discrimination at the workplace, particularly in terms of wages (Srivastava and Srivastava 2010, Bardhan 1989).

In the next round (68th round during 2011-12), the LFPR for rural female declined further to 25.3% but an important change observed was that the LFPR for urban female increased marginally in this period. Another notable thing observed in 2011-12 is fall in the number of casual workers, especially in the agriculture sector. The decasualisation in the agriculture sector has occurred with rise in the number of workers in the Regular Wage Worker (RWW) category. Female casual workers, as percentage of total female population, declined from 8.4% in 2004-05 to 6.6% in 2011-12 and that in the RWW category increased from 2.5% to 2.9% during the same period (Rangarajan et al 2014).

It has happened for the first time in the history of Indian labour market that share of employment in the farm sector declined to below 50% (48.9%) from 59.9% in 1999-00. There was an absolute decline of workers in the agriculture sector in 2011-12. This has created a lot of pressure on the non-agricultural sectors to grow fast enough to absorb this surplus labour. Due to poor quality of jobs created, many women are discouraged from participating in the labour market. This may be one of the reasons why urban educated female preferred to attend to domestic duties in their own households (Thomas 2015). The numbers of women who engage only in domestic duties was 230.5 million in 2011-12 which was almost 39% of the female population. Around 35.3% of all rural females and 46.1% of all urban females in India were attending to domestic duties about five years ago.

At an all-India level, without doubt, such a massive withdrawal of women from the labour force involves a tremendous wastage of talent and huge opportunity cost for the Indian economy. One wishes to look at the position of various States in terms of female participation in the labour market as well as their involvement in domestic work. Such an analysis shows that Bihar has the lowest number of women reporting their status as workers, both in rural (only 5%) as well as urban areas (only 4%) (Table 1).

Bihar is followed by Haryana, which had only 16% of its rural females and 10% of urban females as workers in the labour market. Himachal Pradesh is the State with the highest proportion of workers to female population, both in rural (52%) and urban areas (21%).

Table 1: Workers as a proportion of female population (2011-12)

	Rural Female			Urban Female	
	Non-workers	Workers		Non- workers	Workers
BIHAR	95	5	BIHAR	96	4
HRY	84	16	HRY	90	10
UP	82	18	UP	90	10
WB	81	19	MAHA	87	17
KERALA	78	22	RAJ	86	14
PJB	77	23	AP	86	17
GUJ	72	28	KERALA	83	19
RAJ	65	35	TN	83	20
TN	62	38	GUJ	82	13
MAHA	61	39	PJB	81	14
AP	55	45	WB	80	18
HP	48	52	HP	79	21

Source: Estimates based on NSSO (68th Round).
Note: Non-workers include both unemployed females and those not in the labour force.

In Bihar, among those who were not participating in the labour market (those involved in activities given in code 92 and 93), 50% of the females in rural as well as in urban areas were involved in domestic duties (92+93). Except Himachal Pradesh, all the other selected States given in Table 2 had more than 40% of their urban females involved in domestic work.

If we look at the distribution of rural females as per their education status, we find that Rajasthan had the highest number of illiterate rural females (56%) followed by Uttar Pradesh and Andhra Pradesh (53% in each State). Kerala had the lowest proportion of rural females in the category of not literate.

If we take education status of rural females who are not participating in the labour market and reporting themselves as involved in the domestic duties, we find that Bihar is the State with the highest number,

Table 2: Females involved in 92 and 93 activities in 2011-12 (as % of total female segment-wise)

States	Rural	urban
	92+93	
HIMACHAL PRADESH	10	33
RAJASTHAN	25	44
WEST BENGAL	43	49
UTTAR PRADESH	37	49
HARYANA	45	50
ANDHRA PRADESH	22	44
BIHAR	50	49
PUNJAB	38	50
GUJARAT	37	49
MAHARASHTRA	25	45
TAMIL NADU	27	43
KERALA	37	41

Note: 92 Code refers to the activity status of persons who are engaged in domestic duties only 93 Code refers to the activity status of persons who are engaged in domestic duties as well as activities like free collection of goods, tailoring, weaving etc.

ie. 61% of 'not literate' rural females reporting themselves in the 92+93 category, followed by Haryana (Table 3). Gujarat has the maximum number of rural female graduates, ie. 90% involved in domestic work followed by Uttar Pradesh where 69% of the rural female graduates and 67% of the rural female post-graduates are involved in domestic work.

As per the distribution of Urban Female by their education status, UP has the highest number of urban females in the 'not literate' category, ie. 36% followed by Rajasthan and Bihar (34% and 31% respectively) (Table 4). Himachal Pradesh, Haryana, West Bengal and Kerala have 10% or more than 10% of the urban female population as graduates. Himachal Pradesh has the maximum number of females in the secondary and higher secondary level.

Table 3: Rural females involved in 92 and 93 C as a proportion of total rural females in an education level, State-wise, 2011-12

States	Not literate	Below Primary	Primary	Middle	Secondary	Higher Secondary	Diploma & Certificate courses	Graduate	Postgraduate not above	Total
Bihar	61	29	37	48	61	64	12	55	16	50
HP	10	5	11	9	12	13	12	21	15	10
HRY	49	31	44	49	48	51	39	47	55	45
West Bengal	44	30	45	55	49	41	89	50	26	43
Maharashtra	20	17	23	31	38	47	28	55	78	25
Kerala	21	25	36	51	47	40	34	34	22	37
Tamil Nadu	22	18	24	37	39	43	45	42	17	27
UP	41	14	32	48	44	47	15	69	67	37
AP	18	20	18	29	38	31	9	32	19	22
Gujarat	35	25	41	50	50	59	19	90	10	37
Rajasthan	27	16	28	28	25	28	0	28	27	25

Table 4: Urban females involved in 92 and 93 C as a proportion of total Urban females in an education level, State-wise, 2011-12

States	Not literate	Below Primary	Primary	Middle	Secondary	Higher Secondary	Diploma & Certificate courses	Graduate	Postgraduate not above	Total
Bihar	57	23	47	51	62	54	43	62	16	49
HP	32	11	39	41	49	39	31	26	28	33
HRY	53	22	45	58	62	58	38	65	49	50
West Bengal	42	27	42	59	68	55	47	62	42	49
Maharashtra	35	21	39	53	67	53	26	50	36	45
Kerala	17	22	44	61	52	40	38	35	30	41
Tamil Nadu	34	25	41	54	60	50	41	55	34	43
UP	51	14	44	55	60	56	27	74	69	49
AP	37	29	41	48	64	48	32	57	55	44
Gujarat	39	27	48	60	66	56	26	64	64	49
Rajasthan	43	24	55	59	53	44	7	59	41	44

UP has the maximum number of graduates and postgraduate urban women, ie. 74% and 69% respectively who are not participating in the labour market and are engaged in domestic work. As per the distribution of urban females according to their education status, 8% of urban females in UP are graduates and 4% of the same are of post graduates. Next comes Gujarat, where 64% of both, of the graduate and postgraduate level urban females areinvolved in domestic duties.

Conclusion

This paper has tried to present the structural changes occurring in India's labour market with a special focus on the aspects of female labour force participation. The issue of low and falling female LFPR needs to be studied in detail. Knowledge of the reasons behind low LFPR is required to take appropriate policy actions, both at the central as well as State level. The data on education status of the women engaged in domestic duties clearly shows that even educated women in urban areas, who face less social constraints are not participating in the labour market and instead prefer to engage in domestic duties only. This raises concern over the number and quality of jobs being created in the country.

References

1. Abraham V (2009): 'Employment Growth in Rural India: Distress Driven?', *Economic & Political Weekly*, 44 (16): 97-104.
2. Bardhan K (1989): 'Women: Work, Welfare and Status: Forces of Tradition and Change in India' *South Asia Bulletin, 6*(1), 3-16.
3. Chandrasekhar CP and Jayati Ghosh (2011): Latest employment trends from the NSSO, *Business Line* newspaper.
4. Chandrasekhar CP and Jayati Ghosh (2013): 'Where have all the woman workers gone?', *Business Line* newspaper.
5. Klasen Stephan, Pieters Janneke (2012): 'Push or Pull? Drivers of FLPR during India's Economic Boom', IZA Discussion Paper No. 6395.
6. *National Sample Survey Office* (1986): Employment and Unemployment (All India), *38th Round.*
7. (1997): Employment and Unemployment in India, *50th Round.*
8. (2001): Employment and Unemployment Situation in India, *55th Round.*

9. (2006): Employment and Unemployment Situation in India 2004-05, *61st Round.*

10. (2011): Key Indicators of Employment and Unemployment in India 2009-10, *66th Round.*

11. (2013): Key Indicators of Employment and Unemployment in India 2011-12, *68th Round.*

12. Mazumdar, Indrani and Neetha N (2011): "Gender Dimensions: Employment Trends in India, 1993-94 to 2009-10", *Economic & Political Weekly*, 46 (43): 118-26.

13. Rangarajan, C, Padma Iyer Kaul and Seema (2011): "Where Is the Missing Labour Force?" *Economic & Political Weekly*, 46 (39)

14. Rangarajan, Seema and Vibeesh E M (2014): "Developments in the workforce between 2009-10 and 2011-12" *Economic & Political Weekly, XLIX No 23*

15. Srivastava, Nisha and Ravi Srivastava (2010): "Women, Work and Employment Outcomes in Rural India", *Economic & Political Weekly*, 45 (28): 49-63

16. Thomas, J Jose (2012): "India's Labour Market during the 2000s: Surveying the Changes", *Economic & Political Weekly*, Vol - XLVII No. 51

17. Thomas, J Jose (2014): "The Demographic Challenge and Employment Growth in India", *Economic & Political Weekly*, Vol - XLIX No. 6

18. Thomas, Jayan Jose (2015): 'India's Labour Market During the 2000s' in Ramaswamy, K V (2015) (ed.) *Labour, Employment and Economic Growth in India*, Cambrdige University Press, New Delhi, pp. 21-56.

Corporate 'Handholding' through 'Tax Expenditure'

— Malabika Pal

'TAX EXPENDITURE' or revenue foregone has not received the emphasis it deserves in the analysis of budgetary allocations in India. The first public expression of the term was given by Stanley S Surrey in 1967 when he was the Assistant Secretary of the Treasury for Tax Policy in the United States.[1] The United States Congress had mandated since 1974 that these expenditures be recorded annually as part of the federal budget.[2] It represents the specific tax incentives such as special tax rates, exemptions, deductions, rebates, deferrals and tax credits that are given

1 It was in his book *Pathways to Tax Reform* (1973) that the concept of tax expenditures was scrutinised and brought to the forefront. It remains a seminal contribution in the field. He coauthored *Tax Expenditures* with Paul R McDaniel, which was published posthumously in 1985. Burman and Phaup (2012) argue that Germany had invented the concept - if not the name - more than a decade before the United States and had included tax expenditure analysis in its budget process. Canada and United Kingdom started publishing tax expenditure figures in the late 1970s.

2 This legislative landmark has been attributed to the persistent efforts of Surrey.

to a limited group of tax payers. In the United States, these have also been known as 'tax preferences', while in Europe, these are often referred to as 'tax subsidies'.

In India, the figures have been presented as part of the budget only since 2006-07 to bring in 'transparency'[3] because very often,these tax expenditures have been criticised on the ground that they lack visibility and, therefore, do not receive the policy attention and public scrutiny they ought to get. This is because these expenditures are not treated as direct spending but as reductions in taxes and are simply stated as 'revenue foregone'.[4] To highlight the invisible nature of this component, Howard (1997) had aptly named his book, The Hidden Welfare State, and successfully brought tax expenditure to the forefront of American political economy. The issue assumes significance since there is an enormous amount of discussion and debate in India around the magnitude of 'fiscal deficit' and the rising figure is given as a justification for reduction in spending in important sectors like health and education. We find that each year, an amount ranging between five to six per cent of GDP is 'given away' as 'tax subsidies', which if it were to be collected as 'revenue' would have made more resources available for social sector spending or could even have led to at least a partial elimination[5] of the fiscal deficit or a reduction in the tax rates across the board.

---

[3] Sarma (2006) has, however, pointed out some methodological problems that are present which stand in the way of the Tax Expenditure Statement (TES) becoming a useful document in the analysis of this very important component of the Budget.

[4] The title 'Statement of Revenue Foregone' which had been termed 'disarmingly honest' [see Sainath (2014)] has been changed in the Budget documents of 2016-17 in which it has been termed 'Statement of Revenue Impact of Tax Incentives under the Central Tax System' on the ground that what is actually being analysed is the revenue impact. Sainath (2014) had pointed out that instead of 'revenue foregone' a better term would have been 'revenue forgone' based on the semantic meanings of the two terms. In this paper, we continue to use the term revenue foregone as in done in Rao (2013) and Sarma (2006).

[5] Although the fiscal deficit also remains in the range of 5 to 6 %, the assumption is that elimination of the incentives could lead to a loss in revenue because some industries which would have produced in the presence of the tax incentives, may not do so now. So, there may not be a one-for-one reduction in deficit.

The question then arises, what is the rationale for these 'expenditures'? The general understanding is that tax expenditures are a tool for achieving national objectives like balanced economic development, promoting education, stimulating research etc. In India export promotion, infrastructure development, cooperatives, promotion of 'infant industries'have been considered important. The essential channel through which these are expected to affect tax collections is that these tax incentives would lead to greater investment in those sectors in which tax incentives exist, which in turn would lead to more income and hence greater collection of tax revenue.[6]

This justification cannot be empirically tested with accuracy because it involves investigating the situation that would prevail had the tax incentives not been there. In fact, even the 'revenue foregone' calculations are based on the assumption that the tax base would remain the same if the incentives were removed and that there is no interactive impact of the tax incentives. The world over there has been scrutiny and dissent over the huge amount of 'aid'[7] given to the corporate sector in the form of these 'hidden subsidies'. In India, the proportion of this subsidy has been high and that has been maintained even though there has been a cut in expenditure on sectors such as agriculture and education.As Rao (2013) shows, an increasing percentage of tax expenditure has been going to the corporate sector. There have been attempts in the past to do away with even the taxes that exist in the name of creating Free Trade Zones (FTZs) and more recently, Special Economic Zones (SEZs).[8] The tax concessions extended to them have been substantial. One may ask, why does the private sector need such huge subsidy in a market economy? Even in the presence of all these subsidies, the Finance Minister while presenting the 2015-16 Budget argued: 'We inherited a sentiment of, if I may say so, doom and gloom, and the investor community had almost

---

6 For individual households, tax incentives would raise consumption and savings and thus boost the economy.

7 In the OECD countries, these expenditures are known as 'tax reliefs' or 'tax aids'.

8 This trend however is not new. As Gupta (1984) has argued that tax holiday of 5 years for Free Trade Zones was seen to be inadequate and arguments were made to extend it to 10 years and may be more.

written us off'. Obviously, tax expenditure has not been able to live up to its rationale of being able to 'incentivise' investment.

The ruling party which has a majority in the Lower House of Parliament chose to continue with the policy of providing these indirect subsidies in the 2015-16 Budget. The Finance Minister stated in his Budget speech: 'I wanted to start the phased reduction of corporate tax rate and phased elimination of exemptions right away; but I thought it would be appropriate to give advance notice that these changes will start from the next financial year.' We note that in the Budget Speech of 2009-10, it had been mentioned that the tax base remains low compared to other countries due to the plethora of exemptions. However, as the revenue foregone figures show, the magnitude of these 'subsidies' has only risen over the past few years. On the 20th of November, 2015, the Central Board of Direct Taxes (CBDT), issued a Press Release which gave the proposed roadmap for the phasing out. The 2016-17 Budget announced a one-per cent reduction in the corporate tax rate for companies with a turnover of Rs. 5 crore or less and phasing out of benefits associated with accelerated depreciation and for those available to SEZs. However, the bulk of exemptions and deductions have remained untouched.

There have been reports that defence spending has not increased commensurate with the needs[9] of the sector and that could be used as a justification for permitting the private sector in defence. In such a scenario, where the government has a paucity of funds for even defence spending, it is imperative to look at the justification for doling out such a huge fraction of the GDP to particular groups in the economy. In fact, this point has been highlighted time and again, with an early example being the emphatic position put forward in Bagchi (1974) and

[9] There has been an increasing gap between the resource requirement projected by the Ministry of Defence and successive budget allocations. The amount has increased tremendously from 8 per cent (Rs 12, 453 crore) in 2009-10 to 26 per cent (Rs 79,363 crore) in 2014-15. See Behera, L K (2015), 'India's Defence Budget 2015-16', Issue Brief, Institute of Defence Studies and Analyses (IDSA), March 02. In comparison to other countries such as China, Pakistan, US and Russia, India spends much lower percentage, namely just 1.8 per cent of its GDP, on the military. Russia spends 4.1 per cent of GDP. See Editorial, *The Economics Times*, On 'Guns, Butter and a Great failure', 7 May, 2015.

more recently in a detailed discussion paper prepared by the Centre for Budget and Governance Accountability (CBGA).[10] While the world over, discussion and debate has led to tax reform and is often reflected in the composition of tax expenditures, in India that has not yet happened. We find that while in the United States, the share of the corporate sector in total tax expenditure is about 9 per cent; the figure is around 40 per cent in India.[11] This paper attempts to look at some of the issues that are criticalfor investigating the efficacy of using the tax expenditure route to promote national causes and press for a systematic debate on the issue in a situation in which 'resource crunch' is used as a reason for forcing the public sector to get into partnerships with the private sector (the PPP mode) for almost all the areas which were hitherto under the exclusive purview of the state.

The paper is organised as follows. In the first section, we focus on the hidden nature of 'tax expenditure' which is relegated as a 'not-so-significant' component of the Budget by bringing out its meaning, its magnitude, structure and the trends in India. This is followed by an examination of their rationale and some of the implications of using the tax exemption route of extending state support for particular activities. The third section analyses the reasons why in India these exemptions have persisted despite repeated recommendations for their rationalisation and perhaps removal. In the changing context of the Indian economy, the 'phasing out' question is very significant and this section analyses why the phasing out process needs to be scrutinized. A concluding section looks at some of the directions in which research in this area needs to be undertaken. The example of Stanley S Surrey who single-mindedly pursued this agenda in the United States from about 1932 until his death in 1984 is instructive both for its perseverance and effectiveness.

Hidden Subsidy: Meaning, Magnitude, Composition and Trends

The concept of tax expenditure relates to instances in which the government can give money to certain taxpayers by using a narrowly

---

[10] CBGA Discussion Paper (2013)

[11] We note that due to different methodologies used in the reporting of tax expenditure, the figures are not strictly comparable. However, even a rough estimation would give a difference of about four times. See in this regard, Rao (2013).

directed tax deduction or exemption, instead of using its direct spending route. These are concessions provided which reduce the tax liability. In particular, these include special tax rates, exemptions, deductions, rebates, deferrals and credits. The effect of these is that the taxpayer may get complete relief for a specific tax or be taxed at a reduced rate or be taxed for only a portion of the items subject to taxation. Most governments prefer to promote certain activities through the tax exemption route because if they were to directly spend the money as subsidy for those activities, they would be subjected to greater scrutiny. By giving out the money through the tax expenditure route, both government spending and effective tax rates would be lower. These subsidies are 'hidden' because of the nature of reporting adopted. They are shown implicitly as revenue foregone on the receipts side and not on the expenditure side. This makes the cost of these expenditures seem non-existent, since the amount does not turn up as spending.

The use of exemptions as incentives for facilitating national goals would not have been cause for concern if it had not been of such high magnitude. The total estimated amount of revenue foregone stood at Rs 2.05 lakh crore or 5.6 per cent of GDP in 2005-06, which had risen to Rs 5.73 lakh crore or 5.7 per cent of GDP by 2012-13[12] and in 2015-16stands at Rs 6.11 lakh crore.The focus of the current study is the structure and proportion of tax expenditure going to the corporate sector. A company- wise break-up given in Table 1 shows that for the entire sample, the effective tax rate was 23.22 per cent while the statutory rate was 32.445 per cent in case of companies having income up to Rs 10 crore and 33.99 per cent in case of companies having income exceeding Rs 10 crore. In FY 2012-13, the effective tax rate was 22.44 per cent.

We find from the above that the effective tax rate is lowest in case of larger companies than for the smaller ones. For instance, those with profits greater than Rs 500 crore are in effect paying 20.68 per cent as taxes. This is because when a tax system has a progressive rate structure, a tax exemption in effect saves more money for those in the higher tax bracket. This means that exemptions reduce the progressivity otherwise present in the tax structure.Private companies continued to pay a slightly higher

[12] CBGA Discussion Paper (2013), p.6.

Table: 1: Effective Tax Rate and Size of Company

S. No.	Profit Before Taxes	No. of Companies	Share in Total Corporate Income Tax (CIT) payable (in %)	Effective Tax Rate
1	Less than Zero	228,447	0.50	-
2	Zero	25,624	3.98	-
3	Rs 0-1 crore	278,515	3.41	26.89
4	Rs 1-10 crore	5,613	7.72	25.84
5	Rs 10-50 crore	4,464	9.67	24.99
6	Rs 50-100 crore	853	5.63	24.99
7	Rs. 100-500 crore	808	15.38	23.11
8	>Rs 500 crore	263	53.71	20.68
9	All Companies	564,787	100	23.22

Source: Statement of Revenue Foregone, Union Budget 2015-16.

effective tax rate at 24.44 per cent compared to public sector companies, which paid at the rate of 19.33 per cent, although these were lower than the statutory rate for both categories. Further, the service sector has a higher effective tax rate of 24.37 per cent compared to manufacturing sector which has to pay at the effective rate of 21.96 per cent, both below the statutory tax rate of 33.217.

An examination of the trend over the past few years leads one to look at the ratio of revenue foregone to total gross revenue and examine how it has changed over time. Rao (2013) argues that there have been many refinements over the years so that the series is no longer comparable. She argues that just by looking at the numbers published as part of the Statement of Revenue Foregone by the Government, one can conclude that: '...revenue foregone has increased from around 50% of gross revenue in the pre-slowdown phase to over 65% from 2008-09. It is also apparent that the ratio seems to register sporadic increases after which there is a declining trend.'She further goes on to details about the corrections that ought to have been made because of refinements due to introduction of Minimum Alternate Tax (MAT), the replacement of cooperatives by a larger set comprising of Association of Persons/Body of Individuals or APO/BOI, accounting for input taxes in case of central excise, reduction of revenue foregone estimates to the extent that itis for 'zero-rating' exports, that is, schemes intended to provide a level playing field to Indian exports. After accounting for these refinements, she computes the ratios which are given in Table 2 below.

Table: 2: Revenue Foregone as a Percentage of Revenue Collected

	2006-07	2007-08	2008-09	2009-10	2010-11	2011-12	2012-13
Personal Income Tax	42.8	37.1	35.4	36.9	12.3	12.2	12.7
Corporate Income Tax	31.2	32.2	31.4	29.8	59.9	49.4	44.7
Excise Duty (corrected)	30.5	31.6	32.5	19.0	22.4	15.7	21.9
Customs duty	100.8	93.5	181.6	234.4	127.2	158.6	154.1
Total	53.0	53.3	45.0	46.3	41.1	42.3	39.9

Source: Rao (2013), Table 2, p.24.

She concludes that the reported figures are over-estimates in some cases. She further argues: '... while the revenue foregone associated with corporates seem to be increasing as a percentage of total revenue collections-especially those associated with corporate tax and customs duties-those related to the individual taxpayer, as reflected in personal income tax is declining.'[13] From the above figures, we find that the revenue foregone under customs duty is greater than the actual collections. On the whole, we find that a very high magnitude of tax that could have been collected is 'given away'.

What ever the method of calculation, the significance of such high magnitude of tax expenditure is that they reduce the tax base and requires higher tax rates to raise any given amount of revenue. The composition of taxes shows that a particular class of tax payersbenefits proportionately more compared to others. For instance, the corporations get an exemption

[13] Rao (2013), p.24.

of almost four times that the individuals get. Even within the corporate sector, although the majority of companies are in the Rs 0-1 crore bracket, they end up paying the highest effective tax rates. This has serious equity issues. There are also issues related to allocation of resources. The revenue that was forgone could have been used to fund many important public programmes like health, education and even defence instead of going to just one class of taxpayers, namely the corporate sector. They could be also used to reduce the fiscal deficit. The amount of tax expenditure also has implications for debt. The imbalance between spending and revenue could be partially corrected if the exemptions were reduced and would have helped control the volume of debt.

Rationale and Implications of Hidden Subsidies

The efficacy of tax exemptions in India was analysed in detail by Bagchi (1974). His exposition of the rationale is by far the most effective in bringing out the nature of the justification given for these subsidies in India. He argued: 'Taxation is widely acknowledged as a powerful instrument of state policy and every country in the world makes use of it in varying degrees to further national objectives....From book publishing to family planning, not to mention fostering of growth, export promotion, agricultural development, refugee rehabilitation and scientific research, there is hardly any item on the national agenda that does not find support somewhere in the tax statute.'[14] Over time, many objectives keep getting added. In fact, Bagchi (1974) had put it very aptly: 'Almost invariably, the first act of an individual or a collective body entrusted with or engaging themselves in looking after anything with a 'public' pretention is to ask for tax exemption for themselves and their donors.' The most glaring ones are those related to the setting up of FTZs (and more recently the SEZs). Gupta (1984) elaborated the above point by stating: 'The Committee on Free Trade Zones..., has expressed the view that tax holiday of five years offered to free trade zones enterprises in the 1981-82 Central budget is inadequate. This, according to the Committee, should be extended to ten years and even after that further concession should be granted on a case by case basis.'[15]

---

[14] Bagchi (1974), p.951.

[15] Gupta (1984),p.M-122

There have been many discussions on whether tax concessions rather than direct spending are the best way of promoting the national objectives. The tax exemptions are in the nature of an entitlement, meaning that they are paid out to any individual or company which meets the eligibility rules. Once they are in the tax statute, they automatically get realised. However, any direct spending is discretionary and needs to be approved. It has been argued that from the tax payer's point of view, a tax exemption is preferable if the costs of delivery lead to reduction in the actual value received by the taxpayer. Among the few studies conducted by economists, Feldstein (1980) had derived the result that for a wide range of parameter values, tax expenditures are a more effective policy tool for meeting a given objective compared to direct spending. However, as argued by Rao (2013): '...there could be rent-seeking in gaining access to tax concessions, both at the time of availing the benefit- this process can effectively equalise any differentials that might exist in the benefits derived.'[16]

In fact, we find that over the years, direct subsidy component has been reduced. In such a context, it would not have been politically feasible to push through an expenditure of this magnitude for the corporate sector. Thus the trend we noted regarding the expansion in tax expenditure must be contrasted with the trend in 'discretionary spending'. We find that while the former has been increasing, the latter has been shrinking.The Budget estimates of total expenditure for 2014-15 was Rs 1,794, 892 crore[17] but for 2015-16 the budget estimates are lower at Rs 1,777, 477 crore, due to the drastic reduction in Plan expenditure by Rs 109,723 crore.

The Question of 'Phasing Out'

The most contentious issue regarding tax expenditures is the question of their continuance.

As explained above, these tend to be hidden in the complexity of the tax law and the cost of these tax subsidies are difficult to ascertain. Due to their very nature, these tend to acquire a permanency much beyond what is justified in terms of the benefits for which they were put

[16] Rao (2013), p.21.

[17] The revised estimates were lower at Rs 16, 811, 58. See Expenditure Budget, Vol. I, 2015-16.

in place. Advocacy for their reduction or removal needs to be persistent, like that of Surrey who made it his abiding concern and brought into it 'the intellectual and governmental resources necessary to make tax expenditures a subject that Congress and the Treasury would address in a straightforward way.'[18] In India, there has been conflicting opinions and varied recommendations that have come from Committees set up for Tax Reform. In the early decades of our planning process the environment was one as summarised by Bagchi (1974): 'Seldom does a committee or study group required to look into specific problems of public policy conclude its report without putting down a plea for a tax incentive among its recommendations.'[19] This view was reiterated in Gupta (1984) when he argued that tax expenditures had become so popular in India that practically all government committees had called for introduction, maintenance, extension or enlargement of tax expenditures.

The introduction of tax incentive must be done very carefully since once inserted into the tax law it is difficult to get them out. Bagchi (1974) had argued, even if the rationale for a tax incentive is clear, many of the provisions must be subjected to reappraisal in the light of the experience of their working. However, the question that is pertinent here is how has the issue of withdrawal been tackled in India? Is it always based on economic reasons? One interesting example cited by Gupta (1984) shows that non-economic factors may also play a role. In February 1984, the government decided to withdraw section 80 CC on the ground that the concession plays a negligible role in stimulating investment in certain categories of new equity shares, even though the Economic Administration Reforms Commission (1983) had recommended that the section be made more generous. However, seven weeks after the proposal to withdraw was made public, another announcement was made saying that the proposal was dropped. The reason given was that a further review was needed and, therefore, the concession would be continued for three more years and then be reviewed again. This brings out the importance of doing a thorough background work of both economic and non-economic issues pertaining to a particular incentive before announcing a phasing out.

[18] Wolfman (1985), p.494.

[19] Bagchi (1974), p.951.

Over time, the plethora of exemptions has only expanded and has led to a very complex and non-transparent tax statute. The stand taken by some committees in recent decades has been more towards pruning the multiplicity of tax expenditures and bringing about a transparent system, so that the main function of raising revenues can become the focus of tax policy. The Chelliah Committee, constituted in 1991, had observed that a simple tax system should have a limited number of rates and exemptions and had proposed rationalisation. The Shome Committeein 2001 had drawn attention to the scope for reductionin the number of exemptions prevailing in direct taxes. It had also highlighted the need for minimising exemptions with respect to customs duties, and suggested that the number of export promotion schemes needed to be reduced. With respect to the corporate sector, the Kelkar Committee in 2002 specifically argued that there were excessive exemptions which had led to considerable reduction in the tax base, complexity of the law and encouraged rent-seeking behaviour. It had recommended the immediate or phased elimination of the corporate tax exemptions.

The Direct Taxes Code (DTC), which was meant to come into effect from 2011 aimed at a comprehensive overhaul of the direct tax structure in India. It recommended the removal of most exemptions, both individual and corporate. In particular, it recommended the removal of all profit-linked incentives for area-based investments like setting up plants in a backward area or in the North-East with investment linked incentives in specific sectors such as infrastructure, power, exploration and oil production.

Instead, an increase in incentive by way of a phased reduction of the corporate income tax rate was announced in the 2015-16 Budget from 30 per cent to 25 per cent in the next four years. In the 2016-17 Budget, the corporate tax rate for companies that have a turnover of or less than Rs 5 crore was reduced from 30 per cent plus surcharge and cess to 29 per centand surcharge and cess. A corporate tax rate of 25 per cent was announced for all new manufacturing companies incorporated from 1 April 2016, provided they do not claim any exemptions. Earlier on 20th of November 2015, the CBDT had announced a roadmap for the phasing out by which profit-linked, investment-linked and area based deductions for both corporate and non-corporate tax-payers; it was stated that sunset dates will not be extended and if no terminal date has been mentioned then 31 March 2017 will be treated as the sunset date and finally there will be no weighted deduction from 1 April, 2017.

Patnaik (2015), in his analysis of the 2015-16 Budget, had noted that the fall in the tax-GDP ratio could be attributed to the increase in corporate tax revenue by only 7.8 per cent while GDP increased by 11.5 per cent (between 2013-14 and 2014-15) and gross tax revenues for 2014-15 (RE) was higher than that for 2013-14 (Actual) by less than 10 per cent.He argued that corporate income could not be said to have fallen in 2014-15. He further argued that in any system of progressive taxation as income increases, tax revenue should increase more than proportionately. In such a scenario, Patnaik argues that the corporate tax rate should have been increased. Instead, the Finance Minister had announced a cut in the statutory corporate income tax rate. This cut in tax rate together with the'phasing out' of the exemptions meant that the 'effective tax rate' could still stay at the present level of 23 per cent even after the proposed budgetary changes. In the intermediate period while these changes take place, it would be interesting to see what would be the effective tax rates in any particular year to gauge the full impact of the 'phased' changes.[20] In Table 3, we note the escalation in the effective tax rate for companies, with an effective tax rate for the entire sample at 24.67 per cent, as against the rate of 23.22 per cent reported in 2013-14 (Table 1). It has been argued that this is due to the gradual phasing out of various profit-linked deductions and the levy of Minimum Alternate Tax on companies.

Looking Ahead

From the above analysis, we find that although there has been a call for scrutiny of this very significant part of the Budget, intensive studies have been few and far between. In the current scenario of reduction in spending in important sectors and the withdrawal of the state from important areas on the ground of paucity of funds, the importance of a rigorous examination of the efficacy of the tax expenditure route cannot be overemphasised. The implications for resource allocation are enormous, so

[20] We note that it has been announced in the 2015-16 Budget that the DTC is being dropped.

Table: 3: Effective Tax Rate after the start of phasing out

S. No.	Profit Before Taxes	No. of Companies	Share in Total Corporate Income Tax (CIT) payable (in %)	Effective Tax Rate
1	Less than Zero	254,079	0.47	-
2	Zero	18,080	2.81	-
3	Rs 0-1 crore	276,531	3.25	29.37
4	Rs 1-10 crore	26,9183	7.40	26.99
5	Rs 10-50 crore	5,130	9.48	25.52
6	Rs 50-100 crore	894	5.26	25.14
7	Rs. 100-500 crore	895	15.12	23.97
8	>Rs 500 crore	297	56.21	22.88
9	All Companies	582,889	100	24.67

Source: Statement of Revenue Impact of Tax Incentives under the Central Tax System, Union Budget, 2016-17.

are the distributional consequences. The study has attempted to highlight the fact that it is the hidden nature of these subsidies that allows it to escape public scrutiny. Also, since there are enmeshed in the intricate details of the tax statute, they are not accessible for analysis to a wide section of the population. The practice of relegating the reporting to one of the documents accompanying the Budget and not including it as part of the main Budget makes it appear as if they are insignificant and are being reported for the benefit of experts who deal with public finance.

The research questions that must be taken up relate first to the appropriate methodology that must be adopted to account for these expenditures and the conceptual clarity regarding classification of a particular item as tax expenditure.This exercise becomes pertinent to verify conflicting claims regarding tax expenditure. For instance, Kumar and Das Krishna (2015) have put forward a case that it is dishonest to classify the several fiscal incentives included in the estimates for revenue foregone as giveaways. They conclude: 'Most concessions included in revenue foregone undoubtedly contribute to enhancing public welfare or promoting exports. These should not be included in estimates of revenue foregone. Therefore, the finance ministry would do well to come up with a new methodology for calculating the actual revenue foregone and a new nomenclature for genuinely effective tax incentives.'

As far as the overall revenue foregone estimates are concerned, Rao (2013)states the methodology used in India 'is an ex post calculation of the loss in revenue incurred by the government'.[21] She goes on to elaborate: 'It can also be interpreted as the benefit derived by an incentivised taxpayer when compared to an ordinary taxpayer. It is computed as the difference between the identified "standard rate", i e, a norm, and the rate effective for a specific activity or commodity times the total value of transactions. Here, any behavioural responses of the taxpayers are not taken into account.'[22] The difference in the two rates multiplied by the total value of transactions effectively rules out consideration of any changes in behaviour that may have been the result of the incentive provided. Research must be directed at finding out how the figures can be interpreted given this methodology of estimating revenue foregone.

Refinements in the tax code need to be incorporated to make a particular series comparable with the previous ones in India. More studies along the lines of Rao (2013) are needed to bring about greater analytical rigour into this significant aspect of the Budget. Further, methodological uniformity helps in comparison with other countries so that analysis of trends is more meaningful. The important issue of which sectors need prioritisation must be examined. With continuous addition and few withdrawals of tax incentives, the complexity of the system has become such that what Bagchi (1974) had stated has become an even more serious problem today. He had argued: 'What all this- that is, saddling the tax laws with the task of promoting every conceivable worthy cause- means to the tax administration and the tax system as a whole does not seem to be anybody's concern. No one even bothers to inquire what the cost of a

---

[21] Rao (2013) gives the three methods that are conceptually present in the literature. She uses the above quote from Swift et al (2003). The other two methods are the revenue gain method which 'is an ex-ante calculation of the additional revenue that would accrue from repealing the tax expenditures' and the outlay equivalent method which captures the expenditure equivalent of a tax concession.

[22] Rao (2013), p.21.

tax incentive is to the community, whether the incentive truly begets any benefit to the country or whether allowing a tax concession is the best method of extending state support for a particular activity.'[23] Without specifying the rationale, particularly in the light of the experience and the changing context, it becomes clear that political reasons are dictating the continuance of these tax subsidies.

Further, it is important to view these tax subsidies together with the other subsidies that the corporate sector gets such as cheap land through the state power of eminent domain. Periodic analysis of the efficacy of choosing a particular activity over others would help in moving towards a more equitable allocation of valuable resources. Even in cases where the tax incentive route appears to be the best way, it is imperative to ensure that it has mechanisms to address the issue of eliminating the regressive elements which are brought into an otherwise progressive tax system. Since all these are not easily clear to the average citizen not equipped to read between the lines, it is important to work towards untangling the mazeto bring out the implications in a clear and straightforward way. On the other hand, rigorous analysis must also be done to estimate in some way the revenue impact and the tax buoyancy.

In the United States in the 1970s and 1980s, while direct spending faced retrenchment, tax expenditures experienced vigorous growth. Howard (1997) calls this the expansion of the 'hidden welfare state' and the contraction of the 'visible' welfare state. In the United States, the composition of tax expenditure was such that individuals benefittedmost from these changes. Research should be directed at the changing composition of tax expenditure and public spending.

In India, the state is withdrawing from public provision and almost 'handholding' the private corporate sector into areas which used to be the forte of the state. One can say that in India today while the state is assisting the corporate sector through the hidden tax expenditure route, the size of 'the welfare state' as conventionally understood is shrinking. Also, within the corporate sector, the 'handholding' seems to be greater, the larger the size of the company. This continued support despite the corporate sector doing very well in the past decade shows that the issue

---

[23] Bagchi (1974), p.951.

is more about the continuance of the changed policy stance of the government, no matter which party is at the helms. Bhaduri (2009) had argued in this context: '...the style of industrialisation the government has increasingly adopted...amounts to extending various privileges to the large corporations by the federal and state governments, irrespective of their professed political colour as incentives for promoting corporate-led industrialisation.'[24]

In conclusion, one can say that given the enormity of the issue and the pace at which pressure has been created, it may take a long time to get those provisions out of the tax statute which have long become inefficient entailing higher costs than benefits. However, that does not mean that effective and persistent efforts will not yield fruits. Just like the publication of the revenue foregone statement as part of the Budget was a significant step, many such steps must be taken. The changing context must be analysed rationally. Data on the performance of companies need to be examined to see whether they need these subsidies at all and the 'infant status'of companies must be reviewed for purposes of judging whether the recipients of these hidden subsidies deserve them.Surrey worked hard 'to have the concept capture the imagination and minds of policy makers, economists and lawyers the world over.' Perhaps, in India too, we need to find out how to weed out the unmeritorious tax exemptions first and keep on scrutinising the 'phasing out' process to monitor the direction in which the welfare state is moving and to particularly be vigilant about whether the economy is moving towards a development process that is truly inclusive or veering further from it.

Wolfman (1985), p.491.

[24] Bhaduri (2009), p.38.

*The author would like to thank Surajit Das for helpful inputs.

References

1. Bagchi A (1974), 'Efficiency of Tax Incentives- "Tax Expenditure Analysis". and Its Relevance for India', *Economic and Political Weekly*, June 15, pp.951-960.
2. Bhaduri A (2009), 'A Failed World View', *Economic and Political Weekly*, Vol.44, No.5, pp.35-39.
3. Burman L E and Phaup M (2012), 'Tax Expenditures, the Size and Efficiency of Government, and Implications for Budget Reform', *Tax Policy and the Economy*, Vol.26, No.1, pp.93-124.
4. Centre for Budget and Governance Accountability (CBGA) Discussion Paper on 'Tax Exemptions in India- Issues and Challenges', March 2013.
5. Feldstein M S (1980), 'A Contribution to the Theory of Tax Expenditures: The Case of Charitable Giving', in Henry J Aaron and Michael J Boskin ed. *The Economics of Taxation*, The Brookings Institution.
6. Government of India: 'Statement of Revenue Foregone', Union Budget, various years.
7. Gupta A (1984), 'Management of Tax Expenditures in India', *Economic and Political Weekly*, Vol.19, No.47.
8. Howard C (1997), *The Hidden Welfare State: Tax Expenditures and Social Policy in the United States*, Princeton University Press.
9. Kumar A, Chattopadhyay S, and Dharan, S (2007) 'Fiscal Policy' in *Alternative Economic Survey*, 2006-07, Daanish Books.
10. Kumar, R and Das Krishna, G (2015), 'The Myth of foregone Revenue', *Livemint*, February 26.
11. Patnaik, P (2015), 'Budget 2015-16: Bonanza for the Corporate' *MacroScan*, March 9. (Accessed from www.macroscan.com/the/political.htm on the 10th of May, 2015).
12. Rao K (2013), 'Revenue Foregone Estimates- Some Analytical Issues', *Economic and Political Weekly*, Vol.48, No.13, pp.21-24.
13. Sainath, P (2014), 'How much can we Forego to India Inc.' *Outlook*, July, 20.
14. Sarma E A S. (2006), 'How useful is New Tax Expenditure Statement', *Economic and Political Weekly*, April 8, pp.1322-1324.
15. Swift Z L, Baxi H P and Valenduc C (2003), 'Tax Expenditures: General Concept, Measurement, and Overview of Country Practices' *Tax Expenditures- Shedding Light on Government Spending Through the Tax System*, World Bank.
16. Wolfman B (1985), 'Tax Expenditures: From Idea to Ideology', *Harvard Law Review*, Vol.99. No.2, pp.491-498.

Desirability of Low Fiscal Deficit : Where does the Idea Come From?

— V Upadhyay

IN HIS Budget 2015-16 speech, Union Finance Minister, Arun Jaitley, said: 'We will meet… fiscal target of 4%... I will complete the journey to a fiscal deficit of 3% in three years… for the next three years, my targets are: 3.9% for 2015-16, 3.5% for 2016-17, and, 3.0% for 2017-18.' In his 2016-17 Budget, the Finance Minister has stuck to these targets. He has reduced fiscal deficit as percentage of GDP from 3.9 in 2015-16 to 3.5 in 2016-17. In the Budget 2016-17 speech, he said:

> While preparing this Budget, I have received conflicting suggestions about the FRBM roadmap. Different schools of thought have argued either in favour of fiscal consolidation and stability or for a less aggressive consolidation and for boosting growth. I have weighed the policy options and decided that prudence lies in adhering to the fiscal targets. Consequently, the

> fiscal deficit in RE 2015-16 and BE 2016-17 have been retained at 3.9% and 3.5% of GDP respectively.

This is not an honest statement. Mr Jaitley had no option but to continue along with the declared goals of fiscal reduction targets. This is because he was too sacred of the western credit rating agencies' reactions.

How has the reduction in fiscal deficit been achieved? As we can see from Table 1, taxes and total expenditure as percentage of GDP have been kept unchanged. So, to achieve reduction in fiscal deficit, there have been increases in non-tax revenue (to be achieved from spectrum sale) and capital receipts (to be achieved from disinvestments).

Table 1: Budget 2016-17 figures as percentage of GDP

	2015-16 Revised Estimates	**2016-17 Budget Estimates**
Tax Revenue (net to Centre)	6.98	6.99
Non-Tax Revenue	1.9	2.14
Capital Receipts	0.32	0.44
Total Receipts	9.21	9.58
Total Expenditure	13.16	13.13
Fiscal Deficit	3.94	3.54

Source: Own calculations from Budget 2016-17 figures.

If from total expenditure, we exclude additional payments to government personnel (including defense) due to implementation of the Seventh Pay Commission's recommendations and OROP, the ratio of total expenditure to GDP, in fact, declines. So, if the government claims that it is spending more on rural sector and infrastructure, then it necessarily means reduction in expenditure (in proportional terms) under other heads.

Like other conservatives anywhere in the world, Jaitley must think that reducing fiscal deficit – basically the difference between G (government expenditure) and T (taxes) – is a desirable objective, irrespective of whatever happens to the economy in the coming years.

What is the origin of this notion of the desirability of low fiscal deficit? Does it originate from some economic reasoning, being rooted in established macroeconomic theory? Or, do we have to look for answers in the political arena, in the class relations theory?

Before we explore these issues further, we need to get clarity on the decision-making process about macroeconomic matters in the present BJP-led government. In the BJP or its parent organisation, the RSS, there are only a very few people who can be said to have a decent understanding of macroeconomic issues. The BJP and the RSS have their main focus on identity nationalism, on a strong military and GDP growth. Even though it is a conservative (right-wing) party having its original political base in the trader community, it has, at times, even toyed with non-conservative ideas such as 'Gandhian Socialism' and 'Swadeshi'. How then does a first-ever majority BJP government decide to set a target of continuous reduction in fiscal deficit? The answer is that, sensing an internal talent deficit in domain knowledge, it has outsourced its economic thinking to the thought-to-be sister conservative parties in the US and the UK. To make sure that the ideas of its western counterparts are properly understood and implemented, the government has given charge of economic policy to highly conservative-minded US-based Indian economists. It needs to be noted here that the record of the preceding UPA government was hardly any different.

The conservative parties in the West have a clear stand on this issue: They want to reduce fiscal deficit. But why?

Conservatives are strongly against high taxes on the rich. According to them, high taxes create disincentives for capitalists who are the real wealth creators in society. But more importantly, conservatives are against the idea of a big-size welfare state. They aim to limit the state's functions to a bare minimum like providing security and enforcing contracts etc. They are eager to cut all those government programmes which seek to provide benefits to the poor and the marginalised. In short, conservatives want to cut both T and G. High fiscal deficit thus goes against the very core tenet of their philosophy and that is why they are opposed to it.

Extreme conservatives (the Tea Party-types) are even against the countercyclical monetary policies. The mainstream, pragmatic conservatives are, however, quite favourable to countercyclical monetary and fiscal policies. There is a basic difference between 'expansionary fiscal policy' and 'expansionary monetary policy'. In case of fiscal policy, government expenditure directly impacts the incomes of the targeted sections. In case of monetary policy, the impact is indirect as additional flow of money/credit is through banks and corporations. From the standpoint of conservatives, it is a safe policy as the control of the operation remains in the hands of the elite sections.

The conservative idea of spending cuts is not supported by standard macroeconomic theory. It is true that there are certain situations when excessive fiscal deficit can prove counterproductive. (For example, a nation can face a threat to its sovereignty if its government borrows too much in foreign currency.) But in situations when an economy is weak, high government expenditure and/or tax cuts provide boost to economy. In India, high government expenditure (and subsidies) is necessary to provide support to more than two-fifths of the population who live in conditions of dire poverty.

Notwithstanding the fact that standard macroeconomic theory does not support conservative ideas related to fiscal matters, these ideas continue to hold sway over a large range of public opinion. It is not only the conservative parties like the Republican Party in the USA, the Conservative Party in Britain and the BJP in India, but even the centrist and centre-left parties like the Labour Party in Britain and the Congress Party in India, adhere to conservative (neoliberal) economic viewpoint. These ideas are quite dominant among international financial institutions and credit agencies, as well as also among business and corporate leaders across countries.

What explains this kind of universal acceptability of conservative ideas among elite sections almost everywhere? Major international financial print media plays an important role here. If the *Financial Times*, *The Economist* and the like are ready to help, enough 'empirical' justification can be generated and sustained even for ideas that are patently wrong. Look at how a term like 'expansionary austerity' has become so popular in the West, and look at how a term like 'tax terrorism' has become so popular in the Indian media.

The ideological position of the extreme right is captured by the slogan 'Minimum Government, Maximum Freedom'. The BJP government, in its typical double-speak, has distorted the slogan into 'Minimum Government, Maximum Governance' which is an oxymoron: It does not make sense.

By not making any effort to widen the tax net, which could have allowed increased social spending, the BJP government has revealed its keen resolve to follow the dogma of fiscal consolidation. According to *Economic Survey 2015-16*, only about 5.5 per cent of Indians who earn are in the tax net and only 15.5 per cent of net national income is reported to the tax authorities as gross taxable income. When asked by a newspaper correspondent whether he would consider those who do not pay their taxes as anti-national and not doing duty towards the country, Arvind Subramanian (the Chief Economic Advisor to the Government of India) replied: 'That is not quite right. To get people to pay taxes, people should believe in the legitimacy of the state, that they are getting value for money.' This statement reveals how thoroughly Subramanian has imbibed the values of the American extreme right (the Tea Party or Donald Trump-types).

The government's anti-poor policies are certain to have adverse impact on the living conditions of the poor and the marginalised in India. Unless corrective steps are taken soon, their misery can only be expected to deepen much further in the coming years.

'Make in India': Issues and Concerns

— Satyaki Roy

DWINDLING MANUFACTURING growth has been a major concern for Indian policymakers in the recent past. The present government has launched a 'Make in India' campaign with the promise to jack up manufacturing growth that recorded a negative growth rate in terms of index of industrial production for the year 2013-14. The growth of manufacturing, however, shows a rise in the current year from the revised estimate of 5.5 per cent in 2014-15 to 9.5 per cent according to the advanced estimate of 2015-16. Despite some signs of recovery in manufacturing growth in the current year, India's average manufacturing growth rate for the entire period 2001-2013/14 has been less than the average overall growth rate. This is disturbing precisely because it is estimated that by 2022, 250 million people will join the labour force and manufacturing sector has to be able to absorb at least a 100 million workforce in order to avoid alarming levels of unemployment. The earlier government came up with the National Manufacturing Policy in

2011, which also estimated certain targets that need to be achieved in the manufacturing front.

In order to achieve the required level of employment, estimates suggest that the manufacturing sector has to grow by 12-14 per cent annually, which has not been close to even 7 per cent in the later part of the current decade. The share of employment in manufacturing has been low, at 12.6 per cent according to the latest NSSO figures while the share of services account for 26.8 per cent of the workforce. It is also important to note that the share of manufacturing output in total GDP has remained somewhere around 16-17 per cent as an average for the past two decades, and this share needs to increase to a minimum of 25 per cent in order to achieve desired outcomes. Therefore, policies should aim to enhance manufacturing growth and create employment in the short and medium term. It will also make our growth trajectory far more stable and inclusive. The question is, what could be the contours of the necessary policy interventions? The government launched several programmes such as ease of doing business, Make in India, Invest India, and the e-Biz Mission Mode Project under the National e-Governance Plan. Official websites and huge campaign billboards have come up with the logo of a lion having a mechanical wheel in its belly, but there does not appear to be much substance in terms of policies that would enhance output and employment growth in manufacturing. In the Union Budget 2016, the proposals were basically to reduce customs duties for imported inputs and increasing the same for imported output, special benefits in terms of deduction of profits and relaxing of capital gains tax for start-up firms and so on. This is premised on the assumption that such exemptions and subsidies would increase private domestic and foreign investors to invest in India's manufacturing and value add

As a response to low growth in manufacturing in India, simply appealing to investors to invest and produce is unlikely to motivate them for a 'national' cause. Capitalist economy is primarily driven by the profit motive and capitalists do not invest and produce goods just to satisfy human needs. In fact, capitalists produce whatever generates profit and not necessarily to meet the consumption demands of people at large. However, a proper balance of producing machines and that of consumption goods need to be maintained in order to avoid a potential crisis. The link is the expectation of profit that ultimately guides capitalists to invest in certain projects. If there is a chance of profit being unrealised, individual capitalists would not be inclined to make investment, howsoever it may be necessary for the whole economy. And in that case, the state as a representative of the collective wisdom of the capitalist class, should take charge in gearing up the dwindling levels of investment.

One can also safely argue that bottlenecks in infrastructure, availability of land, administrative red tapes and labour unrests are not really the major obstacles as they have often been projected to be in the discourse on industry. Ample number of studies show how lands transferred to private owners in SEZs and other production sites, with subsidised infrastructures, has not been utilised for production as it should have been. The number of strikes and trade union membership as well as labour disputes have declined drastically in the context of India's changing industrial relations. In fact, labour has lost its voice by all counts. Cheapening of labour in the name of flexibility has been rampant through outsourcing and subcontracting arrangements. This is not to suggest that problems in the supply side are less important. One of the major concerns in this regard is the inadequate supply of required skills. In India, skilled labour is a scarce factor similar to capital, and such situations undoubtedly influence the growth patterns of manufacturing. But what seems to be the most obvious concern for the capitalist producers is the problem of demand, that often gets reflected by a thin market. This might sound untenable in a globalised world where the market is not restricted by national geographies and it has often been argued that stagnating domestic markets can be compensated by high growth in exports.

The 'Make in India' campaign primarily invokes investors to come and produce in India, promising them a favourable environment of easy availability of infrastructure and docile labour. The idea at the core basically is aspiring to emerge as a second China. Because India has excess supply of labour, a situation more or less similar to that of China, it is perceived that a similar growth trajectory can be replicable. Such an idea of replicating trajectories is hardly tenable, once we understand time as a historical and not as a logical magnitude. Histories of development cannot be gauged by years, days and minutes but in light of how certain opportunities emerge in the context of the dynamics of factors that condition future growth. Although the comparison of India with China has become popular these days, it is often done without considering the divergent history and political economy of these two countries. And, apart from the path of dependencies, in any case, all countries cannot gain by selling their products to others because exports should globally balance with imports. Especially for large countries, high export dependence makes economies highly vulnerable to external shocks. Moreover China, unlike India, did follow a strategy which was essentially coordinated by the state and there had been considerable interventions on the part of the state both in jacking up investment demand on the one hand as well as consumption demand through enhancing social wage. Despite successes for about two decades, China faced the heat of slowing down export demand that most of the primary goods exporting countries also had to face. And in such cases, recovery is difficult through exchange rate devaluation because responses are more likely to be fall in imports rather than rise in exports. Let us have a closer look into the Indian manufacturing sector and its major trends which may perhaps suggest a growth trajectory different from the export-led push.

Trends in Manufacturing Sector

Economic theories of development often identify stages of economic growth on the basis of relative weights of sectors in contributing to overall growth of the economy. From lower to higher stages of development, it is argued that the sequence of importance moves from agriculture to industry and then to services. The Clerk-Fischer-Kuznets hypothesis states how demand for services increases over that of manufacturing beyond a certain level of income and hence, the growth of demand for manufacture is generally followed by and not preceded by a spurt in the demand for services. In other words, demand for services increases only when per capita income reaches a certain threshold level.

The other important relationship that is relevant to the current discussion is that between manufacturing and overall growth. Kaldor's first law states that the faster the rate of growth in manufacturing, the faster will be the growth of GDP (Kaldor, 1966, 1967). He proposed a causality saying that, more the difference between the rates of growth of manufacturing compared to overall GDP, the faster will be the growth of GDP. Therefore, manufacturing emerges as the 'engine of growth', in the sense faster it grows, the faster it pulls up the growth of the economy. In the Indian case, the difference between the growth of manufacturing compared to that of overall GDP was much higher than the difference the services growth rate had with the growth of GDP till the eighties. This simply implies that manufacturing was playing the role of the 'engine' till eighties and after that, it was overtaken by services.

But this is not very typical to India. Most of the developing countries having per capita income of comparable range show similar trends of services sector-driven growth. Not only in terms of growth rates, if we compare the sectoral contribution in a larger timeframe, we find that the declining contribution of agriculture in the GDP has largely been captured by the services sector. The average sectoral share of agriculture in GDP declined roughly from an average of 41 per cent in the four decades preceding liberalisation (51/52-89-90) to an average of 21 per cent in the two-and-a-half decades since liberalisation (90/91-13/14), recording a decline of 20 percentage points. During the two reference periods, the share of manufacturing increased as little as by 3 percentage points and that of services recorded a rise of more than 17 percentage points. As mentioned earlier, the percentage share in employment for services is more than double of that recorded for manufacturing.

Table 1: Sectoral Growth Rates over the years

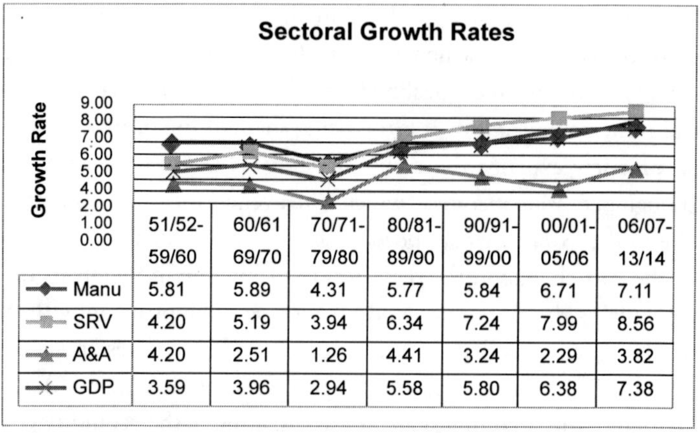

	51/52-59/60	60/61 69/70	70/71-79/80	80/81-89/90	90/91-99/00	00/01-05/06	06/07-13/14
Manu	5.81	5.89	4.31	5.77	5.84	6.71	7.11
SRV	4.20	5.19	3.94	6.34	7.24	7.99	8.56
A&A	4.20	2.51	1.26	4.41	3.24	2.29	3.82
GDP	3.59	3.96	2.94	5.58	5.80	6.38	7.38

Source: Computed from National Accounts Statistics, several years.

The trend seems to be peculiar because this service-led growth is taking place in India when per capita income is much less than what it ought to be, according to the experience of advanced capitalist countries. One important explanation of such a trend is related to definitional changes as well as change in the organisation of work. For instance, the service and the value addition of a security guard or a gardener in a factory was earlier considered to be a value added within the manufacturing sector, as the guard was an employee of the factory itself. Now, when most of such services are outsourced, it is accounted as a service output generated by the company which supplies security guards. The more important reason, however, relates to the growth of financialisation of the economy. Business services and many of the intermediate and finance-related services have increased enormously during this period. The supply of such services has become easier and cheaper, primarily because of the communication innovations and the globalisation of finance. But the question is, what explains the growth of demand for such services?

Studies show that the contribution of growth of 'services exported' to the overall growth of services is only 22 per cent. This precisely implies that India's growth of services has to be explained by growth of domestic demand rather than that of exports. The plausible explanation could be the fact of a significant rise in the share of profit earners in the gross value added, compared to wage and salary earners. According to National Accounts Statistics, the share of employees' compensation and that of mixed income which accounts for income of self-employed and unincorporated business declined over the years while that of operating surplus increased sharply. It is the rising share of the profit earning-class that precisely explains the rising demand for services. In other words, although per capita income—which is an average measure—did not show a rise to the extent that supports such a growth in demand for services, it is the vast change in the distribution of income in favour of the rich that explains the rise in demand for services. The problem with such a growth trajectory is that it is exclusionary and it requires an even faster rise in profit income to sustain the growth of services demand. On the other hand, the declining share of wage income in the economy possibly explains the stunted growth of manufacturing in India.

Problems of Demand

The manufacturing sector primarily grows, depending on the growth of demand for machinery and durable consumer goods in the domestic market, as well as due to the growth of similar demand in the external market.The share of manufacturing product to total exports in India declined from 80.7 per cent in 1999–00 to 61.4 per cent in 2013–14. The share of primary sector, including resources, remained more or less same. The share of petroleum-related products increased although these exports once upon a time had high import content. Moreover, in the current scenario, there is hardly any sign of a massive rise in global demand and that to in the US and Europe which happen to be the major export destinations for Indian goods.The recovery of the US economy is slow, the Euro zone is close to recession and Japan experienced two successive quarters of negative growth. The index of export growth potential as reported in the Economic Survey 2015-16 as the proxy of export demand declines from a growth rate of 3 per cent in 2014 to 2.7 per cent in 2014. In fact there was decline in absolute volume of non-oil exports. Therefore, rise in export demand that could pull up India's manufacturing growth is at least not visible in the immediate horizon. Furthermore in case of India there has been a sharp fall in domestic value added share of gross exports from 87.4 per cent in 1995 to 63.9 percent in 2011. This further weakens the link between exports and employment creation in the domestic economy.

If we take a look on the nature of consumption demand in the domestic economy, it is easily discernible why demand for manufacturing goods is not enough to stimulate higher growth. There is a notion that in the past two decades there has been a significant swelling of the middle class segment and that would have generated enough demand for higher growth in manufacturing.True indeed that there has been a rise in per capita income in India as well as increase in the absolute number of people belonging to the middle class, nevertheless, it is far less than the share of people belonging to comparable income strata in China. Defining middle class by \$2–\$13 per day, the absolute number of people in the middle class increased from 17.3 million in 1990 to 24.1 million in 2005 and during the same reference years, the absolute number of people belonging to the middle class in China went up from 15.3 million to 61.8 million

(Ravallion, 2009). Using a broad measure of $2–$20 per day, as used by ADB (Asian Development Bank), the share of people having more than $4 per day increased from 12 per cent in 1993–94 to 18 per cent in 2004–05 in case of India while the share increased from 18 per cent to 70 per cent during the same reference period in case of China (ADB, 2010). No comparison can exist between the incomes of the middle classes of China and today's India.

Table 2 shows the growth of consumption expenditure by various categories of goods and also their respective shares in the average Indian consumption basket. The average growth of consumption of durable goods during the last decade was 9.9 per cent, which is close to the average growth of the consumption of services. But services account for 35.8 per cent of the average consumption basket while durable goods on an average accounted for only 3.2 per cent of the total consumption expenditure for an average Indian.

This precisely shows that for an average consumer, the demand for durable consumer goods is actually a very small share of the total expenditure and hence even if this demand is growing, it has not created enough expansion of the domestic market. This becomes more evident from household expenditure surveys that show demand for consumer durables only increases very sharply at the top 5 per cent of the average private consumption expenditure distribution. Table 3 shows the monthly per capita consumption expenditure on durable goods by fractile classes for rural and urban areas for the survey year 2011-12. It is evident from the figures that the bottom 90 per cent of the population distribution, ranked by monthly per capita consumption expenditure, together spends close to half of what is being spent by top 5 per cent in buying durable goods. Moreover the expenditure on durable goods for the 12th fractile class is 6.5 times and 7.8 times higher than that of the 10th fractile class in urban and rural areas respectively.

The narrow base of consumption demand also creates constraints for the growth of intermediates and machinery because there has to be some balance between segments producing equipment and machinery and that producing goods for consumption. And a stagnating consumption demand may be compensated by a high investment demand for some time, but once expectation of profitability through investment encounters

Table 2: Growth and Composition of Private Final Consumption Expenditure by Goods

	Growth of Consumption Expenditure by Goods Type										
	2000–01	2001–02	2002–03	2003–04	2004–05	2005–06	2006–07	2007–08	2008–09	2009–10	Avg
DG	8.6	4	-2.3	10.9	34.9	4.4	14.3	7.6	5.5	11.3	9.9
SDG	13.7	-4.4	0	5.2	27.9	13	20.1	4.7	2.4	0.3	8.3
NDG	-2.9	4.4	-2.7	4.7	3	6.5	6.2	5.1	2.2	0.7	2.7
SVC	10.5	9.3	7.8	6.8	11.5	8.1	11.5	11.5	10.6	9.5	9.7
	Share of Consumption Expenditure by Goods Type										
DG	2.8	2.7	2.7	2.7	3.4	3.3	3.5	3.5	3.4	3.9	3.2
SDG	6.5	5.8	6.1	6.1	8.6	9	9.9	9.6	9.3	9.6	8.1
NDG	63.4	63.9	61.9	61.4	49.1	48.5	47	45.8	44.8	43.7	52.9
SVC	27.3	27.6	29.3	29.8	38.9	39.1	39.7	41.1	42.5	42.7	35.8

Source: Computed from National Accounts Statistics, various years

Table 3: Monthly Per capita Consumption of Durable Goods by Fractile Class

	1	2	3	4	5	6	7	8	9	10	11	12
Urban	9.8	14.96	19.11	25.88	31.44	45.64	56.64	79.32	122.55	196.84	320.71	1287.3
Rural	8.68	12.92	13.97	17.45	21.7	25.46	30.81	37.43	51.27	74.63	139.5	586.24

Source: NSS Report on Household Consumption of Various Goods and Services in India, 68th. Round.

a setback, investments also tend to decline. Despite the fact that the share of profits in gross value added increased sharply during the post-liberalisation period, and the average rate of profit was much higher during the period 2005/06 to 2011/12 compared to earlier periods, the rate of profit in manufacturing reached its peak in 2007-08 and then recorded a declining trend. This might be because of the negative impact of global recession that adversely affected the profit rate. The declining rate of profit might have impacted upon corporate investments and the share of private corporate investment in gross capital formation shows a declining trend since 2011-12. A point to note here is that private investors also seem to apprehend a declining rate of profit in the manufacturing sector. This is reflected by the fact of declining capacity utilisation in manufacturing sector in India. As reported by the *Economic Survey*, the July-September 2015 Round of the Order Books, Inventories and Capacity Utilization Survey (OBICUS) of the Reserve Bank of India (RBI) showed that at the aggregate level, capacity utilization of a sample of manufacturing companies recorded a decline. Capacity utilisation in manufacturing declined from 75 per cent in the fourth quarter of 2013-14 to 70.6 per cent in the second quarter of 2015-16. Hence, it is not only about improving roads and ports and enhancing ease of doing business, ensuring zero labour activism by dismantling existing labour institutions. The question of demand and profitability creates the biggest stimulation for capitalist investment. And the 'Make in India' campaign seems to be not at all serious in addressing the issues of demand. This is primarily because, addressing such issues demand redistribution of income in favour of wage earners and that is, of course, a proposition that makes governments committed to neoliberal reforms very uncomfortable. Ironically, this government's commitment to market causes further shrinkage of the market!

Composition of Demand

It is also a fact one has to reckon with that manufacturing growth per se will not necessarily ensure higher growth of employment. Indeed, it is true that manufacturing has a far higher backward linkage compared to services and because the growth of productivity is much faster in manufacturing, it is also true that prices of manufacturing goods rise at a slower rate than that of services. This precisely implies manufacturing growth requires a pace of growth of per capita income, which is at least lower than that required for a faster growth of services. In other words, in countries like India where income distribution is increasingly becoming skewed in favour of the rich, it is very difficult to sustain a higher services growth in the domestic economy until and unless the distribution ensures even higher growth of income for the richer sections of the society. And with a shrinking base of demand it would hardly be possible to sustain a growth, driven by services in the longer run. Moreove,r it is also argued that services require more manufactured inputs than the proportion of services entering into the production of manufactured goods. Therefore, manufacturing growth is also needed for services to grow.

But the growth of manufacturing does not necessarily ensure a higher growth of employment. In the organised sector, there has been a secular decline in the employment elasticity over the years. This is precisely because capital intensity in the manufacturing sector has increased during the past three decades. Capital has become cheaper because of financial integration and sops are given to industries such that they can raise their investment levels. Capital intensity has also increased because excess capacities were created, using capital that are easily available. There is another plausible reason for introducing machines that reduce the use of labour. This is mostly related to inadequate supply of skilled labour. In case of India, skilled labour is also a scarce factor and if that requirement can be met by using skill-replacing machines, industries happily procure such equipment. In many industries, higher order machines have been introduced that require lower levels of skill to operate. In other words, in such cases, capital intensity increases with a process of deskilling. Moreover, because of availability of cheap unskilled and semi-skilled labour, wages can easily be contained which would not have been the case had the employers employed skilled workers.

The moot point however is, how to increase the demand for manufactured goods that employ relatively more labour. And this issue is essentially linked with the composition of demand. Goods that are used by common people, by wage and salary earners, are the goods that are generally produced by using more labour. Tobacco products, apparel, leather and related products, furniture, other manufacturing, wood and related products, textiles, food products, fabricated metal products and repair and installation[1] are the top ten labour intensive sectors in our manufacturing sector. One can easily discern from the list that the demand for these products basically depends on the rising income of the wage and salary earners, but unfortunately that has sharply declined over the years.

The rise in profit income, of course, has a positive impact on the demand for services, luxury goods and high valued imports but the relative proportion of income that is used for buying products listed above gradually declines as the share of profit earners in the national income increases. In this regard one can easily understand that it is not the question of generating more employment—meaning share of people employed within the labour force increasing—it is important to increase the share of wage and salary earners within the total income. If more people are employed in the informal sector and forced to accept lower wages—keeping their total share of wages in national income unchanged—it would hardly have any impact on the demand for goods. Therefore there has to be a redistribution of income in favour of the wage earning class that would in turn increase the demand for manufactured products, and especially those produced with a larger use of labour. In this context, one can argue why one has to depend on domestic demand that requires redistribution, rather, why cannot one think of supplying labour-intensive goods to the global market and derive similar results? Without discounting the fact that the possibility of participating in global production network has increased during the era of globalisation, in case of labour-intensive goods studies show that the barter terms of trade of these goods produced in developing countries vis-a-vis the sophisticated manufactured products produced in Europe suffer a decline. In other words, competition between developing countries tends to reduce the unit price of manufactured products in a bid to raise their export share. Therefore, it is also not very reasonable to think of enhancing labour-intensive production in India that increasingly fetches lower terms of trade and depends on a competition that further tends to push down wages.

Redistribution in income not only increases the demand for manufactured goods but also changes the composition of demand.

---

1 Repair and installation comes under manufacturing as defined by Annual Survey of Industries.

A rise in the income share of wage and salary earners would reduce the demand for luxury and imported goods and also that of low value-added, low quality products, usually produced in the informal segment. This change in composition in demand might increase the demand for goods produced in modern small-scale industries that usually have relatively higher employment elasticity.

However, globalisation in the current phase is a process that not only involves inter-penetration of economies in terms of financial flows and production, but also involves considerable penetration of culture. Our choices and preferences are increasingly homogenised. A homogenisation that favours the culture of the North, their tastes and preferences, are increasingly being adopted as 'standards' or 'global', and hence, technologies that help produce goods preferred in the developed countries are increasingly becoming essential for the production process across the globe. The hegemonic in this case works through setting norms that disfavours a production process using labour-intensive technology. And, in this context, one needs to think of a calibrated engagement with the global economy.

Why is it essential for a country to satisfy the needs of the few rich at the expense of sacrificing demand for goods that are less sophisticated but employ more people, and hence raise incomes of a much larger proportion of the population? Why is the collective goal of creating gainful employment compromised by using labour-saving technologies that actually fits well economies of the North that are capital abundant? Let us refrain from servicing the need of the few; let the high-end needs wait till the vast majority of India's1.2 billion people get the taste of a decent life.

References

1. ADB (2010), Key Economic Indicators 2010, *The Growth of the Middle Class*, Manila: ADB.
2. Kaldor N (1966), *Causes of the Slow Rate of Economic Growth of the United Kingdom*, Cambridge University Press.
3. Kaldor N (1967), *Strategic Factors in Economic Development*, New York State School of Industrial and Labour Relations, Cornell University.
4. Ravallion M (2009), 'The Developing Worlds' Bulging (but Vulnerable) 'Middle Class', Policy Research Working Paper, No. 4816, World Bank.

Foreign Direct Investment for Making India

— KS Chalapati Rao

EVER SINCE India liberalised its foreign investment regime in 1991, attracting large amount of foreign direct investment (FDI) has captivated the psyche of the policymakers to such an extent that regime changes have little relevance for the course the FDI policy has been set upon.* Although occasional concerns are expressed on issues like takeover of pharmaceutical companies and high royalty payments to foreign parents by their Indian subsidiaries, 'regulation' of FDI is discouraged in general for fear of 'sending wrong signals' to foreign investors. This is also understandable because in the context of huge current account deficit, FDI was seen to

* This chapter draws from some of the papers prepared for the ICSSR-sponsored study 'India's Inward FDI Experience in the Post-liberalisation Period with Emphasis on the Manufacturing Sector', conducted at the Institute for Studies in Industrial Development, New Delhi. The author gratefully acknowledges the contribution of Professor BiswajitDhar to the papers.

be a source of stable long- term external funding. In this scenario, critical analysis of the contribution of FDI to India's development endeavours has become a major casualty. Thus, not surprisingly, liberalisation of India's FDI has continued unabated since the present government took office in 2014. (See Box-1)

The changes affected many sectors—the more important ones being construction development, defence industries, insurance and pensions funds, plantations, broadcasting, railways, air transport and retail trade. Going by the signals emanating from the recent Budget and the *Economic Survey*, the process would continue. The policy orientation of the new government towards foreign investors has two components. First, there has been a distinct shift away from prioritising long-term forms of foreign investment, which economists had identified as 'foreign direct investment' (FDI). In the process, the distinction between 'FDI' and other forms of foreign investment diminished further. Secondly, the government has been seeking greater participation of foreign capital in its 'Make in India' project, the first major initiative that the Government of India has taken since the adoption of the Industrial Policy Resolution in 1956 to build the country's manufacturing sinews.

This paper is an attempt to critically assess the government's policy of putting foreign capital in a pivotal position in the country's development strategy. In Section I we would trace some relevant features of global FDI flows. In the light of this international experience, in Section II, we will analyse India's experience with foreign investment over the past decade and highlight some of the key facets of the functioning of FDI companies. In the context of the substantial increase in the reported FDI inflows, we would try to describe in Section III some salient features of the large inflows during September 2014 to December 2015. The likely implications of the government's policy of opening the door wider for the entry of foreign investments in defence industries and the multi-brand retail sector are also presented in this Section. Section IV provides a contextualised summary of the paper.

Box 1: Modifications to India's FDI Policy since the Middle of 2014

Jun 2014	Removed the need for obtaining an Industrial License manufacturing certain items like components, parts, sub-systems, testing equipments falling under the category of defence industries.
Aug 2014	Defence Industries: while raising the general cap to 49 per cent, it was stated that the combined share of FII, FPI, NRI, FVCI and QFI investment cannot exceed 24 per cent. FDI policy for railway infrastructure relaxed.
Dec 2014	Relaxed the policy applicable to the Construction Development Sector.
Jan 2015	Carve out for medical devices and freeing it from the requirement of government approval in case of brownfield investments.
Mar 2015	Insurance: FDI limit raised from 26 per cent to 49 per cent—automatic up to 26 per cent & approval route for foreign share exceeding 26 per cent. The limit is composite for FDI, FPI (FII/QFI), NRI, FVCI and Depository Receipts.
Apr 2015	Pension sector opened to FDI. Conditions same as for insurance are applicable.
Jun 2015	Definition of NRI expanded to include 'Overseas Citizen of India' in addition to 'Persons of India Origin' cardholders. Further, NRI investments 'will be deemed to be domestic investment at par with the investments by residents'.
Oct 2015	FDI up to 100 per cent allowed in White Label ATMs through automatic route.
Nov 2015	100 per cent FDI through Automatic Route allowed in Tea, Coffee, Rubber, Cardamom, Palm Oil tree and Olive Oil tree plantations. Earlier 100 per cent FDI allowed in Tea plantations though approval route. The sub-limit of 24 per cent for portfolio investments within the 49 per cent foreign investment in defence industries was removed. An important addition was that 'Investee company should be structured to be self-sufficient in areas of product design and development. The Investee/joint venture company along with manufacturing facility, should also have maintenance and life cycle support facility of the product being manufactured in India'.

	Broadcasting Sector: FDI limits applicable to the sector relaxed substantially. Caps on FDI in non-scheduled Air Transport Service, Ground Handling, establishment of Satellites, Credit Information Companies removed. Construction Development: Minimum floor area and investment requirements were removed. SBRT: 30 per cent sourcing norm could be relaxed for trading of products having 'state-of-art' and 'cutting-edge' technology and where local sourcing is not possible.
Feb 2016	Budget Speech 2016-17 announced that (i) 100 per cent FDI will be allowed through FIPB route in marketing of food products produced and manufactured in India. (ii) foreign investment will be allowed in the insurance and pension sectors through the automatic route up to 49 per cent (iii) 100 per cent FDI in Asset Reconstruction Companies will be permitted through automatic route (iv) investment limit for foreign entities in Indian stock exchanges will be enhanced from 5 per cent to 15 per cent. (v) the existing 24 per cent limit for investment by FPIs in Central Public Sector Enterprises, other than Banks, listed in stock exchanges, will be increased to 49 per cent. (vi) to ensure effective implementation of Bilateral Investment Treaties signed by India with other countries, it is proposed to introduce a Centre State Investment Agreement. This will ensure fulfilment of the obligations of the State Governments under these Treaties.

Glimpses of the Global Situation

The reported global FDI inflows consist (though not uniformly across all countries) of fresh capital inflows, profits retained abroad and other capital – primarily loans obtained from foreign affiliates. This distinction is important because, not all the reported flows represent actual cross-border investments. On the other hand, while foreign capital is expected to confer benefits on host economies, it also entails certain costs. For the host countries, the direct costs of allowing foreign companies to operate in their territories could be in the form of dividend outflows, payments for using the technologies and brand names, adverse trade balance, international travel expenses, remuneration for expatriate employees, interest payments, payments for a variety of services, capital repatriation etc. Foreign investment also brings with it the serious risk of displacing of domestic investors. Further, FDI companies' dominance, coupled with their huge financial backing may inhibit the emergence of local alternatives in developing countries in the absence of appropriate institutional mechanisms. In the following we shall try to describe these in some detail.

Reinvested Earnings

Reinvested earnings are treated as a part of inflows because these are net additions to the stock of capital held by foreign companies in their host countries. There are two contrasting views about reinvested earnings. The first is that foreign companies' reinvested earnings augment domestic investment in host countries and, therefore, the latter should devise policies that encourage foreign investors to retain more of their profits because dividend remittances act as a drain. The other view is that retained earnings increase the host country's liabilities without actually transferring resources from abroad. In fact, retained earnings are surpluses generated by the foreign companies in the host countries and in domestic currencies that are then converted into foreign assets and can thus become the conduits for larger volumes of dividend remittances in future. Further, if such earnings are used to take over domestic companies or to buy back shares from the public, then they would not add to the existing capacities directly.

Interestingly, UNCTAD said that:

> ...earnings retained in the economy do not automatically translate into capital expenditures. For host countries of FDI, the same measures that promote investment will help maximize the extent to which retained earnings are reinvested. In addition, some countries adopt targeted incentives to facilitate reinvestment. (UNCTAD, *World Investment Report*, 2013, p 36)

Essentially, UNCTAD is suggesting that host countries should (continue to) offer incentives so that the retained earnings lead to further investments. This, however, misses the point that if foreign companies hinder the emergence of domestic alternatives, there will be avoidable buildup of foreign liabilities and continuous drain of surpluses.

It should be underlined that reinvested earnings have emerged as an important dimension of global FDI flows. However, their role is not highlighted probably because of unavailability of disaggregated data, especially for the developing countries. It is only for some time now that UNCTAD has started reporting indicative shares of reinvested earnings. UNCTAD's figures suggest that the share of reinvested earnings has increased progressively during the recent past and by 2013 they constituted two-thirds of the FDI outflows from the developed countries. For select developed countries, the share is reported to have increased to as much as four-fifths of total inflows in 2014. In 2014, a mere 10 per cent of total inflows were accounted for by direct equity flows, with loans making up for the remaining part. Reinvested earnings are also reported to be accounting for a fairly large share of outward investments by developing countries. Since data are not available for some emerging major economies, these could be taken only as indicative. However, it would be realistic to expect that the burden of reinvested earnings increases as companies grow older, even while they receive little additional investment from outside.

An exercise conducted by us provides further support to the above phenomenon. For a set of 15 large developed country global investors, the average share of reinvested earnings in equity outflows worked out to be 57.5 per cent during 2011-2013 – far higher than the corresponding share of 40.6 per cent during 2005-2007, *ie.* the three years immediately preceding the financial crisis. Another important feature is that outflows as a ratio of dividend income, received by the developed countries, declined steeply over the period. In the pre-crisis period, they just matched the dividends. The ratio fell to almost two-thirds in the recent period. Thus, more money was flowing into the developed countries as dividend income than that was flowing out as direct investment, thanks to the past investments.

Payments for Use of Intellectual Property

Further, developed country entities control the market for proprietary technologies and consequently, they are the main recipients of the payments made for using these technologies. Indeed, during 2011-2013, the high income OECD countries accounted for 96.2 per cent of the receipts under the head, 'Charges for the use of intellectual property'. United States alone accounted for about half (51.4 per cent) of the global receipts arising from the use of proprietary technologies. The country's share in payments was only 15.0 per cent.

To the extent technology payments are made for 'use' rather than for transfer of ownership of technologies, extraction of surpluses from foreign subsidiaries and affiliates and royalties on brand names help to perpetuate the position of the holders of technology/brand names. Our calculations show that the average ratio of intellectual property-related receipts to dividend receipts by the 15 large developed economies was 40 per cent during 2011-2013. Even excluding the extreme case of the United States, the corresponding share was 25 per cent. Thus, such payments are another important means of benefiting by the developed home countries. Obviously, the aggregate FDI flows reported by UNCTAD and other international organisations do not reflect the actual resource transfers from the developed to the developing countries and the benefits the latter derive from outward FDI. Freer entry of FDI will have two unintended consequences for developing countries. One, foreign companies would be unwilling to transfer technologies to unaffiliated entities, thereby stifling their growth potential. Second, having complete control over the investee companies, they will have greater freedom to unduly extract surpluses from host countries.

FDI and Capital Formation

In spite of the fact that FDI inflows include a sizeable portion of M&A related flows, most of which do not contribute to capital formation in the immediate or even in the medium term, the ratios of FDI inflows to gross fixed capital formation (GFCF) are used as indicators of the potential contribution of FDI inflows to host economies. Private equity related M&As, in fact, entail regular and huge reverse flows due to periodic encashment of the earlier investments. According to UNCATD, except for 2009, the share of reverse flows on account of encashed investments was close to half or more of the gross inflows. For the ten year period 2005-2014, the share was 57.1 per cent. Thus the reported ratios of FDI inflows to GFCF, which at times may appear to be relatively high, could, in fact, be exaggerating the role of FDI; more so when they are secondary investments by private equity investors or were replacing the domestic investors. In any case, a significant portion of the surpluses that could be ploughed back into the economy would be drained out. Obviously, foreign investment has played a limited role in countries while bulk of the investment was local.

Some Aspects of India's Experience

It is now well-known that India started including reinvested earnings and other capital (loans) in the reported FDI inflows since 2000-01. During the past one-and-a-half decades, re-invested earnings accounted for a substantial share of the reported FDI into India. For instance, a little more than a fourth of the FDI inflows reported by the RBI during 2009-10 and 2014-15 were made up of re-invested earnings. Another major component is the inflows on account of buying out of existing enterprises or investors (both domestic and already existing foreign ones). Official data suggest that M&A-related inflows account for a little over one-fourth of the equity inflows, net of reinvested earnings and the equity attributed to branches of foreign companies and loans. This could, however, be an underestimate as inflows deployed indirectly in acquisitions are excluded from official calculations.

Further, official data show that during January 2000 to March 2015, majority of the FDI inflows (through approval, automatic and acquisition routes) went into non-manufacturing sectors, with construction sector receiving the largest share of 10 per cent of the total, or $24.06 bn. Within the manufacturing sector, which received about a third of the total inflows, four broad sectors, namely, pharmaceuticals ($13.2 bn), automobiles ($12.5 bn), chemicals ($10.4 bn) and metallurgical industries ($8.6 bn) received the largest amounts. Other high-technology industries, namely, electronics ($1.4 bn), medical and surgical appliances ($0.93 bn) and machine tools ($0.7 bn) in which foreign companies are expected to have an edge over domestic enterprises, FDI inflows were relatively much smaller. The share of IT and related sectors, which was among the few services that had earned net foreign exchange for the country, had progressively declined. Between April 1999 and end of March 2008, the

IT and related sectors accounted for 13.1 per cent of the total inflows, but between April 2008 and March 2014, the share of these sectors had halved to below 6 per cent.

In view of the liberal approach adopted by India in defining what constitutes FDI, a good part of the reported inflows do not possess the characteristics that are theoretically associated with FDI such as advanced technology, managerial expertise, brand names, long term interest, etc.—which are the prime attractions for developing countries—as these are made by financial investors, Indian entrepreneurs and Indian diaspora. A study of large tranches of FDI inflows into India by us found that what could realistically be called FDI worked out to about 53.5 per cent of the reported FDI equity inflows during Sept 2004 and March 2014. The remaining was by portfolio investors (32 per cent) and other India-related investors (14.5 per cent). Within the manufacturing sector which accounted for 35.8 per cent of the total, a little more than three-fourths of the inflows can be termed as realistic FDI. Further, the estimates showed that the share of M&As involving manufacturing companies receiving such realistic FDI could have been more than half of the total during 2004-05 to 2013-14. Thus, very little of the total reported FDI contributed to new capacity creation in the manufacturing sector.

Servicing Obligations

The reported FDI consists of investments by a variety of investors, including financial investors who would keep circulating their investments and M&As. Since financial investors seek substantial capital gains within a few years, repatriations are bound to be in multiples of the inflows, for not only do they need not necessarily add to the existing capacities, the outgo on their account results in leakage of domestic resources. It thus follows that actual inflows, which could supplement domestic savings and investment and, therefore, contribute to the country's development, would be smaller.

The leakages on account of FDI occur through dividend outgo, capital repatriation and payments for other services and technology. There is further justification in treating some of the technology payments as avoidable remittances. A few instances suggest that FDI companies in

India could be using such payments as substitutes for dividend remittances either to lower the tax incidence (corporate and dividend distribution taxes) and/or to deny the public shareholders of the companies their due. Since some of the royalty/knowhow payments could have been made by Indian companies not having FDI, we attributed an arbitrary 50 per cent as the share of FDI companies in the annual outflows on their account. During 2009-10 and 2014-15, outflows due to repatriations, dividends and payments for technology have become a major drain: together they worked out to nearly one-half of the equity inflows during this period (Table-1). It is pertinent to note that repatriations/disinvestments alone accounted for more than a fourth of the equity inflows. Surprisingly, India's policymakers seem to be unconcerned about the high servicing burden.

Manufacturing Companies Run Large Trade Deficit

It is widely known that MNCs in India are generally domestic market-oriented. Further confirmation of this dependence comes from the Annual Census of India's Foreign Liabilities and Assets conducted by the Reserve Bank of India. The Census for 2013-14 shows that the surpluses on the trade account generated by the subsidiaries of foreign companies operating in India was possible only because of the companies in the Information and Communication sector. In other words, subsidiaries of other foreign companies together ran a huge trade deficit. What is more striking is that most of the individual manufacturing sub-sectors run negative trade balances (See Table-2). The trading companies too ran deficits. Foreign subsidiaries in manufacturing sectors like pharmaceuticals registered surpluses mainly because they had acquired Indian-owned companies that already had significant presence in international markets. Interestingly, the reported exports by some of the consumer electronics companies, which ran large trade deficits, were actually software exports and thus the contribution of foreign manufacturing subsidiaries could have been overestimated to that extent. Together with the remittances outgo referred to in an earlier paragraph, and other payments, foreign subsidiaries in most cases can be seen to be adding to the vulnerability of India's external payments position.

The nature of FDI flows is such that there is relatively low share of sectors which have the potential to generate surplus on trade account.

Table 1: Ratio of Certain Remittances to Equity Inflows

Year	Gross Equity Inflows ($ mn)	Outflows				Ratio of Outflows to Equity Inflows (%) (6)/(2)*100
		Equity Repatriation/ Disinvestment ($ mn)	Dividends ($ mn)	Charges for use of Intellectual Property ($ mn)	Total (3)+(4)+((5)/2)	
(1)	(2)	(3)	(4)	(5)	(6)	(7)
2009-10	27,146	4,241	4,030	2,017	9,280	34.2
2010-11	22,250	6,514	4,901	2,424	12,627	56.8
2011-12	35,854	13,018	5,264	3,207	19,886	55.5
2012-13	22,884	6,853	3,486	4,159	12,419	54.3
2013-14	25,274	4,786	4,041	3,980	10,817	42.8
2014-15	31,885	9,612	3,679	4,820	15,701	49.2
2009-10 to 2014-15	1,65,293	45,024	25,401	20,607	80,729	48.8

Source: Based on the BoP data provided by the RBI periodically, based on BPM6.

Table 2: Sector-wise Exports, Imports, Trade Balance of 9,081 Foreign Subsidiaries during 2013-14

Amount in Rs billion					
Activity	**No of Cos**	**Exports**	**Imports**	**Trade Balance**	**Share of Imports to Purchases (%)**
(1)	(2)	(3)	(4)	(5)	(6)
A. Agriculture-related, Plantations & Allied activities	**25**	**5.5**	**4.2**	**1.3**	**11.1**
B. Mining	**36**	**7.8**	**9.9**	**-2.1**	**12.7**
C. Manufacturing	**2,166**	**2284.1**	**3,498.2**	**-1,214.1**	**50.7**
Computer, electronic and optical products	56	165.9	536.9	-371.0	78.6
Coke and refined petroleum products	9	414.5	740.1	-325.6	81.5
Food products	92	371.9	668.6	-296.7	68.2
Chemicals and chemical products	160	117.5	172.9	-55.4	46.3
Electrical equipment	132	97.0	151.8	-54.8	36.4
Rubber and plastics products	77	21.5	38.2	-16.7	48.7
Manufacture of paper and paper products	19	7.1	22.9	-15.8	58.4
Basic metals	25	43.5	56.2	-12.7	19.0
Fabricated metal products, except machinery and equipment	79	8.4	15.7	-7.3	38.1
Motor vehicles, trailers and semi-trailers	75	390.1	385.5	4.6	26.3
Wearing Apparel	20	9.9	3.4	6.5	34.7

Table 2 (Contd...)

Textiles	30	16.7	8.7	8.0	40.7
Pharmaceuticals, medicinal and chemical products	100	108.5	80.4	28.1	45.7
Machinery and equipment nec.	355	156.1	119.2	36.9	35.6
Other manufacturing	937	355.5	497.7	-142.2	46.4
D. Electricity, gas, steam and air conditioning supply	72	1.50	5.20	-3.70	25.0
E. Water supply; sewerage, waste management and remediation activities	31	0.30	0.60	-0.30	12.5
F. Construction	187	20.50	31.10	-10.60	22.4
G. Services	4,968	2,580.40	846.70	1,733.70	35.1
Information and communication	1,920	2007.7	202.2	1805.5	25.4
Financial and insurance activities	243	67.0	6.3	60.7	6.9
Transportation and storage	163	63.6	25.3	38.3	25.1
Wholesale and retail trade; repair of motor vehicles	783	153.4	548.2	-394.8	51.3
Other Services activities	1,859	288.7	64.7	224.0	18.1
Total	7,485*	4,900.10	4,395.90	504.20	

Source: Based on the data released by the Reserve Bank of India. (https://rbi.org.in/Scripts/BS_PressReleaseDisplay.aspx?prid=33035)

* Out of the 9,081 subsidiaries 7,485 reported sales.

Note: (i) One is not sure whether the tabulations are for only those companies which reported sales. (ii) RBI does not explain the items covered under purchases.

On the other hand, all investments, irrespective of the sector, would carry with them servicing obligations of one form or the other.

FDI, Infrastructure Finance and Two Classes of Indian Investors

Large-scale substitution of domestic investment by FDI and foreign financial investors dealing with hot money flows, are two major problems that require immediate attention. In recent years, the involvement of financial investors is more in infrastructure sectors, specifically the construction and real estate sector, which was thrown open to FDI in the mid-2000s. It has also been noticed that some of these investors are affiliated to both Indian financial institutions and leading construction companies. Even in the reported FDI in the energy sector, the involvement of India-related entities is significant. Available data are inadequate to conclude whether such investors are bringing back funds stashed abroad or are raising funds abroad like the Chinese companies which do so in Hong Kong. The latter form of inflows would tantamount to disguised foreign portfolio investment. But since they route their investments mostly through tax havens like Mauritius and Cyprus, it raises questions about the sources of their funds and possible income leakages for India.

There are second-order implications of the kind of inflows discussed above. The huge inflows into the construction and real estate sector by investors seeking returns, which are multiples of their initial investments and that too in a short period, have serious implications for the other sectors of the economy in terms of escalating land prices, land acquisition, housing for the middle and lower middle income sections, clamour for allowing FDI in retail trade, increased demand for imported luxury fittings and accessories etc. India needs to rethink about financing its infrastructure through such portfolio and round-tripped investments, disguised as FDI. This point needs to be underlined here especially because the FDI policy applicable to this sector was liberalised further in December 2014 by lowering the minimum land/built-up area, providing exemption from the same in case 30 per cent of the project cost is committed to low-cost affordable housing and by explicitly stating that unlike the earlier three-year lock-in period, repatriation or transfer to other non-resident investor(s) would be permitted, albeit on a case-by-case basis. Further, the secondary investments implied in this policy would give a false sense of the country's ability to attract large inflows as they will only be displacing the earlier investments.

Some may justify round-tripping of investments as it facilitates return of flight capital for national development. But there is a more important dimension to the problem. If the investors are adopting this route merely to take advantage of the favourable tax regime, it shows how domestic investors are at a disadvantage. Secondly, investors who route their investments through other countries can invoke the provisions of the Investor State Dispute Settlement (ISDS) mechanisms included in the bilateral investment treaties (BITs) and can initiate litigations against the Indian government before private international tribunals. The key question before the government is the following: Should Indian investors who contribute substantially to the country's capital formation be discriminated against?

Royalty Payments or Disguised Dividends?

The emphasis on attracting large amount of FDI makes the dice loaded heavily in favour of the foreign investors. Unfortunately, investor rights have come to dominate investor obligations. Foreign investors can sue developing country governments, but the latter feel constrained to act against the former for fear of hurting 'investor confidence'. Investors' obligation, for example, to transfer technology, has remained a non-starter. There are cases where foreign companies have been keeping their Indian subsidiaries under tight control. For instance, Suzuki's Indian subsidiary Maruti Suzuki India Ltd, which has been operating in India for more than 30 years, paid royalties to its parent company to the tune of $2.12 bn. during 2008-09 to 2013-14. Why it did not transfer technology completely or why the company decided to pay royalty for use of brand name should be a matter of concern. It is obvious that the Indian subsidiary, the mainstay of Suzuki globally, will remain dependent on its parent.

Hindustan Unilever Ltd, a foreign subsidiary whose origins in India date back to 1888, decided in 2013 to increase the rate of royalty that it pays to its parent company, that too after the foreign share was increased through buyback. The result is already showing in the payouts: annual royalty payments have increased by 70 per cent. Incidentally, the company started cutting down on its R&D expenditure both in absolute terms and relative to its sales, thus paving the way for continued and greater dependence on the parent. Nestle India Ltd also agreed to hike the rate of royalty paid to the Swiss parent company Nestle SA in 2013. It is relevant to note that Nestle SA has a wholly-owned subsidiary in India called Nestle R&D Centre India Pvt Ltd, which began R&D operations in 2010.

Another important case is that of Samsung India Electronics which has been paying royalties on production that depends heavily on imports of components. The payments made by Samsung India to its parent have far exceeded the initial FDI inflows. The company was, however, quite candid in its admission that 'Considering the rapidly changing industry scenario; need for further strengthening the business...' it was not paying any dividends. The contribution to India's development made by such enterprises that are perpetually dependent on their foreign parents and incur huge deficits on the trade account, since they do not indigenise their production, need to be seriously debated, particularly when the government is emphasising on 'Make in India'. Given the freedom they enjoy, FDI companies would continue to transfer resources to their parents in both overt and covert ways. Payment of royalty is only one such mechanism.

Acquisitions is not an Issue of Competition Only

With the official focus firmly on the volume of inflows, the phenomenon of takeovers is not getting the attention it warrants. India should learn to distinguish not only between foreign investors but also between the sectors in which they invest and the mode of entry. The classic comment on FDI in potato chips and computer chips is still relevant. Will there be any difference in quality between the wheat flour sold directly by a miller located in a semi-urban town and the flour from the same factory being marketed by an American multinational under its brand name, most probably at a higher price—both selling in the same super market? Justification that the marketing MNC would ensure quality treats FDI as substitute to public authorities. Then who would monitor the quality of products marketed by MNCs? Or, is there a need at all? Would Indian consumers have been entirely deprived of quality FMCG products, had there been no MNCs around? The case of soft drink manufacture is relevant here. The exit of Coca-Cola from India during the 'seventies did not leave a vacuum as an alternative in the form of the Parle group had emerged. This Indian group also established itself as a leading bottled fruit juice seller. After having fought tooth and nail against the entry of Pepsi, when Coca-Cola returned following the liberalisation of the FDI policy in 1991, the Indian entrepreneur realised that he had neither the financial muscle to sustain a long-drawn fight with the two MNCs nor the support from policymakers. He then surrendered to the company whom he had succeeded. But the brands he created could not be killed by the foreign acquirer because of their popularity. Recent reports indicate that Coca-Cola is mulling to sell the bottling units for $1 bn. and concentrate on marketing. (*Economic Times,* February 29, 2016.) So someone else will 'Make in India' and Coca-Cola will 'Sell in India' and reap the benefits of the brands that it owns. Incidentally, foreign subsidiaries in the food processing sector are net losers on the trade front (Table-2). Further, bulk of the FDI that came into the food processing sector during 2004-05 to 2013-14 comprised alcoholic beverages, soft drink and allied products. Should India encourage such FDI, which incidentally replaced domestic entrepreneurs and which thrives on the strength of brand names, particularly when that does not translate into earning foreign exchange for the country?

It is significant to note that in the pharmaceuticals industry, the top FDI-recipient manufacturing sector, inflows are dominated by takeover of existing generics businesses and not by setting up of new plants with cutting edge technology. Our estimate puts the share of acquisitions in what could realistically be termed as FDI into the pharmaceutical sector at more than 90 per cent! In many sectors acquisition-related inflows dominated the inflows. Can the takeover of Credit Information Bureau (India) Limited or CIBIL, the credit information company having access to key financial data of an overwhelming portion of individuals and corporations in India, by an American multinational be termed as routine business transaction? Added to this, leading credit rating agencies ICRA and CRISIL have also been handed over to American investors by their respective promoters.

There is a need to introspect when leading seed companies are being taken over one after the other. The taken over companies include both established ones and start-ups, some of them in niche positions. Loss of such companies, which could form the basis for future industry leaders, will have a long-term negative impact on the Indian economy as it could lead to greater dependence on foreign companies whose behaviour, as shown above, is not always in the best interest of the host country.

That large global companies do not follow unethical practices or that they are infallible have proved to be fallacies. The $5.7 billion penalty imposed last year on five large global banks for manipulating foreign exchange market/interest rates shows how the investors behind the large corporations do not stop at anything to maximise their returns. It is possible that Enron has been forgotten by many, but the resignation of the chief executive of Toshiba in connection with the overstating of profits for six years should serve as another example as to how large, globally reputed companies can fall prey to the machinations of individuals.

A number of the non-financial companies are now being controlled by financial investors, at times by a single such investor. The merger of two large American food companies namely HJ Heinz and Kraft Foods was indeed orchestrated by two large private equity investors. UNCTAD also referred to the influence of a large private equity player in the merger of Tim Hortons (Canada) and Burger King Worldwide (USA). Interests of such investors need not necessarily coincide with those of individual countries, their workers and consumers. American corporations are known to have used tax havens to reduce their tax liability. More recently, the United States has had to change the rules to discourage what has come to be known as 'tax inversions' whereby American corporations, while continuing their businesses in the country, shift their headquarters to low tax countries. Will such companies which do not care for even their own home countries promote the interests of host countries like India?

Recent Scenario

As explained in the introductory section, the new government which came into power at the Centre in May 2014, not only continued on the path towards a freer FDI policy, it has also tried to accelerate the process through 'simplification and rationalisation of procedures and processes to attract more FDI'. The planks it has used are 'Ease of Doing Business', 'Make in India' and 'Start-up India'. Pertinently, the *Economic*

Survey 2015-16 stated that the 'FDI reforms reflect a decisive change in philosophy, from viewing FDI as a tolerable necessity to something to welcome'. Earlier, in the context of the acute current account deficit, the then finance minister said in his Budget Speech (2013-14) that

> This year, and perhaps next year too, we have to find over USD 75 billion to finance the CAD. There are only three ways before us: FDI, FII or External Commercial Borrowing (ECB). That is why I have been at pains to state over and over again that India, at the present juncture, does not have the choice between welcoming and spurning foreign investment. If I may be frank, foreign investment is an imperative. What we can do is to encourage foreign investment that is consistent with our economic objectives.

Thus, starting from a limited focus on the manufacturing sector and export promotion in 1991, and finding it to be imperative to meet current account deficits about two decades later, India's FDI policy has travelled a long way to openly welcome FDI.

The *Economic Survey* underlined that after the launching of FDI policy reforms in September 2014, there was nearly 40 per cent increase in FDI inflows during October 2014 to June 2015 over the corresponding period of the previous year. Indeed, more recent data for the period till February 2016 suggests that the inflows already crossed $51 bn during 2015-16, the highest in any single financial year so far(Table-3). The international credit rating agency Moody's attributed this rise to, apart from the further liberalised FDI policy, to the 'Make in India' campaign. A look at the actual equity inflows reported for the period April 2015 to December 2015, however, suggests that the share of manufacturing sector fell drastically while that of the services increased sharply (Table-4). While the omnibus Services sector stands at the top, interestingly, the second position was occupied by computer software and hardware(Table-5). This was followed by trading and construction (infrastructure) activities. The automobiles sector tops the manufacturing activities with 8.7 per cent of the total inflows. Incidentally, official data suggest that the addition to inflows on account of defence industries during April 2014 to December 2015 was a mere $0.08 mn.

Table 3: India's Gross FDI Inflows

($ bn.)			
Financial Year	**Total**	**Of which,**	
		Equity	**Others**
2011-12	46.6	35.9	10.7
2012-13	34.3	22.9	11.4
2013-14	36.0	25.3	10.7
2014-15	45.1	31.9	13.2
2014-15 (Apr-Feb) – "A"	41.6	29.7	11.9
2015-16 (Apr-Feb) – "B"	51.6	38.5	13.1
2015-16 (Apr-Dec)	40.9	30.2	10.7
Increase in "B" over "A" (per cent)	24.0	29.6	10.1

Equity: Inflows through government, acquisition and automatic routes & equity capital of unincorporated bodies.
Others: Reinvested earnings and Other Capital (loans).
Source: Based on data provided by RBI.

Table 4: Sectoral Distribution of FDI Inflows during the Recent Period

(Percentages)		
Sector	**Sep 2014—Dec 2015**	**Apr 2015—Dec 2015**
Services	64.4	72.9
Manufacturing	29.9	20.6
Energy (excl. Petroleum & Natural Gas)	3.9	4.3
Primary	1.8	2.1
All Sectors	**100.00**	**100.0**

Source: Based on the data provided by the DIPP on its website.

Since even the *Economic Survey* expressed reservations about the sectoral classification, we made an attempt to understand the nature of inflows based on the classification of companies which received at least $25 million during September 2014 to December 2015 and those investing in such companies. We could identify 297 companies with a

Table 5: Top Recipients of Reported FDI Inflows during September 2014 to December 2015

Rank	Sector/Industry	Share (%)
1	Services Sector *	15.75
2	Computer Software & Hardware	14.95
3	Trading	10.19
4	Construction (Infrastructure) Activities	9.12
5	Automobile Industry	8.68
6	Telecommunications	3.37
7	Chemicals (Other Than Fertilizers)	3.22
8	Hotel & Tourism	2.89
9	Power	2.04
10	Drugs & Pharmaceuticals	1.96
11	Hospital & Diagnostic Centres	1.92
12	Non-Conventional Energy	1.86
13	Miscellaneous Industries	1.83
14	Information & Broadcasting (Including Print Media)	1.67
15	Industrial Machinery	1.57
	Sub-total	81.0

Source: Based on data provided by the DIPP on its website.
* Includes finance, banking, insurance, non Fin. business, outsourcing, R&D, courier, tech. testing and analysis, etc.

total inflow of $36 bn—72 per cent of the FDI equity inflows received during the period. The main points emanating from this preliminary and limited exercise are as follows:

- The share of manufacturing sector was 25.5 per cent. The next in importance was trading with a share of 20.7 per cent. The construction sector including engineering companies succeeded with a share of 11.6 per cent. Information technology & communications and the transport sectors had almost equal shares of 8.7 and 8.5 respectively. Finance and hotels & restaurants again had almost equal shares – 6.4 and 6.3 respectively.

- Within the manufacturing sector, automobiles stood at the top followed by pharmaceuticals. Most of the inflows into the chemicals were into pharmaceuticals which were either already taken over or are in the process of being taken over. The two industries accounted for more than half of the inflows into the sector.
- Identifying takeover-related investments is a difficult exercise. While it is apparent that investments into taken over companies could be far higher than the official figures indicate, we are refraining from offering any comment in this regard at present.
- E-commerce related investments accounted for an overwhelming portion of the inflows into trading (81.0 per cent). Another 10.7 per cent were on account of wholesale trading companies. It appears that some of the e-commerce related companies might have been classified as computer software companies by the official agencies. Another category of companies which were classified as IT-related ones were actually engaged in providing app-based coordination of passenger transport. Thus, investment into those engaged in software development would be less than half of what even our classification suggests. Interestingly, inflows into trading and the online facilities equal the investments into the manufacturing sector.
- It is noteworthy that leading information technology companies did not make substantial investments either for manufacture or for software development. They were missing even when investments lower than $25 million were scanned. While CISCO invested $144 mn, the investee company's purpose was to provide 'loans/ leases for the IT assets to its customers which are Companies and other Corporate/Legal entities'. It did invest a total of $10 mn in IL&FS Technologies and One Mobikwik Systems. On the other hand, Google invested $9.7 mn in an online portal providing information on housing. Hewlett Packard did invest $174 mn but the amounts were for the reorganisation of existing operations into separate companies. Microsoft, whose India-born CEO visited the country many times in the recent past, brought in $0.02 mn to acquire the shares of Inmage Systems Ltd.

- The multiple small amounts of investments into Oracle by individuals appear to be ESOPs. The high profile Uber received a little less than $20 mn. Another high profile IT company, Facebook, invested $0.03 mn as a part of its acquisition of the startup Little Eye Labs during this period. The overall cost of acquisition is reported to be about $11mn.
- In the backdrop of the above, Computer Software & Hardware, a net earner of foreign exchange, occupying the second position (Table-5) appears to be quite untenable. Such so-called IT companies cannot generate positive foreign exchange balances.
- It is our understanding that most of the investment (72.7 per cent) in the construction development sector went into housing and other activities. The remaining was into infrastructure development (SEZs, Technology parks etc.) and engineering companies. It is important to note that about 31 per cent of the foreign portfolio investment into the sector was through acquisitions. Such investors were not adding to the existing investments in the sector but were either bailing out the promoters and/or were providing an exit for the existing portfolio investors (secondary investments).
- The enhanced inflows could possibly be attributed to policy relaxations with respect to trading and construction activities. It is relevant to note that a single company was reported to have invested as much as $2.25 bn during Oct-Dec 2015 to create facilities for senior citizens. It is highly unlikely that such huge investments flow in regularly. Excluding this investmen,t the shares of different types of investors turn out to be remarkably similar to the pattern observed for the decade 2004-05 to 2013-14: Realistic FDI 55.8 per cent; Portfolio: 32.8 per cent and India-related 10.9 per cent.
- Only 16 out of the 297 companies were incorporated in 2014 or 2015. Since four out of the 16 were incorporated to carry on the activities of the already existing operations, the effective number of newly incorporated companies was only 12 and these accounted for 1.79 per cent of the inflows under study. It appears that only one of the 297 companies was set up during 2014-2015

that took up greenfield manufacturing. This might indicate that the surge in inflows was more due to the past decisions of foreign investors, rather than being a response to policy and procedural changes.

- Out of the total inflows examined by us, about 59 per cent could realistically be treated as FDI having the theoretically expected attributes. 30.7 per cent was by a variety of portfolio investors, some of whom had Indian affiliation. 10.2 per cent of investment could be by other India related investors. Portfolio investment was highly concentrated: 43.2 per cent of the portfolio investment went into trading companies and an additional 12.4 per cent went into web/app based facilities.
- Most of the portfolio investment came through just two countries: Singapore (47.5 per cent) and Mauritius (43.9 per cent). Countries like Cyprus, Cayman Islands contributed another 3.3 per cent, making a total of 94.7 per cent. This will partially address the concern expressed by the *Economic Survey* 2015-16 when it said that:

> These inflows [from Singapore and Mauritius] need perhaps to be examined more closely to determine whether they constitute actual investment or are diversions from other sources, to avail of tax benefits under the Double Tax Avoidance Agreement that these countries have with India.

In the following we shall take a look at the FDI policy towards defence industries and multi-brand retail trade which underwent significant policy changes during the recent past.

FDI in Defence Industries

This is one sector where the policy makers have a lot of expectations. However, the defence industries sector is different from all others in many respects. There is very little chance of foreign governments (not just the corporations) weakening their hold on advanced technologies. Had it been otherwise, India would have attracted a lot of FDI even without raising the cap to 49 per cent as was done in 2014. After all, even the 2013 policy offered 100 per cent foreign ownership, if advanced technology was on offer. Foreign governments and companies made sustained efforts to dilute India's offset policy by offering to take up activities other than manufacturing. It is unlikely that large amounts of FDI will flow into defence industries and production bases will be shifted to India even if 100 per cent foreign ownership is allowed. Official data indeed confirms that very little FDI came into defence industries since September 2014.

Another of our study clearly showed that the foreign partners in the joint ventures, irrespective of their share in equity, tightly control technology and the JVs do not 'own' the technology. For instance, the articles of association of the now disbanded joint venture between Mahindras and BAE Systems, namely Defence Land Systems India Pvt Ltd (DLS), clearly stated that the technology would remain with the respective parties and the JV would not have the right to use it in case the foreign partner withdraws from it. The AoA of DLS had the following provision.

> Intellectual Property provided, licensed, and, or otherwise transferred to the Company by BAE Systems or any Affiliate of BAE Systems *will always remain the property of BAE Systems* or the respective Affiliate of BAE Systems (as the case may be) and the Company [JV] will: (i) use such Intellectual Property in accordance with the terms of the BAE Systems Technology Licence and Consultancy Agreements; and (ii) will not claim any rights or title to or in such Intellectual Property except as may be set out in the BAE Systems Technology Licence and Consultancy Agreements (emphasis added).

Even though a similar condition was applicable for technology provided by the Mahindras, it would not have had any practical significance. Similar right was provided in the AoA of Tata Lockheed Martin Aero Structures Ltd. Thus, in the event of a breakup, the Indian companies will have no right to use the technologies. Incidentally, capping of the foreign shares at 26 or 49 per cent has little significance as far as rights over technology or management are concerned.

The introduction of a condition in November 2015 that the

> Investee company should be structured to be self-sufficient in areas of product design and development. The Investee/joint venture company, along with manufacturing facility, should also have maintenance and life cycle support facility of the product being manufactured in India.

seems to recognise the above constraint faced by the JVs. The proposed defence procurement procedure also aims at encouraging indigenous production. In the context of the foreign companies adopting various mechanisms to retain control over technologies, it might end up as 'Hobson's choice' for India.

The study also underlined that countries, other than the traditional leaders, developed their defence industry mainly through public sector and domestic enterprises with advanced country corporations playing a limited role. Their geopolitical importance was also an important factor in the development of their defence capabilities. FDI policy could only be an enabling mechanism. The real levers lie with the advanced home governments. India should be prepared to do real hard bargaining and also be prepared for some political compromises.

FDI in Multi-brand Retail Trade

Permitting FDI in multi-brand retail trade was one of the most contentious aspects of India's FDI policy making. Prolonged nation-wide debate and discussion preceded it. At one time, the ruling party had put its government at risk and the then Prime Minister addressed a public meeting in the national capital to explain the benefits of FDI. The safeguards in respect of the policy towards FDI in multi-brand retail trade were expected to address the concerns expressed by the opponents. Following pressure from foreign investors, India, however, watered down the conditions relating to all the three critical elements of the policy namely, investment in backend infrastructure, sourcing from small enterprises and the protection provided to traders who are outside the vicinity of large cities with 10 lakh population. Even then the policy did not take off. Notwithstanding the lukewarm response of the foreign retailers, hopes are still being nursed by India to develop critical infrastructure for marketing agricultural produce with their help. *Economic Survey 2014-15* underlined the need to liberalise the FDI policy with regard to retail trade and said:

> In view of the difficulties in attracting domestic capital for setting up marketing infrastructure, particularly, warehousing, cold storages, reefer vans, laboratories, grading facilities etc. liberalisation of FDI in retail could create the possibilities for filling in the massive investment and infrastructure deficit which results in supply-chain inefficiencies.

The Budget Speech 2016-17 followed by announcing that:

> Our FDI policy has to address the requirements of farmers and food processing industry. A lot of fruits and vegetables grown by our farmers either do not fetch the right prices or fail to reach the markets. Food processing industry and trade should be more efficient. 100 per cent FDI will be allowed through FIPB route in marketing of food products produced and manufactured in India. This will benefit farmers, give impetus to food processing industry and create vast employment opportunities.

Will foreign retail majors, who have been opposing the safeguards and who had forced the government to dilute the conditions, especially with regard to the minimum investment in backend infrastructure and how it will be reckoned with, invest in these activities or will they force the suppliers (that means mainly domestic investment) to invest? It is pertinent to note that Wal-mart mandated its suppliers in the United States to cut down on the costs by not making any sales promotion expenditure. It is also reported that the company will be charging most of the vendors for stocking their items in new stores and for warehousing inventory. This was aimed at compensating the increases in the wages to workers. An additional fall out of this would be that the dependence of the suppliers on Wal-mart would be even more complete. Those who are aware of the working of the large retailers – how they squeeze suppliers, employees and the exchequer would be little convinced of the trust expressed in such companies by the Indian policymakers. As was noted above, foreign money is being poured in both by private equity investors and global e-commerce players. E-commerce can hardly make a dent in the 'massive' infrastructure required for Indian farmers. The way things are happening, the FDI policy relevant for this sector will see further dilution.

Conclusion

The policymakers of 1991 and their academic colleagues who argued for an MNC-friendly policy regime might not have visualised that India would face a situation wherein it needs more and more of FDI to service the already invested one. There would probably be no better proof of India's faulty approach towards FDI than the fact that the country is now beseeching even home-grown Chinese companies to invest in the country's manufacturing sector. Contrary to the belief and assertion at the time of opening up, Indian entrepreneurs failed to withstand the competition both in the form of imports and FDI competitors. The MNC-friendly approach, which is not backed by appropriate trade policy, failed to give a fillip to India's manufacturing sector. Many Indian entrepreneurs have now turned into part-traders of imported consumer durables. Instead of going towards building new capacities, most of the FDI went into displacing the domestic entrepreneurs. Even though it could be argued that the acquiring FDI companies would expand the existing facilities subsequently, it can also be said that the incumbent Indian entrepreneurs would not have let the units stagnate. Without changing the overall policy landscape and attitude, India cannot expect to make a success of 'Make in India' with the help of FDI. FDI cannot be a substitute for national efforts and FDI policy cannot be a substitute for domestic policy making.

Far from being satisfied with the quantum of inflows, the policymakers should pay attention to the factors that are contributing to the sell-offs, especially in the manufacturing sector and seek correctives both in terms of the procedures and related matters like trade policy and financing. So far, concern was expressed only with regard to the takeover of pharmaceutical companies. India's long term interest lies in strengthening domestic entrepreneurs. There can be no denial of the fact that there are black sheep among the Indian entrepreneurs whose behaviour imposes costs on the economy. But the alternative of preferring foreign companies for every product and service carries with it its own costs and risks.

What is perceived as the strength of an MNC could turn out to be a drawback, as far as host developing countries are concerned, unless appropriate safeguards are built-in. UNCTAD estimated the annual loss of revenue to host developing countries resulting from inward FDI through offshore investment hubs at about $100 bn. It elaborated that 'There is a clear relationship between the share of offshore investment in host countries' inward FDI stock and the reported (taxable) rate of return on FDI. The more investment is routed through offshore hubs, the less taxable profits accrue'. (UNCTAD, *World Investment Report*, 2015, p 200.) While stating the obvious, what UNCTAD has done is to place a figure on the possible loss of revenue to the developing countries annually, which they should ponder over seriously. With bulk of the investment coming from tax havens, the loss for India is self-evident.

The limited analysis of the FDI inflows during the recent past, present in Section III does not give rise to the possibility of India being able to avoid the 'FDI Trap'. But for the sharp increase in volume, not all of which can probably be attributed to the policy and procedural changes, the script did not change. The FDI dependent strategy is unlikely to augment domestic resources and expand the manufacturing sector. Further, since practically the entire manufacturing sector being already open for FDI, policy relaxations cannot be used to attract more FDI into it. This is extremely important in the context of the reported strategy of the DIPP to increase the contribution of the manufacturing sector to 25 per cent of the GDP by 2020. On the other hand, the 'Start-Up India' initiative being dependent upon financial investors is unlikely to promote enterprises that would ultimately remain in Indian entrepreneurs' hands.

The global situation described above only shows that India's case is not unique and in fact, India's case might help understand the global situation better. Indian policymakers should keep a close watch on international developments which could help them in having realistic expectations from FDI. India should learn to distinguish between different types of foreign investors and the costs and benefits associated with each one of them. The paramount objective of earning net foreign exchange should be sacrificed only if some definite advantages, which cannot be obtained otherwise, are guaranteed. This is particularly important as India seems to be accelerating on the path of perpetual dependence on FDI.

The Global Context

— V Upadhyay

THE INDIAN economy is projected to grow at the rate of about 7.5% in the coming years, thus making it the fastest growing major economy in the world. The high pitch hullabaloo echoed everywhere, that India has overtaken China in growth, is, however, completely out of place. When countries get richer, their growth rates slow down. As the Chinese economy is five times larger than India's, there is nothing much to gain by comparing their growth rates.

The foreign trade policy announced in April 2015 aims at raising India's total exports (merchandise plus services exports) from $465 billion in 2014-15 to $900 billion by 2020-21. At present India's share in global trade is 2%, which is estimated to rise to 3.5% by 2020-21. All these are very laudable objectives. But they are hard to achieve, especially so in the present circumstances where the world economy is projected to experience slow growth in the coming years. As per the latest estimates available, in the first eleven month of the financial year 2015-16, India's merchandise exports were $238.4 billion compared with $286.3 billion in the same period last year. Going by the current trends, merchandise exports in the year 2015-16 will be around $260 billion, a drop of about $50 billion as compared to the year 2014-15.

Although the present government has won its electoral mandate on the basis of a large number of developmental promises, its focus remains largely growth-oriented. Achievement of even these limited growth-related goals depends on suitable conditions prevailing in the domestic economy. Equally important, however, is that it also requires favourable external environment. In this paper, an attempt is made to analyse what different kinds of external challenges the Indian economy faces and how well prepared it is to deal with them.

In former RBI governor Raghuram Rajan's view, capital flow does not constitute a serious external risk for the Indian economy. He sees weak growth in industrialised countries as the biggest external risk, as this has dampening effects on our exports. It is our contention that this assessment—that capital flow is not a serious risk—is not correct. It only reflects overconfidence on the part of RBI in its ability to deal with volatility in the Indian markets.

Rajan thinks that India's foreign exchange reserves were large enough to deal with foreign fund outflows. In April 2015, India held $343 billion foreign exchange reserves. To treat this amount as sufficient enough to deal with any eventuality arising out of capital outflows is to exhibit a false sense of security. Even after about one year, in February 2016, our reserves remain about the same, ie. at $350 billion. To safeguard its currency and other markets, China had to spend about $700 billion of its reserves during 2015. They were able to do so because they hold 10 times larger foreign reserves as compared to us.

In reference to China's devaluation of its currency (Yuan) in recent months, Prime Minister Modi has said:

> *'We have never tried to gain in trade at the expense of our partners. We do not follow "beggar thy neighbour" macroeconomic policies. We have never undervalued our exchange rate (in this manner).'*

This statement has no significance: it only points to a technical difference between devaluation and depreciation. India now does not devalue its currency. The rupee's exchange value is now determined in the market: it either appreciates or depreciates depending on market conditions. In comparison to the yuan, how the rupee has performed over the last three decades is revealed by the figures given in the table below:

Table 1: Exchange Rate (Rupee to Yuan)

Year	Exchange Rate
1990	3.64
2000	5.43
2016	10.38

The US Federal Reserve has held short term interest rates in the US near zero for more than six years now. The Fed increased the rate by 25 basis points in December 2015. But as the rate increase was very small, it did not make money suddenly expensive. Because the increase was long anticipated and was already factored in, it did not cause any panic reaction anywhere in the world. Fed officials have indicated that the Fed might start raising its key rate again in the near future. IMF head Christine Lagarde, however, has warned that the timing and pace of such a move on the part of the Fed could come as a surprise to the market. If interest rates in the US start rising, portfolio re-balancing out of the emerging markets is certain to occur. Even a small unanticipated change in rates can cause havoc in the exchange rate and stock markets around the globe. The unexpected volatility in these markets is so high that a new term 'volatile volatility' has gained currency in recent months. Between 2009 and 2012, emerging markets, including India, received huge amounts of capital inflows which led to substantial rise in bond and equity prices. Lagarde points out that the danger is that vulnerabilities that build up during a period of very accommodative monetary policy can unwind suddenly when such policy is reversed, creating substantial market volatility. In 2013, as a result of mere mention of trimming the Fed's bond purchase programme by Ben Bernanke, a massive global sell-off took place. Several emerging market economies, including India, experienced large scale capital outflows. This episode is known as the 'taper tantrum'. The possibility of a repeat of such a 'taper tantrum', when the Fed decides to act, which cannot be known before hand, is always there.

Raghuram Rajan had warned against the spillover effects of monetary policy actions of larger economies on the rest of world. He has been quite critical of larger countries' central banks' policies, which which according to him, 'almost focus inwards and tend to overlook the spillover effects on the smaller economies'. He advocates that a global consensus should be built on 'how to get better outcomes for the world'. But given that all countries act in their self interest, why would larger, powerful countries heed his advice and act, keeping all countries' (including small) interests in mind?

The fall in international crude oil price during the last one year has helped India to control its fiscal and trade deficits. Due to low crude prices, our current account deficit (CAD) has seen a sharp fall. But, current account still remains in the negative. At present, net capital inflows in the forms of FDI and portfolio inflows are adequate to finance the CAD. But all this does not insulate us from future shocks. Referring to the effects of earlier global crises on the Indian economy, RBI Deputy Governor HR Khan is reported to have said that India was hurt not because history repeated itself, but because we had not learnt from our history. He has stressed upon the need to 'internalise past crises and take effective steps to safeguard against future shocks'. Khan also points out that the impact of the global crisis becomes severe if our own house is not in order. 'The impact of the May 2013 announcement of the Federal Reserve was more pronounced due to domestic vulnerabilities'. The unsustainably high CAD of 5% GDP during that period was the factor behind the aggravated impact of the Fed's taper talk.

Another major external risk the Indian economy faces relates to weak economic growth in industrialised countries as it has negative effects on India's exports. The near doubling of India's exports in a span of seven years, as projected by the recently released foreign trade policy, is contingent upon quick revival of economic growth in the industrialised countries.

The prospects of quick revival of growth in the industrialised countries (the US, Europe and Japan), however, do not appear very bright. The US economy is in a state of 'secular stagnation'. The average annual rate of growth of the US economy during the five years following the recession in 2008-09 has been 2.2 per cent. This is very much in accordance with the growth predictions made by Robert Gordon for the

US economy. Since 2008, Europe has experienced two recessions. The output of the Euro zone is still 2 per cent below its 2008 level. Southern Europe's economic problems echo Great Depression as some southern European countries are experiencing unemployment levels comparable to the levels in the early 1930s. Japan's economy is yet to come out of its 15-year 'doldrums'.

The major problem with the economic decision-making process under the present NDA government (as was with the earlier UPA government for that matter) is that, an extreme neoliberal viewpoint is presented as fact. This conservative message is the one that one constantly hears on TV and reads in newspapers. Most TV panellists and newspaper columnists talk against entitlement programmes, public spending that benefits the poor and fiscal deficit. They invariably favour privatisation, removal of environmental and labour regulations and reduction in tax rates for the rich. In Britain, this phenomenon has been termed as 'mediamacro'. Those who participate in these debates are mostly the economists employed by banks, consultancy firms and credit rating agencies. Economists belonging to academic institutions hardly get any space there.

In the context of India, we have an additional issue. The top three economics positions in the government are being held by US-based economists. These three 'renowned' economists have quite a controlling influence on the economic decision-making process in the country. It needs to be noted here that the situation in the earlier UPA government was hardly any different.

At a meeting of economists organised by the *Economic Times* in January 2015, one of the 'renowned' economists said:

> *'There is a weakening West and a weakening US and a rising China.... I still think we need a strong United States but also backed by a genuinely healthy, economically healthy coalition of partners.'*

It is evident that his mission here in India is to prepare India to play a subservient role in furthering American interests.

Another 'renowned' economist recently said that hopefully, India will have 'full capital account convertibility in a short number of years'.

This is a recipe for complete disaster. He seems to have learnt no lesson from the Asian financial crisis. China's economy is five times larger than India's and China's foreign exchange reserves are almost ten times larger than India's. Despite having so much economic strength, even China doesn't feel confident enough to take fast steps towards capital account convertibility.

According to the US Department of Agriculture's latest macroeconomic projections, India, ranked eighth for 2015, will reach the third place in the world ranking by 2030. India's GDP at that time is projected to be $6.6 trillion. The third 'renowned' economist thinks that this is an underestimate. According to him, the Indian economy is expected to grow at the annual rate of 8-10% in rupee terms for the next 15 years. Calculating in dollar terms, he says that it would be about 11-12%, and by 2030, the Indian economy's size would be about $8 trillion. To arrive at this number, he must surely have assumed that the nominal exchange rate of rupee would stay stable at around Rs 62 to a dollar. Can one ask what the basis of such an assumption is? In a short span of few months after his statement, the rupee fell to a record level of close to Rs 69 to a dollar.

Our Finance Minister and other senior government officials are very fearful of western credit rating agencies. They often argue that if the government increases expenditure on entitlement programmes beneficial to the poor, then our fiscal deficit would increase and that would surely invite downgrading of our credit ratings. In this context, it needs to be recognised that the actions of these agencies (Fitch, Moody's and Standard and Poor's) are politically motivated and 'have nothing to do with a central government's ability to generate revenues and its ability to repay debts'. There is now a move by BRICS countries (India included) to establish their own credit rating agency that will counter the monopoly of the three big western agencies.

A new development is taking shape now that has far reaching implications for the future global economic order. China has taken the initiative to establish a financial institution, the Asian Infrastructure Investment Bank (AIIB), that is to rival the post-IInd world war West-dominated financial institutions like the IMF, World Bank and the Asian Development Bank, that serve as pillars for the West's domination of the global economic order. The main aim of establishing the AIIB is to provide funds for infrastructure projects in Asian countries.

Major emerging economic powers have been asking for quite some time to increase their say in the working of the West-dominated institutions like the IMF and World Bank. But the western powers, mainly the US, have not been accommodative and have refused to concede larger space to them. The establishment of the AIIB is an outcome of the failure on the part of western powers to take cognisance of the rapidly changing ground reality around the world scene.

The United States made serious efforts to dissuade its allies, especially its major European allies, from joining the AIIB. However, ignoring Washington's concerns, most of its allies including the major European powers – Britain, Germany, France and Italy – have joined AIIB. Japan is the only major US ally which has refused to join. Other major countries that have joined this institution include Russia, Australia, the Netherlands, South Korea, Turkey and Brazil. This event – China's establishment of a global-level financial institution and the US's failure in stopping its allies from joining it – is being described as a momentous one. In Lawrence Summers' words, it signified 'the moment the United States lost its role as the underwriter of the global economic system'.

As one of the founding member of AIIB, India could expect to derive benefits from it in terms of funding for its infrastructure needs. This is a welcome development.

For Better or for Worse? India's Trade Policy Shift towards Bilateral and Regional Agreements

— Ranja Sengupta

> *The development challenge is that, in the absence of conscious national policies or fair global rules, no guarantee exists that these benefits will be equitably shared among nations and sub-groups. This challenge is most stark in trade negotiations, where the interests of narrow sectoral lobbies could exert such a concentrated influence upon governments that they offer reciprocal concessions to trading partners in sensitive areas such as services, trade, intellectual property standards and investment measures—with widespread impact* (*The Great Maze* p81)[1].

INDIA HAS now been through more than two decades of economic liberalisation. This has involved not only a gradual liberalisation of goods trade but increasing opening up of services trade and the liberalisation of

---

[1] UNDP (2005): The Great Maze: Regional and Bilateral Free Trade Agreements in Asia; Trends, Characteristics, and Implications, Asia-Pacific Trade and Investment Initiative, UNDP Regional Centre in Colombo, December

foreign direct investment in almost all sectors with key focus on service sector investment. While some of this has been autonomous, India has also engaged in legally binding agreements with other countries. This was originally at the multilateral level in the form of the World Trade Organisation (WTO) where India has engaged actively. But over the past several years, India has increasingly moved towards bilateral and regional trade agreements.

This shift towards Free Trade Agreements (FTAs), as they are generally called, reflects the current mood in the current global trade scenario. With some strengthening of developing country voices, especially those of China, India, Brazil, the WTO has seen more disagreements over key issues in recent years leading to somewhat of an impasse until 2013. With this impasse at the WTO, the world has seen the proliferation of bilateral and regional trade and investment agreements. This has also been actively driven by developed countries, who are seeking to extract from developing countries through the bilateral and plurilateral agreements what they now cannot get so easily from the WTO. In this scenario, there is a feeling of being left behind if one does not join the FTA race. India seems to be subscribing to this belief.

However, the race has become a race for the richest and the strongest, and with a large development lag India has many concerns to address in pursuing this kind of a trade policy. The FTAs involve liberalisation of goods, services and investment and also poses significant challenges to India's policy space that goes way beyond its WTO commitments. The process of negotiations is also undemocratic and secret. Further, India is now moving towards large agreements with several developed countries of much higher economic strength, which are demanding much more coverage (both intensive within and extensive across sectors and issues) than southern partners.

The other interesting aspect is that India's FTA policy seems to be quite at odds with its stance at the WTO. Whereas in the WTO India has often projected itself as a champion of developing countries and resisted provisions seen as a 'threat' to development objectives,[2] it seems to agree to the same under the FTAs. There are

---

[2] Though India often caves in at the last moment.

numerous examples: agricultural liberalisation even with continued unfair agricultural subsidies given by the EU and USA which India had resisted at the WTO; liberalisation of key service sectors, including contentious issues such as investment, government procurement and competition policy (Singapore issues which are now coming under the umbrella of 'new' issues) in trade agreements; raising IPR standards[3] and so on. This dichotomy is beginning to matter as the WTO negotiations are now at a critical juncture where special treatment to developing countries is under threat and there is an effort to systematically multilateralise the provisions of the FTAs. India's policy confusion is worrying as its FTA stance can weaken its WTO positioning considerably.

This essay aims to provide a brief background of the global trade policy scenario, followed by a description and analysis of India's tryst with FTAs.

Current Global Trade Framework and Developing Countries

The Revival of the WTO

The World Trade Organisation, which was signed in 1995 and has 159 member countries, had gone into an impasse in 2008 following differences over the promised 'special' and 'differential' treatment for developing countries. Less publicised was the US stance to not reduce its cotton subsidies.

Though the Doha Development Round (DDR), launched in 2001, was supposed to be about giving special treatment to developing countries, in reality this round has been relegated to harsh negotiations over tariff cuts, eg. in the industrial segments (NAMA) and the refusal of rich countries to give any 'effective or usable' special treatment including concessions on Special Products[4] and a Special Safeguard Mechanism (SSM)[5] in agriculture. In fact, even in the Trade in Intellectual Property

---

[3] India is being asked to comply with TRIPs Plus standards in FTA negotiations with several developed countries but has not agreed yet.

[4] Sensitive products that are not subject to tariff cuts.

[5] SSM allows developing countries to raise import duties to protect against a sudden surge in imports.

Rights Agreement (TRIPS)[6], flexibilities allowed for public health are now being denied to the developing countries.

At the same time, the WTO has failed to regulate and curb speculation in commodities that has been fuelled by rampant speculation and has increased volatility of global commodity prices. This has increased vulnerability of both small producers and consumers. Most developing country governments do not have the resources to provide a buffer against such price volatility.

In the recent period, the moribund WTO has revived itself under the somewhat over-zealous efforts of the current Director General, Roberto Azevedo. However, this reawakening seems to be happening again at the cost of developing countries.

The Bali Agreement, signed in December 2013, represents a lopsided agenda which includes a permanent and binding agreement on Trade Facilitation (TFA) that largely benefits developed countries and China. But issues of importance to LDCs and a food security proposal by developing countries (the G-33 Proposal on Food Security),that asks for removal of unfair WTO restrictions on use of subsidies to developing country farmers for supporting public food stockholding and national food security, have seen little progress. The latter got only a temporary respite from facing disputes in the form of a Peace Clause. This is in spite of the fact that developed countries like the USA and the EU are allowed to give huge subsidies to the tunes of 140 billion USD and 67 billion Euros respectively to their food sector.

The current negotiations before and after the WTO Nairobi Ministerial reveal the hard fight for developing countries. Key developed countries, led by the USA, have refused to advance talks on a permanent solution on the food security proposal nor allow a Special Safeguard Mechanism (SSM)[7] for developing countries. Further, there has been a big push to conclude the Doha Round but without fulfilling its development mandate, and to bring in 'new issues' such as liberalisation of investment,

---

6 TRIPs is an agreement within the WTO that lays down standards for intellectual property rights (IPR) protection, but allows certain flexibilities to developing countries for public health, environment, development-related objectives.

7 The SSM is a proposed instrument to raise tariffs to counter a sudden rise in imports (import surge) which can threaten domestic producers in developing countries.

government procurement, global value chains, environmental goods and services, SOEs and e-commerce. There is now considerable uncertainly about the future of the DDR and inclusion of new issues as there was a lack of consensus among member states in Nairobi. In the Geneva negotiations post Nairobi, the new issues are being resolutely pushed by developed countries. It is important to remember that these are already present in several FTAs (see below) and the attempt is now to multilateralise these provisions. This will have a much larger impact on developing countries and India.

Though India has championed developing country positions at the WTO, India's negotiating position is not helped by Chapter One of the *Economic Survey 2015-2016*[8] which was just released. It asks if India needs the SSM and a permanent solution on food security. In fact, it points out that India needs to move out of providing support to the producers through price support. Further the Report states, '*India and other emerging market economies must make it attractive for trading partners to engage in the WTO. An important part of this will require India playing more of the reciprocity game and using its growing markets as leverage to attain its own market interests abroad...*' (Page 34, *Economic Survey 2015-16*). This could well be signalling a change in India's negotiating stance in the coming days.

A matter of serious concern is the lack of transparency and true multilateralism in the negotiation process. Small-room meetings that exclude most WTO members seem to be the flavour of the season. India's participation in these meetings (for example in the G-5 during the Nairobi Ministerial) and the tendency to do bilateral deals, for example with the USA on TFA, stands contrary to its proclamations on strengthening developing country positions. In this hazy labyrinth of negotiations, the LDCs and in particular the African countries, even though the last ministerial was in Nairobi, are under high pressure to yield to the pressures of the USA and the EU to hastily conclude the Doha Round without actually offering anything of substance to developing countries in terms of development tools. Instead, new issues are being pushed and future rounds at the WTO are likely not to have even a modicum of 'development' in them.

---

[8] Government of India, Economic Survey 2015-16.

The Strategic Use of Plurilaterals to Thwart the Multilateral Framework

The DDR has a principle of single undertaking, where all agreements must go through together. This is creating a problem for the developed countries to get agreements they favour passed, over the others they do not want. The current situation over the TFA vs food security proposal is a perfect example of this. Given this increasing trend and rising, if slowly, voice of developing countries, the developed countries are now trying to push plurilateral (between a few members) agreements in place of multilateral WTO agreements.

Under the WTO, the liberalisation of investment, government procurement (or purchases by the government), and competition policy (that sets common standards for companies) were seen to be sensitive for developing countries. So these were termed the 'Singapore Issues' and were not to be included under the DRR. However, a plurilateral agreement called the Government Procurement was signed under the WTO. Similarly, the International Technology Agreement (ITA), now to be followed by its second Avatar ITA2, the Trade in Services Agreement (TISA), are all plurilateral agreements that are pushing the agenda of the North. These are bypassing the WTO system and creating tremendous pressures on smaller countries to join. The Agreement of Environmental Goods (to be followed by Services) is the latest in this list and includes full tariff liberalisation on a set of goods which are less about environment protection and more about penetrating developing country markets and making it impossible for them to grow in these sectors. For meeting environment standards, what the South needs is technology and not goods.

Rise of Regional and Bilateral Trade and Investment Agreements

The other route to escaping multilateral dynamism has been the push for bilateral or regional (often plurilateral or between a few partners) trade and investment agreements. Globally there are 612 notifications of RTAs (counting goods, services and accessions separately) to the GATT/WTO. Of these 449 are physical RTAs counting goods, services and accessions together, of which 262 are currently in force.[9] In addition, there are 3,236 international investment agreements including 2902 Bilateral

---

[9] WTO Notification, as of 7 April 2015.

Investment Treaties (BITs) or Bilateral Investment Protection Agreements (BIPAs) in force globally (UNCTAD World Investment Report 2014).

The FTAs had started with the coverage only of goods trade but are expanding fast to cover services, investment and intellectual property rights. In addition, a new tendency for large regional agreements is clearly visible. The North American FTA (NAFTA) was one of the first of strong regional agreements. In the recent times, the Trans Pacific Partnership Agreement (TPPA), led by the USA, has just been signed. The Trans Atlantic Trade and Investment Partnership (TTIP) between the USA and the EU and the Regional Comprehensive Economic Partnership (RCEP) between the ASEAN-plus-6 countries including China, India and Japan are being negotiated. All these agreements are likely to create extensive impacts. The developed countries are insisting on including issues in these agreements they could not get passed at the WTO. Box 1 provides a list of these provisions.

Box 1: Provisions in Typical North-South FTAs

- Asking developing countries for almost **complete elimination of tariffs on 85-97% of goods** while maintaining high standard barriers in developed countries. Simultaneously, the EU and the USA has continued with huge agricultural subsidies while asking for market access in developing country agricultural markets.
- **TRIPs plus IPR provisions** which are threatening access to medicines worldwide by eliminating cheaper generic production as well as establishing corporate control over seeds and agrochemicals that gradually pushes developing country farmers out of production.
- **Aggressive liberalisation of service sectors** (like retail) which is threatening employment, especially in the informal sectors, as well as access to critical services by raising costs in developing countries and challenging the provision of key public services including in health, education, water, energy and infrastructure.

- **Strong investment protection clauses**, apparently to attract Foreign Direct Investment (FDI), including the investor-state-dispute-settlement (ISDS) which allows foreign investors to sue national governments in secret arbitration cases in international tribunals for astronomical sums, and is threatening policy regulation even in public interest, public health or environment, worldwide. Such provisions are also included in the BITs and have led to cases involving natural resources (more than 50% of cases) including air, water and land, finance (Argentina faced more than 50% of BITs cases following its economic crisis). Interestingly, the UNCTAD trade and Investment Report 2013 has found no evidence of increased FDI from ISDS.
- **Liberalisation of government procurement** which will prevent preferential treatment to domestic industries, SMEs or disadvantaged sections.
- **Setting competition policy standards** according to western levels, thus threatening prospects of domestic industrialisation, especially for SMEs.

In fact, when regional Southern agreements spill over to include Northern countries or compete with a North-South or a Northern Agreement, the coverage is closely mimicking the latter. The Regional Comprehensive Economic Partnership (RCEP) being negotiated between India and the ASEAN plus six countries (including Australia, New Zealand and Japan) is a case in point. It is likely to follow standards set by the Trans Pacific Partnership Agreement (TPPA), a mega FTA of which USA is the driver. The adverse impact of this trend will be significant on developing countries who are the weak players in this game.

India's FTAs: Intensive and Extensive Liberalisation

The Indian government has clearly been focusing a lot of attention not only on FTAs but on more ambitious and comprehensive agreements called CEPAs/ CECAs/ BTIA (see Box 2 below for the different types of FTAs) which are much more invasive in nature and are significantly greater in coverage than the WTO. The impact can be much more immediate and intense.

Box. 2: The Various Categories of Indian FTAs

- **Goods Agreements:** Cover only trade in agricultural and industrial goods. Include provisions: Import duty reduction to zero (WTO plus) on 80-95% of goods, easing of processes related to standards, rules of origin etc. Example: Sri Lanka, SAFTA, ASEAN (but other chapters are being negotiated).
- **Preferential Trade Agreements (PTA):** Gives some concessions to partners but are not as expansive either in terms of duty reduction or other provisions.Example: Mercosur (Argentina, Brazil, Paraguay and Uruguay), Chile, Afghanistan.
- **Comprehensive Economic Partnership Agreements (CEPA)/ Comprehensive Economic Cooperation Agreements (CECA)/ Regional or Bilateral Trade and Investment Agreements (BTIA):** Include trade in goods + trade in services + investment + chapters on intellectual property rights (IPRs), government procurement (GP), and competition policy (sometimes).Example: Singapore, South Korea, Japan and Malaysia.
- **Proposed North-South FTAs:** Under the categories of CEPA/ CECA/ BTIAs but are often more aggressive in nature and involve both intensive and extensive trade liberalisation, compared to FTAs among developing countries. More emphasis on strong IPRs plus Singapore Issues such as investment, GP, Competition Policy. Example: Signed with Japan while negotiating with the European Union, EFTA bloc (Switzerland, Norway, Liechtenstein and Iceland), Canada, New Zealand, and Australia. Started negotiations on Regional Comprehensive Economic Partnership (RCEP) with developed and developing partners.

Contours of India's Free Trade Agreements

India has signed about 14 agreements and is negotiating about 16 more, bringing the total to around 30 (see Fig 1). Starting from more strategic agreements, mainly on goods trade, India is currently more engaged in several North-South FTAs and one mega regional FTA, namely, the Regional Comprehensive Economic Partnership (RCEP). The Ministry of Commerce is also signalling its interest to join the gigantic TPPA which has just been signed. India's FTAs are based on 'reciprocity', i.e. 'give and take', with limited scope for special treatment unlike the WTO where Special and Differential Treatment (S&DT) for developing countries is still an accepted (though not always operative) principle.

Several of these, especially the agreements signed from 2010 and those that are being negotiated with the EU, EFTA, Canada, New Zealand, Australia and in RCEP, are more comprehensive and include most of the FTA features described under the section on regional and bilateral agreements. These include deeper (compared to the WTO) tariff cuts on agriculture and industrial goods covering 80-97% of goods, deeper liberalisation of services, raising IPR protection standards and going beyond TRIPS commitment (demanded by EU, EFTA, RCEP but not yet agreed to) and more market access and protection for foreign investment.

Figure 1: FTA Footprints

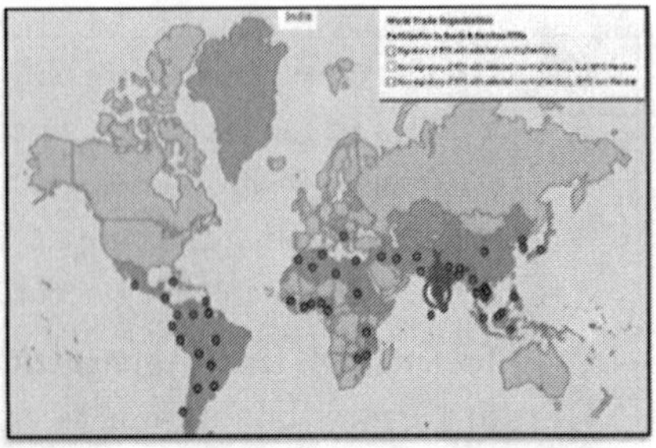

Box 3: Impending Mega FTA: The Regional Comprehensive Economic Partnership (RCEP)

- **16 partners:** 10 ASEAN Countries plusAustralia, China, India, Japan, the Republic of Korea and New Zealand
- 8 Rounds of talks completed, launched in 2013
- **Included:** Goods, services, investment, economic & technical cooperation, intellectual property, competition and dispute settlement
- **Mimics:** Other mega FTAs like the Transpacific Partnership Agreement (TPPA) which lays down high standards of liberalisation
- **Could Impact:** Agriculture and food rights, affordable medicines (through IPRs), livelihoods, environment, internet freedom, copyright, access to critical services, conservation and use of natural resources like land, water, forests, and government policy space

The tariff (or import duty) cuts under these FTAs are based on actual applied tariffs which are already much lower than the bound or maximum tariffs that are negotiated under the WTO and are expected to move towards zero. For agriculture sector India's current (2013) bound duty is 113.5% but applied duty is 33.5% (See fig. 2). For industry the bound is 34.6% and the applied rate is 10.2%.

Figure 2: Bound and Applied Tariff Rates in India for Agricultural Products (%), 2013

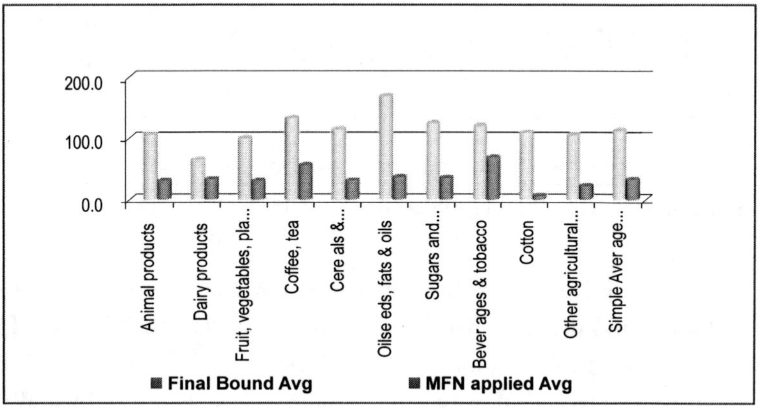

Source: WTO Tariff Profile 2014.

India's Macroeconomic Scenario, Sectoral Issues and the FTAs

Any country's trade policy has to be consistent with its macroeconomic policy scenario. Unfortunately this does not seem to be true for India. Its trade policy, with its high deficit (Fig. 3), has made India more vulnerable to macroeconomic crises. For example, the macro-crisis with the depreciation of the rupee to 68 against the dollar in September 2013 was triggered by US monetary policy that impacted India through liberalised financial markets and drew out foreign portfolio investments from India. This happened from several other emerging markets as well but India was much more vulnerable because of the growing Current Account Deficit and Trade Deficit. Current account deficit (at 88.16 billion USD, 4.7% of GDP by 2012-13, and provisional estimates, 6.5% in Q3 2013-14) and trade deficit (at 190.9 billion USD and 7.9% of GDP in 2012-13) were on the verge of triggering a critical Balance of Payments (BOP) situation.

Figure 3: India's Export, Import and Trade Deficit

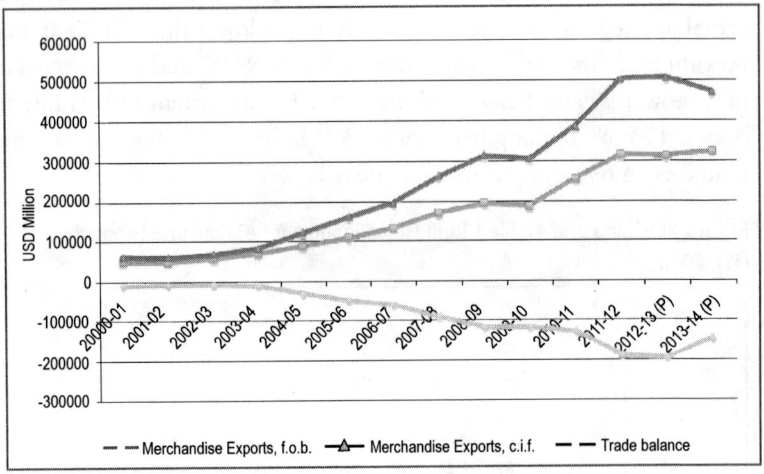

Source of Data: RBI Annual Reports up to 2012-13.

The situation is currently better with the CAD at 32.4 billion (1.7% of GDP), and the trade deficit at 147.61 billion US (7.9% of GDP), based on provisional estimates for 2013-14, but this is due to a fall in imports. The recent improvement in trade balance is driven by a 40% decline in gold and silver imports and a 13.5% decline in capital goods imports and a modest 4.7% increase in exports.

India has experienced unbalanced growth and employment patterns, with high growth in the service sector at 67.4 % of GDP (2012-13) but with the lowest share of employment (25.40% of total jobs, NSS Employment Survey 2009-10). For growth to be inclusive, it must be in sectors with higher employment potential such as industry and agriculture. This has also accentuated income inequality. However, India's trade policy is concentrated only on services (see Table 1) and narrow industrial segments and has further strengthened the unbalanced nature and inequality in the country.

But the question is: does India's FTA policy help to address these issues and provide better options for macroeconomic stability?

The answer is a simple no. With the exception of Singapore, South Asia and Sri Lanka, India has a trade deficit with all its existing FTA partners such as ASEAN, Malaysia, South Korea, Japan and Thailand

Table 1: India's Export, Import, Trade Balance, Services Trade, Curent Account

(US $ million)							
	2007-08	**2008-09**	**2009-10**	**2010-11**	**2011-12P**	**2012-13P**	**2013-14P**
Exports, f.o.b.	1,66,163	1,89,001	1,82,442	2,56,159	3,09,774	3,06,581	3,18,607
Import, c.i.f.	2,57,630	3,08,521	3,00,644	3,83,481	4,99,533	5,02,237	4,66,216
Trade Balance	-91,467	-1,19,521	-1,18,203	-1,27,322	-1,89,759	-1,95,656	-1,47,609
Invisibles, Net	75,730	91,603	80,022	79,269	1,11,604	1,07,493	1,15,212
Services Net (Included under Invisibles)	38,853	53,916	36,016	44,081	64,098	64,915	72,965
Current Account Balance	-15,738	-27,917	-38,181	-48,053	-78,155	-88,163	-32,397
Key Indicators as a % GDP							
Trade Ba;amce	-7.4	-9.8	-8.7	-7.5	-10.1	-10.5	-7.9
Net Services	3.1	4.4	2.6	2.6	3.4	3.5	3.9
Current Account Balance	-1.3	-2.3	-2.8	-4.2	-4.7	-1.7	

Source: Data from RBI Annual Report, 2013-14.

Figure 4: Trade Surplus/Deficit with Key FTA Partners

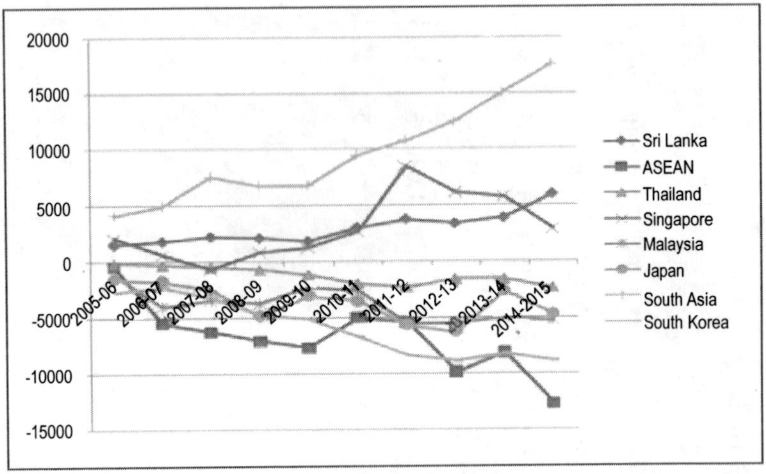

Source: Based on Data from Export-Import Bank, GOI.

(See Table 2). With South Korea and Thailand, the deficit has been continuously increasing. For example, with Thailand, Japan, ASEAN and Malaysia (the last three of which were signed in 2010) the deficit increased after signing of the FTA (See Fig4). With ASEAN the deficit has increased pretty sharply. With Japan the deficit had fallen in 2013-14 but has again increased in 2014-15.

India also has a trade deficit with most of its proposed FTA partners. With the EFTA countries and Australia, its deficit is pretty large. With the EU, it has had a trade deficit over several years, with a surplus from 2010-11 which is declining rapidly. If India-EU FTA becomes a reality, all projections show that the commodity trade deficit will go up in agricultural and industrial segments, except for pockets like textiles, garments and leather.

Interestingly, India's latest *Economic Survey* (2015-16) recognises this problem. The chapter on PTAs says '*against this background of proliferating FTAs and the emergence of mega-regionalism, a review of India's FTAs is overdue. Any reduction in tariff barriers should spur trade between partners, by offering greater market access for firms and encouraging specialization within industrial subsectors. However, the impact of an FTA on the trade balance is unclear, as it may favor one region over the other. Similarly, the*

Table 2: India's Trade Surplus/Deficit with Major FTA Partner Countries (in USD Mln)

(US $ million)										
	2005-06	**2006-07**	**2007-08**	**2008.-09**	**2009-10**	**2010-11**	**2011-12**	**2012-13**	**2013-14**	**2014-15**
Sri Lanka	1446.97	1787.97	2195.47	2069.35	1795.82	3008.33	3741.36	3358.06	3867.42	5947.59
ASEAN	-472.37	-5501.05	-6261.29	-7062.33	-7684.25	-4980.07	-5414.49	-9858.15	-8144.54	-12704.74
Thailand	-136.27	-302.21	-490.06	-765.51	-1191.36	1997.88	-2322.83	-1619.44	-1636.93	-2389.13
Singapore	2071.52	569.52	-743.43	790.07	1137.6	2686.13	8469.22	6132.86	5748.05	2875.33
Malaysia	-1253.75	-3985.09	-3437.64	-3764.81	-2341.37	-2652.41	-5493.28	-5506.99	-5506.99	-5314.76
Japan	-1579.84	-1731.42	-2467.44	-4860.57	-3104.64	-3540.79	-5670.89	-6312.23	-2666.68	-4745.9
South Asia	4134.34	4966.36	7520.41	6749.23	6733.35	9485.77	10771.73	12430.75	15030.86	17575.09
South Korea	-2736.64	-2284.75	-3183.96	-4724.49	-5155.02	-6748	-8459.64	-8902.87	-8261.91	-8925.5
In Negotiation										
Australia	-4126.68	-6074.39	-6662.39	-9658.75	-11022.41	-9075.98	-13101.68	***-10737.05***	***-7522.24***	***-7476.12***
New Zealand	-74.73	230.02	-177.12	-235.12	-244.04	-434.04	-571.08	***-394.56***	***-337.84***	***-269.3***
EU (27)	-2769.37	-3024.79	-3914.73	-3381.98	-2405.07	5346.57	879.36	***3727.4***	***1630.37***	***487.1***
Canada	-101.71	-666.02	-714.58	-1094.24	-974.58	-681.16	-865.22	***-763.64***	***-1111.24***	***-1553.42***
EFTA	-6229.13	-9252.58	-10511.34	-11813.26	-14814.68	-34814.68	-34151.52	***-31736.51***	***-18017***	***-21788.01***

Source: Compiled from Data from Exportr-Import Data Bank, Ministry of Commece and Industry, GOI.
Note: The deficit figures are marked in grey.

impact on welfare can be uncertain' (Page 123, *Economic Survey 2015-16*). Again it points out, 'FTAs therefore require a careful empirical analysis, as their implications for the country's policy are wide-ranging. Do they actually improve welfare? Are the effects heterogeneous across the different types of FTAs, between imports and exports, or across subsectors?' (op. cit) The Chapter goes on to provide the various results that trigger these observations.

However the first chapter of the same *Economic Survey* (2015-16), dresses down India's dismal FTA performance and suggests a vigorous pursuit of FTAs. Para 1.106 (Page 34) says, '*the costs of reluctant engagement need careful review. The US and others are negotiating agreements (the Trans-Pacific Partnership (TPP)) that have excluded India and hence shaped in a way that do not take into account India's important interests (the rules on intellectual property are a good illustration). If and when India joins these agreements, it will be not on India's terms but on terms already cast in stone, terms that India could not influence because of being perceived as not engaging fully*'. The reality is the opposite as India's interests are likely to be compromised heavily in negotiations on Mega FTAs which are controlled largely by developed countries.

If we take a sector specific look, India's agricultural exports are low and now face serious threat even in the home market from subsidised European and western products. Subsidies cannot be negotiated under FTAs as it is a multilateral issue. The EU, for example, is asking for significant import duty reduction on agricultural products but will retain its massive subsidy. Further, they have a host of standard barriers. It is of no surprise that projections for the EU-India FTA show large gains for the EU in all agricultural segments (See Fig. 5), which could threaten rural livelihoods and agricultural production, and will clearly jeopardise the growth of the food processing sector where a significant number of EU products will make an entry into Indian markets. Similar benefits to Australia, New Zealand under the proposed FTAs, or the proposed RCEP, could have a similar impact on dairy products.

India does not have a well-articulated industrial/manufacturing policy either, and it is not supported by its trade policy. Premature liberalisation has already destroyed several industries, for example the

Figure 5: Projected Change in Value in EU-India Agricultural Trade between 2006 and 2020 (S mln)

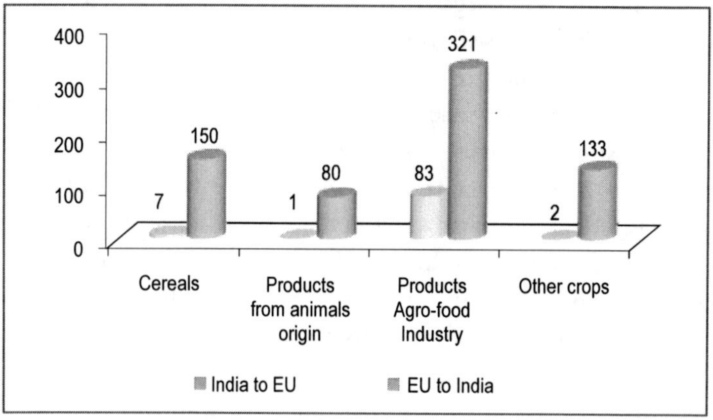

Source of Data: CEPII-CIREM (2007).

nascent manufacturing industries of aircraft, television, radio transmitters and apparatus for line telephony, office and computing machinery India has a negative trade balance in these segments of manufacturing. In spite of a sophisticated software industry, the computer hardware industry has lagged behind. India needs to develop an independent industrial policy and make its trade policy subservient to that framework. Its industrial policy must be for systemic development in keeping with its needs with regard to its labour force, local raw material, local requirements for goods and other domestic considerations. But with FTAs, the policy flexibility is limited. For example, nascent industries need protection and historically no country has developed their industrial sector without tariff protection. The USA had levied 50% import duty and the EU 20-30% duty during their industrialisation. In comparison, India's industrial average import duty is less than 10% and FTAs seek to reduce these almost to zero. Unlike China, India has failed to provide MSMEs the much-needed support to compete with foreign players. India's control over FDI in industrial sectors is also limited by FTAs.

FTAs also tend to lock in 'specialisation', as it becomes more difficult to move up the value chain as imports start coming in. Today India is exporting low-value, low- technology goods and, apart from oil and gold (raw material), India is importing high- value consumption goods.

The technology content of import is low while the import of intermediaries is high. India is facing negative trade balance in this segment in most of its FTAs, except with SAFTA (South Asia).

India's FTAs look to perpetuate the dependence on the service sector and the resultant income inequality. In several FTAs that India is negotiating, India's interest is the service sector, eg. in the EU-India FTA, but the gains are unclear and not easily measurable due to lack of clear data and a host of non-tariff barriers. On the other hand, with the exception of IT and related services, India's other service sub-sectors are not well developed enough to compete in other markets. In terms of inward FDI, a significant focus of the FTAs has been on FDI liberalisation, but uncontrolled and unregulated FDI without conditions can have severe disadvantages. FDI in employment-intensive segments such as retail threatens jobs (especially of women). FDI in banking, insurance, pension, health, education can raise user fees, create inequity in access and aggravate rural-urban divide. The liberalisation of foreign investment in sensitive sectors such as energy or waste can also have security- or environment-related impacts. Earlier, India used to have 'performance requirements'[10] for FDI. But increasingly, and under the FTAs, India has diluted key conditions such as mandatory transfer of technology and local labour use.

The North-South FTA rationale does not work for India.

Since India has begun to focus on FTAs with developed countries, it is important to understand their characteristics and context.

Developed countries already have low average tariffs, duty free lines.

Since the developed partners such as the EU, EFTA, Australia, New Zealand, Canada have low tariffs in most products, India already has access to these segments. On the other hand, additional access through the FTA may not really be significant but India will have to cut its own tariffs.

Current agricultural tariffs in developed FTA partner countries vary between 1.2% to 19% (except Switzerland and Norway) and industrial tariffs are between 0.5% to 4.2% (see Table 3). In comparison, India's

---

[10] Performance requirements are certain performance related conditions that can be imposed on inward FDI such as technology transfer, export component, local content requirements etc which ensure strategic benefits to the recipient country.

Table 3: Current Market Access in Future FTA Partner Countries and India (2013)

Simple Average Applied MFN Tariffs								
(Simple Average MFN Applied tariff)	EU	Swizerland	Norway	Cannda	Australia	New Zealand	Japan	India
Agricultural Products	13.2	35.7	51.3	15.9	1.2	1.4	19	33.5
Non-Agricultural Products	4.2	1.9	0.5	2.3	3	2.2	2.6	10.6
Value of Products Allowed to Enter Duty-Fee								
(MFN Applied)	EU	Switzerland	Norway	Canada	Australia	New Zealand	Jappan	India
Agricultural Products	31.3	30	45.3	59.3	77	72.4	35.9	5.1
Non-Agricultural Products	26.1	20.2	95.3	75.6	45.9	62.5	55.7	2.6

Surce: Complied from WTO Tariff Profiles (2014).

average applied tariffs are 33.5% and 10.2% in agricultural and non-agricultural products respectively. If we consider the products allowed at a low duty of <5%, the access is even more.[11] Moreover these countries allow a significant share of imports to enter duty-free. If we take the example of EU, 72.2% of India's agricultural exports and 68.5% of its non-agricultural exports (value) already enter duty free (WTO, India Tariff Profile 2014, data for 2012). In these large duty-free or low-duty segments, India, even with an FTA, will be at par and not better-off than present suppliers.

In comparison, India allows only 5.1% and 2.6% of its agricultural or industrial goods respectively at zero-duty. In effect, the possibility of a gain just from tariff reduction is huge for the partner but very limited for India.

What blocks Indian exports to these markets are not tariffs but subsidies and standards which cannot really be addressed under FTAs. Mutual Recognition Agreements (MRAs) under FTAs, if at all, provide some harmonisation for technical barriers but does not lower high standards as such. Further, the EU wants the removal of export measures (taxes, quantitative restrictions) which are used for ensuring food security, raw material for industry (eg. leather, minerals).

So on the whole, India's additional market access may be marginal but India may have to significantly open its markets by reducing tariffs and give up other restrictions such as on exports under these FTAs.

Preference Erosion

India is signing the FTAs to get a competitive edge over other countries. However, with the increase in the number of FTAs that are globally operative, the preference margin that India can get from its FTAs will be eroding. Each partner will give similar preferential treatment to more and more partners. As pointed out earlier, 612 FTAs or RTAs were notified to the WTO (until 7 April 2015) of which 262 are in force globally. This is referred to as the 'spaghetti bowl' of FTAs. Experts predict that very soon, FTAs will cease to deliver any benefits in terms of market access.

---

[11] Based on data till 2010. The WTO Tariff Profile has currently discontinued the data for tariff lines with under 5% duty.

But developing countries such as India will end up opening their markets which were protected for strategic reasons such as protection of jobs and incomes, developing productive capacities

North-South FTAs: Specific Features Implications for Development & Policy Space

As discussed, North-South FTAs have key features such as attempting to raise IPR standards, liberalisation of investment, government procurement (GP), harmonisation of competition policy that can have detrimental impact on India's development objectives and tools.

Though India has not yet agreed to raising IPR standards, liberalising GP or harmonising competition policy, there is strong pressure on India to do so. Once the big agreements that are being negotiated are concluded, it is unlikely that India can keep such provisions out.

In the case of **investment,** India has already granted strong protection rights such as the ISDS clause (see Box 1) under its several Bilateral Investment Treaties (BITs) and has included similar chapters under the FTAs with Japan and Malaysia. The EU FTA will involve granting high level of protection to all 27 EU member States. India has already been sued in several cases by MNCs, in secret international arbitration cases and has lost two already. India's first recorded investor-state dispute ((Enron vs the Government of Maharashtra) was initiated by a consortium of US companies including Enron, under the *India-Mauritius BIT* which has already resulted in a billion dollar arbitration award against India. Recently, India has lost a major case to an Australian mining company, White Industries (White Industries Limited v Republic of India) and paid nearly Rs 45 crore under the *India-Australia BIT*. Interestingly, this was lost not on the major clauses but on the ground that there was an inordinate delay in Indian courts to enforce its investment rights.

As in the rest of the world, such investment protection clauses have the serious threat of freezing policy space and discouraging policy regulation, even those for public interest or environmental protection.

If India has to agree to grant ***IPR commitments*** *beyond those it made in TRIPS, it will have a serious impact on access to medicines as India's generic industry, which produces cheap medicines for 67% of the world's population, will be severely threatened by strong patent rights. The impact on agriculture* *through patenting of seeds and agrochemicals will take access to such inputs out of the hands of Indian farmers.* These demands are coming in through the EU, EFTA and in the RCEP negotiations. Further, the EU demand to recognise its Geographical Indications (GIs)[12] will threaten the growth of nascent agro-processed products like cheese. Traditional knowledge and medicine will also be subsumed and go out of reach of communities under such IP protection.

The **liberalisation of government procurement** has been consistently demanded by EU as a 'non-negotiable' in its FTA. India, like other countries, has used GP as a development tool to provide markets to disadvantaged groups such as women, SC/ST, as well as to MSMEs and domestic industry. If GP is liberalised, Indian suppliers will have to compete at par with developed country companies. This will also represent a conflict with the Government Procurement Bill, which allows preference on socio-economic grounds and to domestic producers.[13] But under FTAs, all concessions have to be specifically negotiated. Interestingly, EU's own GP market is heavily protected by standard barriers and is unlikely to be accessible to Indian producers. Further, if India opens up to the EU, it will also have to grant similar access to Japan under a 'non-discrimination' clause, and probably to all future FTA partners.

In **harmonising competition policy standards**, there will be a clear loss of policy space for India to regulate competition to serve its development needs. According to an expert, 'developing countries require special treatment in the sense of being allowed to pursue competition policies which are appropriate to their stage of development'.[14] Level playing field for a developed country (eg. the EU) and Indian firms in India may lead to unequal competition. For example, resource-rich EU

---

[12] GIs refer to a type of intellectual property (IP) and are names of places used to identify where a product comes from and its reputation, such as 'Champagne', 'Feta' Cheese etc.

[13] Ranja Sengupta, 2012, 'Government Procurement in the EU-India FTA', EPW, July 14, 2012 volxlviI, no 28.

[14] Ajit Singh, 'Multilateral Competition Policy and Economic Development: A Developing Country Perspective on European Community Proposals', UNCTAD series on Issues in Competition Law and Policy, UN New York and Geneva 2004.

firms would be able to use the advantage of competition law, but it would be difficult for non—EU firms to use these provisions due to lack of resources and experiences. Harmonisation of competition law and policy would undermine the current development-oriented interpretation of competition law and policy in India.

Process Questions

Finally, there are serious process issues in the way India has conducted its FTA negotiations, which belies the functioning of a democratic country.

By the Constitution, the Indian government is able to formulate foreign policy **without any parliamentary oversight and without consultation with State governments.** In spite of the fact that most of India's partner countries need parliamentary ratification for the passing of such FTAs, governments in India have been able to sign these agreements without any parliamentary process. The governments have not shared information with State governments, even when the subjects fall under 'State' jurisdiction or concurrent lists such as agriculture or health.

FTA negotiation texts are always secret, which **makes impossible any independent evaluation or even public information sharing and understanding** of the impacts of such agreements, even by constituencies they will seriously impact. In spite of claims of having **consultations with stakeholders**, these have been limited to large industry bodies and even then, mainly focused on tariffs but not on standards, subsidies or critical issues like IPRs, investment, GP etc. There has hardly been any consultation with civil society and marginalised constituencies such as women, farmers, indigenous communities, patient groups and others.

Impact assessments, especially of sectors such as agriculture, have been grossly inadequate. Moreover these have broadly been kept secret, out of public scrutiny. No human rights-based impact assessment, especially one that looks at social impacts of FTAs in addition to economic ones, has been conducted. India has **no independent review mechanism** on FTAs and **no compensation mechanism** for sectors, producers and people who lose out. The government had started a review in 2013 in response to industry concerns that FTAs are actually increasing trade deficits, but the result of the review is not yet in public domain.

Table 4: List of Indian RTAs in Force Notified to the WTO(as of April 2015)

ASEAN - India	Asia Pacific Trade Agreement (APTA)	Asia Pacific Trade Agreement (APTA) - Accession of China	Chile - India
Global System of Trade Preferences among Developing Countries (GSTP)	India - Afghanistan	India - Bhutan	India - Japan
India - Malaysia	India - Nepal	India - Singapore	India - Sri Lanka
Korea, Republic of - India	MERCOSUR - India	South Asian Free Trade Agreement (SAFTA)	South Asian Preferential Trade Arrangement (SAPTA)

Source: www.wto.org

Conclusion

India's policy stance to sign FTAs, increasingly with developed countries and mega regional agreements such as the RCEP and TPPA, needs deep introspection. First the government's own stance is unclear. The arguments in Chapter One of the Economic Survey 2015-16 to engage in Mega FTAs such as the TPPA (as well as liberalise more under the WTO) are in conflict with the Chapter on Preferential Trade Agreements which points out the various problems and the need for critical evaluation of FTAs.

Free Trade and Investments Agreements are beginning to impact the lives of Indian citizens through their multiple chapters. The complexity of the language and the inter-linkage between chapters makes it a challenge for development policy analysts, activists and affected groups and even government negotiators to clearly delineate the impacts. Therefore, resisting adverse provisions in one chapter may not be enough as same provisions can come in through another. The inclusion of 'data' (regarded as the core of intellectual property) in the definition of investment in the investment chapter is an example.

The FTAs are clearly founded on the basis of perpetuating inequalities with an obsessive interest on commercial gains for a few, but ignoring the wider socio-economic impacts. With focus on limited service sector-driven gains, mainly through the IT sector that gives high incomes for a few, India's FTA policy is sacrificing the interests of large number of agricultural and industrial producers, workers and their families. The social impacts of FTAs are being felt through the restriction of access to basic resources and services, which goes hand-in-hand with a denial of rights, and the burden is borne by the weak and the marginalised.

The increasingly deep penetration of FTAs into the Indian economy is going beyond simple exchange of goods and services, and influencing whether the government actually can or cannot determine key policies. *The control over policymaking is slipping silently into the hands of multinational companies and developed country governments.* This is also clear, for example, from the urgency to open FDI in multi-brand retail when the EU-India FTA negotiations were at its peak.

The divergent policy stance in India's WTO and FTA positioning is adding to the confusion. The argument that FTAs can be more liberal as they are simply bilateral and, therefore, limited in impact is not borne out by global evidence. In addition, when India is negotiating with a 27-member EU bloc or the RCEP, which has ASEAN plus 6 countries, the impact of FTAs is far reaching. With the battle over development objectives now sharpened at the WTO, hazy and dichotomous policy positions does not augur well for India.

It is not surprising that India is witnessing increasingly visible protests by civil society groups on its FTA policy. Protests on the EU India FTA, the RCEP have been frequent and effective. Protests by South Indian plantation workers, after the ASEAN FTA are also testimony to the growing concern of different constituencies over FTAs. It is clear, India is not even making commercial gains from its FTAs and the social impacts are clearly negative. In this situation the government of India needs to do a serious rethinking of its approach towards FTAs, undertake proper review and consultation and follow a transparent and participatory approach in formulating its trade policy.

The Road to Capital Account Convertibility in India

— Jayan Jose Thomas

WHETHER INDIA should allow full capital account convertibility is a question that has been at the centre of policy debate in India time and again since 1991. Supporters of pro-market reforms insist that full capital account convertibility is a prerequisite for India's emergence as a global economic and financial power. On the other hand, a number of financial crises that occurred during the recent decades—notably in East Asia in 1997 and the global financial crisis since 2008—have pointed to the dangers of liberalising capital flows.

Full capital account convertibility (CAC) refers to 'the freedom to convert local financial assets into foreign financial assets and *vice-versa* at market-determined rates of exchange'.[1] This paper reviews the policy reforms in India in the direction of an open capital account and their impacts so far. It finds that India has substantially liberalised its capital

[1] This definition of capital account convertibility is given by the Tarapore Committee (1997).

account since the 2000s. This has led to relatively large inflows of short-term foreign capital to the country, posing several challenges for the domestic economy.

Opening up the Capital Account: Policy Changes in India

As is well known, there had been severe restrictions on foreign capital flows into India, especially after the implementation of the Foreign Exchange Regulation Act (FERA) of 1973. However, after 1991, greater openness to foreign trade and foreign investment has become one of the main planks of India's economic reform process. Early measures in this direction occurred in 1994 when the Rupee was made officially convertible on the current account.

Full capital account convertibility too was high on the agenda of India's policy makers from the early 1990s itself.[2] The First Tarapore Committee, set up by the Reserve Bank of India (RBI) in 1997, recommended a number of preconditions for implementing CAC in India. These included the reduction of the country's fiscal deficit to 3.5% (of the GDP), inflation rates to 3-5%, non-performing assets (NPAs) of banks to 5%, and cash reserve ratio (CRR) to 3%. However, progress towards full CAC was delayed in India following a crisis in the East Asian countries including Thailand and South Korea in 1997. The crisis was mainly due to the volatility in short-term foreign capital flows ('hot money') to these countries. It provided a sharp reminder to India on the dangers in opening up its capital account too fast and too soon.

India has not yet implemented full CAC. Nevertheless, the country has taken several measures since the 2000s to gradually liberalise the rules on inward and outward flows of foreign capital. In fact, according to Nachane (2007), these measures amounted to a 'creeping movement'

---

[2] Manmohan Singh, the then Finance Minister of India, said the following in an interview he gave in 1993: '...First of all, I believe that there's a lot of capital that goes out of India. If we have capital account convertibility, much of that will remain here, and there will be less need for balance of payments support from outside.... So that's the major reason [for considering full capital account convertibility].... Also, we live in a world where the distinction between the current account and the capital account is increasingly losing its relevance.... Freeing up the capital account would hopefully eliminate the evil of the hawala market.' See Khanna (1993).

in the direction of full CAC. For instance, in the Union budget for 2001-02, the government announced that the limit for overseas investments by Indian companies that had issued global depository receipts (GDRs) would be increased to $100 million. Further, the limit for overseas investments through the automatic route would be increased to $50 million on an annual basis. These were above the limits recommended by the Tarapore Committee (that Indian companies could make direct investments in foreign companies to the tune of $50 million). The rules on overseas investment were liberalised further in subsequent years (the upper limit for overseas investments by an Indian company was raised to 100 per cent of the net worth of the Indian company in the 2003-04 Union budget).

The government raised the limits on investments by foreign institutional investors (FIIs) in government and corporate debt, thus easing the flow of short-term foreign capital into the country. The National Democratic Alliance (NDA) government took concrete steps in this regard in the Union budgets it presented in 2001-02, 2002-03 and 2003-04. The United Progressive Alliance (UPA) government continued this policy of welcoming short-term foreign investments. In the 2004-05 Union budget, the then Finance Minister opined: '...many genuine FIIs... can enhance the flow of equity capital and lend depth to the capital markets'.

By the mid-2000s, India's macroeconomic conditions improved, and the introduction of full capital account convertibility was high on the agenda of reforms again. In 2006, the RBI set up the Second Tarapore Committee to look into the question of full CAC. Two other committees were asked to determine the future course of reforms in India's financial sector: the High-Powered Expert Committee (HPEC) on making Mumbai an International Financial Centre, which was headed by Percy Mistry, and the Committee on Financial Sector Reforms under the chairmanship of Raghuram Rajan. These committees recommended the implementation of full capital convertibility in India.

At the same time, several economists expressed concerns about the many problems the Indian economy would face if the country were to opt for a regime of free capital flows (Rakshit 2003; Nachane 2007; Patnaik 2007; Subramanian 2007). An important basis for these concerns is the well-known trilemma in international economics. That is, a country cannot simultaneously pursue an open capital account, fixed exchange rate and an independent monetary policy.

It appeared that the Reserve Bank of India (RBI) did not share the enthusiasm of the government in shifting to a regime of free capital flows during the mid-2000s. The RBI's cautious approach in liberalising capital flows was evident in the opinions expressed by its then Governor (Y V Reddy) at various points in time. In his own words:

> In brief, given the adverse international experience with unfettered capital account liberalisation, we have been risk averse and have adopted a policy of active management of the capital account. ... Further, prudential regulations over financial intermediaries, especially over banks, in respect of their foreign exchange exposures and transactions are a dynamic component of management of capital account as well as financial supervision.
>
> —YV Reddy, Governor, Reserve Bank of India, Lecture given in June 2005 (see Reddy, 2005).

However, breaks had to be applied yet again on the government's plans during the mid- to late-2000s to implement full CAC in India. The severe financial crisis that affected many western economies and spread to other parts of the world during 2008-09 pointed once again to the problems of liberalising capital flows.

The Impacts of Capital Account Liberalisation

Foreign capital inflows to India increased sharply since 2003-04 onwards, largely as a result of the capital account liberalisation measures. Notably, a large share of foreign capital that India receives has been short-term in nature. These include foreign portfolio investments (FPI), External Commercial Borrowings (ECBs) and bank deposits by Non-resident Indians (NRIs). Capital inflows on account of these three sources combined (FPI, ECBs and NRI deposits) amounted to more than twice the capital flows to the country on account of foreign direct investment (FDI) between 2000-01 and 2013-14 (see Figure 1).

Developing countries like India face severe macroeconomic challenges both when short-term foreign capital flows into and out of the country in large quantities. During periods of heavy capital inflows into India such as during 2007-08, there was pressure on the country's exchange rate to appreciate. The Rupee-dollar exchange rate appreciated to the level of Rs39 to Rs41 per dollar between May 2007 and April 2008 (see Figure 2). The appreciation of the Indian Rupee hurt the growth prospects of export-oriented industries such as textiles, garments, leather and diamond cutting.

To slow down the appreciation of the Rupee, the Reserve Bank intervened by accumulating foreign exchange reserves. Net foreign exchange assets of the RBI increased almost five-fold: from Rupees 2.6 trillion in 2001-02 to Rupees 12.3 trillion in 2007-08. The accumulation of foreign exchange reserves contributed to the growth of the reserve money and to the rise in inflation during the period 2006-08 (see Figure 3)

To reduce the inflationary impact due to the increase in foreign exchange assets, the RBI resorts to sterilisation, which it achieves by decreasing its domestic assets, mainly its credit to the government. The central bank's credit to the government or for 'printing money' is an important way to finance fiscal deficits. However, as shown above, with the need to sterilise the capital inflows, it became impossible for the central bank in India to extend credit to the government during the mid- to late-2000s (see Figure 3). Eliminating the financing of the fiscal deficits by the central bank was also part of the financial sector reforms in India, and an important provision of the FRBM (Fiscal Responsibility and Budget Management) Act.

As the foreign capital inflows into India continued, the RBI too had to continue its intervention in the forex market as also the subsequent sterilisation. For this, the RBI needed to sell government securities in greater quantities. Eventually, it reached a stage where the stock of government securities that could be sold in the market became limited. The solution came in the form of government bonds issued under the market stabilisation scheme (MSS), which the RBI sold to the public as part of its sterilisation efforts. The government paid interest rates on the MSS bonds, but the proceeds from the sale of these bonds were not used to support the government finances (however, MSS balances were used to support the fiscal stimulus measures introduced by the government from 2008-09 onwards).

As a result of these changes, the net RBI credit to the government declined since the 2000s, and was, in fact, negative in 2004-05 and 2007-08 (See Figure 3). In these years, the net flow of credit was from the government to the RBI, and not the other way round, so that the RBI could use the proceeds for sterilising the capital flows.

The economy suffered fiscal costs on account of the intervention and sterilisation operations that the RBI did in response to the large foreign capital inflows. Fiscal costs arose due to the interest payments of the government on the MSS bonds that it issued. Another source of these costs was when the RBI replaced its domestic assets with foreign assets (comprising mainly US treasury bonds), which offered very low rates of return. *The difference between the returns that the RBI could have received by holding domestic assets and the returns it actually received from its foreign assets entailed a cost to the economy.* According to estimates by the RBI, the cost to the Indian economy on account of the sterilisation operations ranged from 0.6% to 2% of the country's gross domestic product (GDP) during the period from 2004-05 to 2008-09 (RBI, 2012, p.90). In addition, there was, of course, the opportunity cost arising from the inability of the central bank to finance the government deficits.

The large inflows of foreign capital also created difficulties for the RBI in monetary management. Given the 'impossible trinity' referred to earlier, it is difficult for any country to simultaneously allow free capital mobility, maintain fixed exchange rates, and be able to pursue independent monetary policy. The Finance Minister admitted this in the 2008-09 Union Budget: 'We have... witnessed capital inflows that are far in excess of the current account deficit. This poses a challenge to monetary management.'

Short-term foreign capital flows into emerging economies are often in search of high returns. A fall in domestic interest rates could, therefore, trigger capital outflow from these economies. This creates pressures on domestic interest rates in emerging economies from moving in a downward direction. In other words, even with greater openness to foreign capital flows, cost of capital for domestic entrepreneurs has not actually gone down in India.

Capital inflows to India were also marked by high degree of volatility. Net inflows of FPI into India turned sharply negative in 2008-09 as foreign investors took the 'flight to safety' out of emerging market economies in the wake of the global financial crisis. Consequently, the Rupee depreciated sharply in 2008-09. Driven by the rapid rise and equally rapid fall in global commodity prices, there were sharp fluctuations in domestic prices too during January 2008 to March 2009 (see *Economic Survey 2008-09*).

Liberalisation of the Capital Account after the Global Financial Crisis

As shown earlier, many of the problems on account of short-term foreign capital flows became evident to India by the late 2000s, especially during the 2007-09 period. Nevertheless, India has continued to welcome foreign capital flows.

Part of the reason is that India's current account deficit worsened since 2011-12 and capital flows were helpful to support the rising current account deficits (see *Economic Survey 2010-11*, p. 17). Therefore, the government further liberalised the rules on short-term foreign capital flowing into the country. In the 2012-13 Union Budget, the limits on FII investments in long-term infrastructure bonds, corporate bonds, government securities, and ECBs were raised. Also, qualified foreign investors were allowed to invest in specified Indian mutual funds and directly in equities. In the 2013-14 Union Budget, the government announced several proposals relating to the capital market that simplified the procedures for FPIs to enter the country.

India's overall macroeconomic situation turned adverse since 2011-12 onwards. The country's GDP growth slowed down considerably, its current account deficit increased, and there was considerable rise in food inflation. In the changed circumstances, outflows of foreign capital became substantial. As a consequence, the Indian Rupee was on a decline since August 2011, and the decline became much sharper after June 2013.

With liberalisation in rules on ECBs, many Indian firms have been borrowing foreign currency loans. This has contributed the most to the rise in India's external debt, which increased from 113 billion dollars in 2004 to 440.6 billion dollars in 2014. The share of short-term debt in overall debt increased sharply from 2005 onwards. The share of ECBs in India's total external debt rose from 19.5% to 33% between 2004 and

2014 (while the corresponding share of government borrowing decreased from 35.3% to 13.8% during the same period). With the depreciation of the Indian Rupee during the 2011-13 period, the external liabilities of firms that had taken foreign-currency loans earlier increased significantly.

Conclusion

Lastly, the opening up of the economy to foreign capital flows has not helped much to rejuvenate productive investments in the economy. As already noted, short-term capital inflows have led to currency appreciation, volatility in domestic prices, and also to rise in inflation and domestic interest rates. In turn, these have created barriers to the growth of manufacturing and other productive sectors. At the same time, short-term foreign capital flows have encouraged the growth of speculative areas such as real estate.

The benefits from even the long-term foreign capital flows have not been that great. Estimates by Rao and Dhar (2011) show that of the total FDI equity inflows into India during 2005-08, manufacturing received a share of only 20.6%, energy received another 4.6%, while services, notably finance, construction and real estate, received the bulk of the foreign investments. They also show that a large proportion – 40.3% in 2006-07—of FDI flows into India in recent years has gone into the acquisition of shares of domestic enterprises by foreign companies (and, therefore, do not represent the building of new facilities) (Rao and Dhar 2011: 25-7).

Public sector gross fixed capital formation (GFCF), as proportion of GDP, increased in India from 6.6% in 2002-03 to 8.5% in 2008-09 but declined afterwards to 7.5% in 2011-12. Private corporate sector GFCF rose from 5.3% of GDP in 2002-03 to 14.3% in 2007-08, and fell sharply afterwards to 9.9% in 2011-12. The decline of public and private domestic investment along with the vulnerabilities caused due to foreign capital flows have been the key to understanding the problems in the Indian economy in recent years.

There are ample indications that the government is yet again considering the introduction of full capital account convertibility for India. The Union Budget for 2016-17 has announced a slew of tax concessions for the International Finance Service Centre (IFSC) in the Gujarat International Finance Tec City (GIFT). According to the budget speech of the Union Finance Minister (on 29 February 2016), the IFSC will be exempt from dividend distribution tax, securities transaction tax, commodity transaction tax, and tax on transfer of long-term capital asset. It is expected that investments by FPIs will migrate to IFSC, once it is set up because of these tax concessions. This can potentially increase volatility in India's capital markets and give global finance a greater control over the Indian economy (Nayak, 2016).

It is clear that India should exercise utmost caution while opening up its capital account any further to short-term foreign capital inflows. At the same time, the country should try for ways to mobilize domestic resources, encourage public and domestic private investments, and ensure fast growth of its productive sectors, especially manufacturing.

Figure 1: Net Foreign Capital Flows to India, in billion dollars, 2000-01 to 2013-14

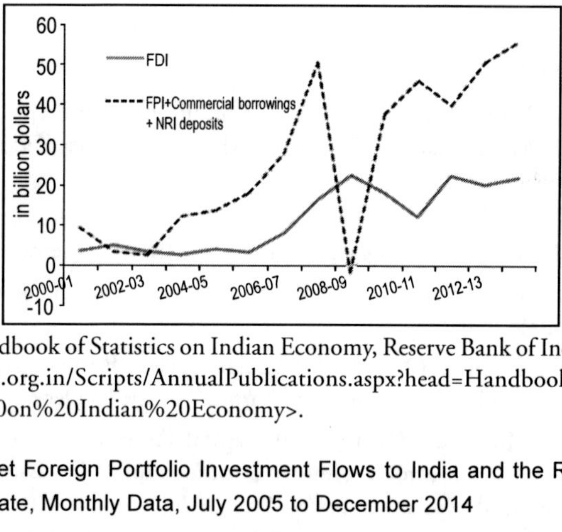

Source: Handbook of Statistics on Indian Economy, Reserve Bank of India, available at <www.rbi.org.in/Scripts/AnnualPublications.aspx?head=Handbook%20of%20Statistics%20on%20Indian%20Economy>.

Figure 2: Net Foreign Portfolio Investment Flows to India and the Rupee-Dollar Exchange Rate, Monthly Data, July 2005 to December 2014

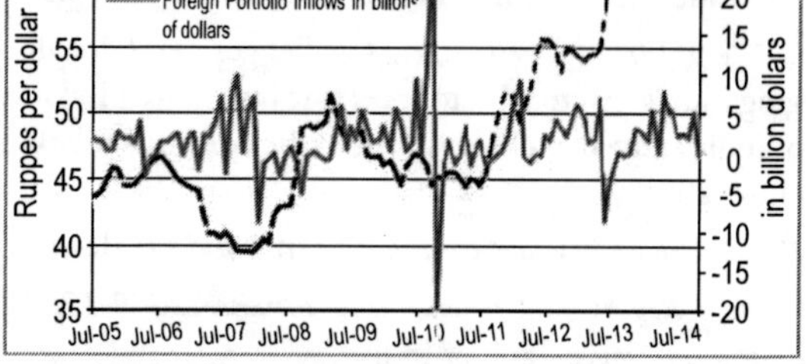

Source: Same as for Figure 1. For exchange rates after May 2011: <http://www.x-rates.com/d/INR/USD/hist2011.html>.

Figure 3: RBI's Credit to Government and its Foreign Exchange Assets, as percentage of Reserve Money in India, 1991-92 to 2012-13

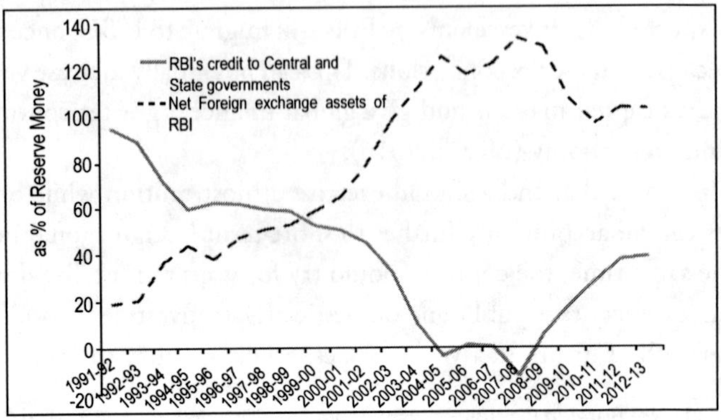

Source: Same as for Figure 1.

References

1. Khanna Vikram (1993), 'India's economic mandarin speaks: Interview with Dr Manmohan Singh, Finance Minister of India', *Business Times*, 24 Novemeber 1993.
2. Nachane DM (2007), 'Liberalization of the Capital Account: Perils and Possible Safeguards', *Economic and Political Weekly*, 8 September.
3. Nayak, Mahesh (2016), 'The Flight to IFSC', *Business Today*, March 27, Vol 25, No 6, p 23.
4. Patnaik Prabhat (2007), 'Financial Crises, Reserve Accumulation and Capital Flows', *Economic and Political Weekly*, 15 December, pp. 45-51.
5. Rakshit Mihir (2003), 'External Capital Flows and Foreign Exchange Reserves: Some Macroeconomic Implications and Policy Issues', *Money and Finance*, April-September, pp. 63-95.
6. Rao Chalapati KS and Biswajit Dhar (2011): 'India's FDI Inflows: Trends and Concepts', Research and Information Systems for Developing Countries, New Delhi and Institute for Studies in Industrial Development, New Delhi.
7. Reddy, Y. V. (2005), 'Overcoming Challenges in a Globalising Economy: Managing India's External Sector', Lecture by Y V Reddy, Governor, Reserve Bank of India at the India Programme of the Foreign Policy Centre, London, on 23 June 2005.
8. RBI (2006), *Report on Currency and Finance 2005-06*, Reserve Bank of India.
9. RBI (2012), *Report on Currency and Finance 2009-12: Fiscal Monetary Coordination*, Reserve Bank of India.
10. Subramanian Arvind (2007), 'Capital Account Convertibility: A Neglected Consideration, *Economic and Political Weekly*, 23 June, pp. 2,413-8.

Food Inflation in India

— Seema Sharma

INDIA HAS experienced a prolonged period of high inflation. This phenomenon can be attributed to a large extent to the persistently high food inflation. The share of food expenditure in total household expenditure in India, like in other developing countries, is relatively higher as compared to the developed countries (Figure 1). As a result, the weight for food in CPI basket is also high.

Figure 1: Share of Food in Household Expenditure (%) in Various Countries

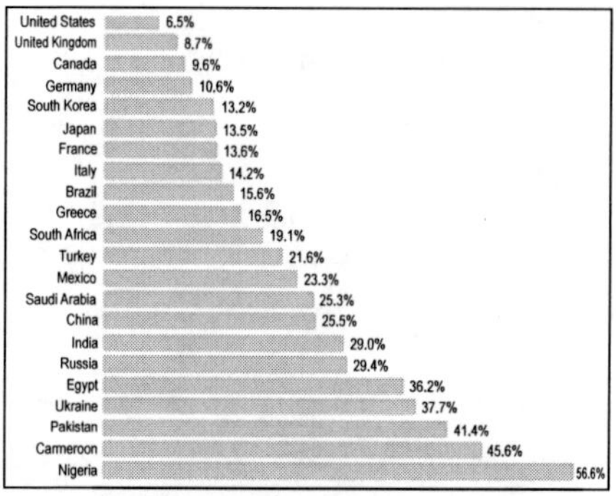

Source: USDA, Economic Research Service, USA; Vox, Vox Media Inc. 2015 USA.

The WPI (wholesale price index) inflation and CPI (consumer price index) inflation figures for India are presented in Table 2. We can see that in the post liberalisation period, the WPI food inflation has been higher than the WPI headline inflation, barring the few years of 1993-94, 1997-98, 2000-01 to 2004-05 and 2011-12. It is worth noting that for all these years, CPI food inflation was higher than CPI inflation except for the years 1999-2000, 2005-06 and 2010-11 (see Table 1 and Figures 2, 3 and 4).

Table 1: Food Inflation and Overall Inflation

Year	WPI	WPI - FOOD	CPI	CPI -FOOD
1990-91	10.3	11.9	11.6	12.4
1991-92	13.7	20.2	13.5	15.6
1992-93	10.1	12.4	9.6	10.4
1993-94	8.4	4.9	7.5	7.1
1994-95	12.6	12.8	10.1	11.8
1995-96	8	8.3	10.2	10.9
1996-97	4.6	12.4	9.4	9.5
1997-98	4.4	3	6.8	5.1
1998-99	5.9	12.7	13.1	14.7
1999-00	3.3	3.8	3.4	0.2
2000-01	7.2	3	3.8	1.5
2001-02	3.6	3.3	4.3	2.9
2002-03	3.4	1.8	4	2.4
2003-04	5.5	1.3	3.9	3.7
2004-05	6.5	2.6	3.8	2.2
2005-06	4.5	5.4	4.4	4.1
2006-07	6.6	9.6	6.7	9.2
2007-08	4.7	7	6.2	8.4
2008-09	8.1	9.1	9.1	12.3
2009-10	3.8	15.3	12.4	15.2
2010-11	9.6	15.6	10.4	9.9
2011-12	8.9	7.3	8.4	6.3
2012-13	7.4	9.9	10.4	11.9
2013-14	6	12.8	9.7	12.3
2014-15	2	6.1	6.3	6.5

Source: Handbook of Statistics on Indian Economy, Reserve Bank of Indiab, Various Issues.

After 2004-05, both the WPI and food inflation rose sharply over the years. Another major observation is that during the period 1999-2000 to 2005-06, inflation has been moderate and below 5%. However, beyond this moderate inflation period, the CPI food inflation and the WPI food inflation have exhibited a steep and increasing trend over the years. From 2005-06, general inflation has also shown a sharp rising trend which continued upto end of 2013. In 2014-15, both the CPI and WPI food inflation rates have shown significant decline and touched single digits.

Figure 2: WPI Headline and WPI Food Inlation (1990-91 to 2014-15)

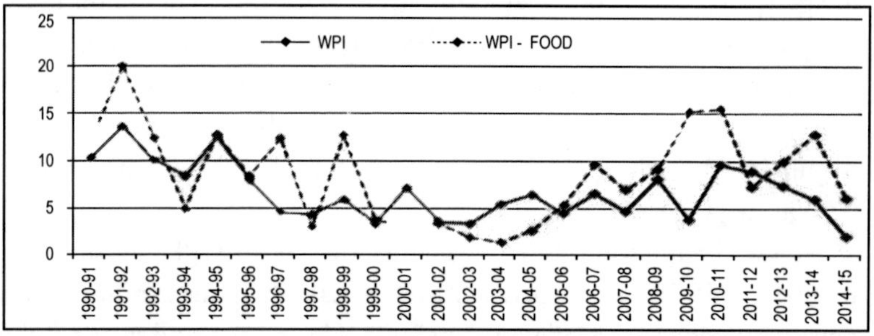

Figure 3: CPI and CPI Food Inflation (1990-91 to 2014-15)

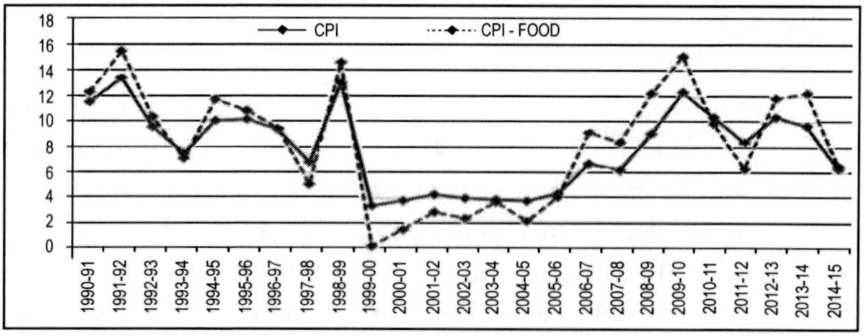

Figure 4: WPI Food and CPI Food Inflation (1990-91 to 2014-15)

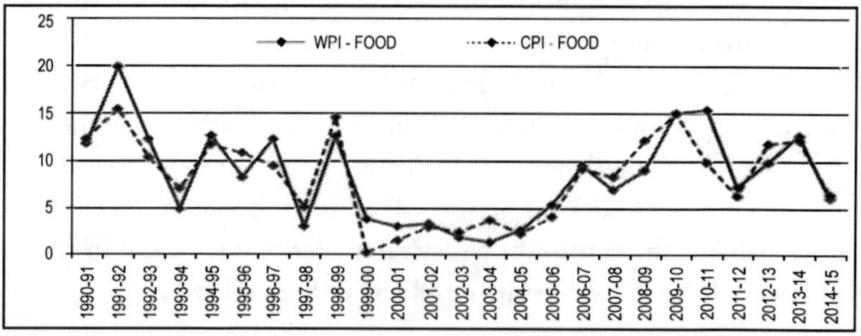

Fall in Food Inflation in India: Sustainable or Temporary?

Our analysis of year on year monthly inflation in India shows that the escalating trend in CPI food inflation in particular, continued upto Nov 2013 and thereafter it has turned into a declining trajectory. The CPI food inflation has fallen from 12.1% in Dec 2013 to 2.9% in Aug 2015 and then reached to 6.7% in Jan 2016 (Table 2). If we further examine the CPI food inflation at disaggregated level, we find that inflation in all food items except pulses has shown a falling pattern over the months (see Table 2 and Figure 5). A deeper look at disaggregated level shows that in the last two years, the fall in non-pulses categories was steeper in 2014 and has been moderate in the year 2015. It is notable that inflation in vegetables has gone up in Jan 2016. Also, It can be observed that there has been sharp increase in prices of pulses. The inflation rate which was at 2.1% in Dec 2013 rose to 43.3% in January.

Now the question arises – whether the fall in CPI food inflation in 2014 and 2015 can be seen as a sustainable turnaround in the persistently rising food inflationin in India. The stability and sustainability of this downturn in food inflation is questionable in future due to following reasons:

(i) The decline in food inflation is greatly due to fall in the global commodity prices (see Figure 6) due to slackening demand and the reduction in oil prices. If this trend reverses, inflation in India will rise again. Also, the examination of monthly CPI food index reveals that the food prices are rising in the country.

(ii) The Rabi crops across north and western India have been victim of unseasonal rains and hailstorm in 2015 and 2016. This in turn has drastically affected the agricultural production in the country. The supply shocks can give rise to inflationary pressures in the economy.

Therefore, the decline in food inflation in recent times should not be seen as a sustainable shift in the behavior of food prices in India. Also, even though, the inflation rate has come down but the prices are still rising. That's why RBI has persistently resisted, due to its concerns for price stability, the cuts in the policy rates. Hence it is crucial to address the causes behind the persistent problem of high inflation.

Table 2: Year on Year CPI Inflation

(Base 2010=100)													
	Dec 13	Jan 14	Dec 13	Jan 14	Feb 14	May 14	June 14	July 14	Aug 14	Sep 14	Oct 14	Nov 14	Dec 14
Food, Beverages and Tabacco	12.0	9.9	8.6	9.1	9.8	9.2	7.9	9.1	9.15	7.6	5.8	3.6	5.06
Cereals and products	12.1	11.4	9.8	9.6	9.7	8.8	7.6	7.5	7.32	6.4	6.0	5.2	3.98
Pulses and products	2.1	2.6	3.5	4.5	5.0	5.4	5.2	5.8	6.80	7.2	7.5	7.5	7.24
Milk and products	9.7	9.8	10.2	11.0	11.4	11.3	11.1	113.	11.70	11.1	10.8	10.2	9.62
Vegetables	38.5	21.9	14.3	16.8	17.5	15.2	8.7	16.8	15.03	8.6	-1.4	-10.9	0.58
Egg, fish and meat	12.6	11.7	9.5	9.5	9.4	10.0	8.3	7.7	7.71	6.4	6.3	6.5	5.24
Fruits	14.6	15.7	16.1	17.2	21.7	22.9	20.6	22.3	24.00	22.4.	17.5	13.7	14.84

(Base 2012=100)

	Feb 15	Mar 15	Apr 15	May 15	Jun 15	Jul 15	Aug 15	Sep 15	Oct. 15	Dec 15	Jan 16
Food, Beverages and Tabacco	12.0	9.9	8.6	9.1	9.8	9.2	7.9	9.1	9.15	7.6	5.8
Cereals and products	12.1	11.4	9.8	9.6	9.7	8.8	7.6	7.5	7.32	6.4	6.0
Pulses and products	2.1	2.6	3.5	4.5	5.0	5.4	5.2	5.8	6.80	7.2	7.5
Milk and products	9.7	9.8	10.2	11.0	11.4	11.3	11.1	113.	11.70	11.1	10.8
Vegetables	38.5	21.9	14.3	16.8	17.5	15.2	8.7	16.8	15.03	8.6	-1.4
Egg, fish and meat	12.6	11.7	9.5	9.5	9.4	10.0	8.3	7.7	7.71	6.4	6.3
Fruits	14.6	15.7	16.1	17.2	21.7	22.9	20.6	22.3	24.00	22.4.	17.5

Note: For each month, the inflation figures are yearly variations.

Source: Calculated from CPI Index Data from RBI Bulletin, Various Issues, Government of India.

Figure 5: Year on Year Monthly CPI Inflation

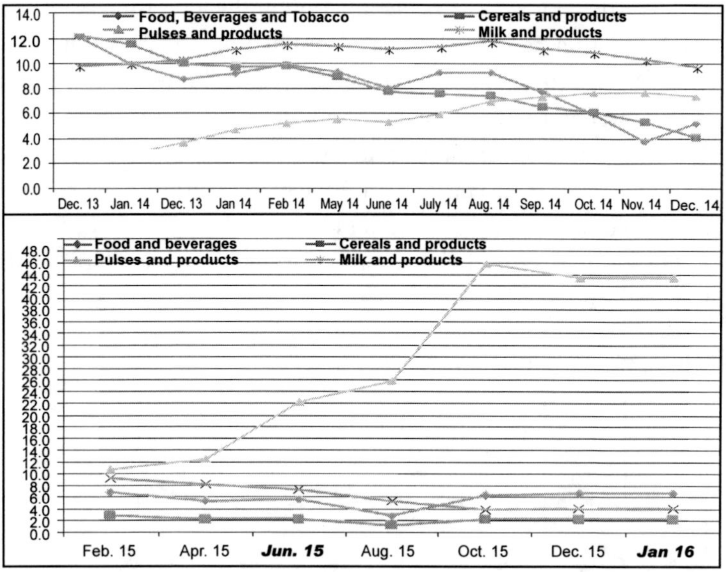

Figure 6: FAO Food Price Index vs. India CPI Food Index

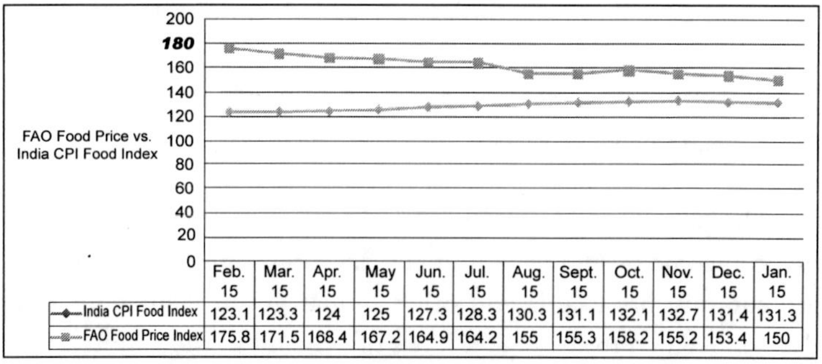

	Feb. 15	Mar. 15	Apr. 15	May 15	Jun. 15	Jul. 15	Aug. 15	Sept. 15	Oct. 15	Nov. 15	Dec. 15	Jan. 15
India CPI Food Index	123.1	123.3	124	125	127.3	128.3	130.3	131.1	132.1	132.7	131.4	131.3
FAO Food Price Index	175.8	171.5	168.4	167.2	164.9	164.2	155	155.3	158.2	155.2	153.4	150

Source: (i) *World Food Situation*, Food and Agriculture Organisation of United States (FAO), 2016.
(ii) RBI Bulletin, 2016, Government of India.

Factors Responsible for Inflation in India

As we know in any country, high level of inflation is a serious concern due to following reasons:

(i) It affects the purchasing power of lower and middle income strata adversely.

(ii) It directly feeds into the wage structure in the country, hence, further adds to the rising inflation in the long run.

(iii) Inflation adds to the cost of production and hence leads to a vicious circle of price rise over the years. This not only affects the lower and middle income group people in the country but also makes exports from the country less competitive. As we can see in Figure 7, India continues to have high inflation when compared to other emerging economies in BRICS.

Hence, it is crucial that food inflation be checked to avoid its adverse effects.

Figure 7: Annual Variation (%) in Consumer Prices

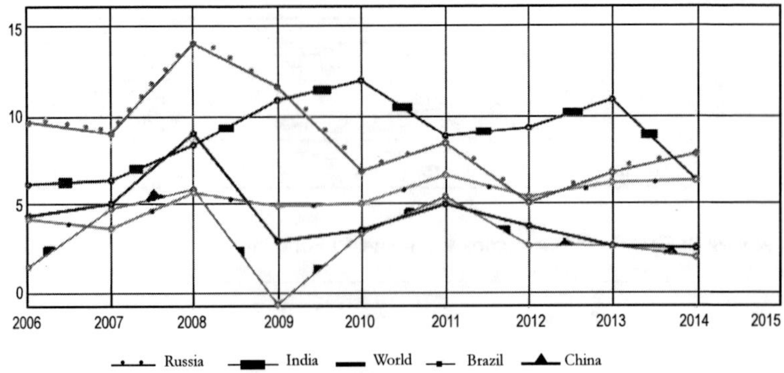

Source: World Bank Database.

The post liberalisation era in Indian economy is characterised by rise in income of middle and upper class. Furthermore, the occasional pay commission awards and other similar government policies have also contributed to the higher levels of demand in the country. On the supply side, Indian agriculture is still predominantly dependent on rains. Approximately 50% of area under cultivation is still rain fed (Figure 8). Even the area under irrigation is also indirectly dependent on rainfall as rains improve the water table. However, lack of irrigation facilities continues to severely enhance the vulnerability of Indian agriculture. As we can see in Table 3, the per capita availability of cereals has declined significantly over the years, which is a great cause of worry.

Table 3: Per Capita Availability per day (grams) of Cereals and Foodgrains over the years

Year	Cereals	Foodgrains
1951	334.2	394.9
1961	399.7	468.7
1971	417.6	468.8
1981	417.3	454.8
1991	468.5	510.1
2001	386.2	416.2
2010	401.7	437.1
2012	408.6	450.3
2013	468.9	510.8

Source: Agriculture Statistics at a glance 2014, Directorate of Economics and Statistics, Ministry of Agriculture, Government of India, 2015.

Figure 8: Area under Irrigation (%)

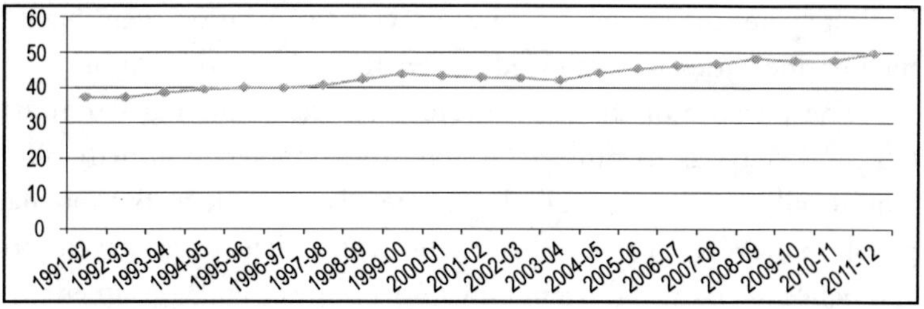

Source: Based on data retrieved from Agricultural Statistics at a Glance 2014, Directorate of Economics and Statistics, Ministry of Agriculture, Government of India, 2015.

Figure 9: Minimum Support Price of Paddy & Wheat (Annual percentage variations)

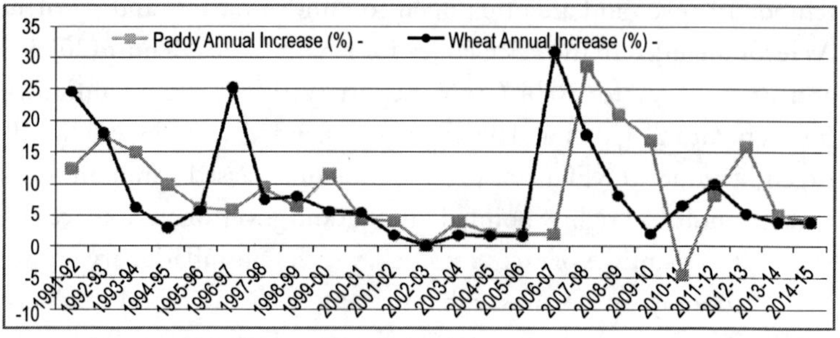

Source: Based on data from (i) Handbook of Statistics on Indian Economy, RBIb, 2014, (ii) Agricultural Statistics At a Glance 2014, Directorate of Economics and Statistics, Ministry of Agriculture, Government of India, 2015.

On the other hand, the cost of agricultural inputs has also increased substantially in the recent period (RBIa 2014). Often, hikes in minimum support prices (MSP) are cited as one of the major reason for food inflation. In view of the high rise in cost of production, the hikes in minimum support prices (MSP) are justified. Nevertheless, if we look at the growth rates of MSP of paddy and wheat over the years, we find that there has been a declining trend in both over the years (Figure 9). Also, how can the increases in MSP be attributed as a significant cause behind inflation when there exists a huge gap between what the farmer gets and what is paid by the end consumer in the market. The farmers get merely 30 per cent of what an end consumer pays for a food commodity. Therefore increases in MSP cannot be held responsible for inflation. So, the irony is that on one hand the food market for end consumers is characterised by high inflation and; on the other hand, the farmer is getting meager returns. So the question arises, who is benefitting from the food inflation? Definitely not the farmer. We must draw the conclusion then that only the intermediaries are getting advantage from the food inflation.

The purpose of the Agriculture Produce Marketing Committee (APMC) Act was to protect farmers from market intermediaries. It requires all produce to be sold through regulated markets. But too many people in the supply chain seek out a shortcut, which exaggerates the price and hence the farmer gets a nominal price and the end consumer pays a hefty price for the product. Further, the poor management of stocks also creates a paradoxical situation of high inflation and at the same time, overflowing stocks with the FCI. Overstocked grains are kept under temporary cover and are often open to rain, snow, rats and pestilence. As recommended in the Price Policy for Kharif Crops Report (2013-14) and Price Policy for Rabi Crops Report (2014-15), the Commission for Agricultural Costs and Prices recommended that there is need to urgently reduce the FCI stock to the tune of at least 15 million tonnes. The Commission rightly pointed out that the government unnecessarily stores large quantities of excessive stock, which puts inflationary pressures in the economy. So we can say that the supply chain of food products in India suffers from high levels of inefficiency. Therefore, there is a need to improve efficiency at various levels of the supply chain. Apart from all the factors cited in the discussion so far, the future trading of food commodities is also one of the contributing factors for food inflation. Higher speculative investment in the food derivative market can aggravate the inflationary pressure through artificially increasing the demand for food commodities. Hoarding of food products is another activity which leads to higher prices.

Conclusion

Therefore, we can conclude that food inflation in India has been substantially high since 2006. Various factors, viz. rising incomes in middle and upper classes, unfavourable rains,rising cost of agricultural production and poor management of food stocks by government, inefficiencies in different stages of supply chain etc. are the major contributory factors. For the last two years, 2014 and 2015, there has been a declining trend in the food inflation. But this phenomenon is not expected to sustain in the future due to the vulnerability of Indian agriculture. Hence it is crucial that some strong and effective measures are taken by the government.

As an immediate step to ease inflation, government should decrease the excessive stock and adopt the optimum stock policy for wheat and paddy. In the long run, more emphasis on R&D for higher productivity, more water harvesting and efficient modes of irrigation facilities such as drip irrigation, creation of better storage infrastructure and a strong anti-hoarding policy is the ultimate roadmap to follow.

References

1. Commission for Agricultural Costs and Prices (2012), *Price Policy for Kharif Crops Report (2013-14),* Department of Agriculture and Cooperation, Ministry of Agriculture, Government of India.
2. Commission for Agricultural Costs and Prices (2013), *Price Policy for Rabi Crops Report (2014-15)*, Department of Agriculture and Cooperation, Ministry of Agriculture, Government of India.
3. Directorate of Economics and Statistics (2015), *Agricultural Statistics At a Glance 2014*, Ministry of Agriculture, Government of India, 2015.
4. *Economic Survey* 2014-15, Government of India.
5. Food and Agriculture Organization of United States (FAO) 2016, *World Food Situation* http://www.fao.org/worldfoodsituation/foodpricesindex/en/ accessed on Mar 10, 2015.

6. International Monetary Fund (2014), "Food Inflation in India: The Role for Monetary Policy, Anand et al.", *Working Paper* WP/14/178.
7. Reserve Bank of India, *RBI Bulletin*, Various monthly issues, Government of India.
8. Reserve Bank of Indiaa (2014), "Analytics of Food Inflation in India', *RBI Working Paper Series*, WPS (DEPR): 10 / 2014, Government of India.
9. Reserve Bank of Indiab (2014), *Handbook of Statistics on Indian Economy*, Government of India.
10. United States Department of Agriculture (USDA) (2015), *Economic Research Service.*
11. *Vox Media Inc. (2015),* 'Map: Here's how much each country spends onfood', Vox, USA.
12. http://www.vox.com/2014/7/6/5874499/map-heres-how-much-every-country-spends-on-food accessed on Nov 2, 2016.
13. World Bank, 'Inflation, Consumer Prices (annual %)', World Bank Database.
14. http://data.worldbank.org/indicator/FP.CPI.TOTL.ZG/countries/1W-IN-CN-BR-RU?display=graph accessed on Nov 6, 2015.

Public Spending on Health in India

— Sharanjit S Dhillon and Ajay Sehgal

HEALTH IS one of the important parameters to assess and evaluate the socio-economic progress of an individual, a society and of a country. Health is regarded as a vital factor in the formation of human resource development that plays an important role in improving the qualities of human beings who are the active promoters of economic development of a country. Health is considered as an important asset of social welfare as it is a means to empower the deprived sections of the society and thus, becomes a vital component in the strategy for poverty alleviation. Good health generally increases the enrolment of children in school, makes them more capable of learning and use in resources that would otherwise have to be spent on treating illness. The improvement in health status enhances the quality of human resources in addition to food and better shelter, especially in a developing country like India. Thus, better health usually contributes in improving the economic status of the poor. The health status of the people is a reflection of the socio-economic development of a country.

The Indian health system is a mix of public and private sectors, with NGOs and civil society playing a small but a significant role.

India has a three-tier public healthcare service, namely, primary healthcare services provided by primary health centres (PHCs) and sub-centres (SCs), secondary healthcare services provided by community health centres (CHCs) and district hospitals, and tertiary healthcare services provided by medical colleges and multispeciality hospitals. In India, health, being in the State list, is the constitutional responsibility of State governments, with centrally-sponsored schemes largely depicting the role of the central government. The States contribute around three-fourths of total public spending on the health sector and the remaining is the contribution of the centre. Health expenditure in India is dominated by private spending which is, to a large extent, a reflection of the inadequate public spending and thus adversely affects current social welfare and labour productivity and, of course, harms future growth and development prospects (Economic Research Foundation, 2006).

In 2002, the central government brought out a new National Health Policy which listed the achievements between the years 1951-2000 in the form of considerable improvements in life expectancy, reduction in crude birth and death rate and infant mortality rate as well as significant improvements in health infrastructure and health personnel in the country. In this policy, the central government has planned to increase the health expenditure to 6 per cent of the GDP, with 2 per cent of GDP being contributed as public health investment by the year 2010 (GOI, 2002). At present, India is spending around 4 per cent of GDP (including private expenditure) on the health sector, in which the public expenditure component spent on health (including 'water supply and sanitation') accounts for 1.3 per cent of the GDP, much short of the target requirement of 6 per cent and 2 per cent of GDP respectively, set out in NHP 2002 (GOI, 2016). Thus, the health sector in India is indeed grossly under-funded, which results in an unsatisfactory distribution of infrastructure and resources in the health sector and this ultimately leads to adverse impact on health outcomes.

In a developing country like India, though the health expenditure is dominated by private spending, even then the government's role in providing and financing health services assumes greater importance from the perspective of social welfare as well as ensuring equity.

Any deficiency in the public provision of healthcare creates a space for the private providers who tend to play by the rules of the market rather than by the needs and priorities of the people, especially those belonging to the poorer segments. Therefore, the unregulated expansion of private sector health services is often due to space provided by the absence of the public sector.

As the public financing of healthcare services in India has to be met out of the scarce public resources, the financing patterns of the governments in India need to be reviewed and analysed to facilitate better understanding and help prioritise allocation optimally to the health sector. Therefore, this paper primarily focuses upon the public spending on health sector in India at national and State levels. Data have been presented for all States including union territories with special legislature in India during the period 1990-91 to 2010-11. Public spending on health includes public expenditure on 'medical & public health' and 'family welfare' by the Central and State governments in India.

State-wise Analysis of Patterns of Public Spending on Health

The constitutional division of responsibilities among the centre and States places the main responsibility for healthcare on the State governments in India. This section describes the analysis of patterns of public spending on health by the States in India during the period 1990-91 to 2010-11, with a view to understanding the inclination of individual governments in committing financial resources to the health sector. Table 1 shows the public spending on health by all States as a percentage of GSDP. All States, on an average, have incurred a very low proportion of their GSDP that ranges from 0.6 to 0.82 per cent on health in India during 1990-91 to 2010-11. Among all the States, Sikkim has spent the highest proportion of its GSDP on health followed by Mizoram while Haryana has incurred the lowest proportion of its GSDP on health, followed by Maharashtra for most of the years during the period of study. Around 2.03 to 5.08 per cent of GSDP has been incurred by Sikkim on health while Mizoram's public spending on health as percentage of GSDP ranges from 2.51 to 4.79 per cent during 1990-91 to 2010-11. Both Haryana and Maharashtra have spent a meagre proportion of their GSDP that varies between 0.38 to 0.86 per cent.

Among all States, only 11 States such as Arunachal Pradesh, Goa, Himachal Pradesh, Jammu & Kashmir, Manipur, Meghalaya, Mizoram, Nagaland, Sikkim, Tripura and Puducherry have managed to spend more than the national average ranging from 0.75 to 0.94 per cent of GDP on health during all the years under study. This analysis clearly reveals that all special category States, except Assam and Uttarakhand, are spending relatively higher proportion of their GSDP on health as compared to general category States. Among these, 9 special category States, 3 States, namely, Arunachal Pradesh, Mizoram and Sikkim have spent more than 2 per cent of their GSDP on health during the whole period of study.

Among 15 major States, Bihar has spent the highest proportion of its GSDP on health in the early years of the study, ie., from 1990-91 to 1995-96, while Kerala has spent the highest proportion of its GSDP on health from 1996-97 to 2010-11. As already mentioned in case of all States, Haryana has been spending the lowest proportion of its GSDP on health for most of the years during the period of study, followed by Maharashtra. Bihar's public spending on health accounts for 0.80 to 1.67 per cent of its GSDP during 1990-91 to 2010-11. Kerala has shown the greatest intent for its spending patterns on health, as its public spending on health as percentage of GSDP has risen sharply from its lowest level of 1.09 per cent in 1990-91 to its highest level of 2.72 per cent in 2010-11. Among major States, only 2 States such as Kerala and Bihar have spent more than the national average in terms of GSDP on health, except for one or two years during 1990-91 to 2010-11.

Except Kerala and Goa, most of the economically developed States such as Andhra Pradesh, Gujarat, Haryana, Maharashtra, Punjab, Tamil Nadu and NCT Delhi have spent less than 1 per cent of their GSDP on health during 1990-91 to 2010-11, indicating that most of the economically less developed States are spending the relatively higher proportion of their GSDP on health to catch up with developed States, and this gives a ray of hope for improvement in the health status of less developed States in the coming years. It also seems that with economic growth, the focus of most of the economically developed States towards healthcare has decreased.

Table 1: State-wise Public Expenditure on Health (As Per Cent of GSDP)

States	1990-91	1991-92	1992-93	1993-94	1994-95	1995-96	1996-97	1997-98	1998-99	1999-00
Andhra Pradesh	0.82	0.78	0.80	0.80	0.72	0.66	0.75	0.78	0.81	0.81
Arunachal Pradesh	2.98	2.73	2.53	2.31	2.58	2.54	2.80	2.94	2.81	2.82
Assam	0.96	1.04	0.91	1.00	0.95	0.95	0.90	0.92	0.75	0.87
Bihar	1.40	1.35	1.53	1.32	1.31	1.67	1.19	1.42	1.43	1.53
Chhattisgarh	-	-	-	-	-	-	-	-	-	-
Goa	2.35	2.17	1.83	1.70	1.45	1.45	1.33	1.19	1.17	1.17
Gujarat	0.75	0.77	0.65	0.66	0.59	0.59	0.55	0.64	0.75	0.79
Haryana	0.56	0.55	0.61	0.60	0.86	0.52	0.51	0.56	0.66	0.56
Himachal Pradesh	1.92	1.84	1.85	1.76	1.72	1.62	1.72	1.71	1.92	1.79
Jammu & Kashmir	1.67	1.83	2.01	1.96	1.92	1.88	1.89	1.92	2.05	2.14
Jharkhand	-	-	-	-	-	-	-	-	-	-
Karnataka	0.88	0.82	0.92	0.87	0.87	0.81	0.73	0.86	0.83	0.87
Kerala	1.09	1.11	1.08	1.23	1.35	1.52	1.59	1.83	1.83	2.14
Madhya Pradesh	0.95	1.00	0.98	0.96	0.96	0.88	0.92	0.89	1.08	0.99
Maharashtra	0.68	0.65	0.61	0.58	0.54	0.52	0.52	0.52	0.51	0.52

Table 1 (Contd...)

States	1990-91	1991-92	1992-93	1993-94	1994-95	1995-96	1996-97	1997-98	1998-99	1999-00
Manipur	1.85	1.73	1.67	1.61	1.58	1.77	1.63	1.63	1.53	2.02
Meghalaya	1.84	1.75	1.94	1.80	1.61	1.72	1.75	1.73	1.86	1.80
Mizoram	3.23	2.63	2.63	2.70	2.91	2.52	3.13	3.02	2.90	3.39
Nagaland	3.03	2.24	1.79	2.20	1.57	2.36	2.41	2.10	2.23	2.76
Odisha	1.01	0.96	0.90	0.86	0.91	0.81	0.89	0.79	0.95	0.92
Punjab	0.81	0.78	0.74	0.68	0.61	0.59	0.63	0.70	0.82	0.80
Rajasthan	0.90	0.94	0.93	1.00	0.96	1.02	0.95	0.94	0.98	0.94
Sikkim	3.26	3.91	4.54	5.08	4.85	4.44	3.69	2.98	4.71	3.52
Tamil Nadu	0.91	0.87	0.85	0.79	0.75	0.75	0.72	0.73	0.80	0.78
Tripura	2.04	1.80	1.70	1.79	1.74	1.62	1.80	1.62	1.50	1.51
Uttar Pradesh	1.06	0.92	0.98	1.07	0.91	0.88	0.84	0.97	0.74	0.71
Uttarakhand	-	-	-	-	-	-	-	-	-	-
West Bengal	1.17	0.90	0.91	0.93	0.82	0.81	0.84	0.75	0.95	0.98
Puducherry	2.62	2.62	2.51	2.56	2.49	2.82	2.09	1.85	1.89	2.36
NCT Delhi	-	-	-	0.29	0.59	0.69	0.64	0.66	0.66	0.75
All States	**0.82**	**0.78**	**0.76**	**0.78**	**0.73**	**0.72**	**0.70**	**0.73**	**0.75**	**0.74**
All India	**0.92**	**0.87**	**0.86**	**0.87**	**0.82**	**0.79**	**0.78**	**0.82**	**0.85**	**0.85**

Table 1 (Contd...)

States	2000-01	2001-02	2002-03	2003-04	2004-05	2005-06	2006-07	2007-08	2008-09	2009-10	2010-11
Andhra Pradesh	0.83	0.80	0.74	0.71	0.69	0.66	0.64	0.71	0.72	0.72	0.73
Arunachal Pradesh	2.86	2.59	2.44	2.60	2.69	2.02	2.99	2.43	3.22	2.91	2.66
Assam	0.94	0.91	0.74	0.76	0.79	0.69	0.88	0.92	1.13	1.56	1.32
Bihar	1.16	0.88	0.86	0.80	0.81	1.23	1.14	1.22	0.91	0.93	0.82
Chhattisgarh	0.30	0.82	0.83	0.75	0.66	0.62	0.62	0.60	0.64	0.80	0.71
Goa	1.16	1.13	1.08	1.06	0.94	0.97	0.88	0.83	0.95	1.01	1.03
Gujarat	0.76	0.54	0.56	0.48	0.48	0.44	0.40	0.42	0.44	0.53	0.58
Haryana	0.50	0.48	0.48	0.43	0.41	0.43	0.38	0.38	0.42	0.49	0.42
Himachal Pradesh	1.76	1.49	1.45	1.54	1.55	1.45	1.46	1.39	1.36	1.41	1.44
Jammu & Kashmir	2.01	2.09	1.86	1.71	1.83	1.92	2.22	2.18	1.92	2.31	2.26

Table 1 (Contd...)

States	2000-01	2001-02	2002-03	2003-04	2004-05	2005-06	2006-07	2007-08	2008-09	2009-10	2010-11
Jharkhand	0.17	0.67	0.56	0.48	0.71	0.87	0.67	0.63	0.89	0.68	0.64
Karnataka	0.83	0.87	0.75	0.68	0.63	0.59	0.60	0.68	0.67	0.67	0.68
Kerala	1.99	2.04	2.02	2.02	1.93	1.90	2.02	2.09	2.42	2.42	2.72
Madhya Pradesh	0.99	0.72	0.81	0.70	0.80	0.80	0.79	0.77	0.70	0.73	0.82
Maharashtra	0.60	0.62	0.54	0.52	0.48	0.45	0.40	0.41	0.46	0.46	0.44
Manipur	1.87	1.87	1.55	1.63	1.30	1.45	1.57	2.28	2.10	2.50	3.33
Meghalaya	1.75	1.77	1.69	1.58	1.54	1.53	1.36	1.53	1.30	1.81	2.04
Mizoram	3.28	3.31	2.90	3.51	2.91	2.59	2.51	2.59	3.82	4.79	2.73
Nagaland	2.22	1.71	1.68	1.66	2.23	1.84	1.77	1.92	1.57	1.68	2.05
Odisha	0.97	0.88	0.92	0.75	0.81	0.55	0.60	0.58	0.63	0.72	0.64
Punjab	0.83	0.75	0.72	0.66	0.63	0.64	0.55	0.50	0.49	0.50	0.54
Rajasthan	0.96	0.96	0.91	0.81	0.84	0.85	0.77	0.78	0.89	0.88	0.76

Table 1 (Contd...)

States	2000-01	2001-02	2002-03	2003-04	2004-05	2005-06	2006-07	2007-08	2008-09	2009-10	2010-11
Sikkim	3.06	3.25	3.03	2.67	3.30	3.00	2.63	2.93	2.75	2.03	2.03
Tamil Nadu	0.70	0.71	0.67	0.62	0.62	0.64	0.54	0.52	0.62	0.72	0.75
Tripura	1.47	1.36	1.34	1.15	1.18	1.57	1.54	1.62	1.59	1.79	1.39
Uttar Pradesh	0.75	0.68	0.72	0.78	0.86	1.05	1.28	1.09	1.11	1.15	1.08
Uttarakhand	0.18	0.73	0.77	0.79	1.00	1.17	1.12	1.01	0.88	0.74	0.82
West Bengal	1.07	0.92	0.83	0.75	0.68	0.69	0.64	0.63	0.64	0.81	0.76
Puducherry	2.17	1.94	1.67	1.61	1.77	1.48	2.17	2.21	1.79	2.25	2.22
NCT Delhi	0.80	0.81	0.82	0.80	0.84	0.79	0.81	0.83	0.88	0.92	0.93
All States	0.73	0.69	0.67	0.63	0.61	0.61	0.61	0.60	0.64	0.69	0.67
All India	0.85	0.82	0.79	0.77	0.75	0.80	0.81	0.82	0.89	0.94	0.91

Source: Computed from data in Combined Finance and Revenue Accounts of the Union and State Governments, GOI (various years); EPW Research Foundation (2009); DCH, Planning Commission (2014).

Table 2 elucidates the State-wise analysis of public spending on health by each individual State in India, in terms of real per capita public expenditure at 2004-05 prices. The real per capita public spending by all States on health, on an average, has increased from Rs 144 in 1990-91 to Rs 294 in 2010-11.Only 12 States such as Arunachal Pradesh, Goa, Himachal Pradesh, Jammu & Kashmir, Kerala, Manipur, Meghalaya, Mizoram, Nagaland, Sikkim, Tripura and Puducherry are spending the relatively higher amount of real per capita public expenditure on health than the national average ranging from Rs 151 to Rs 402 during the whole period of study. Among these 11 States, except Goa and Puducherry, all the States are special category States, indicating that most of the special category States are incurring the relatively higher amount of real per capita public spending on health as compared to general category States during the period of study.

Sikkim has spent the highest amount of real per capita public expenditure on health for most of the years during 1990-91 to 1999-2000 while Puducherry has spent the highest real per capita public spending on health for most of the years during 2000-01 to 2010-11. Bihar is spending the lowest amount of real per capita public expenditure on health, ranging from Rs 58 to Rs 123 during 1990-91 to 2010-11, except during 1999-2000 in which Uttar Pradesh has incurred the lowest real per capita public expenditure on health (only Rs 97). This analysis reveals that the real per capita public expenditure on health in Bihar has been desperately low as it remains within two-digit value (less than Rs 100) for most of the years covered under study.

Among 15 major States, Punjab has spent the highest amount of real per capita public expenditure on health for the first three years from 1990-91 to 1992-93 while Kerala has been spending the highest real per capita public expenditure on health from 1993-94 to 2010-11. Despite the fact that Bihar incurred the highest proportion of its GSDP on health in the early years of study, but, being a densely populated State, it stands last among major States, in terms of real per capita public expenditure on health. None of the major States has spent the relatively higher amount of real per capita public expenditure on health than the national average for all the years during the period of study. However, Kerala is the only State that has made a significant improvement in its public spending on health, in terms of real per capita public expenditure as its real per capita expenditure on health has increased by more than 7 times from Rs 191 in 1990-91 to Rs 1,495 in 2010-11 while Punjab has shown the lowest growth of 1.3 per cent in its real per capita public spending on health from Rs 213 to Rs 277 during 1988-89 to 2010-11.

All States have shown an increasing trend with wide variations in their public spending on health in terms of real per capita public expenditure during 1990-91 to 2010-11. It is observed that most of the economically less developed States like Assam, Bihar, Madhya Pradesh, Odisha, Rajasthan, Uttar Pradesh etc. are spending the relatively lower amount of real per capita public expenditure on health as compared to most of the developed States. The low levels of public spending on health in poorer States arises from the inability of the fiscal transfer system to offset the general fiscal disabilities of poorer States, arising from their low revenue raising capacities. This failure has been compounded by the shortcomings in the design and implementation of the specific purpose transfers under various central schemes. The specific purpose transfers have failed to ensure minimum standards of health services in the low income States and as these are the States with high concentration of poverty, the poor people have little access to healthcare services (Rao & Choudhary, 2008).

Public Spending on Health at National Level in India

Public expenditure on health consists of expenditure incurred by the central and State governments. Table 3 describes the public expenditure on health at national level as a percentage of GDP as well as in terms of real per capita public expenditure at 2004-05 prices. India is spending less than 1 per cent of its GDP on health which also falls short of 2 per cent target as set out in National Health Policy 2002 (GOI, 2002). As a percentage of GDP, the public expenditure on health has declined from 0.92 per cent in 1990-91 to its lowest level of 0.75 per cent in 2004-05 and it has increased to 0.91 per cent in 2010-11. The decline in the public expenditure on health during 1990-2005 is mainly due to the decline in the States' public expenditure on health from 0.82 per cent in 1990-91 to 0.61 per cent in 2004-05 while the centre's public spending on health has shown a marginal increase from 0.1 to 0.14 per cent of GDP during the same period.

Table 2: State-wise Real Per Capita Public Expenditure on Health (in Rs)

States	1990-91	1991-92	1992-93	1993-94	1994-95	1995-96	1996-97	1997-98	1998-99	1999-00
Andhra Pradesh	130	128	127	139	130	125	149	150	172	177
Arunachal Pradesh	497	517	491	511	510	572	599	648	639	606
Assam	147	163	141	159	153	154	147	149	120	141
Bihar	73	66	70	82	88	94	82	91	96	104
Chhattisgarh	-	-	-	-	-	-	-	-	-	-
Goa	957	873	834	806	722	775	758	697	839	861
Gujarat	144	136	145	141	146	152	159	184	230	235
Haryana	143	142	155	154	231	141	148	164	198	176
Himachal Pradesh	397	375	389	378	399	393	437	456	538	527
Jammu & Kashmir	320	350	394	385	382	379	396	416	452	483
Jharkhand	-	-	-	-	-	-	-	-	-	-
Karnataka	131	135	152	151	156	152	147	183	195	225
Kerala	191	197	201	250	296	344	372	435	462	579
Madhya Pradesh	93	90	93	133	134	127	139	138	174	173
Maharashtra	160	152	160	163	152	161	165	171	171	186

Table 2 (Contd...)

States	1990-91	1991-92	1992-93	1993-94	1994-95	1995-96	1996-97	1997-98	1998-99	1999-00
Manipur	271	260	262	247	237	276	265	287	264	389
Meghalaya	319	319	320	316	294	330	330	348	391	402
Mizoram	562	549	576	630	562	567	746	709	701	798
Nagaland	605	466	361	480	367	517	564	531	480	568
Odisha	119	124	114	114	126	116	119	119	143	145
Punjab	220	218	212	200	180	180	203	226	275	276
Rajasthan	130	126	137	135	149	159	161	172	184	174
Sikkim	619	792	931	1108	1074	861	762	659	1113	861
Tamilnadu	176	171	175	174	183	189	187	205	231	234
Tripura	253	221	209	244	229	231	275	264	269	289
Uttar Pradesh	121	104	110	127	111	110	114	127	98	97
Uttarakhand	-	-	-	-	-	-	-	-	-	-
West Bengal	152	123	126	136	125	131	143	136	180	196
Puducherry	631	600	460	597	525	642	619	704	809	1038
NCT Delhi	-	-	-	120	261	302	305	349	356	403
All States	144	135	138	144	142	145	149	159	170	181
All India	161	151	155	160	159	160	167	179	193	208

Table 2 (Contd...)

States	2000-01	2001-02	2002-03	2003-04	2004-05	2005-06	2006-07	2007-08	2008-09	2009-10	2010-11
Andhra Pradesh	195	194	183	190	195	202	215	265	284	294	332
Arunachal Pradesh	657	690	623	734	783	604	868	792	1140	1124	990
Assam	155	152	129	139	150	134	177	191	243	364	325
Bihar	89	62	67	58	71	104	111	123	103	109	110
Chhattisgarh	48	145	144	148	142	135	158	161	184	232	224
Goa	760	778	794	781	797	886	882	825	1041	1148	1369
Gujarat	209	158	174	170	180	187	184	209	229	306	361
Haryana	167	167	173	167	172	194	187	201	236	302	270
Himachal Pradesh	541	474	476	537	582	591	638	649	682	755	829
Jammu & Kashmir	460	475	440	416	466	509	619	638	583	729	740
Jharkhand	26	107	90	83	149	174	134	149	206	170	183
Karnataka	216	227	202	189	189	193	213	270	283	281	314
Kerala	553	592	623	655	700	753	857	956	1156	1254	1495
Madhya Pradesh	157	120	128	121	139	144	153	154	154	173	203
Maharashtra	206	218	200	205	193	206	202	225	256	276	294

Table 2 (Contd...)

States	2000-01	2001-02	2002-03	2003-04	2004-05	2005-06	2006-07	2007-08	2008-09	2009-10	2010-11
Manipur	322	345	273	317	267	317	337	516	488	623	795
Meghalaya	393	408	405	403	420	434	414	488	469	669	816
Mizoram	835	890	821	1047	781	744	755	863	1315	1849	1234
Nagaland	532	435	446	421	723	658	683	751	656	750	949
Odisha	148	141	144	135	164	116	140	148	172	203	193
Punjab	295	269	259	247	234	249	230	224	228	244	277
Rajasthan	171	183	154	175	178	186	185	195	238	249	239
Sikkim	804	770	769	732	957	955	887	1065	1162	1489	1618
Tamilnadu	221	218	210	204	210	244	237	242	300	386	451
Tripura	298	315	320	291	317	436	461	508	547	660	556
Uttar Pradesh	102	92	99	111	126	160	207	186	199	217	215
Uttarakhand	46	188	214	233	276	362	387	403	392	385	461
West Bengal	218	199	184	176	169	180	179	187	196	268	263
Puducherry	974	935	880	894	1017	969	1473	1628	1423	2082	1997
NCT Delhi	434	438	467	470	571	576	654	732	855	950	1017
All States	182	178	173	176	179	195	209	224	243	279	294
All India	212	210	206	214	220	254	277	305	338	381	402

Source: Computed from data in Combined Finance and Revenue Accounts of the Union and State Governments, GOI (various years).

Since the States account for more than 72 per cent of total public spending on health in India, so any rise or fall in the States' health spending has relatively more influential impact on the total public expenditure on health as compared to the centre's health spending. Since 2005, the centre's public expenditure on health has increased from 0.19 to 0.24 per cent of GDP due to the introduction of National Rural Health Mission in April 2005, while the States' public spending on health has increased marginally from 0.61 to 0.67 per cent of GDP during 2005-06 to 2010-11.

The centre's share in the public spending on health as per cent of GDP has shown an increasing trend while the States' share has shown more or less a declining trend. The trends in the overall public expenditure on health as percentage of GDP do not reveal any clear patterns (see Figure 1). The analysis reveals that public spending on health is abysmally low in India. Moreover, health budget is not just about the central budget, it is more about the Sates committing much higher resources towards healthcare and the politics across the States does not seem to indicate a shift in that direction for the time being (Duggal, 2011).

Figure 1: Public Expenditure on Health in India (As Per cent of GDP)

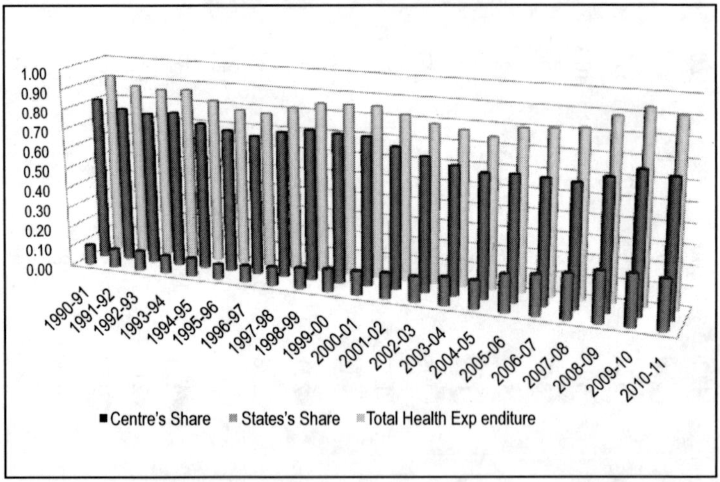

The real per capita public expenditure on health in India has increased by 2.6 times from Rs161 to Rs402 during 1990-91 to 2010-11 that represents a very low amount being spent on healthcare services by the governments in India. The centre has been spending around Rs 15 to Rs108 while the States have been spending about Rs 135 to Rs 294 in terms of real per capita public expenditure on health during 1990-91 to 2010-11. The centre's share in the real per capita public spending on health has increased by more than 6 times from Rs 17 to Rs108 whereas the States' share has increased by more than 2 times from Rs 144 to Rs 294 during the period covered under study.

An important key factor which is critical to higher social spending in general and health spending in particular is the Tax-GDP ratio. Presently India's Tax-GDP ratio for central and State governments combined is less than 18 per cent, which is one of the lowest among emerging economies and certainly very low compared with developed economies (RBI, 2014). Worldwide experience shows that countries with high social spending have Tax-GDP ratios of over 30 per cent (Duggal, 2011). In recent years, there is a large shift of taxation from the rich to the poor through direct tax concessions to the corporate sector and a steep rise in indirect taxes. This is one of the important factors that can be held responsible for widening the gap between the rich and the poor in India. So, there is an immense need to look at the revenue forgone by the government on various tax concessions to the corporate sector and well-off income tax payers.

Total revenue forgone by the central government has accounted for more than 44 per cent of aggregate tax revenue in 2013-14, representing a substantial amount of tax revenue forgone by the government in the form of huge concessions given to the corporate sector and HNIs (GOI, 2015). This shows the bias of government policies in favour of the corporate sector. Thus, apart from the need to increase allocations for the social sector in general and the health sector in particular, there is an imperative need for raising substantially more tax revenues which will make the former possible. To accomplish this, the tax base definitely needs to be expanded substantially, but more immediately, better tax compliance and reduction in revenues forgone through various tax incentives and rebates, especially to the corporate sector and wealth creating sections (HNIs) needs to be focused on. However, instead of giving tax concessions to the wealthy and corporate sector, the government should utilise this substantial amount for welfare of the poorer section of the society by providing better healthcare services to them.

Table 3: Public Expenditure on Health at National Level

Year	Public Expenditure on Health as per cent of GDP			Real Per Capita Public Expenditure on Health (in Rs)		
	Centre	States	Total	Centre	States	Total
1990-91	0.10	0.82	0.92	17	144	161
1991-92	0.09	0.78	0.87	16	135	151
1992-93	0.10	0.76	0.86	17	138	155
1993-94	0.09	0.78	0.87	16	144	160
1994-95	0.09	0.73	0.82	17	142	159
1995-96	0.07	0.72	0.79	15	145	160
1996-97	0.08	0.70	0.78	18	149	167
1997-98	0.09	0.73	0.82	20	159	179
1998-99	0.10	0.75	0.85	23	170	193
1999-00	0.11	0.74	0.85	27	181	208
2000-01	0.12	0.73	0.85	30	182	212
2001-02	0.13	0.69	0.82	32	178	210
2002-03	0.12	0.67	0.79	33	173	206
2003-04	0.14	0.63	0.77	38	176	214
2004-05	0.14	0.61	0.75	41	179	220
2005-06	0.19	0.61	0.80	59	195	254
2006-07	0.20	0.61	0.81	68	209	277
2007-08	0.22	0.60	0.82	81	224	305
2008-09	0.25	0.64	0.89	95	243	338
2009-10	0.25	0.69	0.94	102	279	381
2010-11	0.24	0.67	0.91	108	294	402

Source: Computed from data in Combined Finance and Revenue Accounts of the Union and State Governments, GOI (various years); Handbook of Statistics on Indian Economy2013-14, RBI (2014); World Economic Outlook Database 2014, IMF (2014).

Health Status in India as Compared to Other Countries

The position of India in terms of health status, as compared to other countries, has been analysed in Table 4. In terms of economic growth rate, India performs comparatively much better than the developed countries in the world. During the year 2013, the growth rate of India (6.9 per cent) has been substantially higher than the growth rates of developed countries like the USA (2.2 per cent), the UK (1.7 per cent), Japan (1.6 per cent), Germany (0.1 per cent), France (0.3 per cent) and Australia (2.5 per cent). The growth rates of most of the developed countries vary from-1.9 per cent to 2.5 per cent. However, the per capita GNP of these countries is far more than India, and this is due to the huge population pressure in India. Thus, health expenditure, both in terms of percentage of GDP as well as per capita health expenditure, is comparatively much higher among developed countries. India has spent a meagre proportion (4 per cent) of its GDP while share of GDP spent on health by most of the developed countries varies from a low of 9.1 per cent in UK to 17.1 per cent in USA. The per capita health expenditure in developing countries including India ($61) is extremely low compared with developed countries like USA ($9,146). The share of public expenditure on health both as percentage of GDP as well as percentage of total health expenditure is one of the lowest in India (1.3 per cent and 32.2 per cent respectively) among all the countries under consideration.

Health status in different countries in terms of health attainment indicators, namely infant mortality rate (for the year 2015), life expectancy at birth (for the year 2013) is also presented in this table. Developed countries enjoy a far better health status as they have infant mortality rate less than or equal to 6 and life expectancy at birth more than or equal to 79 years. The condition is very miserable in developing countries, especially in India, Pakistan and Bangladesh as they have high infant mortality rate (38, 66 and 31 respectively) and low life expectancy at birth (68, 66 and 71 years respectively). Among developing countries, Sri Lanka and China enjoy a much better health status as they have lower IMR (8 and 9 respectively) and higher life expectancy at birth (74 and 75 respectively). This analysis reveals that though India is trying to compete with developed countries so far as economic growth is concerned, it still needs large efforts to reach at the levels of health status enjoyed by these countries.

Table 4: Health Status in India as Compared to Other Countries

Countries	GDP Growth Rate (%) 2013	GNP Per Capita Income ($) 2013	Total Health Expenditure as % of GDP 2013	Per Capita Health Expenditure ($) 2013	Public Health Expenditure as % of GDP 2013	Public Health Expenditure as % of Total Health Expenditure 2013	Infant Mortality Rate 2015	Life xpectancy at Birth 2013
Australia	2.5	65,400	9.4	6,110	6.3	66.6	3	82
Canada	2.0	52,210	10.9	5,718	7.6	69.8	4	81
France	0.3	43,520	11.7	4,864	9.1	77.5	4	82
Germany	0.1	47,250	11.3	5,006	8.7	76.8	3	81
Italy	-1.9	35,620	9.1	3,155	7.1	78.0	3	82
Japan	1.6	46,330	10.3	3,966	8.5	82.1	2	83
United Kingdom	1.7	41,680	9.1	3,598	7.6	83.5	4	81
United States	2.2	53,470	17.1	9,146	8.1	47.1	6	79
China	7.7	6,560	5.6	367	3.1	55.8	9	75
Bangladesh	6.0	1,010	3.7	32	1.3	35.3	31	71
India	6.9	1,570	4.0	61	1.3	32.2	38	68
Pakistan	4.4	1,360	2.8	37	1.0	36.8	66	66
Sri Lanka	7.3	3,170	3.2	102	1.4	43.9	8	74

Source: World Development Indicators2015, World Bank (2015).

Conclusion

Health is one of the vital components of the social sector for any nation in the world. Being a core component of the social sector, healthcare expenditure requires a significant contribution from the governments in India. It is widely accepted that health of the people makes a significant contribution to economic growth, human security, poverty reduction, and social development. Thus, the improvement in the health status of the population of a country is instrumental in increasing productivity and economic growth.

The issue of public financing of health has assumed greater importance in a developing country like India mainly due to the changing role of the state in providing healthcare services. On the basis of the aforesaid analysis of patterns of public spending on health in India, it can be concluded that the health sector in India is indeed grossly under-funded, which results in India's failure to achieve the desired targets as set out in national public policies. Though India has currently been recognised as a big economic powerhouse throughout the world, however, a very small amount of public expenditure as a proportion of GDP incurred on health is one of the obvious indicators of inadequacy of public spending on health in India. Furthermore, majority of the States have shown a declining trend in their spending patterns for health as a percentage of GSDP, indicating that government priority for public spending for health has been decreasing over the years. The space is being taken by private investment in this , making healthcare services very expensive and out of reach of the masses.

Despite the low level of public spending on health, majority of the public expenditure has been incurred on curative rather than preventive healthcare in India, which again is a matter of concern. The public spending on preventive healthcare has a pro-poor impact, as the preventive care has significant impact in enhancing the capabilities of the poor. It is also a well-known fact that total expenditure on health in India is dominated by private expenditure, which in itself is an indication of low and inadequate public financing of this vital sector, as reflected by the declining trends in the spending patterns of majority of the States for health in India. Thus, it can be said that along with inadequate public financing of the health sector, the shift towards privatisation has resulted in the absolute neglect of public health services in India.

India has experienced an impressive improvement in the health status in terms of health attainment indicators like IMR, LEB and MMR at the national level since independence. Despite the impressive improvement in these health attainment indicators, the absolute health status of the population in India remains poor which is, somehow, a reflection of supply-side constraints. Thus, India is still far away from achieving the desired targets in terms of health attainments as set out in the National Health Policy 2002,as well as the Millennium Development Goals. At the international level, though India has been trying to compete with the developed nations in terms of the role of economic growth, it still needs concerted effort to reach the levels of health status enjoyed by developed nations.

It is imperative that the government should increase the finances allotted to the health sector with a strong political will. It must also keep in mind that a mere increase in the amount spent might be wasted if it does not contribute to an improvement in the quality of healthcare. Since the States spend around three-fourths of total public health expenditure in India, any rise or fall in the States' health spending influences total health spending much more than the centre's health spending. Therefore, any overall strategy to achieve sizeable increases in total government health expenditure should logically include a strategy to increase the States' spending. The government departments also need to strengthen their ability to spend effectively, along with increased allocations. The study suggests that fiscal targets for health spending should be based on goals for health outcomes and the resources needed to achieve them, which are largely lacking. If the governments in India show a greater political will to rein in the amount of revenue forgone every year,this will generate sufficient resources to meet the budgetary targets for universal access for health, education and other social spending. Reining in more such revenues will give them adequate resources to realise the goals of various flagship programmes and thus, prevent the government and the flagship programmes from sinking in the current morass of corruption and scams.

References

1. Duggal R (2011), 'Changing the 2011-12 Health Budget and Beyond', *The India Economy Review 2011*, Vol. III, Quartely Issue: 15th February-15th May 2011, pp. 26-36.
2. Economic Research Foundation (2006), *Government Health Expenditure in India: A Benchmark Study*, New Delhi.
3. EPW Research Foundation (2009), *Data CD on Domestic Products of States of India 1960-61 to 2006-07*, EPW Research Foundation.
4. Government of India (2002), *National Health Policy-2002*, Ministry of Health and Family Welfare.
5. Government of India (2015), *Union Budget 2015-16*, Ministry of Finance.
6. Government of India (2016), *Economic Survey 2015-16*, Ministry of Finance.
7. Government of India (Various Years), *Combined Finance and Revenue Accounts of Union and State Governments*, Office of Comptroller and Auditor General of India.
8. IMF (2014), *World Economic Outlook Database 2014*, International Monetary Fund.
9. Planning Commission (2014), *Databook for use of Deputy Chairman*, Planning Commission, Government of India.
10. Rao MG and M Choudhary (2008), *Inter-state Equalisation of Health Expenditures in Indian Union*, National Institute of Public Finance and Policy, New Delhi.
11. RBI (2014), *Handbook of Statistics on Indian Economy 2013-14*, Reserve Bank of India.
12. World Bank (2015), *World Development Indicators 2015*, World Bank.

The State of India's Elementary and Higher Education

— Sarbeswar Sahoo

WITH THE promise to bring 'good times' (*achhe din*) for India, the Narendra Modi-led National Democratic Alliance formed the government at the Centre in the summer of 2014. The last one year, the government has done very little to convince the marginalised populations that it is committed to the idea of *sabka saath, sabka vikas* (together with all, development for all). On the contrary, the government in its Union Budgets has cut the social sector spending, particularly in the health and education sector, which has adversely affected the poor and marginalised populations. In 2014-15, the health care budget was slashed by 20 per cent due to fiscal strains. In the education sector, the government has also reduced the budget. While the government has proposed to set up new IITs, IIMs and several other higher educational institutions, it has cut the outlay for the education sector by 2.02 per cent in the Union Budget of 2015-16. While the landmark Kothari Commission Report of 1964-66 had prescribed the expenditure of 6% of GDP for education, fifty years later, the public expenditure on education in India has only been at 3.3% (Human Development Report, 2014).

The strong endorsement of neoliberal policies by successive Indian governments has severely affected the education sector. Not just the funding cut but also growing I privatisation has significantly affected the quality of and access to education. The logic of the competitive market and one's ability to pay determines the access to education; education is increasingly treated as a 'commodity' rather than a social good. Taking this into account, this paper provides an overview of the state of elementary and higher education in India today. The paper argues that having been constrained by the policies of neo-liberalism, the Indian state is gradually withdrawing from social welfare measures and, as a result, increasing numbers of private actors are taking up responsibilities, which were previously the functions of the state. Such a trend towards privatisation is increasingly visible in the Indian education sector.

Elementary Education

The Indian state after independence, following the recommendations of the Sarkar Committee (1946) and the Radhakrishnan Commission (1948), provided a strong emphasis on education for 'development'. Strengthening the higher education was given utmost priority and several IITs were established to contribute to 'nation-building' through advancements in science, technology and economic development (Krishnan, 2014: 64). In the process of developing higher education, elementary education in the country was neglected. At 'the time of independence in 1947, barely 14% of India's populations were literate and only one child out of every three children in the age group of age 6-11years was in school' (Nambissan, 2014: 7).While Article 45 of the Constitution specified that the state shall endeavour to provide a period of 10 years free and compulsory education for children till the age of 14 and the National Policy of Education 1986, revised in 1992, provided momentum to the task, the goal of universalising elementary education proved to be very difficult. The school enrolment rate was very low and by 1991, only a little more than half (52.21%) of India's population was literate.

The major issue was, how to increase the school enrolment rate and achieve universal elementary education. The problem was one of 'deficit' where 'poor families were seen as largely unaware of the importance of education as well as unable to bear the burden of the direct and indirect costs of schooling. The involvement of poor children in work (child labour) was seen as a major obstacle in their education' (Nambissan, 2014: 5). Considering this, the government expanded the school system by establishing both government and government-aided primary schools and provided midday meals, free uniforms, textbooks and scholarships to increase enrolment and prevent dropouts (Chandhoke, 2009: 80). Special campaigns like the Operation Blackboard was also launched to upgrade infrastructure, train teachers and improve the environment. In 2000-01, the government also launched the Sarva Shiksha Aviyan (SSA), a movement to universalise elementary education, in partnership with the state governments, local governments and communities (Chandhoke, 2009: 80).

In 2002, Government of India made elementary education a fundamental right through the 86th Constitutional Amendment and in 2009, it passed the Right to Education (RTE) Act, which stipulated that it is the responsibility of the state to provide free and compulsory education to all children between the age of 6 and 14. Since the 1990s several positive developments have occurred: 'Demand for basic education [has] continue[d] to grow with increasing recognition of the importance of educating children among parents and guardians. Infrastructural facilities have improved over the past two decades, gross enrolment is almost universal, dropout rates have declined even for girls at the primary level, and many more teachers have been appointed. More school incentives (such as free textbooks and the serving of cooked meals) have led to better outreach and coverage' (Kumar and Rustagi, 2010: 1). As a result, there have been improvements in the literary rate of the 7+ age group in the last decade. For example, the total literacy rate for the 7+ age group has increased from 64.8% in 2001 to 73.0% in 2011. In case of the male populations, it has increased from 75.3% to 80.9% and in the case of female populations it has increased from 53.7% to 64.6% during the same period. Similarly, the literacy rate for the15+age group has increased from 61.0% to 69.3% between 2001 and 2011.The data show that the female literacy (from 47.8% to 59.3%) has grown faster than the male literacy (from73.4% to 78.8%) during the same period.

There is no doubt that the literacy rate has increased in the last two decades. The major problem, however, is: how is the quality of elementary education in India? The government's emphasis till now has been on how to increase enrolment and universalise elementary education; very little effort has been made to improve the *quality* of elementary education in schools. Ten year ago, the first ASER report revealed the tragic state of India's elementary education. Successive governments have found it very difficult to accept the findings of the report. 'While the previous government dismissed the ASER reports as "cursory assessments", the current government has called it "a study without a robust methodology' (Madhavan, 2014: 11). Nevertheless, the ASER report (2014) shows two major troubling trends: (1) decline in the quality of education, and (2) increasing privatisation of elementary education.

The Quality of Education

The 2014 ASER report reveals that between 2006 and 2014, increasing numbers of students have been enrolled in school. The percentage of children in the age group 6-14 not enrolled in school has declined from 6.6% in 2006 to 3.3% in 2014. In case of girls it has declined from 7.5% to 3.7%, and in case of boys it has declined from 5.8% to 2.9% during this period. Increasing enrolment has, however, not ensured *good quality* education in schools. In fact, the report shows that the quality of education has drastically deteriorated over the years. For example, in 2008, more than 50% of Standard III students could read a Standard-I level text, but by 2014, it has declined to 40.3%. Similarly, the percentage of Standard III students who could do at least subtraction has declined from almost 40% in 2008 to 25.4% in 2014.

This is an alarming trend. While the government continues to cite inputs in education and enrolment of students as a mark of success, it has done very little to improve the *quality of learning* in schools. The ASER report points out that the deterioration is cumulative, which means that the 'learning decline' gets accumulated because of neglect over the years. The poor quality of education in Standard I pulls down their rate of learning progressively so that by the time they are in Standard V, their level of learning is not even comparable to that of Standard II (Kumar, 2013). For example, the report shows that the percentage of Standard V students who can read Standard II-level text has declined from 58.9% in 2007 to 48.1% in 2014. Similarly, the percentage of Standard V students who can do division has declined from 42.5% to 26.1% during the same period.

While this 'downturn' in the quality of education can be seen both in the public and the private schools, the report shows that the public schools are more affected by this process. In 2008, 46.9% of Standard III students in public schools and 63.9% in private schools could read at least a Standard I-level text, but by 2014, it has declined to 31.8% and 59.0% respectively. Similarly, the percentage of Standard V students who can do division has declined from 34.4% in public schools and 47.1% in private schools to 20.7% and 39.3% respectively between 2008 and 2014. In this context it is important to note that a majority of students in the private schools come from economically better off families.

Similar downturn is also noticeable in language learning. It is frightening to see in the ASER report that English learning in schools have also declined. In 2007, percentage of Standard V students who could read at least words was 59.4%, but it has declined to 49.2% by 2014. Similarly, the percentage of Standard VII students who can read sentences has declined from 53.8% to 38.8% during the same period. This continuous downward trend in the quality of education in our schools raises a much broader question: *how is India going to reap the benefits of demographic dividend and enable its next generation to pick up requisite skills to work in a globalising economy when they lack the basic ability to read, write and do arithmetic?*

The immediate question, however, is what are the reasons behind such continuous decline of learning and how can we fix it? Vimala Ramachandran (of NUEPA, 2015: 13-14) has pointed out the following seven factors responsible for the poor quality of education in our schools.

i. Our system expects teachers to teach according to the curriculum, finish the syllabus within a time frame – regardless of whether the children in the class are learning or not. Teachers are not able to address the learning needs of every child, primarily because of: (a) prevalence of multi-grade classrooms across the country, and (b) frequent absence of teachers and students.

ii. There is no school-level monitoring of teaching-learning process and actual teaching time. Almost all the monitoring is confined to inputs—enrolment, mid-day meals, distribution of incentives and so on.

iii. There is a huge social distance between teachers and students in government schools. Many teachers believe that some children, particularly from poor socio-economic background, cannot learn or that they are not motivated to learn. They blame the family and the community.

iv. The existing system of rote learning is responsible for declining quality of education. A more child-centric and experiential learning process can reverse the trend.

v. The poor quality of teacher – her/his mastery of subjects, pedagogic skills and aptitude to teach –is perhaps responsible for poor learning.

vi. The no-detention policy that ensures children are promoted from one grade to the next is the reason why the school system is not made accountable for the learning of children.

vii. The number of actual teaching days is low and that teachers have many non-teaching duties.

The tragedy is that every year the government spends a huge amount of money in public education. Specifically, the Sarva Shiksha Aviyan, which targets the rural schools, has not improved things. Anit Mukherjee (2015: 16) asks: 'Why is it that higher public expenditure on elementary education has not improved levels of learning?' He argues that, 'after a certain threshold of inputs is reached, increasing levels of learning has very little to do with money. It requires system-wide upgrades and not marginal improvements. It requires a fresh look at norms and standards, monitoring mechanisms and data systems, assessing learning needs of each individual child and tailoring the curriculum to be more aligned with the capacity and the level of teaching-learning process. Some of these require investment in teacher quality, data systems and evaluation mechanisms, while others are intrinsically linked to administrative capacity and commitment'. Ramachandran (2015: 14) argues that, 'it is time that a diverse group of people – including political leaders and administrators—come together to brainstorm and develop a roadmap for systematic reform'. 'The Right to Education is not limited to the right to be enrolled, but to be taught and learn'. The quality of education is essentially about learning.

Privatisation of School Education

The paradox is that while the government is making increasing investments in public education, particularly in expanding the school system, building new class rooms, hiring more teachers and providing incentives like free textbooks, uniforms and mid-day meals, a growing number of parents are pulling their children out of the public school system and sending them to the private ones. It is happening not just in the cities but also increasingly in the rural areas. The 'private sector is making huge inroads into education in rural India' (Kumar, 2013). The recent ASER data show that in 2006, only18.7% of children age 6-14 were enrolled in private schools, but by 2014, it has increased to 30.8%. It also shows that as in previous years, in each age group, a higher proportion of boys go to private schools as compared to girls. In 2014, in the age group of 7-10 years, 35.6% boys are enrolled in private schools as compared to 27.7% of girls. For the age group of 11-14 years, 33.5% of boys are in private schools as compared to 25.9% of girls (ASER, 2014: 81).

The State-wise data show that the private school enrolment has increased in almost all States. This upward trend is seen in States with low as well as high private school enrolment. For instance, it has doubled in low private school States like Odisha, Madhya Pradesh and Chhattisgarh between 2006 and 2014. On the other hand, in Uttar Pradesh where it was high to begin with (30.3% in 2006), it has crossed the 50% mark in 2014 (Wadhwa, 2015: 19).The report shows that five States, viz. Manipur (73.3%), Kerala (62.2%), Haryana (54.2%), Uttar Pradesh (51.7%) and Meghalaya (51.7%), have private school enrolment rates that are greater than 50%.

It is not just the private school enrolment; the report also shows that there is an increasing trend towards private tutoring. Private tutoring is defined as 'fee-based tutoring that provides supplementary instruction to children in academic subjects that they study in the mainstream education system' (Dongre, 2015: 17). The ASER report notes that 'about a fourth of the children in rural India pay for private tutors. At the all-India level this number has remained steady across government and private schools. The interesting thing, however, is that the incidence of private tuition is much higher in States with low private school enrolment. For instance, in Odisha and Bihar, almost 50% children pay for additional help.

In West Bengal, this number is as high as 70%. As a result, the percentage of children with some private inputs in their schooling has increased from about 40% to 48%' (Wadhwa, 2015: 19). According to Dongre (2015: 17), parents and students pay, on average, Rs170 per month, amounting to slightly above Rs 2,000 per annum to attend these tuitions.

The question then is, why do parents shift their children from public schools to private schools and spend extra money to give private tuition? Dongre (2015: 18) has shown that private tuition has had a large positive effect on test scores of math and language (separately or combined) for students in the age group of 6-14 years. He, however, notes that it is primarily because students attending private tuition spend more time studying. Citing the Indian Human Development Survey data, he shows that those who attend tuition spend, on average, 9 hours per week in tuitions. That would mean 1.5 extra school days per week.

The trend towards privatisation of education must be seen in the context of the existing public school system and the wider context of the aspirational politics of neo-liberal globalisation. Ramachandran (2015: 13) found out that even the public school teachers and education administrators do not send their children to public schools. According to them, their children get 'better' education in private schools. 'They had little faith in government schools and the reasons they cited ranged from English medium to excessive non-teaching duties of government school teachers'. Many also argued that the classroom in the government school is so diverse that it is difficult for teachers to teach so many levels at the same time. Added to these, Nambissan (2014: 9) has noted that 'exclusive English medium private schooling is seen as the pathway to elite status and better life chances, and hence these schools have become the centre of competition and striving for positional advantage'.

However, it must be noted that the quality of education in the private schools, as the ASER report shows, is also declining. Nambissan (2014: 14) has rightly pointed out, 'the quality of private education in unrecognised private schools has been of serious concern even prior to 2000'. She further pointed out that 'these schools usually employed untrained teachers, an increasing number of whom had barely more than secondary-/higher secondary-level schooling'. In many of these private schools, 'teachers are so under-qualified that they cannot speak in English, let alone teach in English, one of the biggest attractions for parents in the lower income segment' (Nambissan, 2014: 14-15). Despite such problems, this sector is portrayed as 'better' than public schools. Such portrayal, as Nambissan (2014: 23) argues, is 'driven by powerful financial and political (pro-market) interests that are couched within a neo-liberal discourse of schools markets for the poor'.

The 'most serious and questionable aspect of the low-cost private school advocacy and edu-business is the deliberate misconstruction of 'good quality education' for the poor in increasingly minimalist terms to ensure greater profits. Education that is projected as 'good' for poor/low-income groups is minimalistic in terms of the role of the teacher, and curriculum transacted, with the 'quality of these processes demonstrated in terms of narrow learner outcomes' (Nambissan, 2014: 24). 'If the educational rights of children are to be protected, the purpose of education must be revisited, informed by a perspective of social justice. Such a perspective must go beyond the mere distribution of educational opportunities to ask how socially just the quality of education as well the social relations that constitute it, are' (Nambissan, 2014: 26). It is also essential to note that providing *quality* education is the responsibility of the state and the state cannot shift this responsibility to the private sector.

Higher Education

As discussed above, following the recommendations of the Sarkar Committee (1946), the Indian state after independence provided a lot of emphasis on strengthening the higher education. Several IITs and IIMs were established to contribute to the 'nation building' process. As Krishnan (2014: 64) has noted, 'in addition to their role in furthering science, technology, economic development and self-reliance, the idea of these institutions embodied the national spirit of the post-independence years'. Higher education has been considered indispensable for India's development in a rapidly globalising world. The 12th Five Year Plan notes that: Higher education is critical for developing a modern economy, a just society and a vibrant polity. It equips young people with skills relevant for the labour market and the opportunity for social mobility. It provides people already in employment with skills to negotiate rapidly evolving career requirements. It prepares all to be responsible citizens who value a democratic and pluralistic society. Thus, the nation creates an intellectual repository of human capital to meet the country's needs and shapes its future (Planning Commission, 2013: 89).

Structures and Growth of Higher Education

In order to link education to (economic) 'development' and to provide 'skill-based learning', three kinds of higher educational institutions emerged in India: (1) public institutions, which were established and funded by the state, such as IITs, IIMs, and universities (2) aided institutions, which were owned and established by private individuals, trusts and organisations, but received funding from the state, and (3) unaided private institutions, which were established by private individuals and organisations but did not receive funding from the state; they were self-financing institutions and functioned primarily on the basis of the fees they collected from the students. While the aided institutions were treated as government institutions as they received funding from the state, the unaided institutions were treated as purely private (Krishnan, 2014: 64). As Tilak has argued, the term 'privatisation' applied primarily to unaided institutions, 'which proliferated on account of policy that sanctioned large numbers of private colleges, privatised existing public sector universities or resorted to a greater proportion of private funds (cost recovery) for the running of state-supported colleges' (cited in Krishnan, 2014: 64).

In 1950-51, India had 27 universities, which included 370 colleges for general education and 208 colleges for professional education (engineering, medicine, education) (Kapur and Mehta, 2007: 3). By 2014 India had 712 universities (comprising 42 Central Universities, 310 State Universities, 127 Deemed Universities, 143 Private Universities, 68 Institutions of National Importance, 13 State Open Universities, and others). In addition, there are 36,671 colleges and 11,445 Stand Alone Institutions (GOI, 2014: 3, see Table 1). Data show that while in 1950-51 the total number of students enrolled in higher education was 0.4 million, by 2012-13 this has increased to 29.6 million; of which 88% are enrolled in regular courses and 12% in distant mode. The number of girls per 100 boys in the higher education sector has also increased from 13 in 1950-51 to 81 in 2012-13 (see Table 1).

Table 1: Higher Education Basic Statistics

Year	Total Universities	Colleges	Enrolment (in lakhs)			Number of Girls per 100 Boys
			Girls	Boys	Total	
1950-51	27	578	0.5	3.5	4.0	13
1960-61	45	1,819	2	8	10	21
1970-71	82	3,277	7	26	33	28
1980-81	110	6,963	13	35	48	36
1990-91	184	5,748	15	34	49	46
2000-01	254	10,152	32	54	86	58
2005-06	350	16,982	55	88	143	62
2006-07	371	19,812	60	96	156	62
2007-08	406	23,099	66	106	172	63
2008-09	440	27,882	73	112	185	65
2009-10	436	25,938	83	124	207	67
2010-11	621	32,974	120	155	275	78
2011-12	642	34,852	130	162	292	80
2012-13(P)	665	35,829	133	163	296	81
2013-14(P)	712	36,671	NA	NA	NA	NA

Source: GOI (2014), pp. 14, 16, 29.

The discipline-wise enrolments data show that highest numbers of the students are enrolled in Arts (30.2%) subjects. However, the higher growth rate in enrolment during the 11th Plan period occurred in Engineering; students' enrolment in Engineering grew from 18.06 lakh to 54.68 lakh, a 24.8% growth. Medicine, Nursing and Pharmacy witnessed a 15% growth (from 5.98 lakh to 12.02 lakh). Education subjects grew by 15.9% and Commerce and Management grew by 8.5% (from 22.87 lakh to 34.34 lakh). Data also show that following the enrolment in Arts, the second highest numbers of student are enrolled in Engineering (25%). This is followed by Commerce and Management (15.8%) and Science disciplines (14%) (Planning Commission, 2013: 94; see Table 2).

Table 2: Growth of Enrolment by Field of Study in Eleventh Plan

Faculty	2006-07		2011-12		Growth Rate (Per cent)
	Total (in lakh)	Per cent	Total (in lakh)	Per cent	
Arts	54.86	39.6	65.78	30.2	3.7
Science	25.43	18.4	30.57	14.0	3.8
Commerce and Management	22.87	16.5	34.34	15.8	8.5
Education	6.21	4.5	13.00	6.0	15.9
Engineering	18.06	13.0	54.68	25.0	24.8
Medicine, Nursing and Pharmacy	5.98	4.3	12.02	5.5	15.0
Agriculture and Veterinary Science	0.93	0.7	1.21	0.6	5.4
Law	3.00	2.2	3.48	1.6	3.0
Others	1.16	0.8	2.78	1.3	19.1
TOTAL	138.5	100	217.86	100	9.5

Source: Planning Commission (2013), p.94.

Constraints to Higher Education

Despite considerable progress, the Planning Commission (2013: 90) in the12[th] Five Year Plan states that 'less than one-fifth of the estimated 120 million potential students are enrolled in HEIs [higher educational institutions] in India'. The Commission also states that, 'wide disparities exist in enrolment percentages among the States and between urban and rural areas while disadvantaged sections of society and women have significantly lower enrolments than the national average' Higher education in India today faces a series of constraints, such as how to make education accessible and affordable, meet the growing demand, ensure good quality education, provide infrastructure and well-trained faculty, and other facilities. According to a report published by the British Council, Indian higher education is faced with four broad challenges:

i. The supply-demand gap: India has a low rate of enrolment in higher education, at only 18%, compared with 26% in China and 36% in Brazil. There is enormous unmet demand for higher education.
ii. The low quality of teaching and learning: The system is beset by issues of quality in many of its institutions. a chronic shortage of faculty, poor quality teaching, out-dated and rigid curricula and pedagogy, lack of accountability and quality assurance and separation of research and teaching.
iii. Constraints on research capacity and innovation: With a very low level of PhD enrolment, India does not have enough high-quality researchers; there are few opportunities for interdisciplinary and multidisciplinary working, lack of early stage research experience, a weak eco-system for innovation and low levels of industry engagement.
iv. Uneven growth and access to opportunity: Socially, India remains highly divided; access to higher education is uneven with multi-dimensional inequalities in enrolment across population groups and geographies (British Council, 2014: 4).

Given the inability of the Indian state to meet the growing demands for higher education, a large number of private institutions have emerged in different parts of the country. According to Tilak (2014:34), the higher education system in India is more privatised compared to other capitalist or market economies, for instance, the US, the UK, Canada and Australia. 'In the US, one-fifth to one-fourth of the total number of students in higher education, and about 30% of the global enrolment in higher education, are in private institutions; the remaining students go to public universities'. However, in India private enrolment is much higher. For example, according to the Planning Commission (2013: 90), while the Central institutions catered to 2.6% and the State institutions catered to 38.5%, the private institutions catered to almost 59% of the total enrolments in higher education during the 11th Plan period (see Table 3).The Commission also points out that growth of private institutions was significant during the 11th Plan period. Ninety-eight private State universities, 17 private deemed universities, 7,818 private colleges, and 3,581 private Diploma institutions were set up during the

Plan period (see Table 4). While some of these private institutions offered programmes in arts, sciences and commerce, a majority of them offered professional or vocational programmes almost exclusively.

Table 3: Growth of Enrolment in 11th Plan (enrolment in lakh)

Category	2006-07		2011-12		Increase	Growth rate
	Total	Per cent	Total	Per cent		
By Type of Institutions						
Government	63.38	45.8	89.63	41.1	26.25	7.2
Central	3.10	2.2	5.63	2.6	2.53	12.7
State	60.28	43.6	84.00	38.5	23.72	6.9
Private	75.12	54.2	128.23	58.9	53.11	11.3
By Degree/Diploma						
Degree	123.54	89.2	184.84	84.8	61.30	8.4
Diploma	14.96	10.8	33.02	15.2	18.06	10.8
TOTAL	**138.50**	**100.00**	**217.86**	**100.00**	**79.36**	**9.5**

Source: Planning Commission (2013), p.93.

Table 4: Growth of Institutions in the Eleventh Plan

Category	2006-07	2011-12	Increase	Growth Rate (Per cent)
Central Institutions				
Degree Awarding Institutions	87	152	65	11.8
Colleges	58	69	11	3.5
Subtotal	145	221	76	8.8
State Institutions				
Degree Awarding Institutions	227	316	89	6.8
Colleges	9,000	13,024	4,024	7.7
Diploma Institutions	1,867	3,207	1,340	11.4
Subtotal	11,094	16,547	5,453	8.3

Private Institutions				
Degree Awarding Institutions	73	191	118	21.2
Colleges	12,112	19,930	7,818	10.5
Diploma Institutions	5,960	9,541	3,581	9.9
Subtotal	18,145	29,662	11,517	10.3
TOTAL	29,384	46,430	17,046	9.6

Source: Planning Commission (2013), p.94.

The growing number of private institutions and the growing trend towards privatising higher education has generated intense debates. Krishnan (2014) has argued that the declining public expenditure in higher education is largely responsible for the growth of private institutions. For her, this decline in funding has occurred sharply in the aftermath of economic reforms. Similarly, Kapur and Mehta (2007) and Tilak (2014) have argued that the trend towards privatisation must be understood in the context of neoliberal restructuring. While the growth of private sector has been justified on the basis of (i) increasing access, and (ii) 'good' quality education, Nayak (2014) has argued that there are several myths around these two issues, which need to be busted. The following section will discuss some of these important debates on higher education in India today.

Declining Public Funding

The 12th Five Year Plan acknowledges that there is a huge challenge to funding for India's rapidly growing higher education sector. The Plan document notes that, 'funding from both the Central and the State governments has to be significantly increased and efficiency of its utilisation improved during the 12th Plan'. The Planning Commission (2013: 119) has argued that the government spending on higher education has grown steadily over the years and it is hoped that the government will spend 1.5% of GDP on higher education during the 12th Plan period. However, the Central Advisory Board of Education *Report on the Financing of Higher and Technical Education* (2004) has shown that funding for higher education in India has steadily declined in the aftermath of the economic reform.

The report shows that the budgetary allocation for higher education per student has declined by 28 percentage points between 1990-91 and 2002-03. At the 1993-94 prices, the decline was from Rs 7,676 in 1990-91 to Rs 5,500 in 2002-03. As a percentage of GNP, the decline was from 0.46 to 0.37 over the 12-year period. As far as technical education is concerned, the decline from 0.15% to 0.13% was less drastic (cited in Krishnan, 2014: 65; see Table 5). In 2011-12, the budgetary allocation of Rs 20,000 crore towards higher education reflected a fourfold increase since 2002-03. However, when this figure is calculated as percentage of GNP, it captures the precipitous decline from 0.37 to 0.24 (Krishnan, 2014: 65). Similarly, the allocation of Rs 6,500 crore towards technical education is a considerable decline as percentage of GNP from 0.13% in 2002-03 to meagre 0.07% in 2011-12 (Krishnan, 2014: 65).

Table 5: Expenditure on Higher Education and Technical Education
(As percentage of GDP)

Year	Budgetary Allocation for Higher Education	Budgetary Allocation for Technical Education
1990-91	0.46	0.15
2002-03	0.37	0.13
2011-12	0.24	0.07

Source: Krishnan (2014), p. 65.

The question then is what are the reasons behind and implications of such decline of public funding for higher education? There can be three reasons with regard to the declining funding: (1) since the resources or the capacities of the state are limited, the state needs to limit its spending on higher education, (2) low social rates of return on higher education is cited as one of the reasons for reallocating public expenditure away from higher education (see Kapur and Mehta, 2007: 11), and (3) the neoliberal restructuring of the economy and the increasing importance of the market forces are forcing the state to withdraw from basic welfare services. No matter what the reasons are, the impact of this decline, as

Krishnan (2014: 65) has argued, 'is particularly significant, given the manifold increase in the number of colleges as well as students enrolling in these institutions'. Another implication is that this has given rise to a large number of private higher educational institutions who treat education as a (profit-generating) commodity rather than a social good. Particularly, this impact has had severe adverse consequences for the poorer sections of society.

Neoliberal Restructuring

Not just the declining funding but also the larger trend towards privatising higher education are considered the outcomes of the neoliberal restructuring of the Indian economy. Following the policies of the World Bank and the IMF, the Indian state, since the 1990s has been forced to withdraw from providing basic social services and facilitate the entry of the private market forces. As Tilak (2014: 33) has rightly noted, 'compelled by the[se] policies of the World Bank and the IMF on the one hand, and by the emergence of strong markets and the corporate sector in the country on the other, the state in India had no choice but to reluctantly accept privatisation as an important policy instrument in the development of higher education'. He further notes that 'a big non-violent shift has taken place – from policies of welfare stateism in higher education to a market based approach to higher education'.

In the name of meeting demands and giving everyone access to higher education, the state has justified privatisation. Despite this, there have been many confusions with regard to the state policy towards privatisation, which essentially reflect the ambiguities in the nature of the state itself. On some occasions, the government has argued that privatisation is allowed in higher education but not commercialisation. This could be understood in two ways: (i) by prohibiting commercialisation and profit-making, the government recognises education as a social good, which reflects the welfarist nature of the Indian state, and (ii) by advocating privatisation (which in fact means for-profit) and giving up welfare responsibilities, the state is promoting neoliberal policies. Besides this, on other occasions, the state has advocated for public-private partnership. Most recently, in the 12th Plan, the government has advocated for greater participation of the private sector in higher education. The questions, however, are: how will the government ensure that privatisation is not resulting in commercialisation and commoditisation of education and what implications will this have for the poorer sections of society?

Debates on Access and Quality

The increasing role of the private sector in higher education has been justified on the basis that the public sector is unable to meet the demands, and the quality of education in the public institutions is very low. The private sector has projected itself as an efficient and purely 'merit-based system', which does not compromise on the quality of education. Tilak (2014), Nayak (2014) and Krishnan (2014) have, however, rejected such opinions and argued that these are myths created to justify the privatisation of education.

According to Nayak (2014: 11), the false logic of the 'access' argument can be refuted in three ways:

- Merit vs protective discrimination: Nayak argues that in the name of promoting 'merit', which itself is very subjective, the private sector has denied access to students on the basis of caste, gender, religion and language. The unaided private sector, which functions on students' fees, has provided access to only those students who have the ability to pay the exorbitant fees.
- Loans as enabler: Education loans are projected as enabler for democratising education. However, given the high rate of interests, private institutions attract only students from middle and upper class backgrounds, leaving out large proportions of students from poorer sections.
- Inclusiveness: Given the high fee structure and high rate of interest on loans, the private educational institutions have largely remained socio-economically exclusivist and created a class divide in the education sector.

With regard to 'quality', there is a strong misconception that private education is better than public education. Such perceptions, according to Tilak (2014), are based mostly on impressive buildings of the private educational institutions. A deeper look into the private sector, however, exposes its deficiencies. For example, 'most private higher educational institutions have no libraries, laboratories, or research programmes; they concentrate on saleable courses of study, prefer short-term to long-term programmes, and have under-qualified and underpaid teachers' (Tilak, 2014: 35). Given that most private educational enterprises are self-financing, they are required to generate revenues for their sustenance. In order to generate revenue, they predominantly offer subjects that have higher demands, such as engineering, management and commerce. In so doing, they have ignored other subjects like humanities, social sciences and basic sciences, which has produced 'a distorted, unbalanced and unsustainable higher education system' (Tilak, 2014: 35).

Contrary to the claim that private education is better, several studies have shown that the quality of education in private institutions is, in fact, very poor. The private job market, particularly the information technology (IT) enterprises are not content with the 'quality' of engineering education imparted by the private educational institutions. Following the neoliberal reforms and changes in IT policy, the southern Indian States like Andhra Pradesh, Karnataka and Tamil Nadu experienced an IT boom. In order to meet the demand for skilled workforce, hundreds of private engineering colleges were set up. However, Krishnan's (2014: 69) study in Karnataka shows that 'these [private] colleges do not contribute directly to the IT workforce in the region'. Her study also shows that 'recruitment patterns in Indian IT firms demonstrate that employers' preferences are heavily skewed in favour of graduates from the IITs, the NITs and some highly-ranked private colleges such as BITs Pilani'. As far as Karnataka's private colleges are concerned, only a few top-notch colleges contribute significantly to the rapidly expanding IT workforce. Krishnan (2014: 69) concludes that, 'while the new breed of private colleges produce a large fraction of engineering graduates in the State, they are often deemed as 'unemployable' by IT recruiters, and consequently, do not get absorbed by the IT industry without additional training'. This shows that increasing enrolments in private educational institutions do not necessarily reflect their 'good quality' education.

Questions of Autonomy and Freedom

Besides growing privatisation, the question of autonomy and freedom has also been a major concern for higher education institutions in India. The concept of autonomy is broadly understood as 'the freedom to function to achieve academic excellence and to administer the institution through its own rules and regulations' (Prakash, 2011: 37). However, in India, 'university autonomy in the present context is not absolute as it has to function within the regulatory framework enforced by the state' (Prakash, 2011: 37). A large number of public bodies, such as the University Grants Commission (UGC), the All-India Council for Technical Education (AICTE), the National Assessment and Accreditation Council (NAAC), the Bar Council of India etc. have been set up to govern higher education. According to Tilak (2013: 6), 'as many as 16 professional bodies have been established by the government to deal with accreditation and coordination in higher education. Yet it is widely felt that the system of higher education is highly regulated and least governed'.

The 12th Five Year Plan declared that in higher education, institutional autonomy will be enabled by 'transforming the role of government from command and control to a steering and evaluative role' (Planning Commission, 2013: 92). However, most recently, with the change of the government, several controversies have erupted that have negatively affected the autonomy and academic freedom of higher educational institutions. One such example is the tussle between the UGC and the Delhi University over the four-year-undergraduate programme (FYUP). It must be noted that under pressure from the UPA government, the Delhi University introduced the FYUP haphazardly and without much planning, but the sudden directive of the UGC and the Ministry of Human Resource Development (MHRD) to roll back the programme and return to the earlier three-year-degree system has not only created chaos but also undermined institutional autonomy. Moreover, following the rollback of the FYUP, the NDA government has, in 2015, introduced the Choice Based Credit System (CBCS) at the undergraduate level in Indian universities. The UGC issued a circular to all vice-chancellors of public funded central and state universities to introduce the CBCS with immediate effect. This shows how 'autonomous institutions of higher education in India are just working as custodians of the political agenda of the government' (Thakur, 2016: 21). It should also be noted that both the FYUP and the CBCS programmes 'were initiated in a hurry by the UPA and NDA governments respectively' and 'both programmes adopted the top-down approach for implementation rather than considering a bottom-up approach, ignoring the voices of important stake-holders, namely, teachers, students, educationists and society at large' (Thakur, 2016: 21).

In addition, there have been several allegations that the MHRD has been interfering in the governance structure of higher educational institutions, which has compelled people like RK Shevgaonkar (Director of IIT Delhi) and Amartya Sen (Chancellor of Nalanda University) to offer their resignation even before their term ended. The nuclear scientist, Anil Kakodkar also resigned from the chairmanship of the Board of Governor of IIT Bombay, but was later persuaded to withdraw his resignation. Furthermore, additional secretary (technical education) Amarjeet Sinha was also relieved of his responsibility over some appointments to IITs and IIMs, which the Ministry has termed as a routine reshuffle of portfolios.

Not just interference in the system of governance, there has also been systematic attempts to revise education. The first attempt in this direction was made in the Vajpayee-led NDA government (1998), which 'brought serious changes in the curriculum, education and social science history books' (Puniyani, 2015). The new BJP government has restarted the project where it had left. Most recently, the RSS chief stated that history should be 'saffronised'. Given this right-wing turn in history, historian Sabyasachi Bhattacharya has resigned as the Chief Editor of *Indian Historical Review,* a journal published by the Indian Council of Historical Research (ICHR). Acting towards this saffronisation, the MHRD has replaced the chairman of the ICHR. It has also approved the creation of the Bharatiya Shiksha Niti Ayog (BSNA), which is constituted by the RSS affiliated Shiksha Sanskriti Utthan Nyas, that is mandated to '*suggest corrective steps*' to '*Indianise*' the education system.

Recently, beginning with the JNU controversy, the question of dissent/nationalism has also become very important. The JNU students' union president has been accused of being anti-national and indulging in sedition. He was arrested for allegedly raising slogans on the independence of Kashmir and praise of Pakistan, though some reports suggest that he was doing the opposite and was trying to stop people from raising such slogans (Thapar, 2016: 20). Similarly, the suicide of a dalit research scholar at the University of Hyderabad has raised questions of caste discrimination in higher educational institutions. The students' protest against such discrimination has been supressed by the administration. The government has taken all measures to silence criticism and dissent. As Romila Thapar (2016: 20) writes, 'the ideology central to the BJP-RSS has no space or use for liberal thought and values. Education for such organisation means only what can be called a kind of catechism. This is a memorisation of a narrow set of answers that prohibit any doubt or deviation. The same technique applies to all subjects. Therefore educational centres that allow questioning and discussion are anathema and have to be dismantled'. Such attempts by the government have not only undermined the autonomy and academic freedom but also created institutional crisis and deep cynicism towards higher education in India.

Conclusion

The above discussion has reflected on the various problems that the Indian education system is facing in the present context. While the government has played a major role and taken several steps to universalise elementary education, such as expanding the school system, building new class rooms, hiring more teachers and providing incentives like free textbooks, uniforms and mid-day meals, it has not been much successful in addressing the low *quality of learning* in our schools. The 2015 ASER report has discussed two major problems that our elementary education faces, ie. declining quality and increasing privatisation, which need urgent attention. It is high time that the government acknowledges the gravity of these problems and shifts emphasis from enrolment and inputs in education towards ensuring *good quality* education. As Vimala Ramachandran has rightly noted, 'The Right to Education is not limited to the right to be enrolled, but to be taught and learn'. Once the problem of 'quality' is fixed, this will automatically reduce the trend towards privatisation of elementary education.

Similarly, our higher education system is also marred by several problems. Except a few public institutions like the IITs and IIMs, the quality of education in our public and private institutions is very poor. The funding constraint and the inability of the state on the one hand, and the policies of neo-liberalism on the other, have led to the mushrooming of private self-financing higher educational institutions who consider education as a saleable commodity rather than a social good. The requisite to generate revenue has forced these self-financing institutions to offer programmes in areas that have higher demand. As a consequence, only certain subjects like engineering, medicine and commerce have flourished whereas humanities, social sciences and the basic sciences have suffered; ultimately, as Tilak has pointed out, this has produced 'a distorted, unbalanced and unsustainable higher education system'. Not just commercialisation and commodification, higher education has also been affected by declining autonomy and academic freedom. Given these trends, the challenge before us today is how to meet the increasing demands for education, ensure its quality, restrict profit-making in education and restore the autonomy and integrity of our education system.

I would like to thank Prof KN Kabra and Prof V Upadhyay for giving me the opportunity to contribute this essay.

References

1. ASER (2015) *Annual Status of Education Report (Rural) 2014,* ASER Center, Delhi.
2. British Council (2014) *Understanding India,* British Council India Publications.
3. Chandhoke N and P Priyadarshi (eds.2009) 'Human Development: Health and Education' in *Contemporary India,* Pearson, pp.70-85.
4. Dongre A (2015) 'Do Private Tuitions Improve Learning Outcomes?' in *Annual Status of Education Report (Rural) 2014,* ASER Centre, Delhi, pp.17-18.
5. Government of India (2014) *Educational Statistics at a Glance,* MHRD Publications.
6. Human Development Report (2014) *Sustaining Human Progress,* UNDP Publications.
7. Kapur D and Mehta PB (2007) *Mortgaging the Future? Indian Higher Education,* Brooking-NCAER India Policy Forum.
8. Krishnan S (2014) 'Political Economy of India's Tertiary Education', *Economic and Political Weekly,* Vol.XLIX, No.11, March 15, pp.63-70.
9. Kumar AKS and Rustagi P (2010) *Elementary Education in India,* Oxfam India Working Paper Series, pp.1-34.

10. Kumar GP (2013) 'Why the State of India's Primary Education is Shocking', *Firstpost,* January 22, http://www.firstpost.com/india/why-the-state-of-indias-primary-education-is-shocking-598011.html.

11. Madhavan MR (2015) 'Ten Years of ASER', in *Annual Status of Education Report (Rural) 2014,* pp.11-12, ASER Centre, Delhi.

12. Mukherjee A (2015) 'The "ASER" of Public Finance', in *Annual Status of Education Report (Rural) 2014,* pp.15-16, ASER Centre, Delhi. .

13. Nambissan GB (2014) *Poverty, Markets, and Elementary Education in India,* Max Weber Stiftung TRG Poverty and Education Working Paper Series.

14. Nayak D (2014) 'Understanding the Logic of Neo-Liberalism in Education', *Economic and Political Weekly,* Vol.XLIX, No.13, March 29, pp.10-13.

15. Planning Commission (2013) *Twelfth Five Year Plan: Social Sectors,* Sage Publications.

16. Prakash V (2011) 'Concerns about Autonomy and Academic Freedom in Higher Education Institutions', *Economic and Political Weekly,* Vol. XLVI, No.16, April 16, pp.36-40.

17. Puniyani R. (2015) 'India Should Say No to the RSS Version of History', *Dawn,* April 6.

18. Ramachandran V (2015) 'Can We Fix the Persisting Crisis of Learning', in *Annual Status of Education Report (Rural) 2014,* pp.13-14, ASER Centre, Delhi.

19. Thakur, N. (2016) 'De Facto Privatization in Indian Public Higher Education: A Transition from FYUP to CBCS,' *Economic and Political Weekly,* Vol.51, No.9, February 27, pp.20-21.

20. Thapar, R. (2016) 'Targeting Institutions of Higher Education: Fear of the Intellectual,' *Economic and Political Weekly,* Vol.51, No.10, March 5, pp.19-21.

21. Tilak JBG (ed., 2013) 'Introduction', *Higher Education in India: In Search of Equality, Quality and Quantity,* Orient Blackswan, pp.1-18.

22. Tilak JBG (2014) 'Private Higher Education in India', *Economic and Political Weekly,* Vol. XLIX, No.40, October 4, pp.32-38.

23. Wadhwa W (2015) 'Government vs Private Schools: Have Things Changed?' in *Annual Status of Education Report (Rural) 2014* pp.19-21, ASER Centre, Delhi.

A Decade of Commodities Futures Trading–Regulatory Retrogression

— Tulsi Lingareddy

INDIAN COMMODITY futures markets have been through a rough journey as the requisite path was not laid out with appropriate regulatory and infrastructure systems that would aid in smooth functioning. As a result, the futures markets have been facing frequent roadblocks and diversions during the past decade or so.[1]

Commodity futures, after the operationalisation of the online electronic trade platforms in 2003, have witnessed a manifold growth in trading volumes during the past 12 years despite facing a number of setbacks at frequent intervals.

The volumes have increased manifold from about Rs. 1.29 lakh crore in 2003-04 to a peak of Rs 181 lakh crore in 2011-12, though moderated in the subsequent years rather steeply and reached about Rs 61.7 lakh crore in 2014-15. The fall can primarily be attributed to two factors. One is the levy of commodity transaction tax (CTT) on futures contracts of non-agricultural commodities and the other is the

[1] An earlier version of the paper was published in *EPW* (Lingareddy 2015)

exposure of the Rs 5,600 crore fraud at the National Spot Exchange Ltd (NSEL), incidentally both in July 2013.

The NSEL case has not only affected the trade volumes but also brought forth the concerns over regulatory and monitoring system of commodity markets. Following this, the FMC was brought under the ministry of finance from the ministry of consumer affairs in September 2013. Further, putting an end to a long-term debate, the finance ministry has proposed to merge the FMC with the SEBI during the 2015-16 budget announcements.

But, the question here is will it lead the commodity derivative markets towards their ultimate objectives of efficient price discovery and price risk management? An attempt is made to the analyse issues related to functioning of the Indian commodity markets, particularly in the context of the proposed FMC-SEBI merger.

Major Market Trends

Commodity market volumes witnessed broadly three distinct phases of growth. First Phase, 2002-03 to 2005-06, witnessed a phenomenal and accelerated growth of more than 200% per annum. Second Phase, 2006-07 to 2011-12, recorded a steady and robust annual average growth rate of about 44% per annum. Third Phase, 2012-13 to 2014-15, posted a fall in volumes at an average rate of 28.5% per annum. The important reasons for the steep reduction in volumes were the levy of CTT and the adverse impact from the NSEL fraud.

Although the NSEL fraud was not directly related to futures trading, it has affected indirectly the broking firms, which have been the volume contributors for futures trading, as significant amount of their funds were trapped in NSEL. Further, it has also affected the general sentiments of market participants, making them sceptical about the functioning of the commodity futures market in India.

Trading on Exchanges

Despite the presence of a number of national and regional commodity exchanges, only two exchanges dominate the commodity futures markets.

The first national multi-commodity exchange to offer online trading in commodity futures was the National Multi-Commodity Exchange

(NMCE), in 2002. Following that, the Multi-Commodity Exchange (MCX) and the National Commodities and Derivatives Exchanges (NCDEX) were started in 2003. Apart from these, a number of regional exchanges have been offering futures trading in commodity markets.

Subsequently, three more national exchanges—the Indian Commodities Exchange Ltd (ICEX) in 2009, Ace Derivatives and Commodity Exchange Limited in 2010 and the Universal Commodity Exchange Ltd (UCX) in 2013—were permitted to offer futures trading in commodities. However, volumes have not picked up on these exchanges and as a result, the ICEX and UCX have suspended futures trading operations in 2014. At present, there are four national multi-commodity exchanges that are actively offering commodity futures trade in the country.

Chart 1: Exchange-wise Share in Volumes

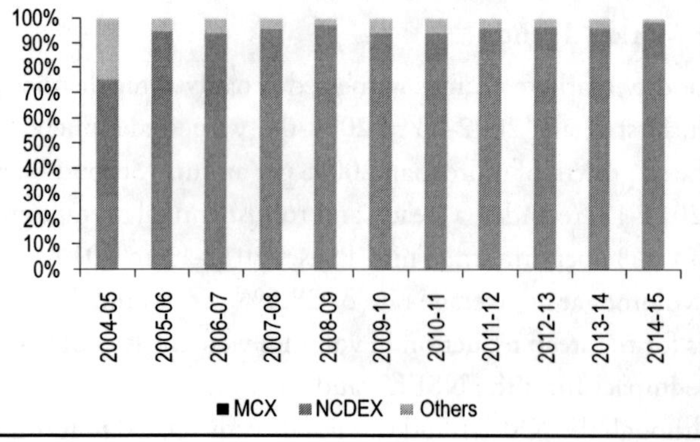

Source: www.fmc.gov.in

Of the four national exchanges, NCDEX and MCX account for more than 95% of the total market volumes in commodity futures. NCDEX gained large volumes in the initial three years from 2003-04 to 2005-06, mainly in agricultural commodities.

However, the volumes on MCX, concentrated in non-agricultural commodities, rose rather steeply from 2005-06 onwards. As a result, the MCX has become the largest exchange in trade volumes in 2006-07 and has remained in the first position ever since with more than 80% of market share. While the market share of the NCDEX stood around 12% on the average, trading on other national and regional exchanges put together accounted for less than 5% of the total futures market volume.

Concentrated Trading

Commodity-wise trading volumes indicated that the share of agricultural commodities has declined steadily from more than 50% to around 12%, while share of non-agricultural commodities has gone up significantly from around 30% to more than 80% during the past 10 years (Table 1). Nonetheless, the share of agricultural commodities has improved marginally during 2013-14 and 2014-15, following the levy of CTT on non-agricultural commodity futures trade in July 2013.

Among non-agricultural commodities, the share of bullion accounted for more than half of the total futures volumes till 2012-13 but declined thereafter to about 35% in 2014-15. Interestingly, the share of energy products trade has increased between 2012-13 and 2014-15 in contrast to the other non-agricultural commodities after the levy of CTT.

Thus, the share of agricultural commodities has been around 12% on the average during the past decade except for the initial few years, while the futures trading is dominated by gold and silver with their high per unit prices.

Table 1: Commodity Share in Total Volume (%)

	Agri-Commodities	Bullion	Metals	Energy	Others
2004-05	68.3	31.5	NA	NA	0.4
2005-06	55.9	36.5	NA	NA	8.5
2006-07	35.8	57.9	NA	NA	6.3
2007-08	23.2	42.5	NA	NA	34.4
2008-09	12.0	56.7	11.8	19.6	0.1
2009-10	15.7	40.8	23.2	20.3	0.0
2010-11	12.2	46.0	22.5	19.3	0.0
2011-12	12.1	56.2	16.0	15.7	0.0
2012-13	12.7	46.1	19.1	22.1	0.0
2013-14	15.8	42.5	17.4	24.4	0.0
2014-15	17.2	35.5	20.7	26.7	0.0

Source: www.fmc.gov.in, Lingareddy (2015).

Note: Data on metals and energy products are not available separately and are included under others till 2007-08.

Regulatory Developments

Regulation of commodity futures markets has a three tier system, with the Ministry (Consumer Affairs earlier and Ministry of Finance now) at the top, the FMC at the middle and the commodity exchanges at the tertiary level.

Need for a stronger and well planned regulatory system was felt from the beginning and concerns were expressed, suggesting the empowerment of the FMC and amendment of the Forward Contracts (Regulation) Act, 1952. Despite the widely expressed concerns, commodity futures trading on online exchanges was allowed without taking steps to strengthen the FMC and without putting well worked-out regulatory mechanism in place (Sahadevan, 2012).

As a result, the FMC, with its inadequate staff and regulatory strength, has only been able to address the problems post their occurance rather than preventing them. For instance, when the futures exchanges were allowed to function, no limits were specified on the number of open positions a client or a member can take per contract. Similarly, there was no regulation towards the compliance of delivery of commodities.

Taking advantage of it, some of the market participants tried to manipulate markets and as a result mentha oil, guar and urad futures witnessed extreme volatilities within a very short span of time during the last quarter of 2005 (Lingareddy 2005). The FMC brought the delivery period concept and brought required regulatory measures on 3 Jan 2006 after persistent complaints.

Similarly, limits on maximum open positions a client or member can take in a futures contract were brought in only after irregularities cropped up, though limits has been a common practice on international futures exchanges such as the Chicago Board of Trade (CBOT) (Lingareddy, 2006).

It is true that any regulatory system evolves continuously as the markets grow, but a certain amount of regulatory mechanism is pre-requisite to ensure efficient functioning of the markets.

While the FMC has been making sincere efforts to address the regulatory issues in spite of the constraints, the commodity exchanges, despite being a part of the futures regulatory system, have apparently not taken any interest in exercising or delivering their regulatory responsibilities but have only focused on raising the trade volumes over the past decade.

FMC-SEBI Merger

The Ministry of Finance has proposed to merge the FMC with SEBI in the 2015-16 budget announcements. The debate on the merger has been going on over the past decade, ever since the start of futures trading in 2003-04.

The idea of bringing the control of derivatives markets under one regulator appears to be convenient as in the case of the US. The merger is expected to solve the problems of inadequate manpower, research and monitoring capabilities.

So far, the cheer comes from the broking firms, with the expectation that the merger will allow them to have a single entity to trade both in commodities and stocks, unlike the existing system of having separate entities to trade on commodity and stock exchanges. It is an issue of concern, if the regulator allows single entity to trade on both commodity and stock markets without keeping the necessary arms length in trading.

Further, in order to ensure efficient functioning of commodity futures markets, it is necessary to address the issues associated with underlying commodity markets, especially that of agricultural commodities.

Issues to be Addressed

Information Asymmetry

Adequate and free flow of information on demand and supply is a pre-requisite for efficient price discovery, monitoring and price risk management.

Currently, a reasonable amount of information flow is seen in case of gold, silver, metals, energy and some of the agricultural commodities from the international agencies like theWorld Gold Council, the US Geological Survey, US Department of Agriculture (USDA), US Energy Information Agency etc.

But, no such free flow of information on demand, supply and stocks is available for majority of agricultural commodities that are largely produced and/or consumed in India.

In the US, the USDA provides demand and supply estimates/forecasts for all the crops and livestock products for the US as well as the other major producing countries on a monthly basis, based on which the spot and futures prices are traded.

But in India, the information on demand and supply of agricultural commodities is very scanty. The department of agriculture releases only output estimates but almost at the end of the season. For hedging purposes, such information is required well in advance.

The system of agricultural output estimation has not changed over decades. An early release and precise estimation of agricultural output numbers, using remote sensing and satellite imagery techniques, may help in providing timely information and improving market efficiency.

In addition, no authentic and reliable estimates on domestic consumption demand are available for agricultural commodities. Under these conditions, it becomes highly difficult to track the right direction of commodity price trends and as a result, agricultural commodity markets in India are vulnerable to market manipulations, both in spot as well as futures markets

Thus, in order to ensure efficient functioning of commodity markets, adequate availability of market information on commodities is a pre-requisite.

Inadequate Physical Infrastructure

Another important aspect that can smoothen efficient functioning of the Indian commodity markets is a wide-spread network of warehouse facilities by independent agency/agencies.

A well-spread network of warehouses across the country under an independent agency, either government or with public-private partnership, can provide a better commodity handling facilities, instead of the existing warehouses attached to individual exchanges. The existing structure can lead to malpractices, as it has happened in the case of the NSEL fraud.

An independent warehousing agency under the purview of regulators may facilitate futures trading and delivery mechanisms. Apart from futures trading, establishment of a network of warehouses across the country may help increase storage facilities in the country, warehouse receipt financing, reducing the wastage, maintaining quality etc.

Conclusion

Commodity futures trading has witnessed a phenomenal growth in futures volumes during the past 12 years, though concentrated only in two exchanges. MCX alone accounts for more than 80% and NCDEX contributes for about 12% of total futures volumes. On an average, agricultural commodities account for only about 12% of the commodities market share.

Adequate and timely flow of market information and unified widespread warehouse network are pre-requisites for facilitating smooth functioning of futures trading as well as overall development of commodity markets in the country, both qualitatively and quantitatively.

Hence, the merger may provide a relatively stronger regulator, but the desired objectives can be achieved only if it is thoroughly supported with better information and warehouse network.

References

1. Lingareddy Tulsi (2005): An Open Letter to the FMC, Dated December 21, 2005.
2. Lingareddy Tulsi (2006): 'Commodities Futures Trading'*Alternate Economic Survey 2005-06*, Danish Publishers.
3. Lingareddy, Tulsi (2008): 'Expert Committee on Commodity Futures: Agreements and Disagreements', *Economic and Political Weekly*, 43(34): 35-42.
4. Lingareddy, Tulsi (2015): 'Commodity Futures Trading at the Crossroads', *Economic and Political Weekly*, 50(24): 113-116.
5. Sahadevan KG (2012): '"Commodity Futures and Regulation A Vibrant Market Looking for a Powerful Regulator', *Economic and Political Weekly*, 47(52): 106-112.

Electricity Amendment Bill 2014: Privatising Profits and Nationalising Losses

— K Ashok Rao

ELECTRICITY IS a product when it is consumed and sold. It has necessarily to be transmitted through a wire from the point of generation to the point of consumption.

In the 1940s, electricity was privately owned in British India and largely restricted to urban consumers who could afford it. The Electricity (Supply) Act 1948 envisaged that the State governments must deliver electricity, either directly (through the State Board) or through private companies. This Act made the Central government, through the Central Electricity Authority (CEA), the regulator. Electricity was thus taken to not just the villages but to the pump sets beyond the villages, enabling the green revolution. The 1948 Act mandated that '*the Board shall, after taking credit for any subvention from the State government, carry on its operations under this Act and adjust its tariffs so as to ensure that the total revenues in any year of account shall, after meeting all expenses, leave such surplus as is not less than three per cent.'* This law was violated by almost all States. The consequence was loss-making State Electricity Boards.

The Electricity Act 2003 was enacted to usher in first generation reforms in the power sector. It promised to reduce, both the transmission and distribution losses ,and financial losses. Neither have been achieved in the last 12 year in any of the States. The magic bullet was to be the dismantling (unbundling) of the State Electricity Boards—separating Generation, Transmission and Distribution. The total losses in the distribution sector, including short term liabilities, are around Rs 190,000 crore (T&D loss 21.46% in 2013-14) which is more than 2 % of the nation's GDP at 2010-11 prices. Other than questionable privatisation, there is nothing much to show by way of achievement under this Act. In Odisha, repeatedly, the private DISCOM licenses had to be cancelled and in Delhi the DISCOMS are desperately resisting a CAG audit for obvious reasons.

The present Bill—the Electricity (Amendment) Bill 2004—seeks to bring in second generation reforms in the power sector. It intends to separate carriage and content, which implies splitting distribution into the business of bringing electricity, by wire to the consumer premises (investment in the distribution network is almost entirely done by the public sector) and the business of metering, billing and money collection (to be done by the private sector, except for one licensee). There would be separate distribution and supply for other licensees. The stated objective is to retain distribution as a 'regulated activity' and bring in market principles in the supply of electricity.

Whose interests are to be served is evident from the following recording in the Energy Standing Committee[1] report which states, '*ASSOCHAM, CII, APP, IPPAI and FICCI were unanimous in favour of the proposed amendment to introduced segregation of carriage and content in the sector.... All PSUs were also agreed to the concept*' Most of the State governments either opposed the amendment or were skeptical of the segregation of carriage and content. The Tamil Nadu government bluntly stated:

---

1 Electricity (Amendment) Bill 2014 Fourth Report – Standing Committee on Energy, 16th Lok Sabha.

With the separation of carriage and content, this Bill in one stroke will make all the State Utilities unviable.... Private player is not going to make any investment into distribution network. Without making investment into distribution network, it is getting best-paying consumers for supply[ing] electricity and that too, without loss. Further, it will cherry pick the consumers in urban areas or high-value consumers in rural areas. The State is against it in totality.

State Governments Mere Silent Spectators?

Electricity is item 38 in the **Concurrent List** or **List-III** (Seventh Schedule) of the Constitution of India.

'If any provision of a law made by the Legislature of a State is repugnant to any provision of a law made by Parliament which Parliament is competent to enact, or to any provision of an existing law with respect to one of the matters enumerated in the Concurrent List, then, the law made by Parliament, whether passed before or after the law made by the Legislature of such State, or, as the case may be, the existing law, shall prevail and the law made by the Legislature of the State shall, to the extent of the repugnancy, be void.'

Taking advantage of this clause, the Electricity (Amendment) Bill 2014 changes the 'concurrent' character of the law and makes the States merely an enforcement agency.

The Bill requires the States, within two years (or seek extension in 'consultation' with the Central government) but not exceed five years, to implement the separation of carriage and content, whether they are in agreement with it or not.

At the heart of the Bill is open access that would enable any consumer to obtain electricity from anywhere without any control or intervention of the State governments. Under the existing Electricity Act 2003, the State governments have repeatedly exercised their right under Section 11, prohibiting export of power from their States. CERC challenged these orders and the entire matter is subjudice in the Supreme Court.

Power tariff is a major political and electoral issue and State governments have regularly issued directives to the State regulators to meet political compulsions . The 2014 Bill requires that the State regulator 'shall **necessarily** be guided by the Tariff Policy for the purpose of tariff determination' The term **necessarily**, instead of mandatorily, has been used to assuage the feelings of the State governments. This term shall, in due course, be the cause of litigation. The tariff policy that has necessarily to be followed would be formulated by the Government of India. Neither the State government, nor the State regulators would be decisive factors, it would be the executive in the Central government.

And to ensure compliance, there is a clause enabling the performance of the State Regulator to be reviewed by a committee to be set up by the Central government, as and when required and whose '*functions and term of reference, including the time period for submission of the report, shall be such as may be prescribed by the Central Government*'.

The stated purpose of the tariff policy is to ensure that the licensees recover cost of electricity without revenue deficit, pass through the effects of fuel and power purchase cost more than once in a year, and incorporating provisions for initiating suo-motu proceedings for determination of tariffs.

Since fuel cost and power purchase costs do not pass through the State government nor the regulators, they have no control over the tariff levied. Further, the accounts of the private licensees are not subject to public audit, therefore, the scope for gaming and litigation is infinite. This apprehension is reinforced by the following facts:

1. According to newspaper reports, '*The Directorate of Revenue Intelligence (DRI) has unearthed a scam involving companies inflating the value of coal imports from Indonesia for their power plants, thus siphoning money abroad. Initial estimates by the agency pegged the overvaluation at Rs 29,000 crore between 2011 and 2014*'.[2] State governments and regulators would have to be silent witnesses whilst the consumers pay for this overvaluation.
2. There would be no incentive for the licensee to do advance planning and ensure purchase from the lowest cost source. At the last moment, since power is a monopoly and shortages prevail, purchase from merchant power stations at any rate that need not even be accurately recorded, will occur.

---

[2] 18 Dec 2014 : *The Times of India* (Mumbai), Power firms inflate coal import prices, Rs 29Kcr scam bared, C Unnikrishnan.

3. In due course, electricity would also be open for forward and future contracts/ market. The Standing Committee states, '*Allowing such forward trading at this juncture in the power sector will result into manipulation/ artificial shortages which will push the price upwards, causing net loss to the common consumer.*'

There is serious danger that there would be of cartelisation between the generators and the supply licensees, and in the absence of public audit, the creation of several layers that would enable financial manipulation since the Bill provides that, '*In case the distribution licensee or supply licensee propose to undertake distribution of supply of electricity through a franchisee, that franchisee shall not require a separate license*'.

As an interim measure, all the power purchase agreements are to be assigned to an intermediary company to be set up by the State governments. However, it would not be the State but the central government that would decide the functions of the intermediary company and the allocation of power purchase agreements amongst the supply licensees. They, in turn, will' supply electricity progressively, based on the load factor of the consumer as specified by the Central government'.

Privatising Profits and Nationalising Losses

The Ministry of Power has stated in writing that, '*Introduction of open access has not progressed substantially, there is no perceptible impact to the power consumers in the agriculture, industrial, domestic sector of the country by access to cheaper power and reliable supply of the same.*' Since the statuary provision of open access was made in the Electricity Act 2003, in the last 12 years, only 3,000 inter-State open access consumers are buying electricity through power exchange by availing open access. The Standing Committee has recorded that, '*the Ministry[has] informed that DISCOMS are resisting to give open access to industrial consumers (bulk consumers) since industrial tariffs are usually high*'. The Bill being introduced is to only meet the concerns of the few thousands of large consumers of electricity.

The obvious consequence is clearly understood by the Bill. It mandates that there would compulsorily be one supply licensee that would be either government-owned or government-controlled, which shall 'shoulder the responsibility, of **last resort** supply licensee, irrespective of the area of supply'. Profits would be privatised, and losses nationalised. This Bill will only accentuate the crisis and drive it into an unmanageable spiral.

In India, there are more than 300 million consumers who have no electricity at all, and even more numbers who do not get proper supply since they have very limited purchasing capacity. However, their electoral power ensures political commitment resulting in, as of now on an average, the distribution companies losing Rs 4 per unit of power they supply. It is rather naïve or outright arrogant to assume that by enacting a law, it will be possible to ensure that the supply licensee will be able to recover the cost to serve, without any revenue deficit. What will follow will be disconnections and arrest of defaulters.

Competition is not possible in shortages.The India power system, in the near future, will be characterised by power shortages despite addition of power generation capacity. The real situation is that only around 48,389 megawatts (Mw) of projects of the targeted 88,537 Mw for 2012-17 have been commissioned and the balance is expected to come on stream during the last leg of 2015-17. Half of the commissioned 46,000 Mw in thermal (coal-and gas-based) projects are stuck mainly because of fuel supply issues.

Where is the Infrastructure?

The Bill assumes that separation of carriage and content requires *merely administrative action* by the State governments within two to five years, completely ignoring the technological aspects. There is a need for extensive metering and extensive computerised data logging in order to ensure that there is no scope for either gaming the system or manipulating it through clever litigation. Such systems require a huge investment. Every country that has introduced such a separation has preceded it with putting technical systems in place.

The Indian grid is incomplete and inadequate. It is incapable of transferring power at will. Transfer of power is severely limited and conditioned by the available transmission and sub-transmission lines. It is *not the market but the technical constraints* that will determine the working of the open access and the ability of supply licensees to transfer power.

Conclusion

During the elections to the Delhi Assembly, addressing a rally of marginal consumers of electrical power, Prime Minister Naendra Modi assured that his government would enable consumers to choose their electricity supply provider as they do their mobile service provider, and be able to change them at will. A politician cannot be expected to know the vital difference between a wireless and a wired system, but bureaucrats' and legislators' glossing over reality is unacceptable.

Political and Electoral Reforms

— Jagdeep S Chhokar

THERE HAS been a lot of discussion and debate concerning electoral reforms in recent months, particularly since the 20th Law Commission of India submitted the 255th report of the Law Commission titled *Electoral Reforms* in March 2015. This, the 255th report, was in continuation of an earlier, the 244th report of the Law Commission, in February 2014, in response to a Supreme Court order in December 2013. The 244th report was titled '*Electoral Disqualifications*' and dealt with two specific issues: de-criminalisation of politics and disqualification for filing false affidavits. The very first chapter of the 255th report reiterates that the two reports, the 244th and the 255th, should be read together to get a complete sense of what needs to be done for reforming India's electoral system.

One of the reasons for the widespread discussion of this issue, among many others, is the dissatisfaction with the state of governance in the country. While governance happens at many levels and many areas, the one that attracts most comment is political governance. Since 'We, the People' adopted and gave unto ourselves, representative democracy as the chosen form of government, through the agency of the members of the Constituent Assembly, and elections are the mechanism through which decisions about who will govern the country are taken; whenever we find something wrong or wanting in the governance process, we tend to think of elections, and how they must be improved so that governance can be improved.

The last year has been an interesting one from the perspective of elections. The country got its first government in three decades with a single party in majority in the Lok Sabha in over three decades, and we have a State Assembly in which a single party holds 67 out of 70 seats. However, the functioning of the Parliament where the ruling establishment and the opposition are constantly at loggerheads, and of the State with this overwhelming majority where the Lieutenant Governor and the Chief Minister and the State Cabinet are having a very public spat, are not pleasing to the public eye, making citizens wonder about the system that gets such people in these temples of democracy. This is what causes them to think of electoral reforms.

The issue of electoral reforms is not new or recent.

A Peep into History of Electoral Reforms

While the talk about electoral reforms rises and goes into oblivion from time to time, it has a long history. The statement below is worth reading:

> Leaving now our laurels alone, it becomes imperative to take stock of the present state of affairs which causes concern and anxiety because of the existence of the looming danger threatening to cut at the very roots of free and fair elections.
>
> The role of money and muscle powers at elections deflecting seriously the well accepted democratic values and ethos and corrupting the process; rapid criminalisation of politics greatly encouraging evils of booth capturing, rigging, violence etc.; misuse of official machinery, ie. official media and ministerial; increasing menace of participation of non-serious candidates; form the core of our electoral problems. Urgent corrective measures are the need of the hour lest the system itself should collapse.
>
> Electoral reforms are correctly understood to be a continuous process. But attempts so far made in this area did not touch even the fringe of the problem. They appeared to be abortive.

> Some of the recent measures like reduction of voting age and anti-defection law are no doubt laudable and the basic principles underlying those measures should be appreciated. But there are other vital and important areas in election field completely neglected and left high and dry.

Though the above sounds familiar and contemporary, it was written in May of 1990 in what has come to be known as the Goswami Committee Report,[1] officially called the Committee on Electoral Reforms. It went on to say, 'All these four decades, especially after 1967, the demand for electoral reforms has been mounting up.'

Following the 'demand of electoral reforms' over four decades, the then Prime Minister, VP Singh called an all-party meeting on 09 January 1990. This meeting decided to set up a committee under the chairmanship of Dinesh Goswami, the then Law Minister with eleven members:

HKL Bhagat	MP (Indian National Congress)
LK Advani	MP (Bharatiya Janata Party)
Somnath Chatterjee	MP (Communist Party of India) [Marxist]
Ghulam Rasool Mattoo	MP (National Conference)
Chimanbhai Mehta	MP
Indrajit	MP
Homi F Daji	Former MP (Communist Party of India)
Era Sezhiyan	Former MP (Janata Dal)
V Kishore Chandra Deo	Former MP (Congress (S))
LP Singh	Former Governor
SL Shakdher	Former Chief Election Commissioner

The Goswami Committee made 107 recommendations. There is no information on how many of the 107 recommendations have been implemented, and to what extent, but it is widely believed that a very large proportion of these have not been implemented, or even considered seriously or even considered at all

[1] http://adrindia.org/sites/default/files/Dinesh%20Goswami%20Report%20on%20Electoral%20Reforms.pdf, accessed on 25 May 2015.

If we go strictly by the limited descriptor 'electoral reforms', the next important event was in 1998 but before that there was a development in 1993 which has a very strong bearing on this issue and which has come to be known as the Vohra Committee Report.[2] It was prepared by NN Vohra, then Home Secretary to the Government of India, who currently is the Governor of Jammu and Kashmir. The committee actually consisted of the following five officials of the government:

Home Secretary	Chairman
Secretary (R)	Member
DIB	Member
Director CBI	Member
JS(PP) MHA	Member Secretary.

The committee was set up 'to take stock of all available information about the activities of crime Syndicates/Mafia organisations which had developed links with and were being *protected by Government functionaries and political personalities*' (Italics added).

Though it was set up as a committee, the Chairman felt, during the first meeting itself, that some of the members were not forthcoming. The report actually says, 'In the course of the discussions, I perceived that some of the Members appeared to have some hesitation in openly expressing their views and also seemed unconvinced that Government actually intended to pursue such matters. Accordingly, I addressed separate personal letters to each of the Members of the Committee seeking their well-considered suggestions and recommendations.' The Chairman summarised their responses, and then gave his conclusions. Interestingly, the Chairman writes, 'In the normal coursethis .report would have been drafted by the Member Secretary and finalised by the Committee. Considering the nature of the issues involved, I did not consider it desirable to burden the Members of the Committee with any further involvement beyond the views expressed by them. Accordingly, I decided to personally dictate this Report.'

The report goes on to say, 'I have prepared only three copies of this Report. One copy each is being submitted to MOS (IS) and HM, the

---

[2] http://adrindia.org/sites/default/files/VOHRA%20COMMITTEE%20REPORT_0.pdf, accessed on 25 May 2015.

third copy being retained by me... After an initial discussion at the level of MOS (IS) and HM, I could send a copy of this Report to FM, before the issues are discussed with him.'

As far as is known, the report has not been made been made public but, given the open society that India is, the report is freely available on the Internet, and its contents have not been denied. The major contribution of the report, in the context of electoral reforms, is the coining of, or at least popularising, the phrase 'criminalisation of politics and politicisation of crime'. It was the first time that the effect of crime, organised and unorganised, on the electoral process was officially recognised, though not made public.

The next formal attempt at electoral reforms was in 1998 in the form of what has come to be popularly known as the Indrajit Gupta Committee Report.[3] This committee, officially called the'Committee on State Funding of Elections' was set up in 1998 with the following members:

Indrajit Gupta	Chairman
Somnath Chatterjee	Member
Manmohan Singh	Member
Madhukar Sarpodar	Member
Vijay Kumar Malhotra	Member
R Muthiah	Member
Digvijay Singh	Member
Ram Gopal Yadav	Member

The Indrajit Gupta Committee report is about the most often-quoted report on electoral reforms and it is always quoted to support state funding of elections, a topic that will be discussed later.

The next, and possibly the most important, document on electoral reforms till date is the 170th report of the Law Commission of India[4] submitted to then Law Minister, Ram Jethmalani, in May 1999. This report, titled *Reform of the Electoral Laws,* was prepared by the 15th Law Commission which was chaired by Justice BP Jeevan Reddy, a retired judge of the Supreme Court of India. Other members of the Commission

---

[3] http://adrindia.org/sites/default/files/Indrajit_Gupta_Committe_on_State_funding_of_Elections.pdf, accessed on 25 May 2015.

[4] http://lawcommissionofindia.nic.in/lc170.htm, accessed on 25 May 2015.

were Justice Leila Seth, a retired Chief Justice of Himachal Pradesh High Court and NM Ghatate. The member secretary of the commission was Subhash C Jain. Given that piecemeal attempts had not yielded anything worthwhile, as we have seen, and given the complexity of our electoral system the Law Commission was requested to take a comprehensive look at the entire electoral system in the country and suggest what reforms were needed to make the electoral system in tune with the needs of the society. The Commission did exactly that and in a very comprehensive manner and studied all components of the entire electoral system before making their recommendations with detailed rationale and justification. Not much has been done by way of implementation of the recommendations.

This was followed by the National Commission to Review the Working of theConstitution, headed by Justice MN Venkatachaliah, former Chief Justice of India, set up by the government headed by Atal Behari Vajpayee on 23 February 2000, consisting of the following as members:

> Justice BP Jeevan Reddy, Chairman, Law Commission of India
> Justice RS. Sarkaria, former Judge, Supreme Court of India
> Justice Kottapalli Punnayya, former Judge, Andhra Pradesh High Court
> PA Sangma, former Speaker, Lok Sabha and Member of Parliament
> Soli J Sorabjee, Attorney General for India
> K Parasaran, Senior Advocate and former Attorney General for India
> Subhash CKashyap, former Secretary General, Lok Sabha
> Shri C.R. Irani, Chief Editor and Managing Director, *The Statesman*
> Abid Hussain, former Ambassador of India in the USA
> Sumitra G Kulkarni, former Member of Parliament, (Rajya Sabha)

The NCRWC, as it came to be called, submitted its report on 31 March 2002. The report[5] had a separate chapter (Chapter 4) which it chose to title as *Electoral Processes and Political Parties*, and made 38 recommendations. Sadly, nothing significant has been done to implement any of the recommendations.

---

[5] http://lawmin.nic.in/ncrwc/finalreport.htm, accessed on 25 May 2015.

The Election Commission of India has been making recommendations to the Government of India from time to time about various reforms in the electoral system that the Election Commission cannot make within its own authority, some of which require making some changes in the Conduct of Election Rules 1961, the Representation of People Act 1951, and other similar rules and legislations. While the government has made some of these changes from time to time but any major worthwhile changes have been consistently ignored. The Election Commission compiled 22 of these ignored recommendations and the then Chief Election Commissioner wrote to the Prime Minister giving details of these recommendations on 05 July 2004, and published these on 30 July 2004[6] to put these in the public domain. There has been no specific reaction from the government to these recommendations.

Then came the report of the Second Administrative Reforms Commission[7] in 2008 which also contained some significant observations on the electoral system, and made some serious recommendations for electoral reforms. Sadly, those recommendations have also not found favour of the government for implementation.

Later still, on 9 December 2010, the then Law Minister, M Veerappa Moily and the then Chief Election Commissioner, SY Quraishi announced in a joint press conference that seven regional and one national consultations will be conducted to evolve a national consensus on electoral reforms, and that will be followed by a comprehensive new legislation on electoral reforms. The seven regional consultations were indeed conducted in 2011, in association with the Election Commission of India, the last one being held in Guwahati on 05 June 2011. These were to be followed by a national consultation for which time has not been found so far even at the time of writing this in May 2015. There were also reports that a draft bill on electoral reforms had been prepared and had been discussed by the Law Minister with the Prime Minister on more than one occasion. During this time, the Law Minister changed twice but there was no known progress on electoral reforms.

---

6 http://eci.nic.in/eci_main/PROPOSED_ELECTORAL_REFORMS.pdf, accessed on 25 May 2015.

7 http://arc.gov.in/4threport.pdf, accessed on 25 May 2015.

The next episode in this continuing saga was the letter that the then, and outgoing, Chief Election Commissioner, SY Quraishi, wrote to the Prime Minister on 13 April 2012, before demitting office in June 2012. Quraishi was personally involved in extensive and repeated discussions with the then Law Minister, Veerappa Moily, before the latter was replaced by Salman Khurshid. Some excerpts from the letter, accessed by filing an RTI application, given below exemplify the frustration of those trying to improve the electoral system in the country:

> Hence allow me Sir, to place before you the *Commission's deep disappointment* over the fact that a necessary legislation in this regard is yet to be materialised despite an assurance given to us by the Hon'ble Minister of Law and Justice.
>
> However, the quality of our elections often gets questioned on account of certain *weaknesses in our electoral process.* Commission's reform proposals have always aimed at addressing this predicament. Though certain minor reforms have been adopted by Government and Parliament, the substantial ones have been actually left out allowing the allegations that *politicians are not keen about the reforms because of their vested interest.*
>
> I would like to bring to your kind notice that some proposals which are of technical nature and require only amendment of Rules within the competence of the Ministry of Law and Justice, have also been pending for a long time. This raises questions about the *lack of political will, which causes us deep distress* (Italics added).

Then come the 244th and 255th reports of the Law Commission on 24 February 2014 and 12 March 2015 respectively, in response to a Supreme Court order of 16 December 2013.

This is a brief history of electoral reforms in the country for the last 48 years, since 1967. Let us now turn to the content of the electoral reforms... what needs to be done and what can be done.

Content of Electoral Reforms

Given the complexity of the electoral system and its intimate linkages with several other systems of the country, it is not possible to go into anything like complete details in a chapter such as this, so of necessity, this chapter will be confined ourselves to some major issues. A good place to begin with is what might be called the 'representativeness' of our electoral system which looks at how representative is the outcome of the election of what might be perceived as the 'will' of the People.

Representativeness

Let us look at a hypothetical scenario. For ease of calculation and understanding, let us assume that a constituency has 100 eligible and *registered* voters. It is important to remember that the number 100 is that of people who are eligible and actually registered to vote, or, in other words, whose names exist on the electoral roll, or what is commonly called 'voter list'. Let us further assume that there are six candidates contesting a particular election in this constituency. Given that voter turnout is usually around 50 to 60 per cent in most elections (thought it does exceed 70 per cent in once in a while), taking the voter turnout to be 60 per cent, 60 out of the 100 registered voters actually vote in the election, making the *votes polled* to be 60. With six candidates in the fray, if one of the candidates gets 11 votes, four get 10 votes each, and one gets 9, the one who gets 11 votes wins, and this win is considered legitimate making this person legally the 'elected representative' for that constituency.

What gets missed out are some vital facts such as the elected person got only 11 divided by 60, ie. 18.33 per cent of the *votes polled*, or, in other words, only 18.33 per cent of those *who voted*, voted in his/her favour. The flip side of this is that 60-11= 49 people can be effectively perceived to have voted *against* the candidate who was elected. 49 out of 60 works out to 81.67 per cent! This is when we consider only the votes *polled*. If we look at the *registered* votes, then we find that out of the total of 100 registered voters, only 11 have voted in his/her favour, which means that 100-11=89, or 89 per cent *did not vote for this candidate*! Can we call a person who has got the active support of only 11 per cent of the total registered voters in a constituency, the duly elected, or truly representative of the constituency? The answer is left with the reader.

The next question, which also each of the readers will need to answer for themselves, is whether it is reasonable to even expect such a person to look after the interest of the entire constituency, or the entire electorate of the constituency.

Why and how does this happen?

This happens because of the 'first-past-the-post' system of election that we have adopted.

First-Past-the-Post

This system when seen in the context of multiplicity of political parties, results in such anomalous outcomes. Leaving the hypothetical example described above behind, actual data is not much different. In the last Lok Sabha election in 2014, a total of 331 Lok Sabha MPs (out of 543, ie. 60.95%) were elected with less than 50% of the votes cast/polled, out of which 239 (44.01%) were elected with votes cast/polled between 41-50%, 99 (18.23%) were elected with less than 40% of the votes cast/polled, and 4 (0.007%) were elected with less than 30% of the votes cast/polled.

If we consider the total number of registered voters, then the percentages are even more revealing. In this case, 539 out of 543 (99.26%) were elected with less than 50% of thetotal registered voters in their constituency, out of which only 37 (a mere*6.81%*) were elected withtotal registered voters in their constituencybetween 41-50%, 475 (87.47%) were elected with less than 40%total registered voters in their constituency, 211 (39%) were elected with less than 30% oftotal registered voters in their constituency, and 19 (0.034%) were elected with less than 20 % oftotal registered voters in their constituency.

It should be clear by now that the current system results in something like 70 per cent or more votes, which indeed is the majority, going waste; and this proportion of the electorate is left without representation or voice in the elected body, Parliament or State Legislatures. How representative such 'elected representatives' are of the entire electorate does not require much imagination.

The Swing

Another outcome of the 'first-past-the-post' election system is that often a party with as little as 30-35 per cent of the total votes cast in the country can end up with as much as 70-75 per cent of the seats in Parliament or State Assembly, whereas another party which may have polled 27-28 per cent of the votes, might get only about 25 per cent of the seats. As a psephologist would say, a 'swing' of 2 to 3 per cent in votes can result in a huge difference in the number of seats won. As we know, though the Bharatiya Janata Party (BJP) got only 31% of the votes cast in the 2014 election to the Lok Sabha, it won in 282 out of 543 (51.93%) of the seats. The outcome of the 2015 Assembly election in Delhi was more bizarre. The Aam Aadmi Party (AAP) won 95.71% of the seats (67 out of 70) with only 54.3% of the votes cast. The case of Bahujan Samaj Party (BSP) is even more curious. It got the third highest percentage of votes at 4.1% (after BJP-31% and Congress-19%) but it did not get a single seat. In its stronghold, Uttar Pradesh (UP), it got nearly 20% of the votes, again remaining third (with BJP 42.3% and Samajwadi Party 22.2%) but failed to get even one of its candidates elected.

The List System

A useful way to judge the efficacy of election systems is to assess how closely they translate national votes into parliamentary seats won. This assessment requires that one looks at both, the vote-seat relationship and the level of wasted votes. After analysing all possibilities,[8] the Law Commission suggested, in its 170th report, a *combination* of the 'first-past-the-post' system and the 'list system'. The proposed addition of the 'list system' would require that the number of seats in the Lok Sabha be increased by 25 per cent, and these additional seats be filled from lists submitted by political parties at the time of filing nominations, in proportion to the percentage of votes polled by parties nationally, the party polling the highest number of votes getting the highest number of seats, and so on.

Divide and Rule

Another outcome of the above is what might be called the fragmentation of the polity. This can also be referred to as the 'divide and rule'

---

[8] The Law Commission, in its 170th report, reviewed all the 212 parliamentary electoral systems listed in *The Global Distribution of Electoral Systems* in order to assess what might be the most appropriate for India at its current stage of political evolution.

phenomenon which is popularly associated with the British government in India. What is often not recognised is that we seem to have also inherited this 'divide and rule' policy, and its operation has continued over the last many years to the overall detriment of the nation.

An interesting question is who is using this 'divide and rule' policy? Why? And How?

The answer is contained in the question itself. Who *can* use such a policy except the rulers? And who has been ruling the country for the last 60-some years? The answer: The Politicians.

Why have the politicians being dividing the nation? Simply because it gets them elected. And they have been doing so by continuing to split political parties into smaller and smaller factions, thereby also fragmenting the electorate and the polity at large.

To begin with the big ones, the Indian National Congress has undergone five major splits since 1969 giving rise to eight different formations in addition to the so-called 'parent' grouping. The greatest achiever in the regard is what was called the Janata Party in 1977. After splitting countless times, the number of formations it has resulted in seems to add up to 24! The regional parties too suffer from such splits. Starting with the DK of Periyar Ramaswamy, we now have the DMK, AIADMK, MDMK, and the PMK in Tamil Nadu. The irony of parties splitting was captured in a newspaper headline a few years ago, 'Further Split in Janata Dal (United)'. Possibly, the ultimate practitioner of this art was once a Young Turk and later Elder Statesman, Chandra Sekhar, who appeared to be in a party all by himself. The last champion of this phenomenon possibly was Subramanian Swamy who seemed to be the sole member of what was left of the Janata Party till he merged this party in the BJP on 11 August 2013.[9] This fragmentation of the polity seems to call for replacement of the phrase 'unity in diversity' with 'utility of diversity' at least for the politicians.

At this juncture, it should be clarified that it is quite common, particularly these days, to put almost the entire blame of the current state of affairs on the so-called political class in the country. But all those who

---

9 "Subramanian Swamy's Janta Party merges with BJP. *The Indian Express*. 11 August 2013, accessed on 25 May 2015

would have us believe that all that is wrong has been caused by the political class seem to overlook the fact that the political class does not exist or develop in isolation or in vacuum, but that it emerges and evolves out of the society at large. Therefore the society at large, of which all of us are a part, cannot escape responsibility for the existing state of affairs. While the so-called political class cannot be assigned the complete responsibility for the current state of affairs, they cannot be entirely absolved of it either. This will be discussed in some detail later but first it should be noted that a substantial portion of the behaviour of the political class can be explained as a logical response to the broader social system within which they have to operate. And the electoral system is a major and immediate part of that broader social system. Consequently, one way to change the behaviour of the political class would be to change the system in which they have to operate and to which they have to respond. This is where a comprehensive view of electoral reforms becomes important.

Right to Reject

There are other proposals for reducing the fragmentation of the polity. One such stems from, but does not end with, the so-called 'right to reject'. The Law Commission, in its 170th report, presented it as 'an alternative method of election'.

It has two major components. One, according to this method, no candidate should be declared elected unless s/he has obtained '50 per cent plus one' of the valid votes cast in the constituency. In case no candidate gets more than 50 per cent votes, then there would be a 'run-off' election between the two candidates receiving the highest number of votes. The rationale for this is 'to curtail the significance and role played by caste and community considerations in the electoral process, since there is hardly any constituency in the country where any one particular caste or community can command more than 50 per cent of the votes. This means that a candidate has to carry with him/her several castes and communities to get elected.'

The second component of the 'alternative method of election' is the possibility for voters to cast what is called a 'negative vote', by which the voter indicates that s/he is not inclined to vote for any of the candidates on the ballot paper. The reason for suggesting a negative vote is 'to put moral pressure on political parties not to put forward candidates with undesirable records such as criminals, corrupt elements, and persons with unsavory background.'

What the 170th report of the Law Commission termed as the 'negative vote' has now come to be called the 'right to reject'. It is also referred to as the demand for a button with the option 'None of the above' or NOTA for short, on the EVMs. A 2013 judgment[10] by the Supreme Court mandated the inclusion of the NOTA button on the EVMs. However, the Election Commission in its implementation of the judgment has only followed the letter of the judgment but has stopped short of ensuring the spirit of the judgment. The result is that as of now, even if 1999 voters, out of a total of 2000, press the NOTA button and just one voter presses the button for a particular candidate, that candidate is declared elected.

The spirit of the judgment would be fulfilled if the Election Commission had laid down the following procedure while implementing the judgment of the Supreme Court, which is an adaptation[11] of the Law Commission's recommendation of 'Fifty per cent plus one' in its 170th report.

1. If NOTA gets the highest number of votes cast, ie., more than any of the candidates, none of the candidates should be declared to be elected, and a fresh election should be held.
2. In the fresh election, the candidates who contested the earlier election should not be allowed to contest since they have already *not been chosen* by the electors, and a fresh slate of candidates should contest.
3. In the fresh election, the candidate who gets the largest number of votes should be declared to be elected, *provided* s/he secures 'Fifty per cent plus one' or more of the votes cast.
4. If the candidate who gets the largest number of votes cast does not get 'Fifty per cent plus one' of the votes cast, then there should

---

[10] http://www.judis.nic.in/supremecourt/imgs1.aspx?filename=40835, accessed on 25 May 2015.

[11] http://www.asianage.com/debate/nota-ble-impact-098, accessed on 25 May 2015.

be a 'run-off' election between the top two candidates who get the largest number of votes cast.

Five per cent of vote

It is in this context of reducing the fragmentation of the polity and improving the representativeness of the electoral system that the Law Commission has made another recommendation in its 170th report, which may be considered somewhat controversial. This is that only those political parties be allowed representation in Parliament who poll at least 5 per cent of the vote on a country-wide basis. The total votes polled by each party are to be tallied at the end of the election and candidates of those parties who have polled less than 5 per cent of the total vote on a national basis will not be declared elected even if they have polled the highest number of votes in their constituencies. In such cases candidates securing the next highest number of votes will be declared elected provided, of course, the political party of such a candidate has polled more than 5 per cent of vote nation-wide.

Once again, this sounds complicated but undeniably the Indian people have the genius to discuss such proposals knowledgably and come to informed conclusions, *provided* there is a true and open discussions on the merits and possibilities of various options. We need to choose a system which is appropriate to our stage of democratic evolution in keeping with our social realities and also our aspirations. But such a debate has not happened so far.

Financing

Another major issue is that of financing. Financing is often thought of in terms of financing of elections and that is where the Indrajit Gupta Committee Report is most often, and very widely, quoted. However, there are two issues involved here: one of financing of elections and the other the financing of political activity in general, and financing of political parties in particular.

State Funding

It is claimed very often, if not universally, that the Indrajit Gupta Committee *recommended* state funding of elections. This is not entirely true. The Indrajit Gupta Committee recommended only *partial* funding of elections by the state, and that too only in kind and not in cash.

All those who quote the Indrajit Gupta Committee report in support of state funding of elections seem to overlook the opening paragraph of the 'Conclusion' of the report which is worth reproducing: 'Before concluding, the Committee cannot help expressing its considered view that *its recommendations* being limited in nature and confined to only one of the aspects of the electoral reforms *may bring about only some cosmetic changes in the electoral sphere*. What is needed, however, is an immediate overhauling of the electoral process whereby elections are freed from evil influence of all vitiating factors, particularly, criminalisation of politics. It goes without saying that money power and muscle power go together to vitiate the electoral process and it is their combined effect of which is sullying the purity of electoral contests and effecting free and fair elections. Meaningful electoral reforms in other spheres of electoral activity are also urgently needed' (Emphasis added).

The issue of state funding also attracted the attention of the Law Commission of India who devoted one full part (Part IV) of their 208-page 170th report to *Control of Election Expenses*. This part of the Commission's 170th report contains an 11-page chapter on *State Funding*. The entire chapter should be read to get a proper understanding of the complexity of state funding, but here mentioning only the concluding paragraph (4.3.4) would suffice. It says:

> Conclusions – After considering views expressed by the participants in the seminars and by various persons and organisations in their responses and after perusing relevant literature on the subject, the Law Commission is of the opinion that in the present circumstances only partial state funding could be contemplated more as a first step towards total state funding *but it is absolutely essential* that *before the idea of state funding (whether partial or total) is resorted to, the provisions suggested in this report relating to political parties (including the provisions ensuring internal democracy, internal structures) and maintenance of accounts, their auditing and submission to Election Commission*

> *are implemented.* In other words, the implementation of the provisions recommended in Chapter one Part three should be *pre-condition to the implementation of the provisions relating to partial state funding* set out in the working paper in the Law Commission (partial funding, as already stated, has also been recommended by the Indrajit Gupta Committee). *If without such pre-conditions, state funding, even if partial is resorted to, it would not serve the purpose underlying the idea of state funding.* The idea of state funding is to eliminate the influence of money power and also to eliminate corporate funding, black money support and raising of funds in the name of elections by the parties and their leaders. *The state funding, without the aforesaid pre-conditions, would merely become another source of funds for the political parties and candidates at the cost of public exchequer.* We are, therefore, of the opinion that *the proposals relating to state funding contained in the Inderjit Gupta Committee Report should be implemented only after or simultaneously with the implementation of the provisions contained in this Report relating to political parties, viz. deletion of Explanation 1 to section 77, maintenance of accounts and their submission etc. and the provisions governing the functioning of political parties contained in chapters I and II of Part IV and Chapter I of Part III. The state funding, even if partial, should never be resorted to unless the other provisions mentioned aforesaid are implemented lest the very idea may prove counter-productive and may defeat the every object underlying the idea of state funding of elections'* (Emphasis added).

The National Commission to Review the Working of the Constitution 2001, headed by Justice Venkatachaliah, refrained from specifically commenting on the desirability or otherwise of state funding of elections but reiterated the point of the 170th report of the Law Commission that the appropriate framework for regulation of political parties would need to be implemented before proposals for state funding are considered. The actual wording of the NCRWC's report is, 'Any system of state funding of elections bears a close nexus to the regulation of working of political parties by law and to the creation of a foolproof mechanism under law with a view to implementing the financial limits strictly. Therefore, proposal for state funding should be deferred till these regulator mechanisms are *firmly* in position' (Emphasis added) (Para 4.14.5).

255th Report of the Law Commission

Electoral and political funding are a major focus of the 255th report of the Law Commission. The first and the longest substantive chapter of this report is titled *Election Finance Reform.* It deals with the issue of election finance very comprehensively, listing out the current law on election finance and the need for reform. This is followed by a listing and discussion of the current laws regulating election expenditure, contributions and disclosure. Next is a comparative analysis of electoral expenditure, disclosure and contribution laws from some of what are considered more mature democracies, United Kingdom, Germany, the USA, Australia, Japan and the Philippines, followed by a comment on state funding of elections. The chapter concludes with comprehensive set of recommendations.

A very important part of this chapter is the section titled *Understanding the reality of election financing today.* In this section, the Commission makes very significant, and realistic, observations, some of which are worth reproducing in full.

> Although there are legal provisions limiting election expenditure for candidates and governing the disclosure of contributions by companies to political parties, the same is not properly regulated, either due to loopholes in the law, or improper enforcement (Para 2.27.1).
>
> This is evident from the 2001 Consultation Paper of the NCRWC (National Commission to Review the Working of the Constitution) on Electoral Reforms, which estimates that actual campaign expenditure by candidates is '*in the range of about twenty to thirty times the said limits.*' In fact, one of the major concerns regarding expenditure and contribution regulation is that the apparently low ceiling of candidate expenditure increases the demand for black money cash contributions and drives campaign expenditure underground,

causing parties to conceal their actual source of funds and expenditure (Para 2.27.2).

Therefore, there is clearly under reporting of election expenditure and opacity of political contribution. Part of the explanation lies in the lacunae in the law, and part in black money and poor enforcement (Para 2.27.6).

There are various loopholes in the laws regarding election expenditure, contribution and disclosure (Para 2.27.7).

Most importantly… the subject of regulation under Section 77 of the RPA only covers individual 'candidates', and not political parties (Para 2.27.7).

Regarding political contribution, the Rs 20,000 disclosure limit can be easily evaded by writing multiple cheques below Rs 20,000 each, or giving the money in cash. Nor is the profit-linked contribution limit of 7.5% a significant restriction for large companies… while the law creates incentives for disclosure vide tax exemptions, it can be outweighed by the disincentive created by the loss of anonymity, especially given that in many instances big donors support multiple parties, or change their support, and do not want this information to be disclosed for fear of reprisal (Para 2.27.12).

'Disclosure norms need to be strengthened… The ECI's transparency guidelines do not have statutory authority and there is no legal consequence for non-compliance. Further, unlike many of the countries… political parties and candidates file their returns with the ECI, without putting up the information online (on the ECI's website) or making it easily available for public inspection (barring an RTI). This is essential to bring about transparency in the public domain and to let the voters know the donors, contributions and expenditures of the parties and candidates. Moreover, in many cases such as compliance with section 29C of the RPA (regulating political party disclosure), the only penalty for noncompliance is losing the income tax exemption. This is not a significant enough deterrent to parties (Para 2.27.14).

The primary rationale followed by the Commission is that, 'Disclosure is at the heart of public supervision of political finance'. Ensuring disclosure, according to the Commission, 'requires strict implementation of the provisions of the RPA, the IT Act, the Company Act, and the ECI transparency guidelines which need to be given statutory backing.' In addition, the evasion or dilution of disclosure 'has to be tackled through a stricter implementation of the anti-corruption laws and RTI and improved disclosure norms.'[12]

The essence of the recommendations made in the 255th report is to amend various laws, the Representation of the People Act (RP Act), the Income Tax Act and the Companies Act. The most significant amendments suggested are to the RP Act. Some of the major recommendations are the following:

- The accounts of political parties should be 'audited by a qualified and practicing chartered accountant from a panel of such accountants maintained for the purpose by the Comptroller and Auditor General.' This differs from the current practice where political parties choose their auditors entirely on their own.
- Today, political parties are not required to disclose the source of any contribution or donation which is less than Rs 20,000. There are instances of parties who declare donations worth hundreds of crores (yes, hundreds of crores), claim and get income tax exemptions on that, and do not disclose the source claiming that each of the donations was less than Rs 20,000. The report recommends that political parties 'disclose such particulars (the names, addresses and PAN card numbers of these donors along with the amount of each donation) even for contributions less

---

[12] This sounds ironic when the highest authority for implementing the Right to Information Act, the Central Information Commission (CIC) says that it 'is bereft of the tools to get its orders complied with'. See CIC's decision of 16 March 2015 regarding non-compliance of CIC's order declaring six national political parties as public authorities under the RTI Act which the six parties have ignored and not implemented even after 21 months have elapsed since the order was issued on 03 May 2013. The March 2015 order of the CIC can be seen at http://www.rti.india.gov.in/cic_decisions/CIC_CC_C_2015_000182_M_149924.pdf, and the original May 2013 decision can be seen at http://www.rti.india.gov.in/cic_decisions/CIC_SM_C_2011_000838_M_111223.pdf.

than Rs 20,000, if such contributions exceed Rs 20 crore or 20 % of the party's total contributions, whichever is less.' It recommends consequential amendments to be made to the Conduct of Election Rules and the Income Tax Act.

- Political parties today are very lax about submitting their election expenditure statements and the Election Commission does not have any explicit powers to take any action or discipline the defaulting parties. As a matter of fact, the Law Ministry, on behalf of the Government of India, stated in an affidavit submitted to the Supreme Court in a case about a year ago that the Election Commission, under Section 10-A, had power only to 'receive' the statement of election expenditure of a *candidate* but not to 'scrutinise' it! The Law Commission report recommends that, 'Express penalties, apart from losing tax benefits, should be imposed on political parties… for the non-compliance with the disclosure provisions of proposed section 29D of the RPA. This should include a daily fine of Rs 25,000 for each day of non-compliance, with the possibility of de-registration if the default continues beyond 90 days. Further, ECI may levy a fine of up to Rs 50 lakhs if its finds any particulars in the party's statements as having been falsified.'

While most of the recommendations in the 255th report of the Law Commission are unexceptionable and some are even praiseworthy, there are a few that could have been different.

The first issue is a ***possible limit or cap on election expenditure by political parties***. While the Law Commission has not made a specific recommendation in this regard, it has mentioned this issue at least at two places which clarifies what the Commission feels on this issue. The Commission observes in Para 2.28.3 of the report, 'Political parties are free to spend any amount as long as it is for the general party propaganda, and not towards an independent candidate. Thus, there is no ceiling on party expenditure. *It is recommended that the law on this point does not change, namely that there are no caps on party expenditure under the RPA* given that it would be very difficult to fix an actual, viable limit of such a cap and then implement such a cap. In any event, as the experience with section 77(1) discussed above reveals, in the

2009 Lok Sabha elections, on average candidates showed election expenditures of 59% of the total expenses limit. There is no reason why the same phenomenon of under-reporting will not transpire amongst parties' (Italics added).

Transparency

It is further observed, in Para 2.28.4 of the report, that, 'Placing legislative ceilings on party expenditure or contributions will not automatically solve the problem, especially without putting in place a viable alternative of complete state funding of elections (which in itself is next to impossible right now). Our previous experience in prohibiting corporate donations in 1969 did not lead to a reduction in corporate donations. Instead, in the absence of any alternative model for raising funds, it greatly increased illegal, under the table and black money donations.'

The above two paragraphs, read in the context of the chapter on Election Finance Reform, give the impression that the Commission is accepting lesser of the two evils, preferring expediency over doing the right thing. The observation of the Commission that 'it would be very difficult to fix an actual, viable limit of such a cap' is debatable at best. It is admitted that it is indeed 'very difficult to fix an actual, viable limit of such a cap' but one also has to go into the reasons *why* it is so difficult. The obvious reason that the Commission seems to have refused to see is *lack of financial transparency* in the functioning of political parties. IF political parties were transparent about their financial affairs or were made to be transparent, it would not only be possible but would actually be quite easy 'to fix an actual, viable limit of such a cap'. How to make political parties financially transparent is the question that needs to be gone into to take this issue to its logical conclusion, which regrettably the Law Commission has stopped short of doing. Some action is already on in this regard as mentioned in endnote xii above.

Reliable Data

There is *no reliable data available* for the expenditure during elections. An analysis of expenditure affidavits of 5,743 candidates after the 2009 Lok Sabha elections showed that only four candidates had declared expenditure above the then limit of Rs16 lakh. Thirty candidates had declared that they had spent between 90 to 95 per cent of the limit. The remaining (5743-4-30=) 5,719 or 99.58 percent said that they had spent between 45 to 55 per cent of the limit. At the same time there is widespread clamour that the ceiling on expenditure is too low and it should be increased. There is obviously a mismatch somewhere, and *all estimates of election expenditure are far above the limit.*

The Law Commission has itself observed, in its 255th report, that '(T)he experience with section 77(1) discussed above reveals, in the 2009 Lok Sabha elections, on average candidates showed election expenditures of 59% of the total expenses limit. There is no reason why the same phenomenon of under-reporting will not transpire amongst parties.' If the Law Commission found that placing limits on the election expenditure by candidates has not served any purpose because of large scale under-reporting, and therefore it came to the conclusion that laying down any limits for the election expenditure to be incurred by political parties would also be of no use as there would be large-scale under-reporting, then it would be logical for it, the Law Commission, to remove the limits from the expenditure by candidates also. The Commission has, of course, not done so and has not stated the reasons for not doing it.

Having limits on the election expenditure of candidates and not having such limits on the election expenditure of political parties is obviously inconsistent. A PIL[13] filed by the Association for Democratic Reforms (ADR) in the Delhi High Court has been admitted and is currently at the stage of arguments. The petition has requested the court to:

(a) Introduce ceiling on the election expenditure of political parties, on and during the Elections;
(b) Direct the Political Parties to submit expenditure statements, beginning one year prior to the elections; and
(c) Direct the Political Parties to submit the Account Statements of Income and Expenditure, periodically, ie. once a month before the declaration of the election, and at least once a week during the elections.

---

[13] http://www.adrindia.org/sites/default/files/ADR_Writ_Election_Expenditure.pdf, accessed on 27 May 2015.

Financing of Political Activity

In addition to funding of elections, a very crucial issue is the funding of political activity in the country in general, and that of the funding of political parties in particular. The financing of political parties remains one of the most closely-guarded secrets in the country despite the almost chilling observations contained in the Vohra Committee report.

When a civil society organisation[14] applied for copies of income tax returns of political parties under the Right to Information Act, it was opposed, and strongly, by pretty much all political parties. The application had to go all the way up to the Central Information Commission who decided, despite arguments by senior advocates on behalf of political parties to deny the information, that the income tax returns should be accessible to citizens.

Information gleaned from the thus disclosed income tax returns, combined with the statement of donations that political parties are required to file with the Election Commission of India under the Representation of People Act to avail of 100 per cent exemption from income tax, revealed that sources or explanations of *sources were available for only 20-25 per cent of the total income of political parties.* Seventy Five to eighty percent of the income is unexplained. In the 20-25 per cent for which sources were disclosed, there were also some cases of large-scale corporate funding, some of which appeared, at least on lifting the corporate veil, to be possibly of foreign origin. The Delhi High Court has held that it has 'no hesitation in arriving at the view that *prima-facie* the acts of the respondents inter-se, as highlighted in the present petition, clearly fall foul of the ban imposed under the Foreign Contribution (Regulation) Act, 1976 as the donations accepted by the political parties from Sterlite and Sesa accrue from 'Foreign Sources' within the meaning of law.'[15] What it means is that the Delhi High Court has held that the BJP and the Congress are guilty of violating the Foreign Contributions (Regulation) Act, commonly known as FCRA, by having accepted

---

[14] Association for Democratic Reforms (www.adrindia.org)

[15] http://www.adrindia.org/sites/default/files/ADR%20vs.%20UOI%20%28Delhi%20High%20Court%20judgment%20on%20foreign%20%20funding%20received%20by%20INC%20and%20BJP%29.pdf, accessed on 25 May 2015.

donations of foreign money. Both the parties have appealed to the Supreme Court and the appeal is underway.

Requests to political parties under the RTI Act to provide information on their financial affairs have been denied on the pretext that they are not 'public authorities' under the provisions of the RTI Act. The Central Information Commission (CIC) decided on 03 May 2013[16] that six national political parties (Congress, BJP, NCP, BSP, CPM, and CPI) are *public authorities* under the RTI Act, and directed all these parties to appoint Public Information Officers within six weeks of the decision and to provide the information asked for within four weeks thereafter. None of the six parties complied with the decision of the CIC.

Complaints were then filed for non-compliance of the CIC's decision. Several hearings took placed but none of the six political parties showed up for the hearings. The CIC then issued 'show cause' notices to all the six parties and did this more than once. All the parties blatantly ignored all the notices of the CIC. After two years of hearings, the CIC decided on 16 March 2015 that 'the Commission is bereft of the tools to get its orders complied with'.[17] A petition[18] has now been filed in the Supreme Court to get the CIC's decision implemented.

The above situation, combined with the Law Commission's observation in its 170th report, that 'people are generally likely to enter politics or contest election for getting rich overnight', raises certain uncomfortable issues. Taking in to consideration the recommendations of the Indrajit Gupta Committee, the Law Commission of India and the NCRWC, and the attempts that political parties make to keep the sources of their finances secret, the inescapable conclusion seems to be that there is something extremely serious in that the entire political establishment is not willing to disclose and will go to any lengths to keep it hidden. This is, to say the least, very worrying and puts the entire democratic edifice in the country at risk.

---

16 http://www.rti.india.gov.in/cic_decisions/CIC_SM_C_2011_000838_M_111223.pdf, accessed on 25 May 2015.

17 http://www.rti.india.gov.in/cic_decisions/CIC_CC_C_2015_000182_M_149924.pdf, accessed on May 25, 2015.

18 http;//articles.economictimes.indiatimes.com/2015-05-19/news/62369089_1_political-parties-such-donations-transparency-law, accessed on May 25, 2015.

No worthwhile measures concerning financing of elections can even be contemplated till there is reliable data about the cost of elections. The largest proportion of election expenditure is presumably done by political parties. As of now, there is no reliable data about the financial affairs of political parties. The foremost requirement for getting a clear and comprehensible picture of financing of elections is to get financial transparency in the financial affairs of political parties. Any discussion of state funding either of elections or of political activity or political parties can only be discussed after transparency of financial affairs of political parties is ensured.

The detailing of this can of course be worked out and a lot of proposals are available. For example, the Election Commission recently got the Institute of Chartered Accountants of India (ICAI) to draw up guidelines concerning the formats, frequency, scrutiny etc. of the accounts to be maintained by political parties. These guidelines should be made mandatory, and any failure to comply with these should lead to automatic de-registration of the party. This has apparently been discussed with political parties and seems not to have found favour with them, just like all other measure for financial transparency as has been discussed earlier.

Functioning of Political Parties

Arguably, the most important issue that critically affects the entire gamut of electoral and political activity in the country is that of the functioning of political parties. It is obvious and does not need any discussion that political parties are absolutely necessary for the functioning of a representative democracy such as ours. The Law Commission has also said that a democracy and particularly, a parliamentary democracy, without political parties is inconceivable. Even the Supreme Court has held that political parties are integral to the governance of a democratic society. They perform the critical function of mobilising and organising public opinion and will, and function as a link between the public at large and the government, particularly its political wing.

While they are a necessary mechanism for the functioning of a democracy, it is interesting to note that our Constitution is silent on the issue of functioning of political parties. As a matter of fact, the expression 'political parties' does not even appear in the main text of the

Constitution, and figures only in the Tenth Schedule, which was added by the Constitution (Fifty-second Amendment) Act, 1985, with effect from 01 March 1985. And this refers to *anti-defection* provisions.

Some of us might find it surprising that the Constituent Assembly did not deem it necessary to mention anything about political parties in the Constitution. A plausible reason for this is that it was a group of principled and high-minded people who drafted the Constitution. In their deliberations for the future of the nation, they were perhaps influenced by their idealism, particularly in the immediate after-glow of independence. It can be safely assumed they must have thought that people similar to them will lead the country even in the years to come. The Indian genius has certainly evolved over the last sixty-eight years and at least in some ways, the socio-political milieu of India has changed almost beyond recognition. Some of the assumptions and expectations of members of the Constituent Assembly are, therefore and unfortunately, not valid today.

This issue of lack of internal democracy in the functioning of political parties also engaged the attention of the Law Commission. While working on its 170th report, the Commission had prepared a working paper which they had circulated widely and also discussed in four seminars across the country. After considering the vast number of responses received in response to their working paper and the views expressed in the four seminars, the Law Commission observed in its 170th report that, 'if *democracy* and *accountability* constitute the core of our constitutional system, the *same concepts must also apply to and bind the political parties* which are integral to parliamentary democracy. It is the political parties that form the government, man the Parliament and run the governance of the country. It is, therefore, necessary to introduce internal democracy, financial transparency and accountability in the working of the political parties. A political party which does not respect democratic principles in its internal working cannot be expected to respect those principles in the governance of the country. It cannot be dictatorship internally and democratic in its functioning outside'(Emphasis added).

After coming the above conclusion, the Commission proposed that a new part titled *Organisation of Political Parties and matters incidental thereto* be added to the Representation of People Act. This would specify things such as regular holding of elections, transparency of financial affairs. Non-observance of these provisions would attract de-recognition as a political party. It would mean that the party will cease to exist legally as a political party and consequently would neither be able to put up candidates for elections nor be entitled to facilities and benefits available to registered political parties. These recommendations, suggesting legal provisions for the functioning of political parties, were possibly the most significant part of the Law Commission's entire 170th report, and this is the most significant and urgent reform needed to correct our electoral system.

The 255th report of the Law Commission has also dealt with this issue in detail. It makes a very important distinction between *procedural democracy* (the practice of universal adult franchise, periodic elections, secret ballot) and *substantive democracy* which it describes 'to refer to the *internal democratic functioning of the parties*, which purportedly represent the people' (Italics added).

It makes a further 'distinction between the regulation of party *practice* and party *ideoloxgy* as components of internal and inner party democracy' and says, 'Of primary relevance in this chapter, is the first concern regarding the regulation of the *practice* of political parties in terms of internal elections, recruitment of party cadres, and development and training activities.'

Noting that 'Currently, there is no express provision for internal democratic regulation of political parties in India', and 'Consequently, there is no mechanism to review a party's practice against the principles enshrined in the Constitution or against the requirements of the ECI's Guidelines and Application Format for the Registration of Political Parties under Section 29A', it follows the lead given by its predecessor, the 15th Law Commission in its170th report. The 15th Law Commission had observed the following in its 170th report:

> On the parity of the above reasoning, it must be said that if democracy and accountability constitute the core of our constitutional system, the same concepts must also apply to and bind the political parties which are integral to parliamentary democracy. It is the political parties that form the government, man the Parliament and run the governance of the country. It is

> therefore, necessary to introduce internal democracy, financial transparency and accountability in the working of the political parties. A political party which does not respect democratic principles in its internal working cannot be expected to respect those principles in the governance of the country. It cannot be dictatorship internally and democratic in its functioning outside (Para 3.1.2.1).
>
> 'With a view to introduce and ensure internal democracy in the functioning of political parties, to make their working transparent and open and to ensure that the political parties become effective instruments of achieving the constitutional goals set out in the Preamble and Parts III and IV of the Constitution of India, it is necessary to regulate *by law* their formation and functioning (Para 3.1.2) (Italics added).

Following the above, the 20th Law Commission, in the current, the 255th, report makes very significant recommendations, two critical ones of which are the following:

- Insert a new Chapter (IV-C) into the RP Act 'dealing with the "Regulation of Political Parties"' and incorporating the (15th Law) Commission's previous recommendations in its 170th Report with certain modifications. Thus, sections 29J to 29Q will deal with internal democracy, party Constitutions, party organisation, internal elections, candidate selection, voting procedures and the ECI's power to de-register a party in certain cases of non-compliance.
- Another section, section 29R should be inserted in the same Part, providing for the de-registration of a political party for failure to contest Parliamentary or State elections for ten consecutive years.

It is clear from the above that there have been repeated recommendations and proposals for putting some order and logic in the functioning of political parties, but the entire political establishment has repeatedly resisted all such attempts. This is the most important and critical reform that is needed to improve the functioning of the entire electoral and political systems.

Reducing Criminalisation of Politics

One of the initiatives which began this phase of electoral reforms that started about fifteen years ago was to reduce the impact of criminalisation of politics. A public interest litigation (PIL) was filed in the Delhi High Court by a civil society organisation[19] in 1999, seeking disclosure of criminal, financial, and educational antecedents of candidates contesting elections to Parliament and State Assemblies. The Delhi High Court upheld this request in a judgment[20] on 02 November 2000 making it mandatory for all candidates contesting elections to the Parliament and State Assemblies to file an affidavit as an essential part of their nomination forms, disclosing if they had any pending criminal cases against them, their and their spouses' and dependents' financial assets and liabilities, and their educational qualifications. The Union of India went to the Supreme Court against the above decision of the Delhi High Court in a special leave petition (SLP). The Supreme Court rejected the appeal of the Government of India and upheld the decision of the Delhi High Court in a judgment[21] on 02 May 2002.

When the Election Commission issued a notification to implement the Supreme Court's judgment of May 2002, not only the government of the day but the entire political establishment of the day was very upset. An all-party meeting attended by 22 political parties on 08 July 2002 decided to amend the Representation of the People Act 1951 (RP Act) to nullify the effect of the Supreme Court judgment. It was also decided that the amendment will be done in that very session of Parliament that was going on. A draft Bill was prepared for the purpose but it could not be introduced in the Parliament as the Lok Sabha was adjourned *sine die* due to repeated disruptions caused by what was called the Petrol Pump Scam. The Cabinet of the day decided to issue an Ordinance. Given that Article 123 of the Constitution gives the President the power 'to promulgate Ordinances during recess of Parliament 'if 'at any time, except when both Houses of Parliament are in session, the President is satisfied that

---

19 Association for Democratic Reforms (www.adrindia.org).

20 http://adrindia.org/sites/default/files/DELHI_HIGH_COURT_JUDGEMENT_NOVEMBER_2000.pdf, accessed on 27 May 2015.

21 http://adrindia.org/sites/default/files/Supreme_Court's_judgement_2nd_May_2002.pdf, accessed on 26 May 2015.

circumstances exist which render it necessary for him to take immediate action'. It is obvious that the Cabinet believed that it was necessary to take 'immediate action' to prevent disclosure of criminal, financial, and educational antecedents of candidates contesting elections to Parliament and State Assemblies! When the President returned the Ordinance, it was sent back to him without any modifications and following the tradition, he had to sign it.

The Ordinance (and the consequent Act passed by Parliament[22]) was challenged in the Supreme Court. The Supreme Court, in a judgment[23] on 13 March 2003, ruled the amendment of the RP Act to be 'unconstitutional' and 'null and void'. It restored its 02 May 2002 judgment. This is how the disclosure of criminal, financial, and educational antecedents of candidates became possible.

There have been several other initiatives to reduce the impact of criminalisation on politics. One very important judgment is what has come to be known as the Lily Thomas judgment[24] which declared 'sub-section (4) of Section 8 of the Act as *ultra vires* the Constitution'. The effect of this judgment is that any MP or MLA, once convicted by even a lower court in a criminal case of imprisonment of two years or more, cannot continue to be an MP or MLA unless the conviction is set aside by a higher court. This was the reason why Lalu Prasad Yadav had to leave Parliament, once he was convicted by the lower court, and why J Jayalalithaa had to stop being the Chief Minister of Tamil Nadu once she was convicted by a lower court and could take over as Chief Minister only after being acquitted by the High Court.

What is Likely to Happen?

The initiation, formulation, and implementation of electoral reforms rest with the government of the day, under the overall guidance and direction of the Parliament. We are, therefore, in the quagmire where

---

[22] The Ordinance was presented to the Parliament in the very next session and was passed *unanimously*.

[23] http://adrindia.org/sites/default/files/Supreme_Court's_judgement_13th_March_2003.pdf, accessed on 26 May 2015.

[24] http://adrindia.org/sites/default/files/Lily%20Thomas%20Vs.%20Union%20of%20India%20(Judgment).pdf, accessed on May 26, 2015.

politicians are the ultimate authority to decide whether reforms which disturb their existing, familiar and comfortable arrangement should be implemented or not. Given the current political milieu of the country, it is anyone's guess what is likely to happen. A realistic view seems to be that it is extremely unlikely that any significant recommendations will be implemented by the political establishment on its own initiative. This because of the peep into history of electoral reforms mentioned earlier in the chapter.

Politics is not, and does not have to be an undesirable activity. Dictionary meanings of politics are 'the science or art of government', or 'the affairs or activities of those engaged in controlling or seeking control of a government.' As has already been said, political activity and political parties are an essential requirement for the functioning of a democratic society because they provide the necessary link between people at large and the government. In a broad sense, politicians serve the function of mobilising and crystallising public opinion and translating it into executive action. If done conscientiously and with due diligence, this should result in the good of the public. It is, in fact, the very highest form of public service. Notwithstanding this, politicians tend to attract derisive comments from their publics the world over. The situation in India seems to be particularly acute. According to the 170th report of the Law Commission, 'there has been a steady deterioration in the standards, practices and pronouncements of the political class, which fights the elections. Money-power, muscle-power, corrupt practices and unfair means are being freely employed to win the elections.'

The events of the last couple of years have not helped in improving the public image of the political class but improve this, we must.

So, what can we, as Indian citizens, do? It seems be clear that unless pressure is created from the public at large, neither the electoral system nor the political class is going to be reformed. What is needed to generate this pressure from the public at large is sensitisation of the public, and mobilisation and organisation of public opinion. Unfortunately this is a task in which the political class specialises. However, 'We, the People', owe it to the country and its future to do whatever we can in this regard.

UID Project: Does Evidence Matter?

—Reetika Khera

THE SALES pitch for the 'Unique Identification' (UID) project had three important planks – corruption control, inclusion, and portability. All three claims were based on a poor understanding of the relevant programmes. Recent experience in several States suggests that the same goals can often be achieved with simpler and more appropriate technologies without the hassles attached to the UID project. On the other hand, UID application pilots initiated by the Unique Identification Authority of India (UIDAI) and others have faced serious challenges. Yet the government has been pushing towards making UID compulsory, and worse, is now moving towards charging for use of (free thus far) authentication services.

I am grateful to Saloni Chopra and Jean Drèze for helpful comments and suggestions. This is a slightly updated version of a piece that first appeared in Yojana.

Selling the Idea

The advertising blitz to 'sell' the UID project made three claims: one, that corruption would be eliminated, especially in the Public Distribution System (PDS) and the National Rural Employment Guarantee Scheme (NREGS). As far as corruption in the PDS is concerned, Tamil Nadu has been running a clean system without UID. Intelligent applications of simpler technologies (eg. computerisation, sms alerts etc), along with other reforms, have contributed to the turnaround of the PDS in Chhattisgarh and Odisha. In these States, estimated 'leakages' of PDS grain have come down from around 50% in both States, to 10% and 20% respectively.[1] The biometric aspect of aadhaar, could have contributed to corruption control by enabling reduction in the number of duplicate, ghost and fake cards in circulation. While such cards are a source of 'leakages' in the PDS (and other welfare schemes too), there is little or no systematic evidence on the size of this problem. In order to understand this, as part of the Public Evaluation of Entitlement Programmes(PEEP). survey in ten States, a pension social audit was also undertaken.[2] Official lists of pension beneficiaries were obtained of sample villages, and the survey teams traced each person on the list to count the number of duplicates, ghosts and fakes on the pension lists.

Out of 3,752 pensioners on the lists for this specific exercise, teams verified 99% of the names. For a large majority (89%), they were able to meet the person or a family member. We found dead persons (5%) and 'other' cases (6%). In many States, since pensions are paid through banks, this meant that the pension of a dead person keeps accumulating in the account of the pensioner, until authorities are notified. Where cash is paid (eg. Odisha), the pension of a dead person could be appropriated by the GP functionary. Among 'no such person was known in the village' and 'other' cases, there was some overlap: it included people who had moved permanently (due to marriage or work), migrants, imperfect matches of names (eg. father's name did not match) and suspected fake names.

---

1 The scope for reducing corruption in the PDS and in NREGA through computerisation, UID and other technologies, achievements of various states so far and the further scope for corruption control are discussed in greater detail in Khera (2010).

2 For more details of the PEEP Survey 2013, see http://web.iitd.ac.in/~reetika/projects.html.

Often the person belonged to another revenue village of the same Gram Panchayat (GP). In a handful of cases, the team visited the neighbouring village and found that the claim was true. Interestingly, in the entire sample, there was only one duplicate name.

While the pension lists did not match the ground reality entirely, mismatches were often a sign of poor record-keeping. Outdated records do open the door to corrupt practices (eg. in Tulasikani GP, Odisha we found that the panchayat secretary had been embezzling the pension of two dead persons for more than a year),[3] but do not automatically imply corruption. Thus, eg. in Jharkhand, if records are outdated (eg.a dead person's name continues to appear on the pension list), because pension is credited into a bank account, it cannot be fraudulently withdrawn.

In the NREG Scheme, the scope for corruption was greatly reduced when wages began to be paid through bank and post office accounts in 2008-9. In fact, NREGA has contributed much to 'financial inclusion' even before UID existed. Yet, corruption continues in the following three ways: coercion, collusion with labourers, and collusion with post office officials. Coercion occurs when labourers' wages are forcibly 'shared' with corrupt officials after being withdrawn from the bank or post office. Collusion can be between implementing officials and labourers: days of work are inflated to defraud the system. In such cases, UID authentication cannot help. Collusion also occurs between NREGS functionaries and post office officials ('identity fraud'), who operate the labourer's account without her/his knowledge. It is only in this case that the UID-authentication can control corruption. (Even here, identity fraud can be controlled further by switching to banks).

Two, UID was supposedly a project of 'social inclusion' for the millions who were excluded from social welfare programmes because they do not have an identity. It is true that millions of Indians are excluded from the government's social welfare programmes, but the main cause for exclusion is not the lack of identity. In the PEEP Survey 2013, we asked people about the different IDs they possessed. In our sample of 1,900

---

[3] Khera, 2013b provides details on the scale of corruption there and action taken.

households (taken from the NREGS job card register), 95% had a voter card, 85% had a ration card, 82% had a bank or post office account and 16% had an *aadhaar number*.

The main reason for exclusion from these programmes is the meager budget and exclusion errors (ie. poor people being classified as non-poor). Rather than the numbers of people in need determining the size of the budget, the budget determines the size of the 'target' population. To make things worse, there are serious exclusion errors,eg. according to National Family Health Survey data from 2005-6, nearly half of those in the poorest 20% did not possess a BPL ration card (Drèze and Khera, 2010). UID alone can remedy neither the budget constraint nor can it reduce exclusion errors.

The National Food Security Act (NFSA) increases the coverage in the PDS (from about half of the population to two-thirds). Independently of the NFSA, there has been a trend towards greater coverage (or 'inclusivity') as State governments, one after another, have rejected the central 'caps' on coverage. Starting with Tamil Nadu, Andhra Pradesh and Himachal Pradesh, which run universal or quasi-universal PDS, Chhattisgarh, Odisha, Rajasthan and even Jharkhand have expanded their PDS by committing State funds.

Portability

The third claim of UIDAI was 'portability' of benefits. In the current system, most entitlements are tied to the recipient's place of residence. When people migrate, they are forced to forego their entitlements. For instance, one can only draw subsidised PDS rations from the PDS outlet to which one is tied. Indeed, the ability to run a PDS which is 'portable' would be a great improvement.

The Food Department in Chhattisgarh took up the challenge of designing a portable PDS, and in April 2012, they launched the Centralized Online Real-time Electronic PDS (CORE PDS). Ration card holders have been given a 'smart card'. Smart cards (like ATM cards) can be used to draw rations at any CORE PDS outlet which has a 'point of sale' (POS) machine. The POS machine is, in fact, a mini-computer with connectivity. Once a smart card is inserted, the machine authenticates it, and sales can proceed. Offline sales are also possible when there are issues related to the server or mobile connectivity. In such cases, the ration card number needs to be entered for sales.

Starting with two shops of Raipur, the CORE PDS now covers 400 PDS outlets of which 40 are rural outlets. About one-fifth of transactions at these shops have used the portability option– ie. ration card holders chose to go to a PDS outlet other than the one to which they were originally allocated. In most cases, portability was exercised within the ward. (The density of PDS outlets in Raipur seemed very high.) Convenience was the prime reason for switching: the outlet to which people were originally tied was not the nearest, tenants who moved residence, when supplies ran out, etc. To cut a long story short, portability has been achieved without UID.

This raises the question of choosing between UID and smart cards for portability. Smart cards are a tested and affordable technology. In Chhattisgarh, it cost Rs 50 per *cardholder* to implement smart cards. (On the other hand, UID enrolment of each *person* costs Rs 50.) Apart from cost considerations, UID has raised other issues: surveillance and tracking, data security, personal and civil liberty concerns, privacy etc (see Drèze, 2011, Abraham 2012, 2013 and Ramanathan, 2013).

The cost of implementing a smartcard-based portable PDS appear to be 'reasonable' – approximately Rs 50 per ration card holder in the 400 shops in which it has already been implemented.

UID Pilots Crash

While State governments have been using simple technology creatively, UIDAI's pilots have faced serious challenges, often crashing. A pilot in Mysore, linking UID with LPG cylinder purchase, was aborted as it did not take off at all (Bhatti, 2013). In Jharkhand, an attempt was made to integrate NREGS payments with UID. Notwithstanding tall claims in media reports, on the ground, the pilot turned out to be miniscule: eg. in just three GPs of Ranchi district, one of three pilot districts; hardly any payments had been made through the new system, and almost always under great scrutiny for the benefit of a visiting dignitary (see Bhatti et al, 2012 and Bhatti, 2012). The pilot was quietly wound up.

The only 'successful' UID pilot is the integration of PDS with UID in East Godavari (see Khera 2013a). It required nearly two years of preparatory work, a large and dedicated team with dynamic leadership (provided by the sub-Collector). In September 2012, the pilot was launched in 5% of PDS outlets of the district. It has not seen any scaling up since. It still does not offer portability.

If the ration card and UID number match, the electronic-POS (e-POS) prompts the cardholder to place one of their 'best fingers' for real time authentication. Five trials are allowed, failing which, a 'one-time password' (OTP) is issued. OTP is an 'override facility' when biometric authentication fails (either due to biometrics, connectivity, etc).Transaction data from the first year suggest that OTP had to be used in 13% of all transactions. This 'failure' rate is not small, but has not been discussed at all.

Yet the UID juggernaut rolls on: in November 2012, the government announced Aadhaar-enabled cash transfers for existing schemes. Seven months later, a review at the PMO acknowledged that preparatory work was complete for only 9% of all beneficiaries. Undeterred, in October 2013, the UIDAI put out its 'pricing policy' approach paper for authentication of services, which were free only until December 2013. Private and public entities will be charged for iris and fingerprint and demographic data authentication, e-KYC etc.

Against its success in generating more than 50 crore unique numbers, there are many questions, even failures, from the UID pilots. Meanwhile, State governments using other technologies innovatively have demonstrated that corruption can be controlled; inclusion and portability can be achieved without the hassles that are a part of the UID package. Evidence, it seems, does not matter.

Conclusion

In recent months, government data has shown that some of the claims about aadhaar made earlier were exaggerated or incorrect. For instance, only 0.03% of those who got aadhaar numbers are people who did not have two pre-existing IDs. The rest already had IDs, which suggests that aadhaar has not reached those who were outside the ambit of government ID documents. Another example is the Dhande committee which evaluated the Direct Benefit Transfers (DBT) for cooking gas in the 300 pilot districts. They found that the extent of duplication in the database was relatively small – 2 per cent. More importantly, the Finance Ministry's data shows that DBT can proceed without aadhaar: eg., 98% of NREGS payments were aadhaar-free DBT into people's accounts. The figures are similar for other welfare programmes such as Janani Suraksha Yojana, maternity entitlements, scholarships and pensions. This is important because a false impression has been created that DBT will be stalled if aadhaar is not allowed.

Further, there is now evidence that aadhaar has become a tool of exclusion. In Andhra Pradesh, when the PDS system was integrated with aadhaar, about one-fifth the beneficiaries did not buy their grain. A government initiated enquiry at five shops found that aadhaar technology was responsible for nearly half of those exclusions.[4] Similarly, in NREGS there have been reports of exclusion from work and payment of wages on account of aadhaar.[5]

Between August-October 2015, the Supreme Court held several hearings on the aadhaar matter. Two outcomes are worth highlighting here: one, on account of the possibility of violation of privacy due to the project, the matter was referred to a Constitution bench. Two, meanwhile, the Court allowed the *voluntary* use of aadhaar for NREGS, pensions, PDS, cooking gas and Employees Provident Fund Organization (EPFO). The government was also instructed to publicise these orders widely. Unfortunately, as before, the government has chosen to turn a blind eye to the voluntary aspect of aadhaar as its down departments continue to exert pressure to integrate the aadhaar number into its various databases.

References

1. Abraham Sunil (2012), Do we Need the aadhaar scheme? *Business Standard*, 1 February.
2. Abraham Sunil (2013), Freedom from Monitoring: India Inc should push for Privacy Laws, *Forbes India*, 21 August.
3. Aggarwal, Ankita (2015), The slow destruction of NREGA, Evidence from Jharkhand, India Together, 16 March. http://indiatogether.org/destruction-of-nrega-with-evidence-from-jharkhand-government, last accessed 18 February, 2016.

---

[4] See Matharu (2015) and Scroll.in (2015).

[5] Khera (2016) and Aggarwal (2014).

4. Bhatti Bharat (2013), A Pilot that lost direction, *India Together*, 20 June, 2013. http://www.indiatogether.org/2013/jun/eco-aadhaar.htm, last accessed 18 January 2014.

5. Bhatti Bharat (2012), 'Aadhaar-enabled payments for NREGA workers', *Economic and Political Weekly*, 8 December.

6. Bhatti Bharat, Drèze Jean and Khera Reetika (2012), 'Experiments with Aadhaar', *The Hindu*, 28 June.

7. Drèze Jean (2010), Unique Facility or Recipe for Trouble, *The Hindu*, 25 November.

8. Dreze and Khera (2010), The BPL Census and An Alternative, *Economic and Political Weekly*, Vol 45, No. 9, 27 February.

9. Khera, Reetika (2016), For NREGA, TN is the only hope, NDTV.com, 2 February. http://www.ndtv.com/opinion/for-nrega-tamil-nadu-is-the-only-hope-1272338, last accessed 18 February, 2016.

10. Khera Reetika (2013a), 'The East Godavari Pilot', *The Hindu*, 11 April.

11. Khera Reetika (2013b), 'Do Government Schemes Ever Work in India?', *Yahoo News*, 22 October.http://in.news.yahoo.com/do-government-schemes-ever-work-in-india—045454251.html, last accessed 18 January 2014.

12. Khera Reetika (2011), The UID Project and Welfare Schemes, *Economic and Political Weekly*, 26 February, Vol 46, No. 9.

13. Matharu, Sonal (2015), AP detects glitches in aadhaar-linked PDS distribution, *Governance Now*, 28 September. http://www.governancenow.com/news/regular-story/ap-detects-glitches-aadhaar-linked-pds-distribution, last accessed 18 February, 2016.

14. Ramanathan Usha (2010), A Unique Identity Bill, *Economic and Political Weekly*, 24 July.

15. Scroll (2015), An official Andhra survey shows why Modi government should stop pushing aadhaar so doggedly, scroll.in, 15 October. http://scroll.in/article/760530/an-official-andhra-survey-shows-why-modi-government-should-stop-pushing-aadhaar-so-doggedly, last accessed 18 February, 2016.

What is at Stake?

— Lal Bahadur Varma

WHAT IS at stake is not only the body but even the mind and the spirit of man today. At stake is our 'being', our 'becoming', our very existence as 'humane' beings as world citizens. We are supposed to be citizens of a democratic sovereign, secular and socialist republic. But are we? Can we be so in a system economically global, politically nationalistic and culturally fascistic? Not only what India has been is at stake, what she could accomplish in that path too.

Let us take obvious and immediate examples from day-to-day life—ordinary examples to illustrate an extraordinary phenomenon.

Can one even imagine of a form without any content? Can any improvement in the form be effective without any change in the content? Can a change in the form necessarily change the content also? Can a city be made smart, whose inhabitants are not smart? Are we not vulgarising the adjectives by qualifying any noun with any adjective or qualifying any number of nouns with one and the same adjective? Do not we lose our grasp on precision by doing so? Does not the quality of our perception go down in so doing, and thus a cultural decline may start, of which we may not be even aware?

Let us be precise. We used to use 'good' to qualify any number of things—food is good, mood is good, weather is good, so on and so forth. At the best, these are positive but very vague and generalised statements. Earlier it was good, then it was 'cool'—somebody is cool, food is cool (even if it is hot), weather is cool (even if it is pleasantly warm) etc. Soon 'smart' might take over—from smart phones to smart cities—it has just started. I too have a so-called smart phone but am not smart enough to even know all its uses.

The governments and their investing partners are bent upon making cities smart. But can overbridges and overbearing 'joints' suffice to accelerate disjointed lives of even the well-fixed people, not to speak of the 'Aam Admi' ?

The growing tendency of getting used to short-cuts is only the superficial expression of a deeper degeneration. All short-cuts and imprecise uses of adjectives may not appear dangerous but they become so, when used and propagated deliberately by vested interest. It is being taken for granted that if the phone is smart, its user is bound to become one. Similarly, if the city is smart, so will be its inhabitants. It means that content is being deliberately neglected and forms are being imposed.

It is this phenomenon of show which was underlined by the French thinker Guy Debord in his scathing book, La Societe de Spectacle (being translated into Hindi by me). The book is a brilliant critique of spectacular capitalism.

Let us take another example. Hurting somebody's sentiment used to be something deplorable. Actually, it should be always so. But if it becomes a tool to grind one's axe, it becomes loaded with explosive consequences. Getting hurt is a la mode now. Anything and everything seems to be hurting somebody's sentiments now a days. And the 'hurt ones' do not stop at just complaining. They try to hurt others harder. This is done without realising that if one hurts others sadistically, one's own self is hurt on a deeper plane—morally.

Reason hurts, science hurts, secularism hurts, even democracy hurts. And instead of registering a sense of hurt the so called 'hurt ones' start brutally hurting others. They cannot understand, much less accept Voltaire who famously said, 'I know what you say is wrong, but I can give away my life for your right to say so'. It was beginning of democracy which means, the right to say even wrong things. That strengthened dissent, dialogue and pluralism. But self-rightousness leads to feellings, I am the only one, the other exists not. This has led to fundamentalism and fascism all over the world. And this seems to be the chosen path of the fraudulent liberal democracy being practiced in India today.

Let me underline the hypocrisy of the present systems. It talks on and on of culture, specially of the 'Hindu' culture. Almost none of the propagandist spokespersons of this system—political, religious or mixture of the two—understand even mythology, not to say, the history of Hinduism. It is far cry if one refers to the philosophical content of Hinduism. And yet they flaunt Hindu symbols. This crooked mockery continues because even more hypocritical politics of spectacle (to use the ironical words of Guy Debord) patronises this 'hide and seek' symbolism for its known vested interest in votebank 'politiking'.

For 'them' what is at stake is power and pelf alone. For people, what is at stake is the very purpose and meaning of life. They are doing everything to remain in power and keep on expanding it, come what may. All power-mongers get united when they are threatened from below and 'outside' by the people, whom they consider lesser beings and more dangerous, when awakened, than even wild animals.

Then, what are, and has been, the choices before the victims. They have been awakened by the more sensitive, more sensible and enlightened ones. It has always been culture that precedes and marches along political pathways. Let us not forget what Premchand said in this regard. When the anti-fascist cultural movement reached India, Sajjad Zaheer succeeded, with the cooperation of several other Hindi and Urdu writers in launching the Progressive Writers Association (PWA) in Allahabad. Premchad, the lighthouse of Hindi literature, then and even now, said in his first presidential address at Lucknow that literature is like a torchlight (*mashaal*), showing the way to politics. It has always been like that. History records an intellectual revolution in France preceding the great French Revolution, so on and so forth.

Can't one visualise some sort of cultural awakening in India to counter the anti-people (ill-liberal) political economy of the day?

Public Health: Current Status and Neoliberal Response

— AK Arun

INDIA HAS drawn the world's attention because of its emerging health profile as nearly 834 million rural people (69% of the total population), half of whom are below the poverty line (BPL), continue to fight a hopeless and constantly losing battle for health and survival. The policies implemented so far concentrate only on growth of economy, *not* on equity and equality or quality of life. As a result the gap between 'urban and rural' and 'haves and have-nots' has been widened. Nearly 92% of all deaths, and 92% of deaths from communicable diseases occur among the poorest 20% of the population. However, some progress is reflected in the improvement in some health indicators. Under the cumulative impact of various measures and a host of national programmes for livelihood, nutrition and shelter, life expectancy rose from 33 years at Independence in 1947 to 67 years in 2015. Infant mortality declined from 72/1000 live births in 1999 to 40/1000 in 2016. Interstate, regional, socioeconomic class and gender disparities however remain high. Despite noticeable improvements it must be stressed that these survival rates in India are comparable even today only to the poorest nations of sub-Saharan Africa. The rural populations are the prime victims of the policies, work in the most hazardous atmosphere and live in abysmal conditions. Unsafe and unhygienic birth practices, unclean water, poor nutrition and degraded and unsanitary environments are challenges to the public health system. The majority of the rural people are small land holders, artisans and labourers, with limited resources that they spend chiefly on food and other necessities. They have hardly any money left to spend on health. The rural farm worker, who strives hard under adverse weather conditions to produce food for others, is often the first victim of epidemics. This present paper attempts to review critically the current health status of India, with a special reference to the vast rural population.

Health in Union Budget 2016

Increase in the total allocation to the health sector represents an increase of 14 per cent from the previous year. This is only because of the significant cut in last year's budget and, in real terms, is even less than what was allocated in 2014-15. This allocation will do little to improve India's abysmal global ranking on public expenditure on health. The specific allocations to the National Health Mission, the flagship programme for the public healthcare delivery system, represent an insignificant change, and possibly even a reduction, from the previous year. It is notable that this amount is less than that committed for the recapitalisation of public-sector banks; in effect, the government has put yet more money into banks that have performed badly than on fixing the public healthcare system, which is witnessing a steady hemorrhage of the population to the private sector. It is perplexing, then, how this budget is expected to address the goal of reducing catastrophic health expenditure, which the finance minister rightly asserted was 'the single most important cause of unforeseen out-of-pocket expenditure which pushes lakhs of households below the poverty line every year'.

Apart from the low investment in the public healthcare system, there are other troubling facts, which indicate the prescription of the budget will not cut the burden of catastrophic health expenditure. First, the beefed-up health insurance scheme needs to cover out-patient expenditure, not that of drugs and diagnostics, as this accounts for the major share of out-of-pocket health expenditure. In the absence of a structural reform of the health insurance scheme, one must assume it will continue to only insure in-patient care. Second, there needs to be a strengthening of the mechanism to hold the private sector accountable, or else even the increased insurance cover will simply be swallowed up into the bottomless pit of irrational and unethical medicine, led by unnecessary hospital admissions and procedures. This would end up as one more example of public money flowing to private hands without any efforts to reduce costs or ensure transparency. Finally, if the health insurance scheme only targets those who live below the poverty line, the significant impact of catastrophic health expenditure on the impoverishment of those who live above this arbitrary line would not be dented at all.

It is after three years of the health budget remaining stagnant in the Rs 22,000-24,500 crore range that estimates are revised towards the end of the calendar year, when the health ministry had asked for Rs 50,000 crore in the budgetary allocations this year.

The ministry hopes to kick start at least its plan to give free drugs and diagnostics under the National Health Mission. The free drugs scheme, first mooted in 2012, was the cornerstone of the health section of the finance minister's Budget speech last year when he had announced Rs 30,645 crore and a plan for 'Health for All'. None could be rolled out for the lack of finances. In the revised estimates, the allocation has been pruned to Rs 24,500 crore, bringing the total health spend in the first three years of the 12th five-year plan to Rs 70,000 crore, way below the 268,000 crore allocation given in the plan document. The department of Ayush, meanwhile, has asked for a more than six-fold raise in allocation from Rs 400 crore last year to Rs 2,700 crore. *(Union Health Budget, 2016)*

Public Health Scenario

Public health is one of the best indicators of a nation's overall growth and human development. It mirrors the past, present and future of its citizens. Its mission is to improve the health of the population and reduce health inequalities. Presently, we are 1.3 billion Indians and our population is growing at a rate of about 18 million every year. With only 2.4 per cent of the world land area, India has to support 16 per cent of the total global population. According to the International Diabetic Federation there are more than 70 million Indians suffering from diabetes (*Indian Diabetes Research Foundation*). The continued intensity of some diseases (HIV/AIDS, malaria, dengue, hepatitis), the resurgence of other communicable diseases (tuberculosis, plague, virulent cholera, meningitis) and the emergence of new ones (SARS, Asian bird-flu, mad cow diseases, foot and mouth disease, Zika virus) have stretched the already weakened health systems, often resulting in sub-optimal response. An increasing burden of non-communicable diseases, mental illness, and incapacity due to injuries and violence has added to the problem. (*WHO 2006, MOH&FW 2009.*)

We have a health system that is underfunded, under-regulated, irrational, hugely inefficient and very expensive. Public provision of health service is inadequately funded, their facilities are plagued by overcrowding, a shortage of essential items and even of skilled personnel. Private involvement in health provision is beset by rising costs and problems of exclusion, huge and growing differentials in the services available to rich and poor, and inadequate supervision associated with various manifestations of moral hazard. There is a lack of strong national policies supportive of public health as an increasing share of the health budget goes to clinical services (*WHO 2007; MOH&FW Govt of India, 2009*). As a result, India's health indicators are among the worst in the world, which explains to a large extent its appallingly low position in the International Human Development Index.

Health Practices and Problems in Rural India

The people in rural India in general and tribal populations in particular, have their own beliefs and practices regarding health. Some tribal groups still believe that a disease is always caused by hostile spirits or by the breach of some taboo. They, therefore, seek remedies through magico-religious practices. On the other hand, some rural people have continued to follow undocumented, traditional medicine systems, in addition to the recognised cultural systems of medicine such ayurveda, unani, siddha, naturopathy and homoeopathy, to maintain positive health and to prevent disease. However, the socioeconomic, cultural and political onslaughts, arising partly from the erratic exploitation of human and material resources, have endangered the naturally healthy environment (eg. access to healthy and nutritious food, clean water, nutritious vegetation, healthy life styles, and value systems and community harmony). The basic nature of rural health problems is attributed also to lack of health consciousness, poor maternal and child health services and occupational hazards. The majority of deaths, which are preventable, are due to infections and communicable, parasitic and respiratory diseases. Infectious diseases dominate the morbidity pattern in rural areas (40% rural: 23.5% urban). Waterborne infections, which account for about 80% of sickness in India, make every fourth person dying of such diseases in the world, an Indian. Annually, 1.5 million deaths and loss of 73 million workdays are attributed to waterborne diseases. (*Park's Text Book of Preventive & Social medicine, 16th edition, 2000:172-5.*)

The following groups of infections are widespread in rural areas.

1. Diseases that are carried in the gastrointestinal tract, such as diarrhoea, amoebiasis, typhoid fever, infectious hepatitis, worm infestations and poliomyelitis. About 100 million suffer from diarrhoea and cholera every year.(*Health Situation in india:2001, VHAI 2001.*)
2. Diseases that are carried in the air through coughing, sneezing or even breathing, such as measles, tuberculosis (TB), whooping cough and pneumonia. Indiais the country with the highest burden of*TB*. The economic burden of TB is extremely high. Between 2006 and 2014, TB cost the Indian economy a massive USD 340 billion. (Revised National TB Control Programme Annual Status Repor and http://www.tbfacts.org/tb-india/#sthash.zACMAQJ4.dpuf). Over 1.2 million cases are added every year and 37,000 cases of measles are reported every year. 3. Infections, which are more difficult to deal with, include malaria, filariasis and *kala-azar*. These are often the result of developmental projects such as irrigation, which brings with it malaria and filariasis, pesticide use has produced a resistant strain of malaria, the ditches, gutters and culverts dug during the construction of roads, and expansion of cattle ranches, for example, are breeding places for snails and mosquitoes. About 2.3 million episodes and over 1000 malarial deaths occur every year in India. (*Health Situation in India: 2001, VHAI, 2001*) An estimated 45 million are carriers of microfilaria,

19 million of which are active cases and 500 million people are at risk of developing filaria. Every third person in the world suffering from leprosy is an Indian. (Nearly 1.2 million cases of leprosy, with 500 000 cases being added to this figure every year.)

Malnutrition is one of the most dominant health related problems in rural areas. There is widespread prevalence of protein energy malnutrition (PEM), anaemia, vitamin A deficiency and iodine deficiency. Nearly 100 million children do not get two meals a day. A nationwide survey called the Rapid Survey on Children (RSOC), conducted by the ministry of women and child development in 2013-14 in league with Unicef, showed that the proportion of underweight children in India was 29.4%, and that of stunted children 38.7%. While these figures indicate high levels of under-nutrition, they show a marked improvement over what the last nationwide survey, the National Family Health Survey (NFHS), had reported in 2005-06: the ratio of underweight children at 42.5%, and the ratio of stunted children at 48%.

3. Increasing trend has been seen in India in Percentage of Institutional Deliveries 70.625% in 2008-09 and 82.864% in 2012-13 (ministry of Health and Family Welfare). Only 30% of women go for post natal checkups, the various State scheme data show.

Agricultural-and environment-related injuries and diseases are all quite common in rural areas, for example: mechanical accidents, pesticide poisoning, snake, dog and insect bites, zoonotic diseases, skin and respiratory diseases; oral health problems; socio psychological problems of the female, geriatric and adolescent population; and diseases due to addictions. Since 1951, the government has been attempting through vertical and imported programs to combat these problems, but to no avail. However, the new National Population Policy 2005 gave emphasis to an holistic approach, for example, improvement in 'quality of life' for all, no gender bias in education, employment, child survival rates, sound social security, promotion of culturally and socially acceptable family welfare methods.

The Challenges of Rural Health Services

The Bhore Committee Report called for an integrated 3-tier health infrastructure to provide basic services for the rural areas. Reviewing past achievements, the Mudaliar Committee Report in 1962 offered financial options for building health services. India's mixed economy attempted to accommodate a welfare policy that led to expansion of health service infrastructure, manpower and public sector drugs and instruments production units. The training of paramedics was a key activity through nursing, ANM and Basic Health Workers and Health Assistant's training schools. After the Third Plan this emphasis was diluted. Investments in health services continuously declined and urban hospital based services got priority over the rural 3-tier system proposed by Bhore Committee. To contain the emerging dissatisfaction in rural areas, the State introduced the Minimum Needs Programme in the Fifth Five Year Plan (1974), the Community Health Workers Scheme in 1979, and expanded and restructured primary health centre network adding Community Health Centres in the Sixth Five year Plan (1981). The acceptance of Alma Ata declaration of Comprehensive Primary Health Care in 1978 , the National Rural Health Mission (NRHM) of 2005, training Accredited Social Health Activists (ASHAs) and now the proposal for a shorter training for rural practitioners, were all meant to strengthen rural infrastructure. Instead of an effective integrated manpower, capable of responding to the needs of rural areas, the state created volunteers of ASHAs with limited skills to provide full coverage. Absence of an effective infrastructure in rural areas failed to inspire doctors to work in PHCs though their numbers continued to rise as private medical schools expanded. Expansion of private medical education led to undermining the public health component of medical education. Concentration in cities and out migration characterised this set of medical personnel. This paucity of personnel in rural areas created a huge gap between needs and availability of public sector providers.

Health Policy and Infrastructure for Rural Areas

The mini-scale and token health intervention during the colonial period introduced in the so-called 'modern medicine' in India. After independence, the state discriminately chose to follow these 'western models' with very little thought. This system, which is highly selective, centralised and top down – not by oversight but by design as a part of the overall approach of not addressing the roots of the problem – and which treats people as objects rather than subjects, has failed to address the needs of the majority, that is to say, the rural poor and indigenous people which contribute the majority in the country. While a significant portion of the country's medical needs, especially in rural areas, have been attended to by the indigenous health systems such as Ayurveda, Homeopathy, Unani, Naturopathy and folk medicine, it has been conveniently neglected by the policy-makers and planners.

The draft of the National Health Policy 2001 did not given due importance to Indian systems of medicine. The concept of a family physician with social accountability, which has traditional roots and acceptance from the rural masses, has diminished with the existing policies and value systems. The present westernised hospital-based medical education and training, which is supported by public funding, has proved beyond doubt that new doctors are not inclined to and capable of meeting the needs of the majority of the public (i.e. rural people), which is where their services are most required. Thirteen years later, in 2015, the Government of India came out with a revised draft of the NHP which says, 'This National Health Policy addresses the urgent need to improve the performance of health systems. It is being formulated at the last year of the Millennium Declaration and its Goals, in the global context of all nations committed to moving towards universal health coverage. Given the two-way linkage between economic growth and health status, this National Health Policy is a declaration of the determination of the Government to leverage economic growth to achieve health outcomes and an explicit acknowledgement that better health contributes immensely to improved productivity as well as to equity'.

The 2015 draft begins with the admission that 'India today, is the world's third largest economy in terms of its Gross National Income (in PPP terms) and has the potential to grow larger and more equitably... India today possesses as never before, a sophisticated arsenal of interventions, technologies and knowledge required for providing health care to her people. Yet the gaps in health outcomes continue to widen.

On the face of it, much of the ill health, disease, premature death, and suffering we see on such a large scale is needless, given the availability of effective and affordable interventions for prevention and treatment. "The reality is straightforward. The power of existing interventions is not matched by the power of health systems to deliver them to those in greatest need, in a comprehensive way, and on an adequate scale."'

It continues, 'the context has changed in four major ways. Firstly- Health Priorities are changing. As a result of focused action over the last decade we are projected to attain Millennium Development Goals with respect to maternal and child mortality. Maternal mortality now accounts for 0.55% of all deaths and 4% of all female deaths in the 15 to 49 year age group. **This is still 46,500 maternal deaths too many** and demands that the commitments to further reduction must not flag. However it also signifies a rising and unfulfilled expectation of many other health needs that currently receive little public attention. **There are many infectious diseases which the system has failed to respond to – either in terms of prevention or access to treatment. Then there is a growing burden of non-communicable disease.** The second important change in context is the emergence of a robust **health care industry growing at 15% compound annual growth rate (CAGR). This represents twice the rate of growth in all services and thrice the national economic growth rate.** Thirdly, **incidence of catastrophic expenditure due to health care costs is growing and is now being estimated to be one of the major contributors to poverty. The drain on family incomes due to health care costs can neutralise the gains of income increases and every Government scheme aimed to reduce poverty.** The fourth and final change in context is that **economic growth has increased the fiscal capacity available.** Therefore, the country needs a new health policy that is responsive to these contextual changes. Other than these objective factors, the political will to ensure universal access to affordable healthcare services in an assured mode – the promise of Health Assurance – is an important catalyst for the framing of a New Health Policy (all emphasis ours).'

Inequality, Inadequacy and Adversity

It is unfortunate that while the incidence of all diseases are twice higher in rural than in urban areas, the rural people are denied access to proper health care, as the systems and structures were built up mainly to serve the better off. While the urban middle class in India have ready, though costly, uneven and may be even unreliable access to health services, even minimum health facilities are not available to the vast majority of rural and tribal people, and wherever services are provided, they are inferior. While the health care of the urban population is provided by a variety of hospitals and dispensaries run by corporate, private, voluntary and public sector organisations, rural healthcare services, mainly immunisation and family planning, are delivered by ill-equipped rural hospitals, primary health centres and subcentres. The basic infrastructure is that one PHC covers 30,000 of the population and one subcentre covers 5,000 of the population. It is obvious that there is a marked concentration of health personnel to maintain the large structures in the urban areas. According to the Medical Council of India (MCI), the total number of registered doctors in the country is 936,488 as on 31 December 2014. 'As per information provided by Medical Council of India and Indian Nursing Council, the total number of registered doctors is 936,488 as on 31.12.2014, and as on 31.12.2013 auxiliary nurses midwives are 756,937 and registered nurses/midwives are 1673,338', Health Minister J P Nadda informed the Lok Sabha in 2014. The minister further said, 'As per the Report of the Steering Committee on Health for the 12th Five Year Plan of the Planning Commission, India has 19 health workers (doctors – 6, nurses & midwives – 13) per 10,000 people in India. WHO norms provide for 25 per 10,000 people. Additionally, there are 7.9 lakh AYUSH practitioners registered in the country (approximately 6.5 per 10,000).' Of the registered medical practitioners of various medical systems in India, over 60% are located in urban areas. As a result, a large number of unqualified people (quacks) have set up medical practice in rural areas. Curative care, which is the main demand of rural people, has been ignored in terms of investment and allocation. The percentage share of health infrastructure for rural areas has declined considerably from 1951 to 1993 (*Bulletin on Rural Health Statistics in India, Govt. of India, 2000*).

Inadequate Public Health Expenditure and its Misallocation

The total expenditure on health in India is estimated as 5.2% of the GDP while public health investment is only 0.9%, which is by far too inadequate to meet the requirements of poor and needy people who are about three fourths of the population. Successive five-year plans allocated less and less (in terms of per cent of total budget) to health. A major share of the public health budget is spent on family welfare. While 75% of India's population lives in rural areas, less than 10% of the total health budget is allocated to this region. Even here, the chief interest of the primary health care is diverted to family planning and ancillary vertical national programmess such as child survival and safe motherhood (CSSM) which are seen more as statistical targets than as health services. According to one study, 85% of the PHC budget goes on personnel salaries (*Health for Million, VHAI, New Delhi, 2000*). The lack of commitment to provide health care for its citizens is reflected in the inadequacy of the health infrastructure and low levels of financing, and also in declining support for the various healthcare demands of the people, especially since the 1980s, when the process of liberalisation and opening up of the Indian economy to the world markets began. Medical care and control of communicable diseases are crucial areas of concern, both in terms of what people demand as priorities as well as what existing socio-economic conditions demand. Along with overall public health spending, allocations to both these subsectors also showed a declining trend in the 1980s and 1990s. In the case of medical research, a similar trend is observed. While 20% of research grants are allocated to studies on cancer, which is responsible for 1% of deaths, less than 1% is provided for research in respiratory diseases, which accounts for 20% of deaths.

Growing Commercialisation of Health

The disillusionment and frustration with the growing ineffectiveness of the government sector is gradually driving poor people to seek help of the private sector, thus forcing them to spend huge sums of money. They are often left to the mercy of 'quacks'. While estimates vary, the government accounts for no more than 20–30% of total health spending. The share of the private sector grew from 14% in 1976 to 67% in 1993. About 67% of all hospitals, 63 per cent of all dispensaries and 78 per cent of all doctors in India are in the private/corporate sector. India is expected to rank amongst the top three healthcare markets in terms of incremental growth by 2020. Indian healthcare sector, one of the fastest growing industry, is expected to advance at a CAGR of 22.87 per cent during 2015–20 to reach USD280 billion. In India, private healthcare accounts for almost 74 per cent of the country's total healthcare expenditure, a 2015 report of India Brand Equity Foundation says. Much has been written on the growing privatisation and commercialisation of the medical practices and their links with drug and medical instrument manufacturers. While WHO recommends about 130 essential drugs, as many as 4,000 drugs are available in the Indian market. Due to this, 'buying' healthcare has gone beyond the reach of the poor. Two all-India surveys (*NSSO 46th round and NCAER, New Delhi*), have shown that medical treatment is the most important cause of rural indebtedness, next only to dowry (Duggal R, 'Health Care Budgets in Changing Political Economy', *EPW,* May 1997:17-24).

Conclusion

Almost two decades into the 21st century, 'Health for all by 2000 AD' remains as a distant mirage. Now the slogan has been rephrased as 'Health for all in 21st Century'. Primary health care, as a paradigm, has been lost on the way. To improve the prevailing situation, the problem of rural health is to be addressed both at the macro (national and State) and micro level (district and regional), in a holistic way, with genuine efforts to bring the poorest of the population to the centre of the fiscal policies. A paradigm shift from the current 'biomedical model' to a 'socio-cultural model' is required, to meet the needs of the rural population. A comprehensive revised National Health Policy addressing the existing inequalities and promoting a long-term perspective plan exclusively for rural health is the current need.

The writer thanks:

Ashok Vikhe Patil, International Association of Agricultural Medicine and Rural Health, Maharashtra.

KV Somasundaram and RC Goyal , Department of Community Medicine, Rural Medical College of Pravara Medical Trust, Maharashtra.

Mohd Miraj, Director Institute of Health & Management Studies, New Delhi.

Imrana Qadeer, Distinguished Professor (Retd), Centre of Social Medicine and Community Health, Jawaharlal Nehru University, New Delhi.

Meera Shiva, Chairperson, Health Action International Asia-Pacific.

NDA's Neoliberalism: Unravelling Assumptions and Implications

— Kamal Nayan Kabra

INDIA HAS completed a quarter century of her pursuit of accelerated economic growth along with a showpiece set of populist measures as tokens of the national concern for the poor with a view to contain discontent, win political support and facilitate low-cost labour supply in an open-economy with private corporate sector-led framework of the neo-liberal economic policies. Both continuing and learning—its lessons from the experience of the United Progressive Alliance governments I & II and of the first NDA government and confirming its ideological and social commitments, the present National Democratic Alliance government of India feels confident enough to continue with more of neoliberal 'reforms' (as shown by the first three budgets it prepared) in order to overcome the remaining shortcomings left unattended by the departing regimes and also to impart fresh dynamism to it during the rest of its term. (See for a critical view Alternative Economic Survey various issues, particularly from 2006-07 onwards.)

It may be noted that from the perspective of the NDA, the main charge against the UPA has been deep-seated cronyism in the process of carrying out the neoliberal tasks, possibly owing to a weak leadership wanting in sufficient authority and presumably lacking a vision as well. In reality and as seen in the three budgets and other major policy initiatives meant to enhance the ease of business and attract foreign direct investment (FDI) under the slogan 'make in India', the NDA does not seem to have a different set of economic policy objectives and policy content, or a different set of economic and social agencies for the cutting edge level operations nor the basic assessment of the underlying challenges (which may be summed up as low and fluctuating per capita income falling short of what is required to overcome persistent problems faced by the economy and also the people). Similarly the agency function, the relationship between the state and the main agency, the global context and India's approach to global issues, seems to have remained largely similar between the two groups of political parties, except for some fine-tuning or rather sharpening of the edge and claiming to do more with superior governance.(Kabra, Moneyfestoes of the Plutocracy, 18-24 April 2014, *Mainstream*.)

Let us by way of introduction sum up the way we look at the entire question of continuation of neoliberal policies by political parties in India under the banner of the NDA. We try to maintain that the neoliberal approach to development, viewed as economic growth, and macro and foreign economic relations policies in the Indian conditions (but also in somewhat similar manner elsewhere too) stands on two distinct but fairly closely inter-connected political economy pillars (the two props of neo-liberal political economy).

The first prop refers to a whole series of measures and manipulations which protect and promote the vital interests of the power block constituted by the rich and the powerful. They are the active agency and major state-supported beneficiaries of economic growth. This main and active prop is supplemented by the second one trying to deal with the real political economy of the first prop excessively leaning on the narrow top economic strata by an attempt to address the compulsions springing from the democratic polity . After all, it is incumbent on the regime to keep the majority of the voters contended and convinced about the democratic and fair credentials propounded publicly by the regime, especially during the elections. Thus, the second prop amounts to adoption and at the stated level of up-fronting various measures to help improve the living conditions of the poor and the marginalised majority of the electorate by a slew of measures to add certain income flows and provide social support facilities. These populist measures to don a human face remain largely sideshows and neither can address the basic disabilities nor can be so effective and extensive as to make the special dispensation for the adversely included redundant over a meaningful time horizon. This is apparent as only a comparatively small part of the direct and indirect state interventions, including even in the infrastructure and public goods and services sectors to address the massive deprivation and adverse inclusion of the masses. However, the absolute amount of state revenue devoted to these populist, highly visible measures are enough to overawe the masses by the sheer huge amounts devoted to these programmes defining what has been called 'democratic deceit'. More on this subject later.The essence of the first prop, the heart of the neoliberal dispensation, is to empower the rich and the resourceful and act as their engines of growth by making use of the state-crafted and sanctioned legal entities (organised as legally constituted joint stock companies) by way of putting together capital from diverse sources under a common banner which permits accumulation and operations for business growth while shifting away of risks and the sacrifices for making savings. (For a critique of the very basic institution of corporations as a special purpose vehicle for spearheading capitalist industrialisation in a manner that serves the interests of the super-rich in a highly partisan manner in so far as the profits are allowed to be excessively pocketed by the controlling, promoter families while the losses, thanks to the exorbitant privilege afforded by the limited liability principle, remain the liability of the legal person called the company and its several stakeholders, rarely with a voice in the decision-making processes, see, Bakan, Joel 2004.) Thus emerges a corporationist market economy, ironically in the midst of a large sea of informal, proto-or incomplete commoditisation—marketisation, to facilitate resource mobilisation and cornering of state support from the entire economy by the companies to use for profitable business ventures.

The entire game-plan is so organised as to insulate the flesh and blood decision-making citizens and their families by adopting the corporate form of organisation for capital accumulation, managerial decision-making and bearing risks while facilitating personal/ family level wealth accumulation with a disproportionately low risk of losing shirt (privatisation of profits and capital gains—that is the lure of the carrot, and socialisation of risks—and thus freeing capitalist entrepreneurs and managers of the fear of the stick). The combination of market and financial power with informal highly personalised and camouflaged linkages (cronyism) and social-ideological makeup enable, motivate and permit the company controllers-promoters to follow their animal spirits, leading to the growth of the economy by means of practices described lately as 'phishing for phools' or by devices such as selling snake oil or simply lobbying for their narrow and specific interests with the power afforded by huge capacity to entice the decision-makers with illegal, under the table gifts and allurements (Akerlof and Shiller, 2009 and 2015). As a result, the narrow top segment of the economy go on to follow their instincts merrily bypassing the social norms and practices inconvenient to their basic game-plan of making use of the social resources, opportunities and market institutions for amassing enormous wealth at the cost of the rest of society, and on a global scale. For these ends, the emergent plutocracts often innovate ways and means of expanding business even by violating social laws and obligations and thus make huge unaccounted hidden profits as grist to the on-going exploitative mill of the present day political economy. (see Kabra, AES, 2012—13 on black economy).

The Free Market Theory

The free market competitive economic theory or neoliberal ideology glorifies all these processes and the patrimonial companies are projected as 'national bulwarks' of economic and technological capabilities and efficiency. They operate hand-in-glove with the democratically elected governments. (For a graphic, widely-prevalent account of such practices in India, spread over decades spanning both the statist, populist and the corporatist neoliberal pre-1990 and post-1990 phases,see among several studies illustrating and explaining such structures, agencies, processes and their outcomes McDonald, Hamish. Ambani and Sons, 2010; also the Radia tape story, *Outlook*. Many parliamentary probes into stock market scams and official and academic studies too corroborate such a reading of the business and neoliberal political bonds. Lately, many court judgments and CBI probe reports on politicians-bureaucrats and corporate linkages-based scams located and originating from various tax havens and the home companies , bring out the horrendous truth.) Related to all such traits is the reality in which the company funds come to play a decisive role in making and unmaking of partner political outfits and the overall political regime. This is the formal fiction of separation of freedom of business and democratic participation in the choice of government and exercise of political, legal powers.

Such practices seem to have taken firm and generalised roots and there emerges the image of a national or social system attaining 'national' economic growth, which is in hard reality mainly a proxy for building up of huge empires of hidden, largely asocial and anti-social, family wealth in the hands of a politically well connected tribe of corporate bosses.(See for understanding the logic behind the wider general spread of or near ubiquity of such processes, the National Bureau of Economic Research, Washington study, *The Geography of Financial Misconduct*, July 2014, Working Paper no 20347. This shows the spread of such 'financial misconduct' and how a firm's tendency to engage in misconduct increases with the misconduct rates of the neighboring firms—representing a kind of 'peer effect'. It is found to be stronger among firms of comparable size and similar age of the CEOs.) Such all-pervasive becomes the force of expansion of such practices and outcomes that in course of time, the distinction between the joint perpetrators of the black economy and the dispensers of political patronage tends to get blurred, if not to disappear altogether with the huge hordes of wealth accumulated by resorting to dubious and surely far from normal and fair means. This is more so because the political class itself enters various businesses, leaving the distinction between the political class and the business class a mere formal one. We have spelled out the bare outline of the actual political economy of neo-liberalism at the outset because without highlighting it,one can hardly make sense of how four different political regimes over nearly a quarter century have loudly proclaimed their actual highly partisan policy choices and posited with them despite socially disappointing outcomes followed by frequent electoral defeats.

A great deal of common practices emerge in these processes and practices. 'Corporatisation' of political parties and political form and content of large business corporations seem to have gone far. Actually, the primacy of growth in a system with a great deal of formal state/social controls, regulations and hand-holding by the public agencies as the prime-enabler becomes, in practice, more or less a system increasingly growing distant from the formal state and business models, as though standing for two different civilisations. Therefore, todaythe aura of ideological and social mysticism of the state as a 'neutral arbiter' and facilitator has worn thin. There seems to be growing recognition of the hard reality of a highly partisan, self-seeking participation in company investment and share speculation, basically as a means for family wealth accumulation. In a fairly parallel manner, politics becomes a kind of family-controlled business and the political parties a kind of corporate entities without any social regulatory framework for disciplining their basic activities and ensuring that the parties work in a democratic manner, especially owing tote huge financial resources they raise, mainly from the corporate houses and organise costly political events Little surprise that in such a mode of growing wealth in the company balance sheets, which ultimately moves to the coffers of the de facto owners of the companies, are presented by the advocates of neoliberal ideology as high voltage national economic growth, modernity and industrialisation. The flip side of this India story is the penury of most citizens in the form of adverse inclusion, that is economic involvement of the citizens constituting the labour force as actual or potential suppliers of labour power and the purchasing power to enable the companies to produce for the market and materialise the profits and surpluses in terms of financial profits on increasingly unilaterally beneficial terms and with a great deal of uncertainty, inadequacy and poor working conditions. It is such social and economic relations spawned and nurtured by the market and business relations which prepare the legal and political ground to enable the operation of the second prop of asocial arbitrary mode of functioning by the so-called entrepreneurial classes in a shallow, formal democratic polity. (Often this second prop, misrepresented as social exclusion, is taken in isolation from the political-legal counterpart. We consider it both appropriate and clear to treat this set of relationships as those of adverse inclusion. Remember the pithy saying of the great economist, Joan Robinson, who maintained that the labour would find it far worse to be left unexploited, that is unemployed rather than be exploited by the employer—that is find work with an employer.) Apparently, such a relationship is facilitated by the roots in and protection from the political-legal sphere which treats material production and the growth in supply of goods and services connected with or derived from capital accumulation by the companies and other entities (irrespective of their counterpart of social relations and outcomes) as the relevant indicator of 'development', ignoring the associated level or rather the inadequacy and uncertainty of labour absorption and working conditions and distribution of income. This then becomes the defining main prop of neoliberal growth architecture. It is a shrinking group of decision-makers who easily ignore, bypass and violate the formal legal rights of the suppliers of labour and voters enjoying the same formal political and civil rights and obligations as those of the promotes and controllers of the companies but manage to win special dispensation by means of luring the political decision-makers to upstage their competitors. That is the way completion works for the super capitalist oligarchs.

Growing Concentration of Wealth in Hands of Few

What emerges is that the neoliberal growth, whether of the kind adopted by the NDA or by any other political party, involves heavy and growing concentration of economic and social resources, capabilities and the highly partisan nature of the so-called collective representative agency called the 'democratic state'. Moreover, given the prop of laissez faire and laissez passé enabled by the neoliberal state in utter disregard of any democratic social discipline and moral framework worth the name, in the course of what is considered capitalist business, and the inability of the social system to enforce at the cutting edge-level the formally accepted ideals of the rule of law applicable equally to everyone, whether vertically divided or suffering from disparities among the horizontally-related people, make the inherently extractive institutions and adversely inclusive processes prevent growth from striking a blow against the worsening social economy.

Thus, the neoliberal economic growth proceeds to reach the second prop of state-company coalescence, directed by the latter to intensify adverse social inclusion. As a ploy to save the democratic credentials of the nation and serve some short-term purposes, a number and variety of popular measures for the welfare of people in order to reduce their misery are generally activated. They simultaneously serve to generate a set of arrangements which remain devoted to further serve the already well-served commanding capabilities of capital. Hence growth is spontaneously devoted to endless consumerism, concentration of multiple powers in increasingly fewer hands, while sharing—in whatever limited manner—the goodies and minimum needs (populism) for a variety of complex ends, with an unspecified huge mass of humanity.

Populism

The adverse inclusion (inadequate, uncertain and on terms and conditions beneficial unilaterally to the better-off controllers of the unit and populist nature of the various so-called welfare programmes by the state and even those undertaken directly by the corporate business entities(the grand façade of philanthropy as can be seen from the tax breaks and public relations exercises by the corporate sector) are basically manifestations of the second prop of the operating political economy model of neo-liberal dispensation. While the total outlays allocated and spent for these populist measures are mentioned and indeed advertised, neither the per capita formal and delivered allocations or the time frame for complete eradication of the disability of all those who are victims of these adversities in order to ensure universal spread of the capabilities to participate in development-related activities and decision-making based on adequate and assured access to the means to be active parts of the socio-economic democratic life of the nation are rarely highlighted. Similarly, the question of relative proportions directed towards the common public needs vis-a-vis the middle and the top layers are simply avoided in the official discourse, relative to the significance of the welfare and pro-poor measures. More seriously, the impact of these measures into reduction of inequalities is simply avoided as any pro-equity measure is anathema to the neoliberal creed.

Populism, after all is in effect, a response to the issues of economic survival and sustenance requirements and diffusion of social democratic pressures, to continue the hold over popular democratic support, consistent with the rulers' democratic credentials. This is done also to prevent a blatant undermining of the term 'liberal'. This is the kind of logic for the second prop of neo-liberalism—a set of populist measures to meet the needs for a satisfied and capable labour force and citizenry along with a somewhat wider market for the realisation of profits and doing the public relations for the regime. Populist measures are doled out also because of the hard economic necessity of keeping social tranquility—as a kind of social infrastructure required for the growth and ease of business, state support and low taxation regime, adding to the growth of corporate profits and of GDP.

This seems to necessitate a differentiated assessment of the relative shares of the intra-dominant classes, strata and other socio-economic and identity/ regions groups in the flows and one-time amounts of gains arising from the neoliberal policies. Given the inherent conflicts, lack of information, a clear and acceptable way of allocation and sharing of the neoliberal terrain consciously or unwittingly tend to create enough grounds which may require tight-rope walking to maintain a certain delicate balance and generate the impression of being even-handed and impartial. Hence either slogans such as *garibi hatao* or *sab ka saath, sab kaa vikaas*. A general overall design of policies, howsoever market-determined and corporate-friendly (at least in the sense of causing fiscal conservatism and restricting spending by the state), do tend to draw attention to state-mediated persistence of unevenness and anti-democratic differentiation among various sections and regions, particularly the discrimination against rural areas. It may happen owing to a variety of factors. Thus it becomes an imperative to ease the tensions and friction over the really prevailing socio-economic position and standing of various state-led freeing up, opening up, and marketisation steps, (including the sale of the public enterprises at throw away prices) even including the ease of doing business which may appear to be discriminatory to various agents.

Political Compulsions

A telling example of this kind of pressures and political compulsions faced by the neoliberal game plan of NDA has come to notice recently in the public face sought to be projected by means of the Union Budget for the year 2016-17. It seems the ease of business, the make in India, the smart cities programmes, Jan Dhan yojana and similar ones propagated with a lot of fanfare could not impress the electorate. Instead, the ruling party was teased on account of the tall promises of unearthing and bringing back home the huge amounts of 'black money ' stashed in any number of tax havens across the globe. It may be noted that all it could do was to set up a powerful legal agency to monitor and guide the anti-black money measures. Effectively however, it could only unearth, by means of a liberal amnesty scheme,less than a negligible amount of under Rs four thousand crore! Another scheme in the 2016 budget entices the black wealth holders to come clean by paying up just 45 per cent due in taxes as all the costs of coming clean. The operational result is, that by the frequently-offered soft treatment, whether one calls it amnesty or something else, the process of tax thieving is rewarded vis-à-vis honest tax payments. On the other hand, the ravaging miseries of the farm sector epitomized by regular farmer suicides sort of symboliszed the rural distress as a major social concern. Hence the budget speech up-fronted the farm sector revival (doubling of farmers' incomes in five years) and welfare steps for the rural folk by a slew of measures. Any cursory overview of these measures and the allocations for them vis-a-vis the rest of the budget allocations show basically more of the same tendency and thus puts a serious question mark on the viability and seriousness of these objectives. A former Prime Minister and a noted economist went on record to assert the impossibility of the achievement of the goal of doubling farm incomes in the next five years. Hence, while one sees the continuation of the second prop, its effectiveness to garner political support remains to be seen.

One reason for it seems to be quite generally relevant because competition—as assumed in the abstract price mechanism-market mechanism models—is hardly found to prevail uniformly throughout the really existing economy. This is likely to be so, particularly in a vast and highly differentiated economy and as a result of the leads and lags in the opening up to the global competition as there are too may divergent presences in various branches of the economy and regions. Thus, even though the overall approach of the different neo-liberal regimes may not be too different, even though it may be led by different groups of the political classes—as in India—because the economy, private players, companies and the bureaucracy etc may be differentiated in their status, power and relationships of the company bosses and the political-bureaucratic strata. The approach may be led by the need to appease social forces, their own absolute and comparative inter se desires/ ambitions and for other reasons as well. This may take diverse forms and tends to involve a modus vivendi , that is a number of steps to live and let live by means of a close mutual understanding, going to the extent of joint action that provides critical and concrete support to each other and yet tries to give the impression of an arm's length, non-crony relationship. Then the vacating of the space rightfully belonging to private-public partnership under a set of arrangements agreed upon by the private companies with the public agencies, opens up the floodgates of enlarging the scope of profit-making while exposing the services or production to the winds blowing from the markets. There is then deliberate mess up by the private partner whose stakes do not go beyond the expected profits and are unmindful of the social and macro considerations. At the other end, in an electoral democracy with intense political rivalry, fairly acute competitive bid for obtaining and retaining power, especially in the face of the observed inability of the GDP-centricity populism to make a perceptible difference to overcome, by way of at least partly denting, the deep-seated adverse inclusion of the general masses. Thus, there arises an inescapable necessity to acquire a public face that keeps at least a majority of voters' happy and ensures an overall social tranquility.

Hence the question whether, how and why the neoliberalism of NDA II can be called a really 'different' ballgame. Is it a sheer electoral and personalities-based exercise to look different without actually being different, may be with an implicit advantage of generating general confusion about the real meaning/content and socio-economic constituency committed to and gaining from it. Is the NDA's game—to be rated on a different footing than the UPA—but continue with similar policy objectives, instruments and the main agency for making investments, however with the promise of superior governance, goodbye to cronyism and better and more fabulous-looking populismraising the hope for better governance? The policies unveiled so far look more of a different packaging and branding than in terms of their substantive content. And general social orientation. Neoliberal growth seems to be the element of continuity the new government expressly wants to maintain.

Historical Background of Neoliberalism in India

Our purpose in the exercise here is to examine briefly the historical and theoretical background and rationale of these choices, their evolution in the changing context up to the present, and examine the case for continuing such neoliberal interventions. The idea seems to be to make them morph into open and near full-fledged market mechanism-directed economy, regulated and brought into balance by local and global competition. This may be inferred from the choice of 'transformation' as the chosen description of the thrust of the new-looking measures.

The choice was made despite the evolution of the organised sector of the Indian economy into nearly oligopolistic direction, preventing unrestricted competition from rounding the rough-edges of the functioning of the markets and compromised state structures and personnel owing to gray crony-political economy taking hold of the organised sector growth in the face of 90 per cent and more labour power in the unorganised/informal sector and disproportionate growth of the private corporate sector in terms of profits, access to state bounties and state support in terms of light tax burden much below the formal level of the levies.

Let us understand how all these culminated in the open choice/ adoption or rather the continuation of full-fledged neoliberal policies in line with the dominant policy of the hegemonic global powers and the Indian super rich aligned to the former. Clearly, the Indian and the foreign companies acting as the two real bosses of the economic policies and change, did extremely well for themselves but without producing and sharing the social and humanist responsibilities of their enormous gains as reflected in the worsening/ deepening inequalities, including in terms of a high and rising level of and share in GDP and the weakened social character of the state. We illustrate the above positions with some factual evidence.

Here we try to provide a terse overview of the policy evolution in a way that may help understand the appropriateness and efficacy of these policies. Thus the analysis tends to provide a historical window to encapsulate the new rationale, if any, for the recycling of the old stories with a new gloss and verbiage as the NDA readies itself to implement further economic reforms at top speed. The main thrust of this exercise is to examine the neoliberal school of the so-called reforms in the context of the present Indian government's declarations and initiatives.

This attempt leads us to see how liberal (Fabian) mixed economy framework prior to 1990 for GDP-centric limited self-reliant development attempted with little success to discipline the mixed agency of the public sector enterprises and the private corporate sector but could not go far. The regulator and the intended object of regulation developed close, hidden and open linkages and are often spoken in terms of the regulatory capture of the state. Actually, the regulatory capture was further compounded by the capture of the development state as well as practically all the infrastructure and capabilities-building investments and arrangements were predominantly directed towards strengthening the capabilities of those who had a powerful presence in the economy, polity and society. It meant, the public facilities and services sorely needed by the adversely included sections remained further neglected. This is a factor that further contributed to inequalities-ridden growth of the economy and further marginalisation of the marginalised. This was also a spill-over effect of super abundant riches accumulated by the corporates, irrespective of the regulations they were subjected to. It is often pointed out that the infectious spread of black economy too was a contributor to such anti-development outcomes, especially owing to the state agencies willingly succumbing to the pressures and temptations offered by the market forces. It is a different story that even with the best intentions and implementation, the scope for really significant gains for the ordinary adversely included citizens was quite limited for several reasons. The pattern of imitative Western-style industrialisation—preferring the growth of GDP over near-full employment of the resources and educational facilities for the poor labour force—was simply unsuitable for the Indian conjuncture in all its diverse complexity as it came to evolve during a prolonged spell of absolutist and colonial state domination of the economy, polity and culture. This bad situation was made worse in view of the caste and gender injustices and social authoritarianism built into India's reality, and this placed especially extremely high value on public sector employment.

In any case, such use of the personal and corporate fortunes for their own specific interests in a market economy is as per the rules of the game. So much so that these outcomes and relationships evolved in course of time acquired a dynamics of their own, leading to corruption and negativities of various sorts. It led to the inevitable growth of the black economy and further mal-development of India . Later on, these took the form of crony capitalism. We examine how the neoliberalism of the NDA brand has to cope with these challenges embedded in the structures, processes and relationships it inherted and accepted for furthering .

In this process, it becomes clear that the specification of the problem of development in terms of a low-per capita income economy is thoroughly unrealistic as it overlooks the basic relationships and mode of common person's participation in the socio-economic and political-administrative processes, owing to a deeply unjust and highly differentiated social structure. In the political democracy, the regime which arouses expectations but frustrates them in practice cannot endure and must destroy itself. Hence a whole series of populist interventions become the second inevitable prop required from the point of view of the common masses, and system sustenance from the point of the political-economic power coalescence.

As we examine the issue of the new incarnation of neoliberalism, at frequent points we face a sort of natural query about the motive and basis of the power tussle between the two major parties, the UPA and the NDA, committed to the same set of policies and by implication, having roots in largely similar set of social forces. Moreover, we examine this in terms of GDP growth, high technology, modernity, smart cities, freedom to carry on private business and a low and stable tax regime proposed or introduced by NDA and supported by the UPA constituents in the Parliament. We look at the content of development, with some high visibility welfare measures to shine the pro-poor credentials of the pro-rich and capitalist regime, itself rolling in riches.

One cannot find enough grounds to distinguish the two parties and their policies from each other in these respects. In fact, their view of the future of India as a 'global economic power house' too do not seem to contain any deep qualitative divide. Of course, they differ regarding the role of Hindus vis-à-vis the other religious groups in Indian polity, economy and society, but it seems that, except now no longer low intensity noises , this is a fight that may easily get out of control as some recent pointers show. Tentatively, it seems, on a pan Indian scale, the two parties seem to represent by and large the top echelons of Indian society and a section of the aspiring middle classes who take the top sections, including those from the rich world, as their role models. This tendency is bound, given so many dimensions of the typical Indian diversity, to subsume many differences, major and minor depending on the context, of course, with some regional and historically-rooted persistent differentiation and with roots in similar social forces and their respective histories.

The two-way basic division of Indian society, with many sub-divisions on different criteria, all seem subsumable under the two major very broad categories. This seems consistent with the logic and manner in which the rich and the powerful view India and her subalterns in opportunist ways. It may be difficult to see any reasons beyond the love and yearning for power, especially with the sections who have made politics and the will to attain power their main agenda. A complex interplay of forces seem to motivate the two sets of political parties dominated by the two-fold basic division of India. In this kind of scheme of things the lower rungs, equally diverse but voiceless, are taken as valuable only as passive, manageable voters to help the political class to capture power. Like the corporates sitting atop huge piles of wealth, the main parties treat politics as a business for personal, familial and group-based sharing. It is a kind of corporatisation of politics coupled with politicisation of businesses. Thanks to the two props of neoliberalism—one provides the power and finances and the other popular support of the citizenry— and the model seems to help our muddling through processes.

Two Props of Neoliberalism

The two props called into being by the neoliberal policy design, owing to its interaction with the ground reality, may well be treated as 'necessary' for the satisfying operation of neoliberalism at the ground level from the mutually reinforcing perspective of those at the top and those at the bottom of the pyramid.

One is the manner and extent to which the compromises, sacrifices and incentives offered to the agency are sought to be reconciled with the perspective of the rich and the powerful. The reality of tax evasion, black economy, meaningless existence of laws and regulations from the perspective of their actual enforcement, and the resulting outcomes and the alternatives which informally emerged are one part of the props required for the GDP-centric status quo, but with a growing volume.

The other prop is the various forms of populism and their concrete manifestations in profusely propagated pro-poor social measures, supposed to address the immediate survival and maintenance of the reserve army of labour and a broadly-beholden army of voters. This evolution of the actual course of development and macro-economic balances happened in a far more open economic context than was opted for initially. This then constitutes the core model as it evolved, based on the functional, ideological and practical political and economic grounds.

Thus, India is facing, in a certain sense, a somewhat curious phenomenon in its political economy. Two bitterly opposed political parties—the country's biggest ones—are both engaged in an all-out political struggle for the control of the Union and State governments. In fact, the struggle seems to have been extended down to the village and ward level. But this struggle at the top, for the top and by the top leaves the lower parts of the social pyramid not high and dry but pushes them deeper into the morass. The worsening of the farm ers' distress over the years is a typical manifestation of the dangerous situation. As far as the main thrust is concerned, nothing can show more convincingly how the two are on the same page than the explicit statement by the NDA Finance Minister—that they would maintain **continuity** with the UPA policies. The two inveterate political foes are, thus, hand-in-glove in order to maintain continuity of their enduring commitment to neoliberalism! It may also be taken to showcase how they both welcome investments that lead to economic growth, irrespective of whether the investor is an MNC or of swadeshi origin—a fair-weather friend enetring the stock market or a durable investor, but with little regard to domestic market and society. Such investors, Indian or foreign, are riveted to the company's profitability prospects and assurance of low taxes, unhindered repatriation and guarantee against state take-over or interference with the market-determined functioning. Thus, a kind of supra-nationalism of 'growth' and global-orientation seems to rule the roost irrespective of the impact on employment or rather its inadequacy.

As a concrete instance of it, a U-turn on FDI in retail has taken place with the recent permission to FDI to enter the marketing of food crops and indigenously processed food.The NDA and the UPA, both have done a double U-turn on FDI in retail. In 2002, the NDA I government wanted to go in for freeing up retail trade for the global retail giants and the UPA leaders said, India should not permit 'reforms' which, instead of generating employment, would destroy jobs. (Manmohan Singh in a letter to an organisation of small traders on 21 December 2002. See Kabra, lock cit.) The UPA double-crossed itself and issued the notorious notification capable of jeopardising the livelihood of millions. Thanks to t he resistance by many State governments, not much mischief could be done on the ground. Now back in power in 2014, it is the turn of the NDA as a strong votary of neoliberal 'reforms' to double cross itself on the retail FDI question and prove its loyalty to neo-liberalism and FDI! The budget 2016-17 has further permitted FDI in the processesd food and farm crops market. Incidentally, in this process it ignores the protest of one of its own supporting organisations too. In the initial position of the NDA II, it was maintained that 'at least the retail trade has been spared for the present. But it is yet to be seen if it is a serious and enduring social commitment and not just an electoral game plan. If so, why not protect the small retailers from the far more rampant and dangerous e-commerce giants inflicting similar blows as are expected from the global megastores?' (From the Prologue, Kabra, Kamal Nayan, 2015, *FDI in Retail: A self-Goal,* revised and updated, New Delhi, Vitasta Publishing.)

Cronyism

What can be seen regarding cronyism and neoliberalism under NDA? It has to be seen that crony relations between the political leaders and the business leaders involve both the players as willing agents/participants; it does not seem to be a case of extortion by way of rent of authority or one of offering allurements for some exclusive favors. Cronyism is a street for joint travel by the two parties. It generally happens when the political leadership itself sits atop huge piles of personal wealth just as the corporate bosses have their personal accumulations outside the company account books—both may make use of these for furthering the party and the company interests, mostly for covert operations. Some allegations against some key leaders are making serious rounds, leading to a prolonged impasse in Parliament. The bad loans to big corporate entities continue to be granted, based on the 'logic' of growth-friendly orientation of public policies. Such huge credit lines are turned into unrecoverable loans, forcing the exchequer to help re-capitalise the banks considered too big to be allowed to fail. In sharp contrast, the loans granted to the farmers and forcible and degrading methods of their recovery, often lead the indebted farmers to suicides. Such shameful national disasters continue even today.

The critical point is that formalities apart, in effect, the party and the company have become one, that is two distinct but closely allied faces of the power structure monopolising all the wealth and privileges The phenomenon of corporatisation of politics (dynastic nature of the political parties) is just one major manifestation of the gray political economy of India and may assume several different variants with the key common feature being narrow unaccountable power and influence structure of the organisations/parties concerned. This is comparable to the family-patrimonial character or identity of a company. It takes place and operates in a similar manner. The most disturbing outcome is the perversion of the democratic processes with negative impact on development and democracy.

All these transformations of business and political equations have struck deep roots in the soil of the basic political economy of India, beginning with the era of development planning. Yes, it would be naïve to assume or believe that nothing of the sort was happening prior to 1990. 1990 was no sudden volte face and such cronyism has been in the works from the very beginning of modern economic growth under the a auspices of the state. The business classes and the political classes have bonded together through elections, party-control and management mechanisms and offering of allurements to the middle class political persons. How companies manage personal and family control and ownership through proxies is a story not often told but well understood even by a regular retail investor. The charismatic leaders are also the clever fund-raisers for the party and/or the clique they control or work for! On both the sides, such personalities are firmly in the saddle. It is not a question of corruption cases surfacing or getting exposed because the eleventh commandment is also equally strongly followed. After all, one reason why no law is enacted to regulate the political parties when even an NGO is not allowed without adhering to a legal framework is a silent testimony of the operational model of party functioning, which is supported by almost the entire political class. Hence, the NDA claim that there has not been any scam in its second innings so far is neither here nor there . The systemic logic seems to remain intact. And so we can say that the basic model of neo-liberalism, with its two pillars or props (discussed above) remains intact even under the NDA regime.

One of the regularly operative facts of life is irregular business-political relationships. One rarely sees the public face of cronyism which involves big discretionary deals, say permission or access to natural resources or special cuts and concessions for certain specific kind of business propositions which can be performed only by big ticket investors, as the resource requirements are too massive to invite a lot of competitive biddings. These mega projects or concessions are not suitable for inviting competitive bidding from many small and medium players that can provide anonymity to the potential service providers. Each of the bidders is known and has been personally in touch with the supervising/granting authority. Obviously, such projects, resources and business opportunities would invoke huge bids and cronyism may come to play a role. When, how and to what extent generally remains shrouded in mystery. But the stories(as narrated by, for example, in the disclosures seen in the Radia tapes) and the emergence of new tycoons—virtual favorites of and known to be close to the powers that be—are telling examples of how new cronies move up to the top slots among the corporate dynasties, typifying the new metods and dimensions of oligopolistic competition. Actually, the entire edifice of the new institutional device called 'public-private partnership' is a camouflaged institutional device to hide privatisation of the state itself, as the private agencies come to operate as state agencies, sharing its powers and privileges with major contribution of the public agencies, including the authority of the state.This, for example, is seen in the way the privatised electricity distribution companies are operating. Whether the much-touted auction can be a way of avoiding crony equations, has to be seen, especially in the context of oligopolistic markets and rampant crony relations between those who are ostensibly two separate sides of the deal. The game theorists here are the relevant experts whose services can be illuminating but of little help to control or contain these scandalous patterns of 'legalised' public loot.. Many interesting cases and situations may arise.

Without insinuating, one wonders what made the NDA government fix lower price for aviation fuel compared to that of petrol and diesel! Similarly, granting/facilitating/ guaranteeing/enabling credit from public financial institutions or making a choice of a private partner for a public-private joint project— the choice of an area for earmarking for the PPP mode, including sharing formulae for costs and gains and so on— are a thousand and one decisions in which underhand practices can easily occur. (The reasoning by Robert Reich in *Super Capitalism* 2009, may be relevant in an era of oligopolistic competition to understand how the nature and scene of competition moves to public policy domain.)

The Black and Grey Economy

The presence of a huge black and grey mixed economy, combined with the policy of letting private investment in public projects is one facilitating factor which can light the dark alleys of cronyism. How illegal funds stashed in various tax havens are the basic source ofthe domestic generation remain sidestepped and also how proliferation of numerous high-yielding economic, political, philanthropic and cultural uses of these massive funds have become the main currency of public life dominated by the plutocrats.

Disclosers by The International Consortium of Investigative Journalists and The Indian Express show how a new frontier has been crossed by the gray political economy of India. It is visible in the form of the accounts maintained by about 500 Indians in various offshore tax havens and operations in the name of shell companies. Their illustrative include many business people, political big-guns, sports and film personalities— that is the rich, powerful and the famous who place their greed over everything else. A cursory look at some of the 'explanations' or excuses given to the media by the named but not shamed guys also shows how they are likely to go scot free. Actually, many new neo-liberal financial 'reforms and freedoms', of course, of great practical-commercial value to the high net-worth persons and those who have built up large assets both in India and abroad (in benami accounts that are operated under fictitious companies registered in jurisdictions meant basically for the black money big cats in places like Delaware in USA where the identity of the promoters is not even required to be disclosed and a company can be registered on-line).With the setting up of such offshore financial centres in Ahmadabad and Mumbai, even the stigma of foreign places is likely to be washed clean. Such companies are the real facilitators of such shenanigans.Hence to blame these anti-national activities by the rich, powerful and famous highly adored heroes and brand ambassadors seen rubbing shoulders with the high and the mighty in governance structures is a futile exercise.The permission to open and operate external accounts and register companies abroad are official decisions and one doubts if the use of these avenues were reported and monitored on an on-going basis to safeguard against their misuse. The main factor is basically the neoliberal external sector relaxations, with their backward and forward linkages spread throughout the system. And it is these practices which are going to become routine, once the strongly advocated capital account convertibility is made fully operative . To cry foul over such policies-induced misbehavior is to hunt with the hounds and run with the hares!This is a typical posture of market-and capital-friendly political parties.

Despite the independent role of the judiciary-directed SIT, the course of the white-collar crimes by the rich, the powerful and the page three celebrities closely aligned with each other do not seem to show any signs of weakening. The outcomes of various amnesty schemes in different avatars under diverse nomenclature and their frequent recurrence pale into insignificance compared to the amounts which continue to be unearthed and by the sundry anti-tax evasion, anti-corruption administrative measures of the routine variety. Yet, often one sees Himalayan reluctance of the ruling parties at the centre and in the States to order prompt and credible enquiries before they disappear from headlines when fresh and different kinds of major corruption and black money charges against the political-business classes surface. The corporate and opaque funding of the political parties and denied public audit and disclosure of the accounts of the political parties, including putting them under the scanner of the right to information law, still remain fiercely resisted by the main political parties. These are, as ever, the symptoms of the deep-seated and chronic malaise of some of our polity and economy.

The fact that there is a large volume of unaccounted for and hidden wealth both, within India as also innumerous tax havens, with hardly any prospects in the near future of their reduced salience tend to show how the neoliberal outcomes are the common features cutting across the political divides. (See Palin, Ronen and others, 2010.) To blame them on enormously expensive elections is nothing but begging the question. As long as political-administrative power and the capacity to raise such enormous funds remain concentrated in few hands, irrespective of public or private or foreign sources, the circumstances for special dispensations remain intact. The prescription of full market freedom without a spring-cleansing and a people-centric development discourse—at least as a marked beginning— cannot but become self-defeating.

It is little surprise that owing to adverse inclusion as the main outcome of India's attempts at national development by means of national planning that the public support base of the political parties is so flimsy. It is often misdirected and mobilised afresh on the basis of emotive issues or a mixture of corruption, threats and inducements to a few for managing the rest. It is on such podiums that the 'managed' support base holds the key to political power. Elections are 'competitive' situations for a small number of ultra-rich who live in glass houses and hence, they can hardly leave any stone unturned to manage political support and participation in subtle and not so subtle ways. Crony relationships give them a fresh lease of life. The logic for breeding cronyism has to be extinguished before we can take anyone's 'moral' postures as serious business. One has only to recall the history of scams, the way many cases were unearthed and the large number of successfully prosecuted and non-prosecuted cases.Enquiries do reveal that it cannot be easy to raise massive loans from public sector banks or get contracts of massive size or gain access to public natural resources without a flourishing black economy-political-administrative nexus. The latest instance of it leading to writing off of a stupendous sum of bad debts of over Rs 4 lakh crores by the public sector banks to the top corporate houses shows, it is not easy to uproot the crony and corrupt linkages linking all the organised segments of the system.

It is also not possible normally to involve a large number of bidders so that no one is in a position to influence the final decision. The insider information access too plays a part, especially when foreign relations are involved, which can proceed only through inter-governmental channels. The scope for discretionary processes on both the sides of cronyism in such matters is infinite. It is literally a herculean task to keep a close eye on and see how decisions are clinched as the modernisation and growth projects involving billions or trillions of dollars take shape. What can then be the main inferences (some weak, some pretty obvious and some likely to unfold themselves) if our reasoning has some meat in it? The inference is that cronyism of various sorts are endemic to neo-liberalism and it is difficult to track or tackle them. Neoliberalism and cronyism are like bread and butter, one embellishes the other.

Briefly, the elite in India always enjoy a special privileged and powerful hegemony over all aspects of our national evolution, especially over lives of the lower sections of society. Hence, even during the first phase of state-led development, understood primarily as growth of GNP, the top echelons of society and political power ensured special dispensation for themselves under the cover of promoting growth and thus bypassing equal treatment of all in terms of the rule of law. The growing size and multi-dimensional spread of the extra-legal economic, social and political processes, according to the dictates and interests of the top echelons, create a wide chasm between the formal-legal and the real ground-level operation and outcomes. Whether it is the stateist-self-reliant mixed-economy kind of growth or the neoliberal-globalised corporate-led growth, the outcomes in the form of huge disparities and deprivation-discrimination infested growth, are generated and perpetuated.

Many of the above may be taken as tentative hypotheses, particularly because the real character of the NDA is still, to an extent, in the making. (For example, the ultimate character of the most anti-people and pro-business move, the land acquisition ordinance, is embryonic owing to the storm it has stirred and seems to have been passedon to the governments of the States to take on. Similarly, though there has been talk of doing away with the tax bounties offered to the corporate sector and other better-off classes (the latest estimateof these bounties to the super rich exceed RS 6 lakh crore), not only the single highest transfer to the smallest section of the population and overall indirect tax imposts are a whopping Rs 97 thousand crore.At the same time, besides the abolition of the wealth tax, the direct tax burden has been lightened by Rs 1,000 crore!.

The real interest rate for the savings of the middle and lower income group and pensioners in India—which hardly spends around 1 per cent of GDP on social security and protection on public account—goes on merrily to support the big companies refusing to make full repayment and timely repayments and often causing massive volumes of bad loans finances. Therefore, India's growth is at the cost of the relatively worse off sections. Actually even a good part of what is shown as 'farm credit' goes to the rich. In the name of agricultural income exceeding Rs 1 crore, thousands of non-farm entities save/avoid paying taxes and such practices remain un-tackled to the present day. Many information and vigilance agencies have remained dormant and hence, many such cases remain uninvestigated. The CAG reports for this one year may well be in the making, but so far they are not in the public domain and remain dormant for all practical purposes. Little evidence of any change in the business-government relations have surfaced so far, nor can one see how and why and in which direction the long-established dynamics of these equations may move. More evidence or a priori reasoning is required on these relationships because, in India, theses have roots in the nature of politics, business environment and modes of their functioning. Nor has vigilance by any civil society group become piercing enough.

Conclusion

The commitment to GDP centrality and big and organised business-friendly fiscal and financial management and infrastructure support is by and large at the cost of the persistent neglect of the needs and growth of the small and medium and the unorganiszed, often own account, enterprises and the vast number of the indigent people, mainly deriving their livelihoods from land based activities in the rural areas with little support of other wherewithal, of reasonably high productivity. Our assessment indicates that not only both the UPA and the NDA but broadly, practically all the regimes since Independence (leaving aside the high-sounding claims of advancing the cause of social justice) have mainly followed similar market-centric and big capital-friendly policies, but with far greater degree and qualitatively higher level of open border economic space after 1990. In order to combine the incentives and commitments to growth by betting on the top market players, they all adopted fiscal policies friendly to the savings and investing classes and kept the Tax – GDP ratio fairly low , say in the range of 10 to15 per cent of GDP. Thus, with severely constrained fiscal abilities and the compulsions following from the institutional choices, the state neither directly, nor indirectly, could create adequate and secure livelihood opportunities and the socio-economic infrastructure necessary for widely participative economic growth and social progress. The major success of Idia's development endeavours can be summed up as the minimum imperative for scaling up the rate of growth of GDP in a positive territory by breaking the stagnation syndrome of the days of the British Raj and create a good part of the basic techno-economic base for modern imitative industrialiszation. However, this falls short both quantitatively and qualitatively of the needs and potential of India.

Such a performance of the Indian efforts towards development can hardly be considered poor-friendly. Such practices indeed change the meaning and thrust of populism as well. It surely changes the content of pro-poor populism in India, like in many other countries. Hene one comes across varieties of populism ((Ref.*Science and Society* and selections from *Comparaive Politics*). For example,budget cuts for pro-poor programmes while lakhs of villages are forced to subsist without any—yes any—civil and common public services even mildly commensurate with the weight of the rural population or their distance from the minimum conditions of civic life worthy of a nation which claims to have arrived on the global scene (the data revealed by the Socio-economic Caste Census , 2011-12) on these dimensions of rural India are nothing short of shocking as even now nearly 88 crore Indians live in rural India. These these social facts tell a tale that has to be read carefully and without the blinkers of the self-centered, aspiring middle classes living in urban areas.Thus it is clear that notwithstanding the claims and counter claims by two major political formations which share a good deal of overlapping support among the top private business classes of India, the point to differentiate the two is not the broad socio-economic content of their brand of neoliberalism, but the competing constituencies of their historically connected constituencies, though the flexibility of business strategies cannot be overlooked. Thus populism and the slogans for marketing themselves (in part as suggested by the PR and strategic consultants hired by offering huge fees) may appear to be different, but their essence remains populist, that is look far more pro-poor, even radical (say by speaking in terms of rights-based approach) than what the rivals (who apart from citing their personal histories or humble origins may promise better, closely monitored delivery, as, for instance , by JAM) may adopt but remain wedded to the basic philosophy and policy content closely derived from neoliberalism and its highly advertised success stories. For example, by citing the saga of east Asian tigers. Notwithstanding their historical inherited core support base and the exclusive marks of differentiation, the neoliberal neglect of genuine people-centric development hardly show any indications of making room for a real turn around towards putting an end to the chronic, multi-dimensional adverse inclusion of the people. What matters is the hollowness of social democratic pretensions or a highly paternalistic—revivalist phraseology to the Potemkin game. One may borrow the terminology of social democracy of the Scandinavian or the third way variety or hark back to the golden era of India's past and put India on the road to real social development jointly by the efforts of the common people, social entrepreneurs and social state.

References and Select Bibliography

1. Klein Naomi 2007, *The Shock Doctrine: The Rise of Disaster Capitalism,* Penguin Books.

2. Rodrigues Joao 2013, *The Political and Moral Economics of Neo-liberalism,* Mises and Hayek1019-1034, Cambridge Journal of Economics, 17(5), September.

3. Bo Curt, Umut 2013,*Neoliberalism with a Human Face: Making Sense of the Justice and Development Party's Neoliberal Populism in Turkey*, Science and Society, 77(3) July.

4. Wetland Kurt 1996, *Neo-populism and Neo-liberalism in Latin America: Unexpected Affinities, Studies in Comparative International Development* 31(3).
5. *Clarifyig a contested concept: Populism in the study of Latin American Politics*2005,Comparative Politics, 34 (1).
6. Kabra Kamal Nayan 2014, Moneyfestoes of Plutocracy, *Mainstream,* April 17-24Balkan Joel 2004, *The Corporation: The Pathological Pursuit of Profitand Power,*The Free Press.
7. Cassidy John 2009, *How Markets Fail: The Logic of Economic Calamities* Penguin Books (*The Hidden Informatonand the Lure of the Real Estate*).
8. Yakunin VI, Bagdasarayan SS, Sulakshin SS,2009, *Economic Policy Ideology,* Nauchnyi Export.
9. Akerlof George A and Shiller, Robert J 2009, *Animal Spirits, How Human Psychology Drives the Economy and Why it Matters for Global Capitalism,* Princeton University Press.
10. Akerlof George A and Shiller, Robert J, *Phishing for Phools, Economics of Manipulation and Deception*, 2015, Princeton University Press, Princeton.
11. Reich Robert 2009, *Super Capitalism: The Battle for Democracy in an Age of Big Business,* Icon Press.
12. Balakrishnan P (edited), *Economic Reforms and Growth in India* 2011, Orient Black Swan and *EPW.*
13. Kabra Kamal Nayan *Development as Growth of GNP; The Trojan Horse of Development Discourse*, (editors: Roy AN and Mathew George, Orient Blackswan, New Delhi.
14. Kabra Kamal Nayan *FDI in Retail: A self Goal,* revised and updated, 2016, Vitasta.
15. Ministry of Finance, GOI, *Economic Survey* for various years.
16. *Alternative Economic Survey :* from 1992-93 onwards, Alternative Economic Survey Group, Indian Political Economy Association, for various years.
17. Palan, Ronen Murphy, Richard and C Havagneux, Christian *Tax Havens: How Globalization Really Works,* Cornell University Press (Indian edition too available).